THE NARRATIVE COVENANT

The
Narrative
Covenant

Transformations of Genre in the Growth of Biblical Literature

DAVID DAMROSCH

1817

Harper & Row, Publishers, San Francisco

Cambridge, Hagerstown, New York, Philadelphia, Washington
London, Mexico City, São Paulo, Singapore, Sydney

THE NARRATIVE COVENANT: *Transformations of Genre in the Growth of Biblical Literature.* Copyright © 1987 by David Damrosch. All rights reserved. Printed in the United States of America. No part of this book may be used or reproduced in any manner whatsoever without written permission except in the case of brief quotations embodied in critical articles and reviews. For information address Harper & Row, Publishers, Inc., 10 East 53rd Street, New York, NY 10022. Published simultaneously in Canada by Fitzhenry & Whiteside, Limited, Toronto.

FIRST EDITION

Library of Congress Cataloging-in-Publication Data

Damrosch, David.
   The narrative covenant; transformations of genre in the growth of biblical literature.

   Bibliography: p.
   Includes index.
   1. Bible. O.T.—Criticism, interpretation, etc.
2. Narration in the Bible.   3. Middle Eastern
literature—History and criticism.   4. Literature,
Ancient—History and criticism.   I. Title.
BS1171.2.D26   1987   221.6   86-43001
ISBN 0-06-061693-8

87 88 89 90 91 HC 10 9 8 7 6 5 4 3 2 1

To my parents
The Reverend Leopold Damrosch
Elizabeth Hammond Damrosch

in love and gratitude

Contents

Acknowledgments

Like the Priestly genealogies in Genesis, a list of acknowledgments seeks to link the modern era of a book's completion to the primordial chaos of its inception. The genealogy of this work is more than usually tied to actual genealogies, both familial and intellectual. In dedicating this book to my parents, I mean to signal not only my many general reasons for gratitude to them, but also the specific fact that this book in a very deep sense stems from their lives and teaching. I owe much to the intellectual and artistic inspiration of my mother, who not only taught me to read but also, in many ways, to think; equally, this book arises from years of observation of the role of the Bible in my parents' lives, and in particular from years of exposure to my father's superb sermons, in which textual explication was combined with a vivid sense of the immediacy of the Bible to the problems of contemporary life. The genealogy could be extended laterally as well, to the many benefits I have received from conversations with my brother Thomas Damrosch, and to the scholarly example of my brother Leopold Damrosch, Jr., whose wide-ranging and elegant eighteenth-century studies have long been a model for my own work.

Among intellectual debts owed, I must give prominence to my teachers: Peter Brooks, who first introduced me to narrative theory; the Egyptologist W. Kelly Simpson; Hans Frei, one of the first and best to integrate literary and biblical study. Their broad interests are reflected in the pages to follow. The greatest of these debts, however, is due two teachers and friends: Michael Holquist, whose brilliant disquisitions on unusual combinations of literature find an echo here, and Nils Alstrup Dahl, longtime chair of New Testament at the Yale Divinity School and an inspiration to many students in all fields of biblical study. In his classes I first became fascinated with the problems faced by historical scholarship, and his essays stand as models of profound and lucid exploration of the hermeneutical implications of the problems of history.

Finally, I come to the era of the book's actual composition, and here I must with pleasure acknowledge the help and support of the friends and colleagues who have read drafts of portions of the manuscript and in many ways encouraged the project: in particular, Robert Alter, Kathy Eden, Hal Freedman, Heather Henderson, Frank Kermode, Tobin Siebers, Laura Slatkin, and Ann Van Sant are to be thanked, as are my tireless research assistants, Nancy Nystul and Cornelie van Linge. My debts to family and to colleagues merge in the person of my wife, Lori Fisler Damrosch, whose legal scholarship started me thinking about the narrrative aspects of law, and whose unflagging encouragement and support have enabled this book to come into existence.

Note

In quotations from editions of ancient Near Eastern texts, I have regularized the sigla used for textual uncertainties in the following manner: square brackets indicate gaps in the text; half-brackets, ⌐ ¬, indicate tentative translations of missing or unknown words; parentheses indicate additions by the editor or myself to clarify the sense or to supply a word left out by the scribe.

Where possible, I have quoted from the most readily available collection of Near Eastern material, Pritchard's *Ancient Near Eastern Texts* (*ANET*). At times I have modified those and other translations to improve the style or sense, though always trying to stay close to the literal sense of the original. For the Bible, in general I have quoted from the Revised Standard Version, out of a perverse love of that translation, but I have modified it as needed on the basis of current scholarship and the *Biblia Hebraica Stuttgartensia*. With secondary literature, I cite translations of foreign works when they are available; when the quotation is from a work cited in the original, the translation is my own. For the sake of simplicity, I give brief bibliographic references in parentheses within the text and notes; full references will be found in the Bibliography.

Introduction

The beauty of the legends of Genesis has always been a source of delight to readers of refined taste. . . . . Scholars have more rarely expressed appreciation of the beauty of these narratives, often perhaps for personal reasons, and perhaps often because the aesthetic point of view seemed to them incompatible with the dignity of science. However, we do not share this prejudice, but, on the contrary, are of the opinion that one who ignores the artistic form of these legends not only deprives himself of a great pleasure, but is unable properly to satisfy the scientific demands of the understanding of Genesis.

HERMANN GUNKEL, *The Legends of Genesis*, 1901

The purpose of this study is to explore the origins and growth of biblical narrative. In a small country, in a society younger and less prosperous than the great cultures of Egypt and Mesopotamia, literary composition reached a degree of power and beauty previously unknown in the Near East. Soon after the unification of the country, not one but two extraordinary bodies of material were created: the first historical accounts of the monarchy, and the first versions of the materials that became the Pentateuch. How did the biblical writers come to produce the greatest historical writing ever seen in the ancient Near East?

In seeking to answer this question, it is necessary to address several different problems together. The first has to do with the manifest superiority of biblical narrative over the historical prose of neighboring countries. Can any viable relation be shown between Hebrew narrative and the older Near Eastern literatures? A second question, closely related to the first, is how the developing Hebrew tradition took on an independent life of its own and gradually built up the two great bodies of narrative that eventually resulted: the Pentateuch and the Deuteronomistic history (Joshua through 2 Kings). Problems of dating and conflicting divisions of the texts' reconstructed sources have made literary scholars wary of entering into the study of the literary history of the great biblical narratives. Can literary scholars find anything of value in historical source study? A further question follows from this: If their intricate literary history is to be emphasized, can books like Genesis and 1–2 Samuel still be read as unified texts? Can readers make use of the discoveries of historical criticism without reducing most of the books of the Bible to anthologies or even pastiches, with the texts disintegrating into their separate and often conflicting sources?

This study seeks to give affirmative answers to these questions. First, I hope to show that biblical narrative does have close and meaningful links to Mesopotamian literature, links that help to show both the origins of biblical narrative and its particular individuality; second, I argue that source study does not deserve its continuing neglect by literary students of the Bible but, on the contrary, is essential to understanding the dynamics of literary transformation that produced the canonical form of the text; third, I argue that a better understanding of the origins and growth of biblical narrative gives us important assistance in reading the text in its canonical form.

At the heart of my project is the application of structural and genre analysis to the historical problem of the development of biblical narrative. I have called this book *The Narrative Covenant*, but I could simply have called it *Genre*, for genre is the narrative covenant between author and reader, the framework of norms and expectations shaping both the composition and the reception of a text. Genre is always a shaping force, though never a determining one in the case of truly creative work, and it can be studied in its uses, its adaptations, its transformations, and even its repressions, over the history of the composition and rewriting of biblical narrative.

The historical study of genre requires the integration of three fields of study that have generally proceeded quite separately: the comparative study of Near Eastern literature, the historical study of the sources within the biblical texts, and literary analysis of the text as it develops into its canonical form. Comparative study is essential, as Mesopotamian, Canaanite, and Egyptian narratives provide our best sources for evidence of the literary norms out of which, and against which, the Bible developed. These literatures have long been mined for surface parallels and used as contrasts to the specific excellences of the Bible, but there has been little work to date that makes full use of the great advances that Assyriologists and Egyptologists have made in the last two generations in the recovery and analysis of these texts. Further, the Bible's relation to these materials is often elusive, given cultural differences, historical shifts, and theological reworkings, so that direct parallels have only limited value. Thus the great historical narratives like the David story cannot be compared directly to earlier historiography like the Babylonian Chronicles or the Hittite "Apology of Hattušiliš." Rather, I believe that biblical historiography can best be understood as the result of a confluence of the techniques and themes of prose historiography with those of poetic epic. The assimilation of historiography and epic toward each other was already under way in Mesopotamia in the second millennium B.C., and this process accelerated and was redirected in the Hebrew tradition.

Early in the first millennium, Hebrew narrative took two decisive steps: first, the full translation of older epic into historicized prose; second, the application of poetic epic perspectives to historiography proper. The first of these steps will be discussed using the example of the reworking of the Babylonian creation-flood epic traditions in Genesis 2–11; the second step is visible in the early stages of historical writing. In this study I will focus on the story of King David in 1–2 Samuel, which provides an ideal instance of the development of historical prose, as several stages of the text's growth can be recovered. After a discussion that attempts to clarify the tangled relations between the Yahwistic and Deuteronomistic bodies of material (chapter 4), the fifth chapter describes the full flowering of Hebrew historiography through the composition of early narratives concerning Saul and David and their later reworking by pre-Deuteronomistic and Deuteronomistic writers.

The study of genre is an important aspect of the analysis of this process of growth, for many of the issues raised by compositional history involve questions of genre. Why has the folk tale of David and Goliath been inserted at the start of the David story? What are the relations between the Pentateuch's legendary tales and the historiography of the monarchy? How should we understand the parallels between Aaron and Jeroboam I, or the echoes of the mythic stories of Eden and the Flood in the legends concerning Moses and in the history of David's reign? Scholars have generally discussed the Deuteronomistic historical works in isolation from pentateuchal narrative, logically enough if evidence of influence is to be sought primarily in retellings of stories. This is not the whole issue, however, for the structural and thematic shaping of material can be traced even when very different stories are told. As I hope to show, the historical study of literary patterning in biblical narrative reveals a process of mutual influence between the Pentateuch and the Deuteronomistic history. The early Yahwistic pentateuchal material influenced the shaping of the David story, and the David story in turn influenced the Priestly reworking of the Pentateuch. Attention to this process of mutual influence gives aid in interpreting many passages and yields new insights into the dynamics of the development of both bodies of narrative.

The newly epic historiography produced by the Yahwists and Deuteronomists underwent a second great literary revolution at the hands of the Priestly writers who brought the Pentateuch to its full form: the interweaving of historical narrative and law. Chapter 6 discusses the consequences of this new transformation of genre. I argue that Leviticus, contrary to general opinion, is full of literary interest, with the laws taking on a pronounced narrative aspect and with the ordination of Aaron and his sons showing a subtle interaction of the ritual order with several different orders of history. The surrounding epic history of the Exodus, in turn, is reshaped through the influence of the ritual values expressed in the laws, and the Priestly writers are led to revise the older Exodus account accordingly. In so doing, they redirect the older presentation of the Exodus against the background of the story of the Flood, exploiting the flood story in very different ways from its use in the earlier Exodus story.

All of the topics taken up here are both literary and historical, but they have resisted analysis on both literary and historical grounds. Most of the historical evidence a literary critic would ordinarily use in support of textual analysis is missing, or ambiguous at best. We lack Hebrew texts apart from those in the Bible itself to testify to the milieu in which these texts were composed, and such basic questions as the dating of texts remain the subject of fierce debate.

The literary evidence within the Bible itself is highly problematic, as the texts are the products of long and complex histories of creation and revision, histories that the later writers in the series have actively worked to conceal. Historians of the composition of the Bible have emphasized repetitions, gaps, and contradictions created in the canonical text by the bringing together of disparate materials, and they have generally narrowed their focus to analysis of small subunits and separate compositional strands, with results that literary scholars tend to view as atomistic and unusable in reading the text in its final form.

The difficulty in dealing with textual history leads in one of two directions. A critic can ignore the history of the text altogether and carry out close readings and structural analyses of the overall text without reference to its complex compositional history, an approach that historians often view as fostering arbitrariness and over-reading. Or the critic can bow before history in silence, confining the analysis to some small, discrete unit, preferably one with an uncomplicated compositional background. One can then explore structural patterns, imagery, and themes with a clear conscience, moving within the familiar bounds of a unified text. Some of the best literary work yet done has followed this route, including remarkable essays by Roland Barthes and Jean Starobinski (see Bibliography), each of whom deals with a passage of only a few verses in length. As fine as such narrowly circumscribed studies are, however, they necessarily avoid the literary-historical issues involved in studying how the biblical texts came to be created in the first place.

Working largely in isolation, both historians and literary critics have had little way to account for the emergence and growth of biblical narrative. Historians often show an uncomfortable sense that the whole is a good deal greater than the parts they can account for historically. This awareness is seen in E. A. Speiser's discussion of parallels between the Bible and the most developed Babylonian historical texts, though he passes over the problem at the very moment he acknowledges it: "That even this superior work does not approach the high level of biblical historiography is a fact too obvious to need special emphasis" ("Ancient Mesopotamia," 67). More concerned to account for the difference, Gerhard von Rad points to several important broad cultural forces, but on the fact of biblical narrative as a literary phenomenon he can only suggest, tautologically, that the authors seem to have possessed "narrative talent." He concludes by emphasizing the miraculous suddenness with which biblical narrative emerged: "All at once it is there, mature and artistically fully developed to an extent which makes it impossible to envisage further development in this direction" ("Beginnings of Historical Writing," 171, 193). Confining themselves to the final form of the text, literary scholars have had little to add on this question. In one recent assessment of the comparative material, the literary theorist Meir Sternberg concludes that "the surface similarities only heighten the wonder and conviction of strategic novelty: the Bible's poetics appears to have sprung full-blown" (*Poetics of Biblical Narrative*, 232).

This can hardly be the case, but it is evident that literary students of the Bible have had difficulty making effective use of the insights of comparative and historical criticism, without which little progress can be made in recovering and understanding the literary history of the Bible. There are certainly good reasons why so little integrative work has been done to date, reasons that go beyond the difficulties of mastering the necessary Near Eastern material and the separate bodies of contemporary historical and literary biblical scholarship. The first order of business, then, will be to consider the reasons for the continuing conflict between literary and historical analysis.

Apart from the pure, lurid fascination of the topic, I have several purposes in tracing the reasons for the sharp and occasionally acrimonious debate still under way between the two schools. As the present study seeks to combine these approaches, it is important to face up to the difficulties that have stood in the way of rapprochement between historical and literary study even when parties have sincerely wished it. Further, I hope to show that there does exist a substantial common ground between historical and literary study, a territory largely consisting of areas neglected by both approaches. The study of the literary history of the Bible is not a matter of importing yet another rival into the already crowded field of combatants, but instead involves a systematic and integrated application of principles and insights already widely found in scattered fashion within both schools of biblical study.

It should be understood that my aim is to be suggestive rather than exhaustive; there is much here that is tentative, subject to revision in light of better understanding of text-historical issues and further readings in the texts themselves. At the same time, I believe that it is high time to begin the work of integrating the fields of comparative, text-historical, and literary study. The chapters to follow will attempt to show that a unified use of the three approaches can produce valuable results that cannot be achieved by isolated study within one approach alone. Together, they can do much to illuminate the origins and growth of biblical narrative, and a better understanding of these matters can in turn aid us greatly in understanding the texts in their canonical form.

1. History Versus Structure in Biblical Study

The Quest for History in Textual Analysis

Eighty years ago, Hermann Gunkel discussed the desirability of a literary-historical understanding of the Bible. "Down to the present time," he wrote, "there is, properly speaking, nothing that can be called a history of Hebrew literature" ("Fundamental Problems," 57). This was scarcely surprising, given the absence of most of the evidence normally required by the literary historians of his day, who were interested to recover the milieu and personalities of the authors they studied and to trace the reflection of the authors' minds and lives in their artistic creations. Such evidence had always been scarce, at best, and the rise of the historical-critical method perfected by Julius Wellhausen in the 1880s dealt the last blow to any hopes for this sort of literary history, since it became clear that most of the narrative books of the Bible had not been produced by single authors at all. If a text like Genesis was the product of varied schools of thought operating over a period of several hundred years, it seemed impossible to say anything meaningful about the literary shape of the text as a whole. As for the parts, even if one were to shift one's efforts to trying to describe the schools behind them, very little evidence could be found about these schools, apart from oblique deductions from the stories themselves. The later redactors, indeed, had done their best to conceal the very fact of the texts' complicated compositional history, and historians interested in the original form of a story, and the nature of the circle that produced it, could not apply the usual norms of internal coherence and authorial intention. Indeed, scholars must actively exploit textual incoherencies, working against the intentions of the later authors and editors in order to recover what they had so long concealed.[1]

Faced with this dilemma, Gunkel proposed a form-critical model of analysis with interesting analogues in the structuralist methods dominant in literary study of the Bible to this day. Generic form, not authorial intention, was to be the attainable object of analysis, and Gunkel, writing a generation before the birth of structuralism as such, described his project with a wholly structuralist analogy to linguistic rules:

The prime task of a history of literature in Israel must therefore be to determine the *literary types* represented in the Old Testament. . . . To the people of Israel the laws of literary form were as familiar as the rules of Hebrew grammar. They obeyed them unconsciously and lived in them; it is only we who have to learn to understand them. ("Fundamental Problems," 59–61)

In the very act of calling for a new literary history, however, Gunkel set the stage for the divorce of literary and historical study. In concentrating on the earlier, oral phase of composition, where he hoped to find those deep structures that would preserve the ancient faith of Israel under the accretions of later revisionists, Gunkel only furthered the Wellhausian move away from large-scale literary analysis. After all, he thought, these stories were transmitted for "the ancient listener, whose reception power was very limited. . . . The most ancient Hebrew national ballad is contained in one or perhaps two long lines— that was all the average hearer of the day could grasp at a time" (62–63).

Although more recent studies in several fields have broadened our idea of the capacities of the ancient audience, we still face the difficulties that Gunkel encountered in the study of genre. The recognizable genres the Bible uses tend to be small-

---

[1]As Robert Polzin has said, "To study the Bible with such an uninvolved and 'objective' stance is still to discover a message that was apparently not meant to be understood in such a way. . . . the result of this kind of decoding of the text is the recovery of an original message that reads, 'Do not decode this in the way you have' " (*Moses and the Deuteronomist*, 8).

scale affairs: anecdotes, legal codes, psalms. Very quickly, these identifiable small units are built up—or thrown together—into vast, seemingly shapeless constructions far beyond the purview of traditional genre analysis. As John Barton says,

A work which consists of narrative mixed with poems and hymns and laws, which contains two or even three versions of the same story set down with no apparent awareness that they are the same, and which changes style so drastically from paragraph to paragraph and from verse to verse, cannot in a certain sense be read at all: you simply don't know where you are with it. (*Reading the OT*, 22)

Faced with this problem, historical study of the biblical text has generally proceeded by a process of subtraction as it seeks the historical reality beneath centuries of literary accretion over the original primitive text. The subtractive method persists even when attention is given to the later growth of the material. A classic expression of this perspective is found in Martin Noth's path-breaking *History of Pentateuchal Traditions* of 1948:

The chief task . . . is to ascertain the *basic themes* from which the totality of the transmitted Pentateuch developed, to uncover their roots, to investigate how they were replenished with individual materials, to pursue their connections with each other, and to assess their significance. Thus the task is to understand, in a manner that is historically responsible and proper [*geschichtlich zutreffend und damit sachgemäss*], the essential content and important concerns of the Pentateuch. (3)

The seductive calls of responsibility and propriety have led many historians to abstract the essential message from the surrounding verbiage, seeking out "the smallest literary unities" as the formal bearers of these messages.[2]

Hand in hand with this orientation went the view that the redactors who assembled the final text had not substantially altered the separate materials they had received. Thus, to Martin Noth in 1948, "it is clear that the result was simply a com-

---

[2] This tendency has roots in the Enlightenment quest for the historical truth "behind" the text; see Hans Frei, *The Eclipse of Biblical Narrative*.

pilation in which not only the narrative materials but also the theological concerns are juxtaposed and interwoven with one another just as plainly and incongruously as the individual sources had presented them" (*History,* 250). If the sources themselves were seen primarily as expressions of aspects of Israel's faith as orally transmitted in cultic situations, then it was the cult that determined the expression, and once again there were no authors but only very modest compilers.[3]

The circumspection of the redactors was believed to be reinforced by the presence of a strongly developed impulse toward canonicity from an early date. The gradual weakening of the classic documentary hypothesis merely displaced this idea of canonicity onto the oral tradition, as in Speiser's discussion of the Yahwist:

His task was to retell, not to originate. . . . the lives of the patriarchs had already become part of an oral canon some time between the period that was being depicted and the date of their earliest written presentation.

Now canon implies sanctity. . . . The patriarchal narratives must have acquired such a status well before the date of the literary work in which they were incorporated; otherwise the writer would have felt free to recast them in terms of his own time and environment. ("Biblical Idea of History," 206–7)

Speiser goes so far as to claim that "the canonical tradition among the people of the Book must be older than the age of the Pentateuchal writers, older indeed than the time of Moses himself" (209).

Recent scholarship has argued forcefully against such assertions of the great antiquity of canonicity in a fully binding sense. It seems clear that the idea of canon as Speiser presents it can only be positively demonstrated in the later stages of

---

[3]A good example is found in Walter Beyerlin, *Origins and History of the Oldest Sinaitic Traditions,* 164: "All things considered it is clear to what extent the Sinaitic tradition continued to be determined by Israel's festal-cult right into the monarchical period . . . the literary work of the source-authors, on the other hand, contributed only a little to the final shaping of this tradition."

biblical production. Certainly a group of central traditions arose at an early date and became the subject of later usage and commentary, as Michael Fishbane has demonstrated within the later biblical tradition.[4] The concept of a truly fixed and sacred canon that would guarantee the unchanged transmission of old material, however, only arises in postbiblical times, as James Barr has shown in his recent study *Holy Scripture: Canon, Authority, Criticism*. Thus some of the leading historians of the past two generations appear to have imported an anachronism in the characterization of the history of traditions.

Two reasons for this neglect of the dynamics of canonical development particularly suggest themselves. Most apparent is the historians' desire to reassure themselves of the accuracy of their sources by positing an unchanged transmission of very ancient material. In addition to this factor, though, the turn away from literary history is a function not only of the historians' view of literature but also of their view of history. The interests of the historians might, in other words, have retained an openness to *literary* history, however conceived, but for a further factor: that their real interest has generally been in *political* history.

This interest has been pervasive in scholarship on the development of biblical narrative and lends a political cast to a wide variety of areas, including theological and literary discussion. This interest is so widely shared that it has rarely even been questioned, yet it runs through historical study from the beginning of the century to the present. Often, Christian scholars have sought refuge from uneasiness about the morality of much of the Hebrew Bible by stressing the politics of Israel as a neutral ground on which to do justice to the Hebrew tradition. Thus Gunkel, comparing Hebrew and Christian ethics, concedes that the Hebrew Bible's morality

---

[4] In his article "Revelation and Tradition," Fishbane argues for "an incipient canonical consciousness" from early times; he develops this argument at length in *Biblical Interpretation in Ancient Israel*. See also Gerald T. Sheppard, "Canonization."

is on a lower level, for in its pages religion deals in the first instance with national life, although it was out of this national religion that the higher religion of the individual gradually arose. But at this level of national religion thoughts were born which are still of great value for our time. Chief among these is the thought of the *direct interest of religion in political affairs.* ("Fundamental Problems," 42; his italics)

Later discussions of the origins of biblical narrative have often been shaped by comparable political concerns. Thus the Yahwists who put together the initial account of the patriarchs have often been seen as closely tied to the Davidic court and essentially concerned to give a theological explanation for the rise of the Israelite empire under David and Solomon.[5] This orientation can be summed up in the title of a 1968 article by Walter Brueggemann: "David and His Theologian."

Rolf Rendtorff, one of the most creative contemporary students of pentateuchal composition, touched on this matter in a lecture in 1966 on literary criticism and tradition history:

Throughout our putting of these questions a process of "historicizing" is visible. Many investigations seek to offer a contribution to the *history* of Israel. . . . What more and more attracts our interest are historical connections, developments, tendencies, and so forth: political history, intellectual history, religious history, cult history, and literary history. . . . That is what truly fascinates us and draws our attention. ("Literarkritik," 152)

The noteworthy point here is the order of priority, in which biblical study seeks first the political, and last the literary, history behind the text.

There is no question that the political level is of major importance in biblical narrative, but it is not self-evident that politics should so often be the master-trope from which to view the other aspects of the text. Yet examples of this process

---

[5]See particularly Gerhard von Rad, "The Beginnings of Historical Writing in Ancient Israel." Von Rad develops his political reading of Genesis in relation to Leonhard Rost's highly influential political reading of the David story itself, in *Die Überlieferung von der Thronnachfolge Davids.*

abound, in comparative study as well as in direct discussion of the Bible. A good example is E. A. Speiser's widely read essay, "The Biblical Idea of History in its Common Near Eastern Setting." The topic is one of great interest from a literary point of view, and Speiser, author of the Anchor Bible volume on Genesis and a leading student of Mesopotamian literary texts, is certainly an ideal scholar to assess the ideas of history underlying the different strains of Near Eastern historiography.

Speiser's essay centers on political ideology, and here he draws a sharp contrast. Israel found itself between two dominant cultures, from which it had to choose its model: Assyria-Babylonia on the one side, Egypt on the other. Speiser sees the essence of the two cultures in their governmental structure, with the absolute rule of the divine pharaoh contrasted to the protodemocracy of Babylon, where the king consulted with a council of elders. This political difference was paralleled in religious views, with the Babylonian Council of the Gods as opposed to the supremacy of Ra in Egypt. Having described this difference, Speiser goes on to view the life of the individual in these societies as fundamentally affected by this difference in political ideology and structure: "The dominant factor . . . was the underlying concept of society and the place of the individual in it. Egypt and Mesopotamia were as mutually incompatible as totalitarianism and democracy—and for precisely the same reasons" (207).

This essay, written in 1957, should not be dismissed as a pure cold war fantasy, though the modern analogy is certainly directly made. The patriarchs, leaving Ur "for a healthier religious climate" (210–11), become a kind of amalgam of the Pilgrims and modern refugees from Stalinism, with Abraham making his move "for precisely the same reasons" a modern émigré would opt for democracy over totalitarianism. Modern though the analogy is, it may be grounded in substantial evidence; Speiser's knowledge of Mesopotamia was unexcelled, and he has written persuasively on the importance of the highly developed Babylonian legal system. So let us suppose that the modest limitations on the power of the Babylonian king had far-reaching social consequences, and that the average Babylonian citizen looked forward with serene confidence to the ultimate establishment of independent judiciaries and universal suffrage, a short four millennia later. Granting this,[6] we may note the process by which Speiser reaches his conclusions. He makes three seamless transitions: from the religious to the political, then to the social, and then to the historiographic; and the dominant force here is the political.

A similar perspective is often found even when discussions are less directly centered on political structure, for theological issues are easily translated into speculation about cult politics. So strong is the attraction of a political reading of events that it is not infrequently advanced as the logical explanation even when it is admitted that the political background is too obscure to permit us to know anything at all about it. Martin Noth accounts for the role of Aaron in making the golden calf in this way: "Later rivalries between various groups in the priestly-cultic sphere evidently occasioned the prominent position of Aaron in the polemical narrative of the 'golden calf,' though we can no longer ascertain what lies back of this" (*History*, 182).

---

[6]The sharpness of Speiser's contrast would in fact be difficult to maintain, on several grounds. First, the historical fact of difference between Egypt and Mesopotamia was surely not so absolute as he claims, and readers of the essay will note the degree to which his argument is affected by a classic case of an Assyriologist's anti-Egyptianism. This leads him into quite gratuitous asides, such as a description of the pyramids as "impressive but jejune." Secondly, if there was some difference in political structure that modern historians can reconstruct, it remains to be shown that the authors of the Bible perceived this difference at all, to say nothing of giving it decisive importance. It seems to me that, in the biblical view, Mesopotamian rulers like Nebuchadnezzar and Belshazzar rather closely resemble Pharaoh, as capricious, arbitrary, and extremely powerful autocrats. Finally, it may be questioned how deeply the biblical historians are interested in issues of democracy and autocracy, or even in political issues as such, at all. Though it is often claimed that 1-2 Kings condemns tyrannical rule, I would say that religious issues of loyalty to God and proper cultic practice are uppermost in the minds of the Deuteronomistic historians as they evaluate the kings, rather than any secular issues of economic oppression or curbs on freedom of individual autonomy.

Toward the Systematic Study of Literature

In recent years, historians have tended to modify the earlier emphases on the earliest traditions, on the minimal contributions of the redactors, and on the overarching significance of political history. Emphasis has increasingly shifted to the period around the Exile in the sixth century as decisive for the shaping of much of biblical narrative, a notable change from the earlier concentration on reconstructing a patriarchal age in the second millennium; examples of these newer historical studies will be discussed in chapter 4.

Along with the emphasis on the later history has come a rehabilitation of the redactors and a more integrated sense of the later stages of the text.[7] These changes have paved the way for a revived interest in the story aspect of biblical narrative. A good indication of this change can be seen in two presidential speeches to the Society of Biblical Literature. As recently as 1968, James Muilenberg virtually had to apologize for even mentioning artistry as one feature of biblical composition: "In numerous contexts old literary types and forms are imitated, and, precisely because they are imitated, they are employed with considerable fluidity, versatility, and, if one may venture the term, artistry" ("Form Criticism," 7).

So rapidly did things change over the ensuing fifteen years that Krister Stendahl devoted his presidential address to the Society in 1983 to the subject of the study of the Bible as literature. He began his talk by noting the change:

Thirty years ago there was hardly any attention to an alternative like the Bible as a [literary] classic and the Bible as Holy Scripture. . . . Now there has been a shift from history to story: the Bible as story, theology as story. For both philosophical and literary reasons the focus

---

[7]Already twenty-five years ago, Hans Wilhelm Hertzberg called for a study of the posthistory (*Nachgeschichte*) of biblical texts as a complement to the study of their prehistory ("Die Nachgeschichte," 79).

on language and on forms of literary criticism demand the center stage. ("The Bible," 3)

Whereas shifts among many historians over the past twenty years have laid the groundwork for literary study, it is striking how often biblical scholars themselves now slight history when they turn their attention to literary issues. Surveying current biblical scholarship, a literary critic is likely to feel caught in something of a time warp, as the norm of literary study is taken to be an ahistorical structuralism that has scarcely been seen in general literary studies for the past fifteen years.[8] Why has this happened?

Within biblical studies, an important factor is certainly an element of rebellion against the atomistic tendencies often found in earlier historical work. In this respect, contemporary literary study of the Bible resembles the New-Critical rejection of historical-biographical literary study in the 1930s.[9] A case in point is the new interest in "canonical criticism." A number of biblical scholars, led by Brevard Childs, have begun to give

---

[8]Examples will be found in many of the issues of the journal *Semeia*. A whole series of structuralist and anti-historicist manifestos appears in the two volumes of *Literary Interpretations of Biblical Narratives* edited by Kenneth R. R. Gros Louis. In his introduction to the second volume, Gros Louis flatly asserts that historical study "must, I believe, be rejected by any student of literature" (II, 13). A similarly absolute choice is posited by many of his contributors, as can be seen in the title of Ira Clark's essay, "Balaam's Ass: Suture or Structure?" (II, 137–44). Less polemically, but to similar effect, John Hayes and Carl Holladay say in their recent handbook that "literary criticism . . . recognizes the real value in momentarily suspending consideration of authorship, historical-cultural setting, and other issues in order to focus on the text itself" (*Biblical Exegesis,* 68). Edgar V. McKnight's *Meaning in Texts* expresses a desire to combine historical and literary study, but literary study is so closely equated with a rejection of historical reference that no meaningful interaction is actually envisioned. "A way of combining narrative semiotics and New Testament study may be to forsake the aims of traditional New Testament study and replace them with a 'meaning' which may be obtained only in the discovery of a narrative grammar" (268); in literary study in general, "reference will not be made to real, verifiable historical factors, but to something else" (273).
[9]This analogy has been thoughtfully discussed by John Barton in *Reading the OT,* esp. chap. 10, "The 'New Criticism' " and chap. 11, "The Text Itself" (140–79).

primary emphasis to the study of the final, canonical form of the text. Wishing to aid theology in understanding the text as a whole, Childs seeks to show that the originally disparate source materials have been fundamentally transformed by their inclusion within the Jewish and Christian canons.[10]

The approach has its dangers, as the canonical emphasis can lead to cutting the text off from its compositional history in favor of a modern understanding of the canon and its meaning. In one recent assessment,

Canonical criticism, in at least some of its forms, can be seen as implying an attempt to expel all influence of the history of religion from biblical interpretation. There is scripture itself, and there is theology; theological interpretation is done direct from scripture, and there is no intermediary. (Barr, *Holy Scripture*, 94)

In stressing textual relations in the final form of the text, canonical criticism is open to the objection that it favors the theological concerns of the modern interpreter, with insufficient attention to the discipline involved in trying to reconstruct the historical context of the text's production.[11] In this way, a desire for living truth may bring the canonical critic rather close to the hermeneutic relativism of poststructuralist and deconstructionist literary theorists, who apply a Nietzschean philosophy of language to argue for the radical indeterminacy of all meaning.

In short, Childs may be father to de Man. No one could be less pleased with this implication than Childs himself,[12] but it

---

[10]Childs has set forth his program most fully in his *Introduction to the OT as Scripture* and has recently extended his methods to the New Testament, in his *Introduction to the NT as Scripture*.

[11]See John Barton's comments on Childs in *Reading the OT*, chaps. 6, 7, and 10, and see James Sanders, *From Sacred Story to Sacred Text*, esp. chap. 8, in which he argues for the integration of canonical and historical criticism.

[12]Far from abandoning historical study or the pursuit of authorial intentionality, Childs wishes to show the historical importance of the canonical intentions of the shapers of the final form of the text. In his theory, history is not so much denied as subsumed within textuality: "A religious community emerged which found its identity in terms of sacred scripture. Israel defined itself in

remains true that dissatisfaction with historical study on theological grounds has led the canonical critics rather close to a
relativistic hermeneutics whose validation depends on the
shifting currents of subsequent theologies, or later literary tem-
peraments, rather than on the original world of the text's creation. This tendency within canonical criticism has inspired a
fair amount of strongly negative reaction, and John Barton has
gone so far as to say that Childs's work "gives the impression
of a fulfilment of an inner death-wish of liberal criticism" (*Reading the OT*, 148). When a canonical approach can be applied in
a balanced way, however, it represents a much-needed correc-
tive against the long-standing de-emphasis on the final form
of the text, and interesting results have been produced in the
exegetical work of Childs himself and of others influenced by
his perspective.[13] At the same time, both the canonical movement itself and the criticisms it has inspired testify to the for-
midable difficulties scholars have been having as they attempt
to reconcile historical criticism with an interest in the text in its
received form.

The Historical Study of the Text

While historical critics have been struggling with issues of
history and canonicity, literary scholars have as yet found little

---

terms of a book! The canon formed the decisive *Sitz im Leben* for the Jewish
community's life, thus blurring the sociological evidence most sought after by
the modern historian. When critical exegesis is made to rest on the recovery
of these very sociological distinctions which have been obscured, it runs directly in the face of the canon's intention" (*Introduction to the OT as Scripture*,
78). The interesting thing is that this emphasis on the questionability of traditional historical criticism comes very close to structuralist justifications for
ignoring history altogether: see Polzin's similar statement cited in note 1,
which introduces a structuralist study grounded in the qualified hermeneutic
relativism of Hans-Georg Gadamer. See also Childs's most recent discussion
of the theological uses of his methods, *OT Theology in a Canonical Context*.
[13]Childs's long commentary *The Book of Exodus* is full of fresh readings and takes
advantage of historical criticism while giving priority to the received form of
the text. An impressive example of the application of Childs's ideas is Rolf
Rendtorff's 1983 book *The OT: An Introduction*. Rendtorff reverses customary
practice and gives priority to overall meanings in the received form of the
texts, discussing source history only in passing.

foothold in text history. To be sure, in contrast to the canonical critics, literary scholars may be relatively untroubled by the theological problems raised by conflicts among the component elements of a text. They may, however, be unnerved by the sheer scope of controversy among the historians and must wonder how on earth they are to find any usable historical information when every conclusion is no sooner raised than disputed on several sides.

To some extent, this hesitation is natural to anyone entering a new field of study. As Helen Gardner has said of literary criticism itself, "The ordinary cultured reader, picking up such a journal, feels like someone entering a cinema in the middle of a gangster film, baffled about the antecedents of the battle which is raging, and uncertain who is fighting on whose side" (*The Business of Criticism*, 3–4). All the same, it must be said that the warfare is more general, and the ground less certain, in historical biblical criticism than in most other fields. As Morton Smith put the matter some years ago,

Any honest review of the present state of OT studies must report that there is no prevailing fashion at all; the actual situation is unparalleled in the study of any other body of documents from the ancient Mediterranean world. . . . Palestine itself has no more impressive ruins than those that litter the history of biblical archaeology. ("Present State of OT Studies," 19, 31)

The most devoted historians can testify to the uncertainties attending their work, and many a preface contains a sobering disclaimer such as this:

Concerning the demonstrability of the presentation I have no illusions. The phenomena with which one can work are for the most part of a hypothetical nature. In this area one can surmise much, but prove little. It lies in the nature of the matter and for the present cannot be changed. (Smend, *Yahweh War*, 12)

The literary marshal, newly arrived in town, must wonder how to get any grip on these phantasmal but still highly combative citizens. It would be a bold critic who would not feel a tremor of hesitation, for example, in reading the introduction to Heinrich Valentin's recent study of the early traditions concerning Aaron. Valentin, who is dealing with some two chapters' worth of biblical material, complains with evident distress that financial pressures have forced him to cut down his manuscript from seven hundred pages to a severely constrained four hundred fifty. He then notes that his research was made harder rather than easier by the mass of work on the topic by previous scholars:

Their sweepingly hypothetical and often sharply conflicting results have only increased the undiminished dilemma [of Aaron's origins]. . . . If I had surveyed the scholarly situation at the beginning of my study of Aaron, I would probably not have attempted to take up the topic. (*Aaron*, 25)

Given this alarming situation, little wonder that it has been structuralists who have rushed bravely in where literary historians must fear to tread.

Further, it may well be that the longstanding hold of political history has weakened, and literary history, so often subsumed within political history, has shared its eclipse. Krister Stendahl suggested something like this in accounting for the turn toward structuralism: "The glamour, the glory, the Shekinah has moved away from history" ("The Bible," 3). The dispensability of history was already visible twenty years ago in an early literary study of the Bible by Luis Alonso Schöckel. He raises the compositional history of the story of the ten plagues only to dismiss it:

No one can reasonably doubt that the author of the story as we now have it utilized preëxisting narrative material, some of which was contained in the Yahwistic account, while other elements pertained to the Priestly tradition. . . . The role of the personages involved, the tenor of the refrains used, as well as some other fixed formulas, were also different in the "J" and "P" traditions. But this does not matter: Our author took the two versions as the basis and source for his own composition. (*The Inspired Word*, 203)

By a sleight of hand, Alonso Schöckel turns the two sources

into the single "basis and source" of the final account, which is all he needs to discuss, even though he admits that the materials have not been seamlessly united: "We will not stop here to point out other ways in which the differences in the preëxisting accounts are smoothed out or covered over (not always successfully)" (203).

The sheer denial of history is, however, hardly a satisfactory basis even for close reading of the text, and more recent critics have begun to grapple directly with the problem. Perhaps the most striking and instructive instance can be found in the extended methodological reflections in Meir Sternberg's book *The Poetics of Biblical Narrative*. This remarkable volume, an elaboration and synthesis of twenty years' work, is the fullest and most ambitious structuralist study of the Bible that has yet appeared and sets a new standard for literary study of the Bible. I would like briefly to trace Sternberg's sincere effort to do justice to history, an effort whose drama is increased by its rapid and complete failure, and I would like to show some of the difficulties the collapse of history creates even for such excellent rhetorical/structuralist work as Sternberg's.

At several points in his introduction, Sternberg offers a judicious account of the necessary interdependence of historical and literary study of the Bible. Thus one paragraph opens by expressing surprise that the two approaches should ever be thought of as separate, much less incompatible:

Literary analysis, we often hear, has no truck with textual prehistory. This is neither reasonable nor quite true. Why anyone should wish to deny himself a universal resource for explaining a text's incongruities, whether by appeal to its transmission or to any other framework, remains a mystery. (13)

This generous assessment is, however, immediately followed by a sweeping critique of the entire field of historical study:

Or rather, it would remain one were it not for the incredible abuse of this resource for over two hundred years of frenzied digging into the Bible's genesis, so senseless as to elicit either laughter or tears. Rarely has there been such a futile expense of spirit in a noble cause . . . rarely have so many worked so long and so hard with so little to show for their trouble. . . . Small wonder, then, that literary approaches react against this atomism by going to the opposite extreme of holism. (13)

He follows this broadside with a note of compromise: "But the excesses and fruitlessness of traditional source criticism no more legitimate the waving aside of its available data than they illegitimate its goals" (13). Perhaps the historian may be heartened by this assurance, but the literary student will scarcely be led to feel that there is any point in investigating a field that in two hundred years has borne no fruit beyond the occasional senseless excess. One almost wonders whether paragraphs like these have not been compiled from two quite different sources, one vaguely but ineffectually hospitable to historical study, the other openly contemptuous of it.

In principle, Sternberg is open to historical accounting for gaps and contradictions in the text, but in practice he is opposed to the use of such information, for it threatens to deprive him of the material with which he most likes to work. For many close readers, especially those raised on modern literature, gaps and ambiguity are the stuff of rhetorical drama, the very basis of literary experience. This is implicit in much literary biblical study, and it is Sternberg's particular theme: gaps and ambiguities in the text mirror the mysteries of experience faced by the biblical characters themselves as they struggle with God. Thus our reading process mirrors the lives of the characters and accounts for the richness of biblical narrative:

The ubiquity of gaps about character and plot exposes us to our own ignorance: history unrolls as a continuum of discontinuities, a sequence of non sequiturs, which challenge us to repair the omissions by our own native wit. . . . Far beyond the normal demands of interpretation and with no parallel in Oriental literature, therefore, the world and the meaning are always hypothetical, subject to change from one stage of the reading *process* to another, and irreducible to any simple formula. With the narrative become an obstacle course, its reading turns into a drama of understanding. . . . The only knowledge perfectly acquired is the knowledge of our limitations. (47)

As Sternberg develops this argument, it comes to sound remarkably close to Stanley Fish's thesis about Milton in *Surprised by Sin:* that Milton's seeming contradictions and his inability to keep us from sympathizing with Satan are a deliberate ruse first to seduce us and then to reform us. Fish's perhaps over-ingenious argument is, at any rate, applied to the work of a single and highly self-reflective author. Sternberg extends the argument to the entire range of biblical narrative, convinced that there is *a* poetics of biblical narrative extending through all the major narrative texts, despite the large number of authors and the seven hundred or so years of composition involved. But perhaps, after all, a literary reader can only make some such assumption or else face the loss of the sense of the whole text?

An important issue in addressing this question is the frame of reference in which we are to view the activity of the biblical authors. Sternberg consistently asserts the independence of their techniques from ancient practice in general, and further dismisses the idea that anything can be learned from the putting together of the Bible's own sources. Yet these dismissals do not leave Sternberg free to examine the Bible "in itself," free from any exterior context: rather, they allow him to view the Bible consistently within the context of early modernist literary technique. A good example of this occurs when he discusses the use of artful narration by characters within the Bible. As self-aware speakers, competent or incompetent shapers of language, biblical characters can be compared to the artists who appear as characters in modern novels:

Artistic norms thus operate as a general measure of a character's reliability throughout James's exposure of the dilettantish Gilbert Osmond in *Portrait of a Lady*, [or] Joyce's citation of Stephen Dedalus's theories in *Portrait of the Artist*. . . . The Bible is hardly so literate. But since its inhabitants employ words or even persuasive tools, they are no less subject to implicit judgment in their roles as speakers. (155)

Thus, inconsistencies and other problems in story telling are meant to testify to the characters' distance from the author's own godlike omniscience and skill, drawing the drama of our reading ever closer to the drama of the characters' experience. Composition history fades away before "the game of art, whose name is difficult coherence."

This is plausible if the text really is a fully unified and self-consciously artful composition, the work of a single author like Henry James or James Joyce. Suppose, however, that the cataclysm of the First World War had left us with only fragments of the two novels just mentioned, with no clear memory of their original nature. Suppose that a later editor, finding the fragments and believing them to be versions of a single story, had pieced together the *Portrait of a Lady as a Young Man*, by someone known only as "James," or "J." No doubt, a sufficiently skillful editor might put together a text that later scholars could read in a unified fashion. Even the hero/heroine's frequent changes of sex could to some extent be thematically justified by reference to the theme of androgyny in "James's" oeuvre, and further understood by comparison to other modernist literature, such as Woolf's *Orlando*. All the same, there can be little doubt that various problems in the text could best be solved by unraveling the two strands of "J," distinguishing the Henry James contributions from those by James Joyce.

At its best, Sternberg's perspective produces marvelously rich and sympathetic accounts of the subtle modulations of many biblical stories as they shift point of view and other narrative techniques and manipulate our knowledge of what is going on. Often, on the other hand, we seem to be watching the literary critics of Tlön, in Borges's tale, as they take two books from different shelves, postulate a common author, and then speculate about the broad and mysterious range of this author's interests and modes of expression.[14] The wide range

---

[14]"A critic will choose two dissimilar works—the *Tao Te Ching* and the *Thousand and One Nights*, let us say—and attribute them to the same writer, and then

of technique observable in biblical narrative is unified in an account that draws no distinction between the earliest and latest elements, between the simplest and the most complex. Clearly Sternberg's arguments could be refined in light of the historical evidence he admits in theory but dismisses in practice. But how are these disparate fields of study to be reconciled?

Toward the History of Biblical Literature

For all their differences, historical and literary study of biblical narrative have had much in common all along. Well-meaning affirmations of general similarities have not, however, proved enough to achieve any real rapprochement so far. What is needed, I believe, is a recognition of a different series of similarities: the aspects of literary history that both sides have jointly neglected. In the balance of this chapter, I will focus on four such aspects, methodological matters that underlie the chapters to follow and that form a large part of the common ground between historical and literary study. In all four cases, I would again stress that it is not a matter of inventing a new field of study, but of emphasizing neglected areas that have been entered only sporadically and usually unsystematically by historians and literary critics alike.

The Importance of the Near Eastern Literary Background

Since the end of the last century, biblical scholars have made use of the large and still growing body of rediscovered literary material from the ancient Near East. From the beginning, though, the use of this material was characterized by haphazard and uncritical examination. Several factors undoubtedly account for this, including the sheer difficulty of mastering the relevant languages, and the foreignness of the cultures so re-

---

with all probity explore the psychology of this interesting *homme de lettres*"
(Jorge Luis Borges, "Tlön, Uqbar, Orbis Tertius," 28).

cently brought to light. Beyond this, it has to be said that most scholars who took up the comparative material exhibited one of two opposite tendencies: a naive enthusiasm that led them to see parallels everywhere (the reductionism of which Sternberg complains), or else a cultural imperialism that led them to analyze comparative material only to set up the qualitative superiority of the Bible on almost every count.

Thus, in the first instance, Peter Jensen produced a thousand-page study at the turn of the century claiming that the *Gilgamesh Epic* was the source for the stories of Abraham, Isaac, Jacob, Joseph, Moses, Samson, Saul, David, Jeroboam, Jesus, Paul, Odysseus, and Mohammed, among others.[15] A later and less global work by Alexander Heidel, *The Gilgamesh Epic and Old Testament Parallels,* can stand as representative of the second sort of comparative work. Parallels are carefully noted, but Heidel frequently draws an absolute contrast between worldviews that are "as far apart as the east is from the west" (223). Throughout his study, the refined Hebrew text is set off against the theological and literary primitiveness of the Babylonian story, which is "steeped in the silliest polytheism" (268).

Though early attempts at comparative study perhaps inevitably showed difficulties in critical balance, it is remarkable how persistent the same patterns are even today. Overstressing of parallels is still common; thus, when R. N. Whybray finds an Egyptian analogue for a motif in the David story, he discusses it exclusively, without considering earlier examples of the same motif in the Bible itself.[16] Stark contrasts to compar-

---

[15]Peter Jensen, *Das Gilgamesch-Epos in der Weltliteratur.* He followed this with an inflammatory little pamphlet asserting that the early church had largely invented the stories of Jesus and Paul on the basis of the Gilgamesh model (*Moses, Jesus, Paulus: Drei Varianten des babylonischen Gottmenschen Gilgamesch*). Twenty years later, his enthusiasm for his topic undiminished, he pursued his ideas on relations to classical culture in *Gilgamesch-Epos, jüdäische Nationalsagen, Ilias und Odyssee.* Some relation between Gilgamesh and Odysseus is actually perfectly imaginable, as the parallel openings of the two works already suggest, and a number of later scholars have drawn on Jensen's work; but direct parallels to Jesus and Mohammed are another matter.

[16]He argues that the Succession Narrative is uniquely literary and owes its

ative material are also widely found. James Barr (in "The Meaning of 'Mythology' ") and Herbert Schneidau (in *Sacred Discontent*) discuss pagan myth from very different perspectives, but each is primarily concerned to stress the Bible's absolute break from mythic thinking.

Often, a parallel is cited only to be denied. Thus R. E. Clements devotes a chapter to a discussion of relations between early Yahwism and Canaanite religion, and then assures us that the parallels have been so entirely transformed as to be virtually irrelevant:

> It was not the outward features, either of names or cult, that distinguished Israel, but the fact that such names and practices had been filled with an entirely new content. Whatever Israel borrowed in its allegiance to the god of Mount Sinai was of no real importance beside the fact that they worshipped him as the God, who, out of sheer grace, had delivered them out of slavery and called them to be his people.
>
> This gave birth to what was essentially a wholly new religion, although . . . there were woven into this many features of earlier belief and cult. (*God and Temple*, 20)

It is fair to say that comparative material will receive short shrift at important points when the researcher is influenced by a programmatic desire to demonstrate a qualitative break between the materials to be compared.

The Flexible Use of Methods

Unified work has often been hampered by the championing of one critical method as the long-desired key to a true understanding of the issue at hand. Within biblical study, the techniques of form criticism, tradition history, "literary" (textual) criticism, source criticism, and redaction criticism have often assumed quite separate lives. Of late, there has been a new

---

power to the influence of Egyptian wisdom narrative and Egyptian-inspired texts like Proverbs. Thus David's problems in handling his sons illustrate the wisdom motif of the need to discipline one's children, a theme Whybray discusses in relation to Proverbs without mentioning its importance in 1 Samuel or in Genesis (*The Succession Narrative*, 83 ff.).

and welcome emphasis on the necessary interaction of these methods, as notably seen in Wolfgang Richter's *Exegese als Literaturwissenschaft.*[17]

Even in recent literary discussions, however, there still remains a pronounced tendency to assert the need for a sharp choice between historical and literary methods. Robert Polzin opens his ambitious structuralist study of Deuteronomy by acknowledging the pervasive presence of this choice: "The very first question that today confronts anyone who attempts to analyze biblical material in a scholarly context is: Should one's approach be primarily historical or literary, diachronic or synchronic?"[18] The question would better be how these perspectives can interact, rather than which is to be master.

A movement toward a genuine interaction of method can be seen in John Barton's notable study *Reading the Old Testament.* Even here, however, the essence of literary study is taken to be classic, ahistorical structuralism, studying "the text *in its finished form,* as it lies before us, and not in hypothetical earlier stages of its growth" (127). Literary history is little more than a species of redaction criticism, whose value is limited at best:

More often than not it is either unnecessary, because the text is a unity anyway, and we are competent to read it, or unsuccessful, because the inconsistencies that remain . . . are such that we remain in doubt as to how it should be read in its finished form. . . . the redactor's mind is far more opaque to us than we should like to think. (58)

Barton argues that canonical criticism moves in the right direction but has not gone far enough: it should free itself of its lingering attachment to authorial intention and devote study to

---

[17]Richter makes a heroic effort to order these methods, showing their distinctness and their interdependence. At the same time, his effort to construct a linear and unvarying progression from the use of one method to the next brings a little too much order to the scene, as in his claim that "the ordered sequence of methodological steps cannot be reversed" (72).

[18]Robert Polzin, *Moses and the Deuteronomist,* 1. Polzin admirably discusses the necessity of combining structural and historical study, though he still sees them as quite distinct phases, and in practice gives a pronounced priority to structural study.

the generic forms created, by whatever historical processes, within the received text. Barton makes a strong case for the value of structuralist study, notably in his discussion of the ways in which the radically negative elements in Ecclesiastes are softened by the orthodox context in which the book has been placed. As he wittily concludes,

So determined by context is the meaning that the author himself cannot force the text to bear a meaning that the setting will not allow: Qoheleth may well be gnashing the teeth he would not have expected to find in Sheol over the way his bitter words have lost their edge by being included in the orthodox framework of sacred Scripture. (102–3)

The example of Ecclesiastes is, however, a kind of limit case; the canonical context (as Barton elsewhere admits) is very far from determining meaning in most cases, but rather allows for a range of possible meaning. Given this fact, structuralist criticism can be of great assistance in helping to define the range of meaning permitted, but it will not in itself give much guidance in assessing the different possibilities. The study of genre and structure only reaches its full force when it is linked to historical study of the generic possibilities that existed before, during, and after the time of a given text's creation. The problem is that structuralist readings, like all readings, are never actually innocent of history; if the ancient context is left unexamined, then the alternative, seen in case after case, is the importation of modern generic norms and expectations. It is in recognition of this fact that poststructuralist thought rarely pretends any longer to an objectivity beyond history, and although some theorists have followed Derrida and others into a stance of full relativism, much poststructuralist thought has, to the contrary, sought out a renewed connection to the historical contexts so often obliquely inscribed within the texts themselves.[19]

---

[19]As one indication of this shift, witness the title of the ambitious series now appearing from the University of California Press under the editorship of

Literary-critical methods really cannot replace historical-critical techniques; nor can they simply come in at the end of the series to do a cleanup operation on the final form of the text. Rather, as will be evident in the chapters to follow, what is needed is a continual back-and-forth among different methods and different levels of the text. This is nothing new, as even studies subtitled "Eine formgeschichtliche Untersuchung" or "A Structuralist Reading" have often employed a range of method in the actual working through of the argument. What is new is the possibility of fully developed literary-historical analysis. The union of structural and historical study should not be dismissed, as Barton does, as an effort that "merely adds structuralist ideas to the historical-critical tool-box" (131); on the contrary, such a combining of methods is precisely what is most needed.

The Bible Is Not a Novel

The Bible is highly *literary* at almost every moment, but only sporadically and incidentally does it happen to resemble fictional literature as such. This sounds like a truism, but it is widely denied in practice. If we approach the Bible as literature—as very many introductory college courses do, whether given in religion or English departments—an unfortunate corollary almost immediately appears. Much of the Bible reads like very good novelistic literature indeed; but much of it reads like rather *poor* literature. Our natural tendency is to begin skimming rapidly over large stretches on our way to the good parts, skipping whole books as we gain confidence that Genesis or 2 Samuel will give us rich literary pleasure, whereas a book like 2 Kings is limited at best. And as for Leviticus . . .

Biblical scholars who take up literary analysis turn just as gladly as literary scholars to novelistically satisfying episodes

---

Stephen Greenblatt: The New Historicism. See also Norman Gottwald's interdisciplinary study, *The Hebrew Bible: A Socio-Literary Introduction*, esp. 595–609.

like the Joseph story and the story of King David. Indeed, no book on biblical literature, this one included, thinks itself complete these days without an extended reading of at least one of those two stories, whereas fully three quarters of the Bible is visited sporadically at best.

The problem here is twofold. First, very few of the biblical writers seem to have thought they were writing literature, and we inevitably distort our view of what they were doing if we pass quickly over most of what they did in fact write. Second, granting that the body of 1–2 Kings will never grip us the way the Succession Narrative of David does, the later history of the monarchy provides an essential context for understanding the David story itself. Further, and more surprisingly, the material of Kings is often in the background in the story of Moses as well—an aspect of the theme of reciprocal influence that will be developed in the following chapters.

The presence of the legal material in the Pentateuch is a case in point. Christian scholars have long tended to minimize the importance of biblical law. Thus one recent writer sees an either-or choice between law and narrative, and opts with relief for the latter: "Recognizing the nonlegalistic aspect of the use of the word Torah is an aid in understanding how even the Pentateuch itself, the Torah par excellence, is basically a narrative, a story, rather than a code of laws" (Sanders, *Torah and Canon*, 3). In this viewpoint, the writer follows such earlier scholars as Speiser, who tells us, speaking of the essence of the Pentateuch, that "law enters into it only indirectly, in so far as the inner content requires a shell of formal regulations."[20]

If the legal passages are approached (or avoided) with such a perspective, it is unlikely that much progress will be made in grasping their inner life and meaning. In his introduction to

---

[20]E. A. Speiser, "Idea of History," 207. Thirty years earlier, C. H. Dodd had called the Law "the bony skeleton which supported the warm flesh and blood of prophetic religion" (*Authority of the Bible*, 154). Whether the metaphor is endoskeletal or exoskeletal, the common theme is ossification.

the Old Testament, Otto Eissfeldt notes the literary problem posed by law, one might say by the accretion of all this formal shell-work:

> It is one of the tasks of Pentateuchal criticism to explain how this interruption of the narrative by large blocks of law took place; it appears inept from a literary and aesthetic point of view, and even the young Goethe took exception to it. (*The OT,* 157)

In practice, once scholars have noted that the mixing of law and narrative serves the ideological purpose of giving Sinaitic authority to the laws, they say no more about the issue. It is certainly true that any reading inevitably involves selection, and it would be absurd to claim that one could *only* study episodes in Exodus and Numbers in the context of the law, but the wholesale neglect of such a large body of material must in the end distort our view of the Pentateuch even as narrative.

Critics who pass lightly over the law as not of the essence should be aware that they are perpetuating in new terms the early Christian polemic against the value of the law. I doubt that most literary analysts would be likely to treat an equal body of material in the New Testament so cavalierly. To take the most direct parallel to the Pentateuch, it is fair to say that the essence of the Gospels is the historical story, especially the story of Christ's passion, death, and resurrection. It has rightly been said that Mark's Gospel is a passion narrative with a long preface. Yet this emphasis has not led analysts to ignore Christ's teachings wholesale. There may indeed have been an emphasis on the more literary aspect of his teaching, especially the parables, but no one would seriously claim of Matthew's Gospel that the centrality of narrative history would render the Sermon on the Mount irrelevant to any and every literary inquiry. Indeed, much of Matthew's narrative is shaped around that central body of teaching, and many studies of the thematics and shape of his narrative proper are informed by the teachings of the Sermon on the Mount.[21]

---

[21]The argument is occasionally made that Jesus' teachings are eloquent ethical

If this is so in the New Testament, where the Sermon occupies a small fraction of Matthew's Gospel, it is not inconceivable that it might be all the more true of the pentateuchal law, on which Matthew's sermon is obviously modeled, and which occupies such a large part of the Torah. Perhaps the very extent of the legal material has been part of the problem. The lawlike teaching in Matthew is sufficiently limited in extent that a literary critic can at least read through it without starting to think of something else. Encountering the Sermon repeatedly in the course of rereading the Gospel narrative, the critic is gradually brought to perceive its centrality and its broad literary relevance to the rest of the Gospel, and carries on from there. But fairly few literary readers seem to have read attentively through Leviticus as a regular matter on their way from Exodus to Numbers.

The more famous stories are justly famed and are sure to retain a dominant literary interest, but large stretches of less novelistic biblical narrative will amply reward literary study for their own sake. There will perhaps always remain intractable ground, such as "the Death Valley of the Chronicler," in Morton Smith's phrase ("Present State of OT Studies," 29). But the fertile microenvironments of the more enjoyable materials are never entirely isolated from their surroundings. In the case of law and narrative in the Pentateuch, the pervasive presence of blocks of law has a variety of literary consequences. From a developmental point of view it can be said that the laws were added to the stories, but from the point of view of the people who shaped the text as we have it, it is truer to say that the stories have been preserved as a useful setting for the Law, indeed as commentary on the Law. The mixing of law and narrative was not a crude blunder by incompetent editors whom even the young Goethe could only deplore; rather, it was the most important generic innovation of its age. It can fairly be

statements, not at all comparable to the dry legalisms of the Torah; this is only another version of the appearance of religious polemic in the guise of aesthetic judgment.

compared with the revolutionary mixing of prose and poetic values by the Yahwistic writers, and has had far-reaching effects on the narrative material around it. As I hope to show, a legal collection like Leviticus has a pronounced narrative aspect itself, and the workings of the story around it cannot be fully understood without a sustained literary study of that least literature-like of books.

The Complexity of Generic Development

The final area in which I wish to explore the possibility of greater cooperation between historical and literary scholarship has to do with the meaning of genre in the ancient world and the nature of generic transformations in biblical times. The difficulty scholars have had in making effective use of comparative material and in studying the complex generic form of the Pentateuch goes beyond the possible presence of a cultural agenda, and also involves the difficulties inherent in sorting out the transformations of genre in the Near East. Generic development cannot always be accounted for simply by uncovering earlier examples of what is taken to be the genre in question. The problem is that when all is said and done, the Babylonian Chronicles, for example, are far less rich and compelling pieces of writing than the biblical narratives for which they must in some sense have stood as models. This problem can be dealt with in two ways, if one stays within a linear model of generic development. Often scholars are unwillingly led toward the reductive assertion of an immediate and direct influence; on the other hand, they may throw up their hands with the baffled admission that the biblical text remains immeasurably superior to its identified predecessor. This leaves us with a general sense of the ineffability of the whole mystery but no real clue as to how the biblical writers made their great leap forward.

A way out of this dilemma lies in the recognition that major generic development often occurs not by the isolated modification of an existing genre in itself but by the *merging* of formerly separate genres. To take an example from Greek historiography, it is true that the highly developed history writing of Thucydides is scarcely imaginable without the earlier, simpler stage of historiography seen in Herodotus; and Thucydides is very direct in acknowledging his debt to, and his distance from, his predecessor. At the same time, Thucydides did not simply refine Herodotus alone in the alembic of his immortal soul but added a variety of thematic and compositional elements borrowed from Athenian tragedy. *The Peloponnesian War* could no more have been written without Sophocles than without Herodotus.[22] A comparable development underlies the growth of biblical narrative. The process is a complex one, but not irrecoverable if one uses the wide range of comparative material available and attends to the dynamics of generic interaction whose effects are clearly visible in the various stages of the Bible's development.

The four areas outlined here can provide the basis for a fully developed and effective literary-historical approach to study of the Bible. Through the historical study of the evolution of generic forms and other structural patterns one can mediate between the final form of the text and the world of its creation without falling prey to a naive intentionalism or resigning oneself to a hermeneutic relativism. Genre is, however, not an easy subject of study. Genres have often been fluid constructs, liable to change over time and at different hands in given periods, so that the historical study of genre raises theoretical problems of its own. Before proceeding to specific studies in Near Eastern generic development, I would like in the balance of this chapter to advance some general considerations concerning the nature of generic transformation in the ancient world.

Genre in the Ancient Near East

The norms of genre are fundamental to the construction of meaning in texts, but at the same time, paradoxically, they are susceptible of constant alteration, deliberate or inadvertent, as

---

[22]See F. M. Cornford, *Thucydides Mythistoricus*. A similar point can be made concerning Herodotus himself, who revolutionized the genre of Halicarnassan chronicle by importing and modifying a wide variety of other literary forms.

new authors attempt to adapt old forms to changed circumstances and purposes. In studying the generic form of ancient Near Eastern texts, it is necessary to rely on direct textual evidence, supplemented by occasional indications of a text's purpose, authorship, or audience; what we do not have is any explicit theory of genre. Such categorization of texts as existed at the time tended to be based not on specific genre qualities of form or content but rather on the media of performance or inscription. Thus, in Akkadian, *zamaru,* "song," is used of any sung or chanted composition and can equally refer to epics or hymns. At the same time, a text like the *Gilgamesh Epic* can also be called an *ishkaru,* "lesson" or "series of tablets," among other words designating the text's physical form. In Egyptian, similarly, there are words for "song" and for "book" but no overall word even to distinguish literature from factual writing, unless one considers the term *mdt nfrt,* "beautiful speech," to some extent equivalent to "belles lettres" but also including any sort of elegant rhetoric. That the Egyptians had no theory of literature is, of course, a very different thing from supposing that they had no literature. Apart from the inherent literariness and fictionality of many Egyptian stories, direct indications of the use of literature as entertainment are occasionally found, as in the titles of some collections of secular love poetry, such as "The Songs of Excellent Enjoyment"; the fluidity of terms is seen here too, however, as other collections of love poetry are called "sayings" (Lichtheim, *Ancient Egyptian Literature,* III, 181).

Similarly, the Bible records general categories of "song" (*shir*) and of "book" (*sepher*), the latter sometimes used in contexts in which the natural translation would be "history" or "chronicle." Some more specific designations are also found, such as "psalm," *tehillah,* and "proverb," *mashal,* but there are no recorded indications of any overall interest in classifying genres or even in formally distinguishing such categories as epic, historiography, novella, or fable. In the absence of such labels, our sense of the texts must be derived purely from the thematic and formal shape of the text and from any indications there may be as to the purposes for which it was produced and the ways in which it was used.

Of particular concern in the following chapters will be three general categories of genre: epic, chronicle, and history. The major narrative forms in Mesopotamian literature of the second millennium B.C. were poetic epic and prose chronicle. Each of these forms can be subdivided as well, but to begin with, something should be said about the overall categories. By "epic" Assyriologists refer to long narrative poems, written in an elevated poetic style with pronounced use of rhythm and poetic parallelism, meant to be sung or chanted in public performance, dealing with mythic stories of the interactions of the gods or of the gods and mortals, usually in early times. By "chronicle" I will refer to the common forms of recording of historical events, usually focused on the military exploits of kings, written in a spare prose style, with little interest in portrayal of character or complexities of motivation, concerns much more common in epic. Chronicle typically focuses on the political/military achievements of a specific king or dynasty rather than on deep existential issues of the meaning and limits of culture. One common way of distinguishing epic from chronicle is to contrast the mythic emphasis in epic with the earthly, historical focus of chronicle. As will be discussed in the next chapter, this distinction does not hold up in any absolute sense, as historical concerns are often found within poetic epic and "mythic" representations of the interactions of gods and mortals are common in Near Eastern chronicle. A certain difference of degree may be recognized, however, in that poetic epic tends to concern itself largely with the activities of the gods, whereas chronicle focuses largely on recording specific historical events, in which the power of the gods is manifested relatively indirectly in most instances.

In contrast to the limited and heavily tendentious recording of events in the different forms of chronicle,[23] by "history" or

---

[23]Within the overall category of chronicle in its broad sense, several genres or subgenres are commonly distinguished. The most common of these are an-

"history writing" in its full form I follow many scholars in referring to the flowering of complex historical prose in Israel and in Greece beginning in the first half of the first millennium B.C. "Historical prose" in this period does not necessarily mean a neutral, or even accurate, recording of events on the basis of personal knowledge or the careful weighing of sources, though some degree of drawing on older chronicle is found within the history of the Israelite monarchy and, to a greater and more explicit extent, within Herodotus. What is signified above all is a new openness to narrative representation of character and action, an attempt at a fully realized portrayal of events and their meaning, admitting multiple and sometimes ambiguous causal factors, and showing negative as well as positive aspects of events and of protagonists' characters. What is important is not the objective accuracy of the narrative but rather its claim to represent the full historical truth.[24] Historical prose in this sense would include both the Deuteronomistic history of the nation in Joshua through 2 Kings and also the Yahwistic reworking of old legendary material into the extended "history" of the patriarchs in Genesis.

The great question is how the Hebrew writers came to write such rich and ambitious historical prose, apparently beginning almost as soon as a scribal elite was established in the early monarchy and very rapidly outstripping, in length, complexity,

---

nals, year-by-year accounts of a king's reign, often told in the first person in the voice of the king; building inscriptions, describing events leading up to the construction of a palace or temple or to the bringing of booty or tribute to a temple; and chronicles proper, in the narrower sense of the term an official court record, written in the third person, of events during kings' reigns. See the extensive survey of forms of Mesopotamian historiography by A. K. Grayson in his contribution to a series of articles, "Histories and Historians of the Ancient Near East," titled "Assyria and Babylonia."

[24]See Meir Sternberg's excellent account of the importance of distinguishing between the truth value of a text and its truth claims (*Poetics of Biblical Narrative*, 23–35). The mere fact that a biblical tale cannot be historically true in a modern assessment does not mean that it was produced or read as fiction. The Yahwists and Deuteronomists are absolute in their assertion of the truth of their accounts, in which the idea of "fiction" can only be applied to lies and stories invented by characters within the narrative.

and literary power, any known examples of historical prose in earlier Near Eastern chronicle. The thesis of this book is that the origins of Hebrew historical prose can be traced in Mesopotamian literature of the second millennium, but not through a direct comparison of historical writings alone. Rather, the Bible's historical writing can best be understood as the result of a far-reaching transformation of earlier genres, resulting in a combination of many of the values, themes, and formal properties of historical chronicle with those of poetic epic. Scholars who have sharply separated epic from chronicle, and myth from history, have thus unduly restricted the Near Eastern evidence that can, and should, be used in assessing this movement, since the background to the confluence of epic and history can already be shown within Mesopotamian literature itself, as will be seen below. All the same, however, even once the earlier materials have been examined together, there remains a pronounced novelty to Hebrew historical writing. Biblical narrative cannot simply be understood as a translation of epic into prose, an analogy that has occasionally been made with unconvincing directness. In periods when revolutionary transformations of existing genres are undertaken, the older forms are subverted even as they are renewed, and biblical narrative is the product of a rich mixture of direct use, thorough adaptation, and outright polemical rejection of earlier narrative practices.

The Crossing of Genres

Radical transformations of genre such as those to be discussed here are the product of different forces than those that lead to more limited and orderly variation within given forms. Two different kinds of impetus appear to have been at work in ancient Israel: first, extraordinary historical events, which created the need for historical narratives to explain and justify a rapidly changing situation; second, ideological shifts that led to dissatisfaction with existing narrative forms. Two tumultuous periods of Israelite history have often been considered to have provided a particular impetus for literary composition: the establishment of the monarchy under David and Solomon (c. 1000–930), and the destruction of the nation of Israel and the exile into Babylon in 587–520. Analogies to the heightened interest in historical narrative in both of these periods can readily be found. Nearest to hand might be mentioned the two great flowerings of Babylonian literature: first, in the period of large-scale social and religious reform under Nebuchadnezzar I in the late 1100s, and second, in the late period in which Babylon was controlled by foreign Hellenistic rulers, a time when Berossus and other writers were moved to collect and preserve the literary heritage of their threatened civilization.[25]

Yet the texts produced in these periods of Babylonian literary history generally show advances within existing genres rather than the sweeping recombinations found in the biblical writers. For an analogy to their fundamental reconstruction of a literary heritage, one must turn elsewhere, and perhaps the best comparison would be to the situation in Greece and Rome in late antiquity. The classic study of the impulse to novelty in the Alexandrian era is Wilhelm Kroll's essay, "Die Kreuzung der Gattungen," a title that might best be translated, in a botanical sense, as "the cross-fertilization of genres." In this period, old, well-established genres largely ceased to suffice in the shaping of literary structure. Poets were moved to radical transformations and recombinations, writing epics in which dramatic, rhetorical monologues predominate over narrated action and traditional dialogue, and writing lyrics in which there appears an influx of techniques from drama, like stychometheia.

Kroll discusses two different factors behind this broad pattern of generic change. The first is a change in the means and purpose of production, as lyric poetry lost its traditional direct connection to music, becoming for the first time primarily a

---

[25]These are the periods that A. K. Grayson identifies as the principal eras of the production of historical epic ("Assyria and Babylonia," 187–89).

written form, meant to be read rather than performed. Though the poets still considered themselves "singers," they were no longer composing song lyrics, and as a result the lyric form could be opened up to the use of elements previously confined to other performance media like drama or epic.

Along with the changed conditions of production there went a "modern" desire for novelty. Kroll sees in poets like Ovid, Catullus, Propertius, and Horace a search for surprising effects, a result of their "striving to appear modern at any cost" (202). The driving force was a desire to find individual expression for personal experience. The popularity of the elegy in this period, and at the same time the great changes made in the elegy itself, had much to do with its suitability as a medium for private expression; as Kroll says, "above all, it reflected subjectivity, and hence it appeared as a modern genre, adaptable to the most varied contents" (208). Though old forms could also be developed relatively unchanged (with traditional epic still practiced by figures like Apollonius of Rhodes and his successors), the importation of elements of elegy and tragedy into the metrical form and mythological context of epic created a very new form, *epyllion*, virtually an anti-epic form, which served to personalize and subjectivize the traditionally objective and suprapersonal form of epic.

Something comparable is at work in the creation of biblical narrative as well. Though the sense of modernity has different roots and finds different expressions in the Bible, it is certainly true that the new creation of a united Israel and the development of the new, monotheistic conception of God together led to a sense of Hebrew culture as distinctively new, indeed as "modern" in opposition to the surrounding ancient cultures.

The idea of modernity first becomes both explicit and central for the Deuteronomists. The famous creedal formula accompanying the harvest festival offering in Deuteronomy 26 begins with a bold assertion of the continuity of modern Israel with the history of the Exodus and the conquest of Canaan, symbolized by the figure of Jacob/Israel: "A wandering Aramean was my father; and he went down into Egypt. . . . and the Lord brought us out of Egypt with a mighty hand and an out-stretched arm, with great terror, with signs and wonders; and he brought us into this place and gave us this land, a land flowing with milk and honey" (26:5–10). The worshiper asserts his direct linkage with the patriarchal age, collapsing the in-tervening centuries in the affirmation of Jacob as "my father." In this respect the allusion to "my father" creates a union with the past, and might in other contexts suggest the very opposite of a consciousness of modernity; but the rest of the statement construes the past origin of the Hebrew people as arising through a radical break with previous history. Before God's saving acts in Egypt and the wilderness, Israel is portrayed through its eponymous ancestor as wandering, *'oved*, a term elsewhere used of stray cattle and lost property. The very iden-tification of Israel's origins as an Aramean emphasizes the break with cultural roots. Israel *was* what he no longer *is*: an Aramean from Syria, cut off from his own people, a solitary figure or clan who wandered down to Egypt, where "he be-came a people [*goy*], great, mighty, and populous" (v. 5). By contrast with the older societies around them, societies that were genuinely ancient and that exaggerated their antiquity even further, the Deuteronomists portray their genuinely young culture as much younger than it really was. In this way, the affirmation of Jacob as the worshiper's immediate ancestor actually heightens the emphasis on modernity: Israel has only just established itself as a unique culture, and this new cultural identity is both modern and contingent, since the Hebrew who fails to worship God properly will rapidly slip back into one or another form of the ancient general Canaanite culture and lose the newfound identity as one of the people of God. The ritual, as is often said, reactualizes the past, but the emphasis here is on the reactualization of the originary break with existing cul-tures and previous history.

Few would now agree with Gerhard von Rad's bold hypoth-esis (in "The Form-Critical Problem of the Hexateuch") that the entire structure of Deuteronomy grew out of this brief creedal formula, but there is no question that here (as often) von Rad perceived a poetic truth. In a very real sense, Deuteronomy and the whole Deuteronomistic historical enterprise grow out of the emphatically modern historical perspective succinctly expressed in the alliterative formula 'arammi 'oved 'avi, "a wandering Aramean (was) my father."

A sense of modernity does not necessarily produce "modernist" literature, however; often, it produces an archaizing, pseudepigraphical effort to recreate ancient values through the imitation of ancient forms. Even when modernity is expressly asserted, the actual practice of literary creation need not share the radicalism of the theory. A good example of this is found in an Egyptian wisdom text, "The Lamentations of Khakheperre-sonbe," which probably dates from the nineteenth century B.C. It is a measure of the antiquity of Egyptian culture that a scribe writing not long after the close of the third millennium could already see himself as a modern, as heir to, and even oppressed by, the thousand years of literary tradition before his time. Khakheperre-sonbe begins his text with the classic "modern" lament of the difficulty of saying anything not already said so often before him as to have become a cliché:

Would that I had unknown speeches, erudite phrases in new language which has not yet been used, free from the usual repetitions, not the phrases of past speech which our forefathers spoke. I must wring myself dry of what is in me, giving free rein to all I have to say. For indeed whatever has been said has been repeated, while what has been said has been said. There should be no pride about the literature of the men of former times or what their descendants have turned up since![26]

His desire for a new language to express a new perception of reality leads Khakheperre-sonbe to assert a break with the older forms of wisdom literature; he will not recall the lessons of past

_____

[26]Text in Sir Alan Gardiner, *Admonitions of an Egyptian Sage;* translation adapted from Simpson, *Literature,* 230–33.

history, and he also will not direct his wisdom toward oracular prophecies for future use. Instead, he will record, honestly and directly, the reality he has seen for himself:

What I say has not been said. One who will speak now speaks. . . . Not a tale of telling after the fact: they did it before. Nor yet a story for future telling; this is a vain endeavor, it is lies, and no one will recall such a man's name to his people.

I speak these things just as I have seen them, (while) from the first generation down to those who come after, they imitate that which is past.[27]

The irony in Khakheperre-sonbe's ringing assertion of literary novelty, of truth to his immediate and personal experience, is that most of the actual contents of his lamentation are known from earlier texts. Khakheperre-sonbe's assertions thus serve to claim novelty for what is in fact a quite conservative reworking of old topoi from earlier lamentations and wisdom compilations.[28]

Egyptian culture was unusually conservative, but a degree of caution must be used in assessing the idea of modernity in the Bible as well. The ideological importance of novelty in the biblical tradition, stemming from the writers' desire to assert an absolute break from Canaanite religious and social practices, often served to mask cultural continuities that persisted, rather than to inspire genuinely new productions. As regards narrative form, important continuities with earlier epic tradition will be discussed in the following chapters. At the same time, how-

---

[27]Ibid., 230. For the last sentence I follow Lichtheim's rendering (*Ancient Egyptian Literature* I, 146), which produces a more coherent reading than Simpson achieves; but the sense is not entirely certain.

[28]See Simpson, *Literature*, 230, for further references. Miriam Lichtheim (*Ancient Egyptian Literature* I, 145–46) even doubts that the chaotic social conditions described in the lament were those of Khakheperre-sonbe's own day. In her view, his laments "are either purely literary, designed to enlarge the literary possibilities of the theme, or they may have conveyed a covert political criticism, of a kind that could not be made openly and hence was wrapped in metaphor." In this case, then, the assertion of fidelity to literal experience is itself a purely metaphoric trope.

ever, it is clear that biblical narrative did in many ways decisively break with earlier narrative modes, and it did so through profound transformations of oral, epic, and chronicle traditions, creating hybrid forms unlike anything seen before. The difference from Khakheperre-sonbe's practice lies in the fact that along with the biblical assertions of modernity there went a troubled view of the past that did not permit the biblical authors to use, unchanged, the old forms of epic and chronicle for the expression of their understanding of Hebrew history and of the human condition at large.

The Bible as Anti-Epic

As a result, though it can be said that the fundamental mode of much of biblical narrative is epic, it is necessary to add that these same narratives are also a form of anti-epic, subverting the norms of the genre to which they give new expression. One of the basic functions of epic has often been to explain, justify, and celebrate the establishment of a culture. A people's god or gods are shown establishing the modern world order, either in a mythological *Urgeschichte* of creation, or in a later account of the realigning of relations among existing divine and human societies. Biblical narrative serves this function well, yet it resists many of the norms of epic even as it carries out the epic task of showing God's creation of the universe and his forging of a special relationship with the children of Abraham (in the Yahwistic narratives) and then with the house of David (in the Deuteronomistic history).

A remarkable expression of the unusually complex attitudes toward past history in Deuteronomic times can be seen in the opening verses of Psalm 78. The psalm recites the glorious salvation history of the Exodus and the Wanderings, culminating in the permanent establishment of the Davidic monarchy. The psalm can be dated to Deuteronomic times, as it refers to the fall of the North in 721 and the assertion of the eternal establishment of David's house dates it before the fall of the South in 597–587. Like the Deuteronomistic history, it emphasizes the people's repeated faithlessness during the entire time and pointedly alludes to the downfall of the Northern Kingdom as resulting from the people's infidelity.

The poet begins by describing the psalm to follow as his "teaching" (*torah*, v. 1), but the lesson to be taught is far from simple:

I will open my mouth in a parable,
  I will utter dark sayings from of old;
things we have heard and known,
  that our fathers have told us.
We will not hide them from our children,
  but tell to the coming generation
the glorious deeds of the Lord, and his might,
  and the wonders which he has wrought.   (vv. 2–4)

A note of uncertainty is struck from the beginning: history is seen as a riddle or parable (*mashal*), as "dark sayings" (*ḥidot*), clearly not something to be understood easily, and in fact something that one might consider covering up, hiding from one's children. God, however, wishes his people to remember their inglorious history along with the Law:

He established a testimony in Jacob,
  and appointed a law in Israel,
which he commanded our fathers
  to teach to their children;
that the next generation might know them,
  the children yet unborn,
and arise and tell them to their children,
  so that they should set their hope in God,
and not forget the works of God,
  but keep his commandments;
and that they should not be like their fathers,
  a stubborn and rebellious generation,
a generation whose heart was not steadfast,
  whose spirit was not faithful to God.   (vv. 5–8)

These verses could fairly be called the blueprint for an anti-epic. Memory is still the guiding muse, but the guidance is to be negative: the people must learn to refuse to imitate the deeds of their ancestors, and only by knowing the disasters visited upon the people in the past can the people hope to avoid repeating them in the future.

Within the psalm, this perspective has interesting narrative consequences. The poet is so unconcerned to construct a normal narrative progression that he tells events out of order, first describing the people's most insistent murmurings against God, in the wilderness (vv. 13–41), then going back to describe the plagues in Egypt (vv. 42–55), and then moving ahead to the history of the loss and recovery of the Ark in the time of Saul, concluding with the anointing of David (vv. 56–72). God's saving activity is, of course, presented in glowing contrast to the rebellious infidelity of his people, but even God's actions in history are mysterious, only barely comprehensible, and his activity is described in terms that are hardly reassuring. His anger against the Egyptians is hardly distinguishable from his fury at his apostate people. At the end of the psalm, after he has allowed the Philistines to capture his Ark, destroy the principal shrine at Shiloh, and murder his priests, his eventual action on behalf of his people is described with a disturbing image:

Then the Lord awoke as from sleep.
  like a strong man shouting because of wine.
And he put his adversaries to rout;
  he put them to everlasting shame.   (vv. 65–66)

Hardly a comforting picture of the God who acts in history!

This anti-epic perspective, with its prophetically influenced negative judgment of the bulk of Israelite history, is not the only one at work in biblical narrative, even in Deuteronomic times; it coexists with more positive conceptions of the past, particularly as represented by the figure of David, who can serve as an epic hero to a greater degree than any of the later kings. Even his story, though, is complicated by the exploration of moral flaws that could account for the troubles of his reign, most notably the civil war instigated by his son Absalom. As an anti-epic, the Deuteronomistic history is still a form of epic, reoriented to monitory rather than (or as well as) to celebratory emphases, and relying for its effect upon meditations on closely observed specific historical events.

The factor of rapid cultural change, together with the complex view of past times, provided a fertile ground for the creation of a rich narrative prose with qualities of both poetic epic and prose chronicle, yet not for a direct reworking of either form alone. These factors accelerated movements already under way in Mesopotamian literature of the second millennium, movements that led toward occasional epic expansion of historiography and, even more, toward a greatly increased historical dimension within poetic epic. We can now turn to an examination of these developments, whose literary expression had profound implications for the rise of Hebrew narrative.

2. History and Epic

If the origins of biblical narrative can in part be understood as a process of the mixing of genres available in existing Near Eastern literature, a twofold task presents itself. First it will be necessary to describe the salient features of Near Eastern prose history and poetic epic, both those features that have been taken up into biblical narrative and those features that have not been used. Secondly, it is necessary to inquire why such a combination was ever made, and particularly why it was made the way it was. Within Mesopotamian literature, poetic epic remained the dominant mode of literary expression, and the confluence of epic and chronicle produced more remarkable results in the form of historical poetic epic than in the more limited poetic-epic enlargements of prose chronicle. In contrast, the Bible proved to be much more open than any Mesopotamian chronicle to the creation of an "epic" historiography.

This difference in literary form has tended to obscure the very real continuities in underlying concerns. If Mesopotamian literature of the second millennium is examined in its own historical development, however, it becomes clear that thematic shifts in the direction of biblical solutions to problems of historical representation are already well under way within Babylonian literature itself in the second half of the second millennium. Thus there is more organic development from Mesopotamian literature to the Bible than has been recognized by scholars who have promiscuously mingled together Sumerian, Old Babylonian, and Standard Babylonian texts to produce an artificially static picture of Mesopotamian literature. It should be said that Bible scholars can scarcely be blamed for their tendency to foreshorten a thousand years of literary production;

Mesopotamian specialists have often done the same thing themselves. Thus, the most widely available German translation of the *Gilgamesh Epic*, by Schott and von Soden, silently mixes together the Old Babylonian and the Standard Babylonian material, a practice also followed in the Penguin paraphrase of *Gilgamesh* by N. K. Sandars (1960). Even the scholarly translation by E. A. Speiser freely inserts Old Babylonian material to fill gaps in the Standard Babylonian version.[1]

This tendency to blur Mesopotamian literary history is reinforced by the lack of comprehensive editions of many of the major Mesopotamian texts, which often leaves their textual development obscure. The issue is broader than this problem, though, as even *ANET* has for thirty years given the basic material needed for a better understanding of Near Eastern literary history, even if in a somewhat selective form. The univocal treatment of Mesopotamian literature in biblical scholarship ultimately rests on the confluence of two different sets of prejudices: those of Bible scholars and those of the ancient Mesopotamians themselves. The Mesopotamians were only too happy to cover up the traces of their own historical evolution, as the writers of the Bible did also. Modern scholars have long been concerned to see past this revisionism in the case of the Bible, but it has often served their arguments to suppose that what was fiction in Israel was truth in Mesopotamia. This gave license to the neat contrast of the dynamic novelty of biblical traditions against the stable and unchanging background of all previous cultural life.

Once the continuities between Near Eastern and Hebrew literary history have been clarified, the very real contrasts that remain can provide important clues as to the reasons for the specific ways in which genres were combined by the writers of the Bible. A need for change was felt precisely because no existing genre was adequate as it then existed. Further, it is the

---

[1]Speiser's translation appears in the most widely used anthology of Near Eastern literature, James B. Pritchard's *Ancient Near Eastern Texts Relating to the Old Testament;* citations from this anthology will be abbreviated as *ANET* in the text.

pressure of each genre upon the other that has often helped to determine what has remained of interest for the new combined form and what has been de-emphasized or excluded.

Narrative Aspects of Near Eastern Historiography

Overall, Near Eastern historical texts are notably lacking in narrative fullness. Their concern is to provide a concise record of kings' reigns and major deeds, particularly military conquests and building projects. Violence is the major locus of energy, with a cheery slaughter of one's miserable opponents providing the most common dramatic interest. A typical example can be seen in an account of the pharaoh Kamose's wars against the Hyksos in the sixteenth century: "I sailed south in strength of heart, joyful, destroying every rebel who was on the way. Oh what a happy journey south for the Ruler—life, prosperity, health!—having his army before him! There was no loss of them; no man missed his companion" (*ANET*, 555).

The description is idealized, to say the least—all the enemy troops destroyed, without a single loss among Kamose's men—but this idealization does not preclude moments of close observation and lively reported speech. Thus, when Kamose attacks the Hyksos ruler's fortress,

I saw his women upon his roof peering from their ⌐loopholes⌐ toward the shore, without their bodies ⌐stirring⌐ when they heard me. They peered out with their noses on their walls like the young of *inhet*-animals from inside their holes, while (I was) saying: "⌐This is the attack!⌐ Here am I. I shall succeed. What is left over is in my hand. My lot is fortunate. As the valiant Amon endures, I will not leave you, I will not let you set foot in the fields unless I am upon you! So your wish has failed, miserable Asiatic!" (554)

Along with moments of vivid narrative detail, we also find occasional examples of well-developed historical portrayals of cause-and-effect relations, stressing the rapid passing of time in crisis situations and the importance of quick and decisive choices among conflicting options. These features are all prominent in a chronicle of Thutmose III's first campaign in Palestine (c. 1468, about a century after Kamose). In this account, Thutmose has gone to Palestine in person, to quell a concerted uprising of many of the city-states of the region against Egyptian domination. As he approaches Megiddo, where the enemy awaits him, Thutmose consults with his advisers about the best route. Most direct is a narrow mountain pass, but Thutmose's advisers fear ambush and recommend either of two broader but more roundabout routes. Fearlessly, Thutmose rejects their cautious advice: "Let him of you who wishes go upon these roads of which you speak, and let him of you who wishes come in the following of my majesty! '⌐Behold⌐,' they will say, these enemies whom Re abominates, 'has his majesty set out on another road because he has become afriad of us?'—so they will speak" (*ANET*, 235–36).[2]

Clearly aware that his troops will fear the narrow pass, Thutmose takes the bold and unusual step of leading the way in person. As it turns out, the enemy has guarded the other two routes, not expecting an attack over the pass. A palpably relieved Thutmose is now only barely restrained from an impetuous surprise attack on Megiddo, even though much of his army is still filing through the mountains. ("Then they said to his majesty. . . . Let our victorious lord listen to us this time, and let our lord await for us the rear of his army and his people.") The next day, they attack and rout the enemy.

The text presents a dramatic story, with a full sense of contingency and a well-developed and flexible relationship be-

---

[2]It is interesting that the king does not choose the pass for the physical advantage of a surprise attack, but rather as a form of psychological warfare: the enemy will be cowed on seeing the king's boldness and confidence in the protection of Re; conversely, they would take heart if the Egyptians were to seem hesitant. The motif of tailoring action to the enemy's probable assessment of it also appears in the Bible, as when Moses urges God not to destroy the Hebrews after the making of the Golden Calf, lest the Egyptians be able to say that God had brought the Hebrews out into the wilderness only to destroy them (Exod. 32:12).

tween the king and his counselors. Indeed, the text even admits of miscalculation in the midst of battle, noting with regret that the Egyptian army lingered to take spoils as the Canaanite warriors fled and were pulled up by their clothing over the walls into their city: "Now if only his majesty's army had not given up their hearts to capturing the possessions of the enemy, they would [have captured] Megiddo at this time, while the wretched enemy of Kadesh and the wretched enemy of this town were being dragged (up) ⌐hastily⌐ to get them into their town" (236).

Similar in emphasis to Egyptian chronicles, Mesopotamian texts typically narrate the storming of a town in a single phrase, often then pausing to note the bloody fate of the inhabitants and the kinds of tribute exacted. A good example is Shalmaneser III's account of the taking of a city in Palestine in the mid–ninth century: "I stormed and conquered (it). I slew with the sword 300 of their warriors. Pillars of skulls I erec[ted in front of the town]. I received the tribute of Hapini from the town Tilabna, of Ga'uni from the town Sa[ll]ate, (and) of Giri-Adad (to wit): . . . silver, gold, large and small cattle, wine" (*ANET*, 277). The report, though spare, shows careful attention to detail, and the chronicler even rises to a sort of bloody lyricism on Shalmaneser's behalf in describing the final defeat of the enemy:

I fought with them (assisted) by the mighty power of Nergal, my leader, by the ferocious weapons which Ashur, my lord, has presented to me, (and) I inflicted a defeat upon them. I slew their warriors with the sword, descending upon them like Adad when he makes a rainstorm pour down. In the moat (of the town) I piled them up, I covered the wide plain with the corpses of their fighting men, I dyed the mountains with their blood like red wool. I took away from him many chariots (and) horses broken to the yoke. I erected pillars of skulls in front of his town, destroyed his (other) towns, tore down (their walls) and burnt (them) down. (*ANET*, 277)[3]

---

[3]Later in the campaign, Shalmaneser ingeniously fords a deep river by constructing a bridge out of the corpses of his enemies (279).

Mesopotamian historical texts are not without homier moments as well. The memorial stela of the mother of the Babylonian king Nabonidus (mid–sixth century) records that the god Sin granted her a hundred and four years of vigorous life in reward for her piety: "My eyesight was good (to the end of my life), my hearing was excellent, my hands and feet were sound, my words well chosen, food and drink agreed with me, my health was fine and my mind happy. I saw my great-great-grandchildren, up to the fourth generation, in good health and (thus) had my fill of old age" (*ANET*, 561).

As these examples should suggest, the Egyptian and Mesopotamian chronicles amply show that historical prose was perfectly capable, from the middle of the second millennium onward, of vivid characterization, lively dialogue, careful recording of facts, and detailed and incisive analysis of historical sequence. And yet these writers consistently chose to employ all these rich devices within a narrowly delimited sphere, and this fact is highly suggestive culturally.

To be sure, it is possible to read too much into this self-limitation, as in the rather frequent claim made by Bible scholars that the older Near Eastern societies had no genuine sense of history at all. The classic modern expression of this view is found in Gerhard von Rad's seminal essay of 1944, "The Beginnings of Historical Writing in Ancient Israel," in which he contrasts the richness of Hebrew historiography with the Egyptians' and Mesopotamians' "striking inability to think historically" (167). As von Rad describes the issue,

A historical sense is a particular form of causational thinking, applied in practice to a broad succession of political events. It therefore involves a particularly acute perception of the realities of a nation's situation. It is not difficult to show that most peoples of antiquity were not impelled to analyse their situation in this way. Their historical existence, that is to say their existence in an irreversible time-sequence, presented no problem to them. They were in no position to see great political events in terms of historical contingency, and did not find it necessary to fit these events into a wider pattern of historical cause and effect. (166)

There is certainly an element of truth in these statements, and in its context the paragraph serves a useful function in introducing von Rad's penetrating analysis of aspects of the history of King David. Further, it must be said that Assyriologists and Egyptologists themselves have often been content to give similarly foreshortened and absolute characterizations of their material, perhaps because their concentration has been on reconstructing the history behind the texts rather than on detailed analysis of the texts as historiography.[4]

In recent years, several studies have appeared that begin to fill this need, most notably Bertil Albrektson's *History and the Gods* and John Van Seters's *In Search of History*, both of which argue for substantial continuity between Mesopotamian and Hebrew historical thinking. This new interest in understanding Mesopotamian historiography is welcome, as a nuanced view of Mesopotamian ideas of history can aid us in understanding

---

[4]As recently as 1970, the cuneiformist A. K. Grayson noted, "Ancient Mesopotamian historiography is an exceedingly complex and badly neglected subject. Its complexity is not surprising when one remembers that it evolved over a period of more than two thousand years and was written in two languages, Akkadian and Sumerian. . . . That such an intriguing subject should have been generally neglected by modern scholars is mystifying." He mentions one book, from 1916, and three more recent articles and concludes that "apart from these few studies no one has concerned himself with the broad questions of origin and purpose in Mesopotamian historiography" (*Assyrian and Babylonian Chronicles*, 2).

Given the cogency of these remarks, it is somewhat surprising to find Grayson himself five years later falling back into just the sort of simplified and static terms he had deplored. In his introduction to *Babylonian Historical-Literary Texts*, he says that the best thing the Mesopotamians ever expected from life "was a long, peaceful reign by a pious king. This ideal was never questioned or doubted. . . . It was a simple philosophy clothed in an elementary logic. It was the belief shared by the majority of ancient Babylonians. They, like mediaeval Europeans, looked to palace and church for guidance and security" (3). Thus the Babylonian philosophy of history joins hands with the timeworn fiction of the simple "medieval mind." Again in 1980, Grayson repeats his claim: "Causation, that bogey of modern historiographers, was no problem to the ancient Mesopotamian: all things were ordered by the gods" ("Assyria and Babylonia," 191).

the specificity of biblical historiography. We have already seen, in the attack of Thutmose on Megiddo, a great political event presented in terms of historical contingency, and if it remains true that the chronicle does not admit the possibility that Amon-Re could ever be defeated, the same can be said of the Bible's view of Yahweh. Further, for all the Mesopotamian emphasis on fate, historical texts could envision the gods as changing their minds and altering their plans for human events. A particularly striking instance is found in the seventh-century inscriptions of Esarhaddon, king of Assyria. Marduk becomes enraged when his own people plunder his temple in Babylon in order to raise funds to hire mercenaries to fight against Assyria. He decrees a punishment of seventy years of slavery for his sinful people (a period with an interesting parallel in Jeremiah's prophecies a few decades later), but then he changes his mind and rewrites his own text: "Seventy years as the measure of its desolation he wrote. But the merciful Marduk, whose heart calmed down instantly, reversed (the figures) and ordered its restoration in the eleventh year."[5] As often in Mesopotamian chronicle, this vivid presentation of divine action refers to a single historical event, but larger-scale historical ordering, though less common, was not unknown, particularly in the triadic form of a good king or dynasty being followed by one or more bad kings, with a subsequent restoration by a later good king.[6]

---

[5]Quoted in Albrektson, *History and the Gods*, 91; translation in D. D. Luckenbill, *Ancient Records of Assyria and Babylonia*, 2 vols. (Chicago, 1926–27), 242 ff. The cuneiform sign for "seventy" is composed of two elements that, if reversed, form the sign for "eleven."

[6]This pattern was already remarked on in ancient times. Herodotus's Egyptian informants tell him of good times under Pharaoh Rhampsinitus followed by the impiety and economic mismanagement of Cheops, who was succeeded by his equally wicked brother Chephren. The two brothers ruled for a total of a hundred and six years, and order was only restored by the next king, Mycerinus (*The Histories*, 2.124–29). Strangely, von Rad ("Beginnings," 167) has cited these same informants as evidence for the lack of awareness of history on the part of the Egyptians, who told Herodotus that nothing had changed in three hundred forty-one generations except for a few changes in the position

Further, it is by no means true that existence in an irreversible time sequence was problematic only for the Hebrews; this problem is one of the fundamental leitmotifs of the Mesopotamian poetic epic. The problem of death is constantly tied in the epics to the problem of irreversible causality, and here it might be noted that the immortality that Gilgamesh loses when the serpent steals the magical root at the end of the epic is immortality in the form of rejuvenation: precisely the reversing of time.

Consequently it is not a question of a cultural "inability" to be concerned with large issues of causality and temporal development; rather, the evidence strongly suggests a generic division. Whereas Near Eastern historiography already contained all the tools for the construction of larger patterns of meaning, these patterns were developed only sparingly in the chronicles; it was in epic that the Mesopotamians pursued "historical" issues in von Rad's sense in their full extent; in Egypt these concerns were developed within wisdom literature and related mythic prose tales.

This generic division has often been misunderstood because it can be mistaken for an ideological division: Mesopotamian historiography has been thought to deal with the dry facts (and tendentious propaganda) of day-to-day existence, whereas the separate sphere of mythic epic dealt with a different and higher world, a different time (the *Urzeit*), and a different relation to the numinous, concerning itself—unlike the chronicles—with the ultimate meaning of life.

No such ideological distinction exists, however, for Near Eastern historiography constantly asserts the unbroken continuity of *Urzeit* and present time, of the world of the gods and

---

of the sun's rising (2.142). Von Rad draws too broad a conclusion here, as the priests are not actually making any overall claim one way or the other but simply saying that during that time no god had ever assumed mortal form. He is quite right that the Egyptians wished to schematize their history heavily, but at the same time, their schemas, like the Deuteronomist's, could perfectly well treat historical changes over several generations.

the world of daily life. As Albrektson has forcefully argued, no sharp division can be drawn between the divinely ordered world of nature and a separate, secular world of human historical activity (*History and the Gods,* chap. 4). Consequently, Mesopotamian literature collapses the sort of distinction made by Frank Cross between epic and history: "In epic narrative, a people and their god or gods interact in the temporal course of events. In historical narrative only human actors have parts. Appeal to divine agency is illegitimate" (*Canaanite Myth and Hebrew Epic,* viii). This definition has some applicability for historiography in the tradition of Thucydides, including much modern historical writing, but would force us to classify every ancient Near Eastern chronicle and king list as epic, while passing over the more fundamental distinctions that link the chronicles much more nearly with Thucydidean history than with poetic epic.[7]

The chronicles of Shalmaneser and Thutmose, discussed above, are explicit in connecting their heroes to their gods, and in so doing they very directly present a framework for understanding the meaning of life as reflected in historical process. After Shalmaneser describes his final victory with the aid of Nergal and the weapons given him by Ashur, he concludes the account of the episode as follows:

At that time, I paid homage to the greatness of (all) the great gods (and) extolled for posterity the heroic achievements of Ashur and Shamash by fashioning a (sculptured) stela with myself as king (depicted on it). I wrote thereupon my heroic behavior, my deeds in combat and erected it . . . at the foot of the mountains of the Amanus. (*ANET,* 277)

As this paragraph shows, Shalmaneser's chronicle should not be read purely as propagandistic self-aggrandizement by the

---

[7]Presumably only deists or atheists can write history in Cross's sense. Any modern history of biblical times that alluded to Christ's resurrection as fact rather than fiction would suddenly be converted into epic, and virtually every ancient and medieval chronicle would have to be counted as epic as well.

king; it is also, and indeed first of all, a testimony of praise and gratitude to the several major gods (Nergal, Ashur, Shamash) who have brought about these victories.[8] Indeed, at the climactic moment in the initial description of the battle (see above, p. 55), Shalmaneser compares himself to Adad, the storm god. This is no dead metaphor, but one of many such references at crucial points in Mesopotamian chronicle. By the comparison, Shalmaneser enrolls himself metaphorically within the ranks of the gods, and he clearly sees his actions as an earthly counterpart to their glorious heavenly deeds.

The same is true of Thutmose's account six centuries earlier. The text was inscribed on the walls of the Temple of Karnak, in praise of Amon-Re's granting of victory. The king's boldness in choosing the narrow pass, which seemed a suicidal course to his counselors, is in fact an expression of his greater (and justified) faith in his patron god: "I [swear]," Thutmose tells his advisers, "as Re loves me, as my father Amon favors me, as my [nostrils] are rejuvenated with life and satisfaction, my majesty shall proceed upon this Aruna road!" (*ANET*, 235).[9] In the form of the god's standard, Amon-Re physically accompanies and protects the king on the dangerous path: the king advances "carrying my father Amon-Re, Lord of the Thrones of the Two Lands, [that he might open the ways] before me, while Har-akhti established [⌈the heart of my victorious army⌉] and my father Amon strengthened the arm [of my majesty]" (236).

Thus the chronicles of Thutmose and Shalmaneser closely tie history to the order of ritual and the world of the gods whose heavenly battles are described in poetic mythic texts. As prose hymns to the power of the gods (and of the kings as the gods'

---

[8] As Albrektson says, "The wording is noteworthy: Shalmaneser extols the heroic achievements of the gods by recording *his own* deeds. The military successes of the king are in reality the gods' " (*History and the Gods*, 42).

[9] The motif of boldness in battle as a sign of faith in God is, of course, also well attested in the Bible; in chapter 5, I will have occasion to discuss the theme in relation to David's defeat of Goliath.

servants or sons), these chronicles are not directly interested in ambiguities of character and action, nor do they need the degree of descriptive subtlety we find in the Yahwistic narratives or in 1–2 Samuel. Rather, they present historical process and the meaning of history in ways that more closely resemble the representation of historical events in Psalms.[10]

This understanding of the larger meaning of much Near Eastern history writing should help to clarify the intimate connection between Mesopotamian historiography and epic and, at the same time, can guide us in understanding the nature of the division of ideological labor between the two genres, as well as the beginnings of a collapse of the entire generic distinction in later Babylonian literature. Even recent defenders of the richness of Mesopotamian historiography have largely stayed within the limits of prose chronicle in their discussion of Mesopotamian historical thinking.[11] And yet, since the chronicles portrayed contemporary history against the mythic pattern of the heroic lives of the gods, the natural staging ground for broad speculation concerning the meaning of life, indeed also for detailed discussion of social tensions, was found in narratives of the deeds of the gods in early times. It is true that this mythic orientation often led to a truly antihistorical repression of any complex historical sense in the timeless order of the *Urzeit*. What must be stressed, however, is that the mythic order itself was capable of historicization, and this happened in

---

[10]Their religious dimension usually results in a limiting of narrative interest; in Speiser's witty formulation, "Assyrian historiography suffered not so much from the conceit of the ruler as from his excessive piety" ("Ancient Mesopotamia," 67).

[11]Thus Van Seters mentions epic only in passing in his extensive survey of Mesopotamian historiography, dismissing its relevance to the Bible on the narrow grounds that the Hebrews lacked a poetic epic tradition of their own (*In Search of History*, 18–31, 224–27). Interestingly, however, he is perfectly prepared to envision in Hittite literature the sort of generic relations he never considers in the case of the Bible: "interaction between epic and prose historiography often occurs, with influence going in both directions" (96); "while the Hittites did not develop a poetic epic genre, the annals may have been the Hittite equivalent of the Akkadian historical epics" (108).

certain areas in certain periods. The chief literary product of such a merging of myth and history, as Cross rightly notes, is epic (*Canaanite Myth and Hebrew Epic*, viii). The purpose of the following section will be to examine the nature of the most developed epic tradition of the period before the composition of the Bible: the body of Akkadian epics produced in Mesopotamia during the second millennium.

Mortality and Knowledge in the Mesopotamian Epic

The first point to note in comparing the epics to the chronicles is the major difference in their form: the chronicles are written in prose and the epics are in verse. In contrast to the historical chronicles, the poetic epics display clear use of strophic forms and metrical patterns, often employing unusual word ordering so as to produce effects such as trochaic line-endings. They also employ epic formulae and, in general, show signs of an "epic-hymnic dialect." These features, first discussed in detail fifty years ago by Wolfram von Soden ("Der hymnisch-epische Dialekt des Akkadischen"), have recently received an extended analysis by Karl Hecker, the first synoptic analysis of the thirteen known Akkadian epics (*Untersuchung zur akkadischen Epik*).

Presumably these features reflect a longstanding oral tradition behind the eventual literary codification of Akkadian epics in the Old Babylonian period (2000–1600). They were retained as traditional elements in the purely literary reworking of older material in the Middle Babylonian period (1600–1000). The persistence of this formal difference long after the material had taken on a life within the written tradition reflects an inclination to use poetry when a narrative was to explore deep social and existential issues through stories of the activities of gods and human beings in early times. This raises the question of the relation of the poetic epics to the other major source of elevated poetry, religious ritual. It has often been thought that the mythic poetic epic texts may have arisen directly out of ritual. Against this view, Hecker argues that mythic stories appeared in writing several centuries before rituals began to be written down, and that, furthermore, an active ritual connection is rarely suggested in the epic texts, in contrast to the clear link seen in etiological mythic tales like "The Worm and the Toothache."[12] Hecker argues that myth and ritual can best be thought of as parallel forms, at times directly linked, other times not.[13]

In their variable relation to ritual, the poetic epics are analogous to the prose chronicles. The chronicles do not have an inherent, ineluctable link to ritual, and are clearly built up of elements, like daily records from military campaigns, that had only a direct daily reference and no wider significance in themselves. Indeed, the briefer chronicles, annals, and inscriptions need never have reached beyond an elementary record-keeping function. More extensive historical texts, however, like those discussed above, are assimilated toward ritual, both in their thematic elaboration and in their usage; their inscription on temple walls, or the depositing of the text in a temple sanctuary, has clear implications for the general context in which the text would be read, whether or not within actual ritual settings.

---

[12]In this text (*ANET* 100–101), the mythic story of the origins of toothaches in the descent of a hungry spirit into the teeth forms a prologue to the ritual for curing the toothache. This, however, is a brief tale rather than an independent epic. It is likely that epics could also have been used ritually: the creation epic *Enuma elish* was read during the New Year's festival, and (a less certain case) the emphasis on childbirth medical/ritual practice in the *Atrahasis Epic* strongly suggests that, in the form we have it, this epic was being retold within a ritual setting. These are, however, the only clear examples of a ritual linkage among the thirteen surviving Akkadian epics, and in the latter case the inorganic relation of the childbirth information to the creation-flood story as a whole suggests, if anything, that an existing epic was adapted to ritual use, rather than that the ritual occasion gave rise to the composition of the epic. Often the epics were composed, or at any rate transmitted, for private use, as subjects for reflection and personal piety, as their wisdom-oriented colophons indicate.

[13]He concludes that "myth and ritual are forms of equal value and in origin are entirely independent from each other; rather, they are parallel expressions of primitive ways of living and manners of thought" (22).

Similarly, the poetic epics develop large existential issues, of the sort addressed timelessly in ritual, within narrative sequences concerning the history of early times. Mesopotamian epic thus shows a family resemblance to the representation of mythic prehistory seen in hymns and ritual drama, but develops the mythic material in the direction of history; conversely, the more extensive historical chronicles begin to enlarge recent history toward myth.

If the Akkadian epics of the Old Babylonian period are examined with a view to the later development of the tradition and the eventual composition of biblical narrative, two points in particular stand out. The first is that the epics present among the gods the sorts of staging of complexities in political and social relationships that the Bible will present in human terms, as in the stories of the patriarchs and of King David. The second point is the regularity with which these themes are associated with the problem of mortality, which is the chief locus in the epics for developing the double theme of the origins and nature of human culture.

The same narrative can be utilized to reflect different structural tensions: thus, *Nergal and Ereshkigal* tells of a power struggle between two rivals who in the end become husband and wife; a parallel story, *The Descent of Ishtar*, recasts the story as a conflict between sisters. The setting is the same in each case: the underworld. In the first story, Ereshkigal, queen of the underworld, seeks to kill her brother Nergal, who has not done her honor. Summoned down to her palace, Nergal prepares himself by taking along seven disease demons, and he overpowers Ereshkigal. He is about to slay her, but she pleads with him to accept her as bride instead and become king of the underworld. He gladly accepts, and they are reconciled to each other (*ANET*, 103–4).

The Descent of Ishtar, like its Sumerian prototype *The Descent of Inanna*, gives this story in a yet more violent form. Inanna/Ishtar, goddess of fertility, willfully invades the underworld territory of her older sister Ereshkigal, but with less success than

Nergal. At the seven gates to the underworld palace, her seven items of regal clothing are stripped from her, and she is brought naked into her sister's presence. In the Sumerian version, the underworld judges fix on her the eye of death, and her corpse is hung from a stake on the wall. In the Akkadian version, Ishtar has a direct encounter with Ereshkigal, who orders her vizier to imprison her and torment her with disease. In the end, she is released in exchange for a new prisoner, evidently Dumuzi/Tammuz, who unwillingly becomes the underworld king.

A leitmotif of biblical narrative, the struggle of the younger sibling to overcome the elder, is clearly evident here, though interestingly Ereshkigal has no difficulty in overcoming her younger sister. It would not be at all surprising if the Hebrew version were a reversal of established pattern in this respect, if we assume that the triumph of the younger sibling expresses the Hebrew writers' sense of Israel as the unexpectedly chosen leader among nations despite its youth as a social and political entity. Though the Bible modifies the theme, it differs most of all in its preferred setting, earth; encounters with the underworld are almost entirely lacking in biblical narrative. Yet the image of the underworld had been growing in importance as Mesopotamian epic developed, as can be seen by comparing the Akkadian *Descent of Ishtar* to its Sumerian antecedent, the *Descent of Inanna*. The Sumerian version centers on political issues and gives no special thematic treatment to the underworld scene, which serves simply as a setting for the political struggle depicted. The epic begins by emphasizing the political theme: as she invades her sister's territory, Inanna abandons both her heavenly position and her earthly realm. The text lists the seven earthly cities she ordinarily protects and is now deserting, and then describes the seven royal insignia with which she adorns herself as she prepares her royal descent (*ANET*, 52–57, lines 1–26).

The Akkadian *Descent of Ishtar* replaces this political introduction with an existential meditation on the nature of the underworld. The text opens with an extended scenic description, really part description and part reflection on the meaning of death:

To the Land of No Return, the realm of ⌜Ereshkigal⌝,
Ishtar, the daughter of Sin, [set] her mind.
Indeed, the daughter of Sin set [her] mind
To the dark house, the abode of Irkal[la],
To the house which none leave who have entered it,
To the road from which there is no way back,
To the house wherein the entrants are bereft of li[ght],
Where dust is their fare and clay their food,
(Where) they see no light, residing in darkness,
(Where) they are clothed like birds, with wings for garments,
(And where) over door and bolt is spread dust.

(ANET, 106–9, lines 1–11)

Further reorienting the emphases in the story, the Akkadian text omits any description of Ishtar's regal preparations and plunges directly into the drama of her demand for entry to Ereshkigal's palace. Informed of Ishtar's sudden arrival at her gates, her sister scornfully rejects the idea of accepting a lesser status in the underworld. Even this speech plays down the political and instead emphasizes the negativity of underworld life, for everyone but the pitiless queen:

"What drove her heart to me? What impelled her spirit hither?
Lo, should I drink water with the Anunnaki?
Should I eat clay for bread, drink muddied water for beer?
Should I bemoan the men who left their wives behind?
Should I bemoan the maidens who were wrenched from the laps of
    their lovers?
Should I bemoan the tender little one who was sent off before his
    time?
Go, gatekeeper, open the gate for her,
Treat her in accordance with the ancient rules."   (lines 31–38)

The problem of mortality is perhaps the most pervasive theme in Akkadian epic, and it inspires the furthest developments in characterization and scenic presentation in the Akkadian epic tradition. Often, the presentation centers on the sheer horror of the fact of death, with little probing of the origins of mortality. In such accounts, death is a sheer, incomprehensible given, as in the haunting "Lament for Lulil." In this text, the young god Lulil has died, leaving him deprived of all force but not of all consciousness. His young sister Egime does not understand death and begs him to arise. He replies:

Let me be, my sister, let me be!
Sister, do not upbraid me,
  I am no (longer) a man who can see.
Egi-me, do not upbraid me,
  I am no (longer) a man who can see.
O my mother Ninhursaga, do not upbraid me,
  I am no (longer) a man who can see.
I lie on my bed, the dust of the Nether world,
  among the most down-and-out of men,
I lie down to my sleep, a nightmare,
  among the most wicked of men.
My sister, I cannot rise from my bed!
     (Quoted from Jacobsen, "Death in Ancient Mesopotamia," 22)

Occasionally, there are accounts that suggest a reason for the fact of death. In the *Adapa Epic*, the chance for immortality is lost through the hero's error in refusing the offer of bread and water of life, which he has been misinformed are bread and water of death (*ANET*, 101–3, lines 60–70). In the *Atrahasis Epic*, the Old Babylonian account of the Flood, it now seems likely that a poorly preserved passage shows the god Enlil instituting human mortality as a form of population control, to keep his sleep from being disturbed by the rambunctious noisiness of the rapidly multiplying human race.[14]

---

[14]W. G. Lambert has recently drawn this conclusion on the basis of a reconstruction of *Atrahasis* III, vi, 47–50: see his "The Theology of Death." He concludes: "Thus the institution of death in *Atra-ḫasīs* is similar to that in the garden of Eden. In each case man was first created without any limit being fixed on his life-span. As a result of misdemeanour death was laid upon him" (58). "Misdemeanour" perhaps overstresses the parallel, as the *Atrahasis Epic*

Whether analyzed in its origins or in its essence, death figures above all as the sign of difference between gods and mortals. As the *Adapa Epic* says in introducing the creation of Adapa by the god Ea, "To him he had given wisdom; eternal life he had not given him" (*ANET*, 101, line 4). The absence of this issue in Mesopotamian chronicle, and its prominence in the epics, reflects a generic division of theme. Near Eastern historiography before the Bible stresses human similarity to the gods: in his boundless wisdom and bravery, the king is the earthly image of the divine. The epics, in contrast, turn to the problem of difference: what is the meaning of power and of wisdom in light of the brevity of existence?

This problem leads in the epics to scenes of great beauty, and to a development of interiority and inner conflict unknown in the historical chronicles' depictions of character. These issues reach their furthest development in the Gilgamesh cycle but can be clearly seen in earlier, briefer instances. A good example comes from the *Atrahasis Epic*. Atrahasis, whose name means "Exceedingly Wise," is the hero of this version of the flood story. Enki, the underworld god of wisdom, warns him of the impending destruction of the world by the irritated, sleepless Enlil. Following Enki's instructions, Atrahasis constructs an ark and brings on board his family, animals, and craftsmen. As the storm rises, he feeds his people, but his heart is torn:

. . . he sent his family on board,
They ate and drank.
But he was in and out: he could not sit, could not crouch,
For his heart was broken and he was vomiting gall.
The appearance of the weather changed,
Adad roared in the clouds.

. . . .

---

does not record any specific divine prohibition on noisemaking, an act that in any case is less ethically charged than the eating of the forbidden fruit in Genesis. Nonetheless, the structural parallel is clear, more so than it was when Lambert and Millard newly edited the epic in 1969, when the passage in question was entirely obscure.

The winds became savage as he arose,
He severed the hawser and set the boat adrift.

(Lambert and Millard, Atra-Ḥasīs III, ii, 42–49, 54–55)

Brief though this scene is, there is nothing like it in the chronicles. Atrahasis's restless movements and physical distress reflect both the coming universal upheaval and the inner torment resulting from his unique understanding of events. His wisdom even outstrips that of most of the gods, who have blithely gone along with Enlil's destructive plan and only realize the full horror of the cataclysm once humanity is destroyed.[15] At the same time, however, the gods' overwhelming power is set against him. In the chronicles, Shalmaneser will be identified with Adad as he storms a city; here, Adad storms against all humanity, including Atrahasis and his countrymen.

The importance of the theme of wisdom in the story of Atrahasis has other, less direct narrative corollaries. Wisdom literature characteristically focuses on the here and now, the immediate practical and ethical problems of daily life. Whether as a consequence of this, or whether in a parallel expression of a growing interest in history, the *Atrahasis Epic* shows a new interest in realistic narrative detail. In a significant modification of the stylizations of earlier Sumerian epic, the epic shows moments of scenic expansion along realistic lines, expansion not necessary thematically but aiding the reader/listener in constructing a vivid mental image of the events described. Thus Enki's specifications to Atrahasis include concrete practical details: "The tackle should be very strong, / Let the pitch be tough, and so give (the boat) strength" (III, i, 32–33). Such brief details are the first suggestions of historical interest, helping us to imagine what it would have been like to be there our-

---

[15]See the moving lament by Nintu, goddess of childbirth, in III, iii, 28 ff. She wonders at herself: "In the assembly of the gods / How did I, with them, command total destruction? . . . / As a result of my own choice / And to my own hurt have I listened to their noise" (III, iii, 36–37, 42–43). By a nice irony, in her view the divine debates over the noisy humans are seen in retrospect as only so much more destructive noise.

selves, and they receive considerable expansion in later retell-ings. These hints of historicization of the mythic epic bring a degree of immediacy to the presentation of large and timeless themes, still centered in the abiding Mesopotamian leitmotif of mortality.

The Confluence of Epic and Chronicle

With history playing an increasing role in poetic epic at the close of the second millennium, for the first time epics came to be written in response to specific events in modern history. Two different circles produced such poems: court poets, who composed verse accounts of kings' mighty deeds in a kind of merging of chronicle and panegyric, and religious poets, who wrote theologically oriented narratives dealing with the mean-ing of historical crises. In different ways, each kind of writing shows a first merging of epic and chronicle within Babylonian literature at about the time that prose narrative was beginning to be written in Israel. Two examples can serve to indicate the ways in which history played a new role in these two forms of epic: the best-preserved court epic, the *Tukulti-Ninurta Epic*, and an extraordinary historical-theological work, the *Erra Epic*.

The *Tukulti-Ninurta Epic* was composed in the aftermath of a specific historical event, the sacking of Babylon in 1235 by the Assyrian king Tukulti-Ninurta (reigned c. 1244–1208). This event involved, or followed, the breakdown of treaty relations between the two countries, and the epic stresses that Tukulti-Ninurta himself loved peace and tolerated various abuses by his southern neighbor, the Babylonian king Kaštiliaš. Finally, however, Kaštiliaš's own gods became so enraged at his willful disregard of his solemn treaty oaths that they deserted Babylon and went over to the Assyrian side. In the battles that ensued, they fought on the battlefield on behalf of the Assyrians, whom they then encouraged to plunder Babylon and remove their images, and the royal library, to Nineveh.

The epic serves several purposes: to celebrate the Assyrian

victory; to counter opposition within Assyrian circles against the growing power of the monarch, and perhaps also to the sacking of Babylon; and to assert the preeminence of Assyria as the new spiritual and cultural center of Mesopotamia. Peter Machinist, who has studied the text at length, argues that the epic itself is meant to demonstrate the cultural possibilities of the north, which had long taken a second place to the refined culture of Babylon. In Machinist's view,

> Proof of Assyria's new position is the fact that it can now compose a text like the Epic—one which more than all previous efforts can delve at will into the full range of southern literary traditions, combine them subtly with others, particularly inherited Assyrian themes, and build out of the mixture a new composition of striking literary refinement and power. ("Literature as Politics," 472)

Machinist goes on to draw an analogy to the literary activity of the court of David and Solomon, in which there was a similar need both to consolidate the power of the monarchy and to establish a sense of the value and individuality of the writers' culture.[16]

The *Tukulti-Ninurta Epic* is thus an important product of the growing interest in using epic in the representation and explanation of recent historical events. It employs a skillful interweaving of a variety of literary forms and shows the gods working closely with mortals in the ordering of historical change. The gods must have participated, as human action alone could not have shifted the balance of power, still less the cultural hegemony, from the ancient religious and cultural center of Babylon. As Assyria's own gods were in part taken directly from the Babylonian pantheon and in part syncretistically iden-

---

[16]This analogy may well be applied to the History of David's Rise and related texts directly concerning the establishment of the monarchy. Less persuasive, however, is the direction in which Machinist himself takes the analogy. Staying within a narrow generic model, he looks for a Hebrew poetic epic tradition to serve as a direct corollary to the *Tukulti-Ninurta Epic*. He makes his parallel to the hypothetical "Yahwistic Epic," citing in support of this conception only those few scholars who still maintain that such an epic ever existed. (See chapter 4 for further discussion of this question.)

tified with Babylonian gods, then the Babylonian gods themselves must have willed the overthrow of Babylon. Though the
poet has no sympathy at all for the perfidious Babylonians, he
does emphasize the gods' regret: "Marduk abandoned his au-
gust sanctuary. . . . / He cursed the city of his love" (I, 38'–
39').[17]

Along with this theological explanation go detailed accounts
of the glorious battles by which the war was won. In content,
these descriptions closely resemble the more developed prose
chronicles of similar events. The poet describes how the cow-
ardly Kaštiliaš shifts his forces through difficult terrain in order
to avoid a decisive battle. When Tukulti-Ninurta writes him a
letter pointing out that the outcome of the war is in the hands
of the gods, so that Kaštiliaš might as well come out and fight
in the open, Kaštiliaš craftily delays writing a reply until he can
maneuver his troops into position for a surprise attack. This
stratagem is observed by the vigilant Assyrians, and a pitched
battle follows, with the Babylonian gods themselves fighting
against their former subjects:

The lines of battle were drawn up; on the field of strife the battle was
    joined.
A fierce frenzy ensued, in which the servants quivered among them-
    selves (in anticipation).
Aššur in the vanguard went to the attack; the fire of defeat burned
    upon the enemy.
Enlil . . . ⌜in the midst⌝ of the foe, (and) sent flaming arrows smok-
    ing.
Anu pressed the unpitying mace upon the wicked.
The heavenly light Sin imposed upon them ⌜the paralyzing weapon⌝
    of battle.
Adad, the hero, let a windstorm pour down over their fighting.
Shamash, lord of judgment, dimmed the eyes of the armies of the
    land of Sumer and Akkad.

---

[17]The fullest edition of the text appears as chap. 2 in Machinist, "*The Epic of
Tukulti-Ninurta I.*"

Heroic Ninurta, first of the gods, smashed their weapons.

(V, 31'–39')

After the gods come the Assyrian troops. Tukulti-Ninurta him-self fires the first arrow, and then his heroic armies charge for-ward: "The warriors of Aššur declare: 'To the fight!' (and) go to meet death. / They give the shout: 'O Ishtar, be merciful!' (and) in the melee praise their mistress. / They rage wildly, be-come strange in form like Anzu" (V, 43'–45').

As the battle continues, the heroic tone and scale are main-tained, in ways comparable to battle scenes in the *Iliad*. Though the outlines of the battle could be duplicated in many prose chronicles, the poetry of the description is wholly epic, making full use of vivid imagistic detail and effectively counterpointing the human figures against the scenic background of natural upheaval:

The ferocious, heroic men played ⌜with sharpened weapons⌝;
⌜And⌝ destructive monster winds blew at each other like attacking lions.
⌜T⌝he confusion of swirling dust storms whirled about in the battle.
Death (was) in the eyes of the warriors just as when they sate them-selves on a day of thirst.

(V, 49'–52')

The application of poetic epic form and techniques to the sub-ject matter and purposes of prose chronicle produces interest-ing modifications of older representations of the relations be-tween the gods and humanity. Tukulti-Ninurta, as might be expected, is portrayed in terms paralleling the descriptions of the gods ("When he raises his weapons like Ninurta, the re-gions everywhere are thrown into panic," Ia, 15'), but the text nonetheless holds back from a simple identification. Enlil raises him *as if* he were his real father (Ia, 20'), and the king is not divine but "the eternal image of Enlil." Enlil's "image," ṣalmu, is normally the term for his temple statue; it is cognate with the later Priestly description of Adam as created in the "image of God," *tzelem 'Elohim* (Gen. 1:27; 9:6). Further, even as Tukulti-Ninurta is depicted as Enlil's divine image, he is also shown as a democratic ruler: "He alone is the eternal image of Enlil, attentive to the voice of the people, to the counsel of the land" (Ia, 18'). As Machinist says, this line shows the king's need to reassure his nobles that he was not going to become overbearing in his newfound power.

For all its interest in the poetic depiction of historical events, the epic retains a heavily programmatic, polemical bias that keeps its essential mode of representation well within that of traditional chronicle. On the two poles of resemblance to the gods, power and knowledge, no ambiguities or uncertainties are admitted at any point. Characterizations are absolute: the just and moderate Tukulti-Ninurta is the greatest hero on the face of the earth (Ia, 22'–23'), and conversely his opponent Kaštiliaš, "the wicked, the obstinate, the disobedient" (II, 26'), is a craven traitor and knows it. The action, though gorgeously described, is straightforwardly understood as predetermined by the contrasting moral qualities of the antagonists. In a long monologue, Kaštiliaš is even made to recall all his crimes and to despair of victory: "Many are my sins before Shamash; [⌜great are my⌝] misdeeds. / Who is the god who would save my people from ⌜d[isaster]⌝?" (III, 37'–38'). As Grayson says, Tukulti-Ninurta's epic "is really a panegyric of the king, in poetic narrative style" ("Assyria and Babylonia," 186). In this, as in the other court-oriented historical epics of the time, the complexities of characterization and causality, of knowledge and power, in the older poetic epic tradition are foregone in favor of a chronicle-style emphasis on the godlike strength and virtue of the heroic monarch.[18]

The *Erra Epic* makes a most interesting comparison to the *Tukulti-Ninurta Epic*, as it too deals with contemporary history but is far less concerned to support any particular figure in power. At the same time, though the author's stance is in a

---

[18]Several very fragmentary court epics have been published by Grayson, *Babylonian Historical-Literary Texts*.

sense apolitical, the interpretation of events is informed by a deep interest in political affairs, an interest that coexists with more traditional mythic explanations for the causes of events.

The historical events in question are twin disasters that befell Babylon at about the same time: civil war within Babylon itself, and the overrunning of several of its client cities by nomadic invaders, a disaster that the strife-torn imperial city was unable to prevent.[19] For the author, the two events were linked not only causally but also in their effects; among a variety of forms of devastation wrought both in Babylon and in neighboring cities, in both cases the plundering of temples is the culminating crime. It was evident to the poem's author, identified in the text as a priest named Kabti-ilani-Marduk, that this shocking sacrilege committed against several of the major gods could not have taken place if the gods had been extending their customary protection over their cities as a whole and their own temples in particular. As a devout and patriotic Babylonian, he was not willing to admit the possibility that Marduk and the other gods had simply been defeated by hostile gods; on the contrary, his epic can best be thought of as a response to religious doubts along those lines.

The alternatives open to Kabti-ilani-Marduk were two: that the gods had themselves ordained the disasters as punishment for wickedness among the people, or that the gods had somehow been distracted and had their attention turned elsewhere during the crucial time. The first of these explanations was the simpler and might have been less problematic, but in this particular case the historical situation posed difficulties, as the sacrilege against the gods' own temples would more readily suggest their own defeat than their desire to punish their erring peoples. This left the option of the gods' absence as a probable cause, and Kabti-ilani-Marduk set himself the task of probing the reasons for Marduk's departure from his city.

---

[19]There is considerable doubt concerning the dating of these events; estimates range from 1100 to 750. Albrektson (*History and the Gods*, 32) follows Lambert in positing the mid–ninth century as the time of the epic's composition.

The theory of Marduk's absence was a relatively neutral ground for explanation of the disasters, but in its very neutrality it would tend to become associated with one of the two poles of divine will between which it was situated: that Marduk actively wished the destruction and so abandoned his city to its fate, or else that he actively wished to prevent the destruction but was defeated by superior forces. Though the second of these explanations was absolutely unacceptable to a loyal Babylonian, the first could easily take an anti-Babylonian turn as well, as can be seen in the *Tukulti-Ninurta Epic,* which portrays Marduk and the other major gods as deserting to the Assyrian side in advance of the battle.

Writing for the victors in the Assyrian-Babylonian conflict, the author of the *Tukulti-Ninurta Epic* had little difficulty in casting the war in black-and-white terms. In contrast, writing on behalf of the victims of civil war and defeat at the hands of the Aramean nomads, Kabti-ilani-Marduk is impelled to a far subtler representation of events. He uses the classic theological explanation of the wickedness of his own people, but this explanation is given only secondary status, as he expands the horizons of his work both politically and historically.

Both the political and the historical dimensions are advanced within the overall framework of myth, through stories about the interactions of the gods among themselves (in the political explanation) and of the gods with humanity (in the historical explanation). But Kabti-ilani-Marduk has not produced myth in the sense of a representation of a timeless order; rather, in ways directly parallel to aspects of biblical narrative, he uses the mythic setting, and the epic form, for a searching exploration of very earthly political issues, and for the assessment of modern history against the model of the primeval history of the Flood.

The epic begins with the political discussion. The question at issue is how and why Marduk came to be absent from Babylon. Kabti-ilani-Marduk wishes to portray Marduk neutrally in this initial stage of events, so he presents the motivation for

Marduk's departure as coming from a source other than Marduk himself: the god of death, Erra (=Erragal or Nergal). By focusing on Erra, Kabti-ilani-Marduk can avoid giving any credit at all to the gods of the nomads; moreover, an exploration of complex relations among the Babylonian gods themselves provides the best means for accounting for the breakdown of civil order within Babylon. An older poetic epic might have developed this solution simply by portraying Erra as a blind, elemental force of destruction, who would have lured Marduk away from Babylon out of an inherent need to wreak havoc, a need that could be portrayed but not explained. The *Erra Epic* proceeds rather differently. Kabti-ilani-Marduk still operates within the fundamental Babylonian acceptance of the gods' will to destruction, but he subjects the gods' activities to a developed political-military analysis as well.

In the opening section of the epic, the focus is nominally on Erra, but the real protagonists are the seven disease demons, his lieutenants.[20] Ordinarily, these demons are nothing more than the tools of the underworld gods, but in this epic they are represented as the real instigators of the action against Babylon. Erra himself, far from yearning for war, is tired, and his thoughts have turned to private pleasures: "He asks himself: 'Should I get up? Should I stay in bed?' . . . / he tells the Seven, heroes without equal: 'Go on home!' / . . . . with Mami, his wife, he gives himself to pleasure" (I, 16–20).[21]

Faced with their lord's inaction, the Seven become restive. They come to Erra, speaking as his generals, and urge him to undertake a war. Their chief motivation is a purely military concern, one that might more readily be associated with earthly

---

[20]The seven disease demons, who have a later analogue in the Four Horsemen of the Apocalypse, are personifications of such debilitating conditions as Stroke, Fever, and Plague.

[21]Text and Italian translation in Luigi Cagni, *L'Epopea di Erra*. In general I follow Cagni, occasionally adopting suggestions from René Labat's French translation in *Les Religions du Proche-Orient asiatique*, 114–37.

generals than with their heavenly counterparts: things have
been too quiet, and they are getting rusty.

We, who know the mountain passes, have forgotten the way.
Across our weapons the spider has spun her threads;
our trusty bow rebels against us: it is too stiff for us to bend!
The sharp point of our arrow is blunt,
and our sword, lacking blood, is covered with rust! (I, 87–91)

The disease demons, in short, are presented as a kind of military-pestilential complex; they need a little war just to keep
their weapons in top order and to hone their battle tactics.
Though this is the culmination of their appeal to Erra, it is
reinforced with other considerations both military and political.
The desire to keep the war machine in good working order does
not in itself dictate Babylon as the object of hostilities, but the
Seven recommend attacking Babylon in particular for a second
military reason: as a protective first strike. "O warrior Erra, we
appeal to you, and may our words [not offend you]! / Before
all the mortals' lands become too strong, may you listen to our
appeal!" (I, 78–80).

The Seven preface their request with a mixture of flattery,
cajolery, and thinly veiled threats. They begin by praising the
life of the warrior as helpful for Erra's personal development.
In language common to the military recruiters of all ages, they
portray the warrior's life as a sort of sanguinary Outward
Bound program:

Why are you staying in the city, like a senile old man?
Why do you stay at home, like a helpless child?
Like stay-at-homes, are we to eat women's bread?
Should we fear and tremble, as if we did not know battle?
For young men, going out into the countryside is like (going to) a
    feast!

. . . .

City bread cannot compare to biscuits baked in ashes,
sweet našpu-beer cannot compare to water out of doors;

a terraced palace cannot compare to the huts of [shepherds]!

(I, 47–51, 57–9)

They stop short of claiming that military experience will help Erra get a good job in the private sector, but the Seven do hint broadly that a spectacular little war may aid him in keeping the political office he now has: "Whoever stays in the city, even a prince . . . / he is mocked by the mouths of his people, his person is scorned" (I, 52–53).

These arguments are "as pleasant as sweet oil" to Erra (I, 93), both because they rouse his bellicose nature and because the war will provide a vehicle by which he can gain dominance over the other gods—a political agenda of his own. He goes to Marduk and points out that his statue in his temple has become rather dilapidated. Marduk, who might be aroused by this observation to anger against the tenders of his temple, instead excuses them by saying that only he can restore his earthly image, as he has hidden the materials away in distant places. Erra then suggests that Marduk go and take care of this matter and volunteers to govern Babylon while he is away. When Marduk agrees to this plan, Erra finds himself in the seat of all power, as Marduk is the king of all the gods and Babylon is his throne (IIIc, 44). By causing upheavals in Babylon and throughout Mesopotamia, he is now able to demonstrate his power both to human beings and to his fellow gods; the lesser gods (the Igigi), the underworld gods (the Anunnaki), and even the great gods Anu and Enlil. As his lieutenant Ishum says to him,

Warrior Erra, you hold the reins of heaven,
you are the absolute master of the whole earth, you reign over the
 lands;
you disturb the oceans, the high lands are all yours;
you govern [humanity], you give the livestock grazing;
Esharra is at your disposition, Engurra in your hand;
you control Shuanna, you give orders in Esagil.
You have gathered all powers; the gods fear you,
the Igigi are afraid, the Anunnaki tremble before you;

when you give judgment, Anu himself listens,
and even Enlil obeys you.   (IIId, 3–12)

To demonstrate his absolute, destructive power, Erra takes human form and enters Babylon, where he incites the people to
riot and induces the governor to turn his troops indiscrimi-
nately against his own people:

seeing (Erra), the troops put on their arms,
and the heart of the governor, Babylon's protector, is enraged:
he mobilizes his troops as if to pillage an enemy,
and he eggs on the army's general to evil:
"In this city where I send you, man,
fear no god and dread no mortal;
young and old together, put them all to death,
do not spare a single babe or suckling!
Strip away Babylon's riches as your plunder!"

                                                            (IV, 22–30)

The epic gives a grim picture of social upheaval and disintegration, in terms familiar from lamentations in many periods
and countries of the ancient Near East. (See esp. IIc and III, 1
ff.) Specific to this epic, however, is its analysis of these upheavals as caused by the conjoined pressures of the military
needs of the disease demons and power politics among the
gods.

    Along with this developed political interest goes a new
awareness of the monitory value of past history. The gods
themselves are shown reflecting on the lessons of the past as
they assess the strife in Babylon against the model of the primordial history of the Flood. This theme is introduced even
before Marduk leaves Babylon. When Erra asks Marduk why
his statue is tarnished, Marduk replies: "There was a time, long
ago, when in anger I left my throne, and I created the Flood; /
by leaving my throne, I upset the governance of heaven and
earth; / the heavens quaked, the stars changed their position"
(I, 132–4). Once order was restored, he found that his statue
had been tarnished by the flood waters, and he had to renew

it by great efforts. Now he hesitates to go away to retrieve the materials a second time, lest the upheavals of the Flood time should recur (I, 170–78). This is just what does happen once he goes off and Erra takes his place on the throne. Erra is actually encouraged in his destructive frenzy with the traditional explanation for the Flood, that the Anunnaki were outraged by the noisiness of humanity and wished to have peace and quiet restored. This, however, is now only one of the many arguments advanced by the self-interested disease demons (I, 81–82), and nothing is said in the epic to indicate that humanity really is interrupting the gods' sleep.

When Marduk returns to his self-destructing city, he expresses his shock and horror in a moving sevenfold lament, in which he compares Babylon to such objects as a palm tree of his planting, now withered by the wind, and says that he used to hold the city in his hand like the tablet of destinies (IV, 40–49).[22] He says that this new destruction is even worse than that caused by the Flood, as the nomads have overrun the sacred city of Sippar, "the eternal city, across whose boundaries the Lord of the Lands (Enlil) did not extend the Flood; / its walls are destroyed, its ramparts ruined, against the will of Shamash!" (IV, 50–51).

To some extent, Marduk has only himself to blame for the destruction of his city and the Aramean depredations, as he has failed to heed the lesson of history that he himself recalled before leaving Babylon. At the same time, he has fallen victim to the treachery of Erra, though even here the implication is that one should expect nothing else from the god of death. After he has spent his rage—and achieved his political ends— Erra is the first to admit that he has not acted honorably:

Indeed, in this past fault I plotted evil;
my heart burned with rage, and I ravaged mankind.
Like a hired hand I stole the leader of the flock,

---

[22]The city as text is a theme also found in the *Gilgamesh Epic*, as will be seen in the next chapter.

like one who has not planted I did not hesitate to cut;
like one who sacks a land, I made no distinction between good and
   evil; (everyone) I laid low.
Yet one cannot tear a corpse from the mouth of a roaring lion,
and where one is in a transport of rage, another cannot offer counsel!

(V, 6–12)

Erra's free admission of his arbitrary fury may make Marduk's
earlier trust in him look naive, but it frees Marduk from what
was to the author a far worse imputation: that Marduk himself
could have been the blind force of destruction at large in his
own city. This belief is expressed within the poem by the governor of one of the sacked cities, who complains bitterly, "The
people are treated like cattle, and their butcher is their god!"
(IV, 93). Further, Marduk's own servants, his temple priesthood, are cleared of the charge that their neglect of Marduk
and the decay of his temple image were the causes of his rage.
This charge too is leveled within the poem itself, but in such
a way as to deprive it of credibility. As Erra plans his destructive spree, his counselor Ishum asks why he would wish to
destroy the great city, and Erra advances the neglect of Marduk
as the cause of his ire: "The humans, the black-headed ones,
are showing contempt. / Since they do not fear my name, / and
since they have rejected the word of Prince Marduk . . . / I will
enrage Prince Marduk, I will cause him to abandon his throne,
and I will destroy the people!" (I, 120–23). This very speech
bears out the poem's overall view, that Erra is really concerned
that humanity and the gods do not sufficiently fear his own
name; the neglect of Marduk is only a convenient pretext, and
Marduk's long speech explaining how only he himself can re-
furbish his image completes the exoneration of his priesthood.

Several different purposes are served, then, by the fore-
grounding of Erra and his military advisers, and the complexity
of the representation extends to the treatment of Erra himself.
Far from being a pure, melodramatic villain, Erra is revealed at
the epic's end as the generous guarantor of Babylon's future
greatness. Once his wise counselor Ishum has finally calmed

his rage, Erra promises restoration to the surviving remnant of the people and future victories over the temporarily triumphant nomads (V, 20–30)—a passage with interesting analogues in the Bible. Remarkably, at the close of the epic Erra becomes the gracious patron of the *Erra Epic* itself. His counselor Ishum announces that he has revealed the epic, in a nocturnal vision, to "the composer of these tablets, Kabti-ilani-Marduk, son of Dabibu," ordering him to write it down in the morning, omitting nothing and not adding a single line to what he has been told (V, 42–44). On receiving this report, Erra, in the closing lines of the epic, pronounces a sweeping series of blessings on all who learn the epic by heart:

The god who cherishes this song, his sanctuary will prosper,
but one who rejects it will never savor incense!
May the king who exalts my name reign over the universe;
may the prince who praises my valor have no rival!
The poet who chants this song will not die violently,
and his words will please both prince and king!
The scribe who learns it by heart will be despised by the enemy, but honored in his own land;
in the holy place of wise men, where my name is said continually, I will give revelations.
In any house, where these tablets are placed, if Erra grows enraged, and the Seven threaten,
the blade of destruction will not come near, and all will be secure.
May this song last forever and endure eternally!

(V, 49–59)

Thus Erra promises not only prosperity but also protection from his own depredations to those who hear the poem gladly, learn it, and treasure its tablets.

This poem has more features of interest than those discussed here, but enough has been said to indicate something of the depth of historical and causal reflection underlying this striking text. In Kabti-ilani-Marduk's presentation, the mythic world of the gods is a fully realized political arena, and the historical world of human existence and divine-human interaction is assessed both against the world of the gods and against the primordial earthly history of the Flood. As remarkable as the epic's content are its formal properties: its flexible use of poetic parallelism, its vivid speeches, its subtle and ironic characterizations, and its easy changes of scene. The epic form has become a fully viable vehicle for the exploration of historical events through their narrative representation.

In some ways, the *Erra Epic* closely resembles the *Tukulti-Ninurta Epic*, but in many ways it far outstrips it, not only in poetic power, but also, and relatedly, in subtlety of historical reflection. Two points in particular may be stressed in considering this difference. One is the likelihood that it was the double pressure of civil war and Aramean invasion that impelled Kabti-ilani-Marduk to probe more deeply than was necessary for the victorious Assyrians who commissioned and composed the *Tukulti-Ninurta Epic*. This provides an interesting analogy to consider in debating the importance of the period of the Exile for the rise of Hebrew historiography (on which, more below, in chapter 4). The second point to note is the prominence of the figure of Ishum, Erra's wise counselor. As the "real" author of the epic, Ishum is of considerable interest as a character within the story. He twice questions Erra's destructive intentions, though he is powerless to do anything to alter the course of events until Erra's fury has spent itself. The figure of wisdom, then, has crucial, but limited, power. He cannot control events as such, but he has the ability to understand them and to compose a powerful poem with an apotropaic function.

The poem is not only a protection in dealing with the gods, moreover; it can also serve as instruction for the monarchs who will hear it and whose reigns will prosper as a result. The value of the poem to monarchs lies not only in its instruction in the nature of the gods but also in its presentation of the dangers inherent in behaving as Marduk and Erra have done. Without quite criticizing Marduk directly, Kabti-ilani-Marduk makes it clear that civil disorder naturally follows from such a neglect of rule. This point is made through the inquiries of Ishum. When he first asks Erra why he plans to destroy Babylon, Erra gives the answers discussed above: it is his nature to be violent; the mortals have neglected Marduk; and they do not fear Erra himself sufficiently (I, 106–23). Later in the poem, however, Ishum asks the same question once again, and now Erra stresses Marduk's own responsibility:

The King of the gods has left his throne:
how then should all the lands remain stable?
He has deposed his own sovereign crown:
kings and princes, ⌈li[ke sl]aves⌉, forget their duty!
He has untied the chain (which hung down) from him;
broken are (the links between) god and man,
and they are difficult to retie!   (IIIc, 44–49)

In Kabti-ilani-Marduk's hands, poetic epic is the fully adequate form for the exploration of complex patterns of causality in human affairs, for the justification of the ways of the gods (and their priests) in very specific historical situations, and for the admonition of princes as well. Within court circles, as the *Tukulti-Ninurta Epic* and the other surviving court historical epics show, the epic form remained closely linked to propagandistic purposes. In wisdom-oriented temple circles, however, the epic became the vehicle for profound historical reflection. It will be evident that in many ways biblical narrative is heir to these developments in Mesopotamian epic tradition, to some extent presumably through a direct awareness of Mesopotamian traditions, to some extent through independent but parallel development under similar circumstances. In the absence of any direct evidence of connection, it is enough to consider a text like the *Erra Epic* as an illuminating analogy to what was happening in Hebrew "epic" historiography at about the same time.

Like the *Tukulti-Ninurta Epic* and the *Erra Epic*, but to a greater degree, the major biblical narratives are expanded into comprehensive surveys of the boundaries and meaning of human culture in general, and of Hebrew culture in particular. The best analogy to this most ambitious aspect of Hebrew narrative is to be found in the greatest of the Akkadian epics, the *Gilgamesh Epic*. Here, moreover, close thematic parallels to the Bible are also present, both in the flood story and in aspects of the story of Gilgamesh and Enkidu. In the *Gilgamesh Epic* can be seen the full emergence of historicized poetic epic on a grand scale, the mirror image of the poeticized prose histories in the great biblical narratives. Further, in the different versions of *Gilgamesh* we are fortunate to have a uniquely detailed record of changes in a single story over the full course of the second millennium. The historicizing of epic is dramatically visible as the story of Gilgamesh develops from its Sumerian roots at the end of the third millennium to its fullest form a thousand years later. This late, standard form of the epic provides unique testimony to generic transformations in many ways parallel and complementary to those that produced the Yahwistic corpus and the David story some three centuries later. Often cited for its thematic parallels to the opening chapters of Genesis, the *Gilgamesh Epic* has received little attention for its narrative qualities. In the next chapter, I will attempt to show how an extended analysis of structure and theme in this text can provide a valuable point of reference for the analysis of early biblical narrative, and I will argue that Genesis 2–11 provides an important analogue both to *Gilgamesh* and to *Atrahasis* in the transformation of the poetic epic tradition into historical prose.

3. Gilgamesh and Genesis

History and Myth in the *Gilgamesh Epic*

The *Gilgamesh Epic* is the longest and the most beautiful of the Mesopotamian epics to have come down to us, and it provides the fullest example of the treatment of historical concerns within the epic tradition. The full richness of this text has rarely been appreciated, as biblical scholars have usually examined it only cursorily as a source for surface parallels to the Flood story. To be genuinely effective, however, a comparison must treat the Mesopotamian text as fully as its biblical counterpart. The first half of this chapter will accordingly develop an extended close reading of the *Gilgamesh Epic*, as only in this way can one properly appreciate both the text's beauty and its relevance to the Bible.

The comparison needs to be developed not only with similar care in both cases, but also with similar methods: like Genesis, the *Gilgamesh Epic* can best be understood through an examination of its historical development.[1] The epic's intricate compositional history has been slighted in accounts that focus on the theme of mortality, which has often been treated as the epic's sole concern. The problem of mortality is indeed the hallmark of the Old Babylonian version of the epic, but this theme gradually loses its dominance as the epic develops over the course of the second millennium. The epic's eventual standard form, produced around 1250, interweaves a whole series of themes in a synoptic exploration of the limits and meaning of culture. It is this final form of the epic that is closest in time

---

[1]See Jeffrey Tigay for a discussion of ways in which the evolution of the text of *Gilgamesh* can provide analogies to the evolution of the biblical texts (*Empirical Models*, 21–52).

and in theme to Genesis. Consequently, a close examination of the development of the epic can tell us much about the Bible's debt to the old epic tradition as well as its differences from it.

According to the Sumerian King List (*ANET,* 265–66), Gilgamesh was the fifth king of the first dynasty of Uruk, a city-state in southern Mesopotamia; he would have lived around 2600. Inscriptions indicate that he was regarded as a god by a century or two later, and by the twenty-first century he was identified as king and judge of the underworld. It is, of course, difficult to say that much of the story really stems from the historical Gilgamesh, around whose name much later (and perhaps also earlier) material has gathered. Sumerian poems from the close of the third millennium tell various stories about Gilgamesh and his adventures both above ground and in the underworld. The popularity of the figure of Gilgamesh is attested not only by the survival of several separate stories about him but also by the recovery of these stories from different sites around Mesopotamia, including Uruk and Ur. In a recent study, *The Evolution of the Gilgamesh Epic,* Jeffrey H. Tigay has shown that the first unified Gilgamesh epic was formed on the basis of these old stories and written in Akkadian in the Old Babylonian period (2000–1600).

Versions of this text circulated widely, and several portions from the Middle Babylonian period (1600–1000) have been found, not only in Ur but also in Palestine: Akkadian fragments from circa 1400 in Megiddo and in the Hittite capital Hattusha (Boghazköi), which has also yielded fragments of translations into Hittite itself and into Hurrian, the language of the Mitanni empire in central Mesopotamia. The standard late form of the epic was eventually produced, in around 1250, through an extended literary revision of the Old Babylonian text. The late version is the longest and richest, but the wealth of surviving material from the earlier stages is of great value for the assessment of developments in Mesopotamian epic traditions into biblical times. Specifically it allows us to see the late version as parallel and complementary to the Bible in the generic combining of history with mythic epic.

In respect of genre, both the *Gilgamesh Epic* and Genesis 1–11 can best be understood in relation to an ancient literary form: the epic story of primordial times, from the creation of human beings to the Flood. Both the *Gilgamesh Epic* and Genesis 1–11 owe much to this genre and also distance themselves from it in its classic forms, through a process of adaptation, suppression, and outright polemic. The creation-flood narrative was a major and long-established genre; surviving examples are found both in Sumerian and in Akkadian. A given epic may range over the whole of this period, with a focus on the Flood, as in the case of the *Atrahasis Epic* and the Sumerian "Flood Story,"[2] or it may concern itself only with primordial history up until the creation of humanity, as in the case of *Enuma elish*. These texts remain closely linked, however, and it could be said that the flood stories represent a historicizing extension into human history of primordial conflicts depicted among the gods in *Enuma elish*.[3] We do not have enough evidence to say whether an older, purely heavenly tradition developed human-history analogues in Sumerian times late in the third millen-

---

[2]"The Sumerian Flood Story," M. Civil, ed., in Lambert and Millard, *Atra-Ḥasīs*, 138–45, 167–72. Though the text is incomplete, missing its beginning and large sections thereafter, the extant portions describe the initial pre-deluge building of cities and establishment of agriculture, as well as the Flood.

[3]Notably, the cause of conflict is the same in each case. In the *Atrahasis Epic*, it is the noisiness of the humans that determines Enlil to destroy them, and in the creation epic, the tumultuous younger gods disturb the rest of the first-generation gods, leading Apsu, the primordial sky god, to exclaim to Tiamat, the sea goddess:

> Their ways are verily loathsome unto me.
> By day I find no relief, nor repose by night.
> I will destroy, I will wreck their ways,
> That quiet may be restored. Let us have rest!

(*ANET*, 61, lines 37–40)

The beleaguered younger gods, led by Marduk, finally defeat and subdue Tiamat, who figures as their chief opponent, though the hostilities have been initiated by Apsu. As Tiamat is the primordial ocean, this struggle itself is a heavenly version of the human effort to survive the waters of the Flood.

nium, or whether the two variant traditions coexisted from much earlier.[4] In either case, as Claus Westermann says, "the creation and the flood are the themes which occur most often in the stories of primeval times. . . . creation and flood complement each other" (*Genesis 1–11,* 5).

Four fundamental story elements appear in the creation-flood epics: the creation of the world, the creation of human beings, the cataclysm of the Flood, and the establishment of the post-Flood human order, symbolized in the *Atrahasis Epic* by the reestablishment of ritual and in *Enuma elish* by the building of a temple for Marduk in Babylon. All these elements are taken up into Genesis 1–11, though with major thematic alterations, as will be seen below. If Genesis 1–11 develops away from this ancient paradigm, the *Gilgamesh Epic* develops *toward* it. In the process, the text loses its former exclusive emphasis on the problem of death and becomes a wider meditation on the limits of culture; in this there is a notable parallel to the movement from the problem of mortality to the theme of knowledge in Genesis 1–11.

The earliest Gilgamesh stories, in Sumerian, described the heroic adventures of Gilgamesh, who was sometimes accompanied by his servant Enkidu. These unconnected stories were refocused in the Old Babylonian period into an exploration of the problem of mortality. Enkidu is elevated from Gilgamesh's servant to his best friend, enabling the author to unify the epic around the tragedy of Enkidu's early death. As Tigay says, "The epic is not a study of friendship per se. The motif of friendship serves as a device whereby Enkidu's death can be made to shock Gilgamesh into an obsessive quest for immor-

---

[4]The creation epic *Enuma elish,* at least as we now have it, actually appears to be of later date (1600–1200) than the *Atrahasis Epic* (2000–1600) and its Sumerian antecedent. It is thought to have been composed at this late date as a celebration and justification of the new prominence then being given to Marduk. It may have been created purely through a retrojection of Flood motifs into prehuman primordial history, or both strands of tradition may go far back in time, with some variants dealing with the time of creation and other variants setting similar conflicts and themes at the time of the Flood.

tality" (28). As alternative to the immortality Gilgamesh fails to achieve, the Old Babylonian version suggests a *carpe diem* policy, expressed in a speech by a barmaid. She tells him to eat well, make every day into a feast day, have good clothing, and enjoy his wife and children.[5]

The late version of the epic, though usually viewed as having the same theme, in fact redirects it altogether. The barmaid's hedonistic speech is displaced and de-emphasized, a prologue and epilogue with a broader wisdom perspective are added, and a series of striking additions to the body of the epic expand the scope of the work. Three of these are particularly noteworthy: an extended description of the creation and early life of Enkidu; a marriage proposal from Ishtar to Gilgamesh; and a long account of the Flood, retold by its hero Utnapishtim, whom Gilgamesh visits in search of immortality.

These scenes have usually been viewed as inorganic accretions; even Tigay, who gives a spirited defense of the importance of the increased emphasis on Enkidu, merely notes the new material on Ishtar without attempting to account for it; of the longest addition, the flood story, he suggests only that it serves as a delaying device to heighten our suspenseful interest in knowing how things will work out after the interruption.[6] All three of these additions, however, take on coherent meaning and unified purpose if they are seen in relation to the creation-flood epics; for the consistent effect of these additions is to assimilate the *Gilgamesh Epic* toward this genre.

[5]For the barmaid's speech, see Tigay, *Evolution of the Gilgamesh Epic*, 50. This form of *carpe diem* wisdom was not uncommon in the Near East; particularly good parallels survive from Egyptian, in the genre known as "Harper's Songs"; see Miriam Lichtheim, *Ancient Egyptian Literature*, I, 193–97, and II, 115–16.

[6]Unable to see the flood narrative as having any direct connection to the epic, Tigay thus tries to make a narrative virtue of its very irrelevance. Tigay himself is aware that this interpretation is somewhat forced, noting that it is "obviously speculative" (*Evolution*, 240). It is difficult to see suspense as a primary consideration in the text, which begins by giving away its plot. Further, the subsequent "denouement" of the loss of the root of immorality is briefly told, not developed as a dramatic climax; the flood narrative gets much more space. Any retarding effect it may have must be a secondary consequence and not the motivating force for the story's insertion.

The remarkable thing about this assimilative process is its occurrence at the very time that the poetic epic tradition reaches its furthest degree of historicization. Already the Old Babylonian version of the epic exhibited historicizing aspects of the sort noted above in the *Atrahasis Epic* and the *Erra Epic*. These tendencies were developed much further in the late version, but not, as one might have expected, through a simple abandonment of the mythic tradition. Rather, the late version takes up the mythic epic tradition in its fullest form, the creation-flood epic, not in order to remythologize but in order to carry through a far-reaching process of self-definition vis-à-vis the mythic tradition. In this way the late version explores the nature and limits of human culture and history through an explicit process of separation from divine culture and divine ways of acting, as represented in the older creation-flood epics.

This process is of direct value in assessing the relation of Genesis 1–11 to its polytheistic past, as a related effort at separation and self-definition can also be observed there. The similarity here between Genesis and the late version of the *Gilgamesh Epic* is neither a chance occurrence nor necessarily a sign of direct dependence of one tradition on another, but is a natural feature, perhaps almost an inevitable feature, of the self–definition of historical epic as it separates itself from the trans-historical patterns of myth. In this respect, indeed, the *Gilgamesh Epic* has as much in common with the *Iliad* as with Genesis; some of these parallels will be noted below. The *Gilgamesh Epic*, like the opening section of Genesis, is very much a transitional form, and this may indeed be an aspect of its compelling power, as it gains in richness, almost producing an effect of parallax, from the coexistence of elements that had formerly been separated and had now been mixed but not yet collapsed into each other.

Enkidu and the World of Nature

The first major narrative expansion in the late version, the early story of Enkidu, introduces the theme of the definition and meaning of culture. In this instance the epic defines culture against precultural life. Enkidu has become more than just a friend, his Old Babylonian role; now, he begins life as an image of the primitive human being, and his early adventures suggest the forces distinguishing primitive life from "civilization," as exemplified by the city life of Uruk.

At the start of the epic, Gilgamesh is terrorizing his own city-state, oppressing his people in various ways.[7] The nobles pray to the gods, who decide to create Enkidu as a companion for Gilgamesh, to contend with Gilgamesh and quiet him down. Enkidu could simply have been placed at the gate of Uruk, but instead the author uses the episode as an opportunity to meditate on the origins of human culture. Enkidu is created in the form of a primordial man, covered with shaggy hair "like a woman" (I, ii, 36), looking like Nisaba, the goddess of grain. He roams naked across the steppe in the company of the animals, eating grass and drinking at watering holes. In his primitive union with the animals, Enkidu is actually hostile to human culture: he tears up the traps that the shepherds have set for the animals that prey on their sheep. Enkidu has perhaps been made more fully in Gilgamesh's image than the gods had planned: as Gilgamesh disturbs civil order in Uruk, Enkidu disturbs the pastoral order in the countryside.

The shepherds develop a plan, which Gilgamesh ratifies, to separate Enkidu from the animals: they send a temple prostitute to him. He sleeps with her for six days and seven nights. At the end of this time, his powers are diminished, and he cannot run as well as before; still worse, the animals are now afraid of him. If we suspect a hint of a parallel to Eve's seduction of Adam and the loss of Eden, the parallel becomes direct when the harlot speaks to the "fallen" Enkidu: "You are [wi]se, Enkidu, you have become like a god!" (I, iv, 34).[8] Enk-

---

[7]Gilgamesh's oppression seems likely to include some or all of: forced labor, heterosexual or homosexual rape, and sporting contests in which he as victor would enslave his opponents or their women.

[8]The parallel to Genesis may be a little overstated in this translation, as the

idu's sexual knowledge has brought him godlike wisdom and separated him from the state of nature. In this respect the parallel is very close to the Eden story, though with a direct development of the sexual aspect that is only indirectly present in Genesis. The scene in the *Gilgamesh Epic* differs markedly in its effects, however, as society can counter the loss of nature with equal or greater compensations. Seeing Enkidu's new wisdom, the harlot suggests that he should abandon his limited rustic life for the wider scope and greater pleasures of the city:

"Why with the wild creatures do you roam over the steppe?
Come, let me lead you [to] ramparted Uruk,
To the holy temple, abode of Anu and Ishtar,
Where lives Gilgamesh, accomplished in strength,
And like a wild bull lords it over the folk."
As she speaks to him, her words find favor;
His heart enlightened, he yearns for a friend.

(I, iv, 35–41)

Thus, though deprived of his animal friends, Enkidu will find in the city a bull-like man for a new companion.

A temple prostitute is a somewhat unusual bearer of wisdom for Near Eastern literature; certainly in the Bible, when Tamar disguises herself in that fashion in order to bring her father-in-law, Judah, to acknowledge his duty, the success of her ruse depends on Judah's not looking for instruction from that corner (Genesis 38). The epic does not altogether endorse the harlot's hedonistic view of the values of the city, in fact, but goes on to show such views as limited (on this, more below). At the same time, the harlot's perspective is perfectly valid, so far as

---

phrase "you are wise" is a reconstruction. It is, however, a plausible one, followed as well in the German translation of Schott and von Soden, and if true would make a nice folk etymology for "Enkidu" in the word "wise," *enqata;* see further below on the quasi-renaming of Adam as "subtle" at a similar point in the Genesis story. Even apart from the conjectural "you are wise," however, the parallel to Genesis is quite clear enough in the second phrase, "you have become like a god," a phrase repeated when the scene is recapitulated on the next tablet: "As I look at you, Enkidu, you have become like a god" (II, ii, 11).

it goes, and suits her limited understanding of the drama she is involved in: presumably she knows that her job is to divert Enkidu from terrorizing the countryside, but presumably only the gods know that her advice serves their larger plan of restoring Gilgamesh to proper behavior.

This dynamic of knowledge and concealment is comparable to the problematics of understanding that Meir Sternberg has shown to be at work in various biblical narratives, such as the story of the wooing of Rebekah (*Poetics of Biblical Narrative*, 131–52). It also shows that the Babylonians, at least in their epics, displayed a more complex sense of causality than a simple naive faith that one prays to the gods, who give clear and immediate aid. The shepherds, terrified and bewildered by Enkidu, devise a stratagem to neutralize him, with no way of knowing that the gods themselves have created this evil as a way of responding to the prayers of Gilgamesh's oppressed subjects. Indeed, the shepherds' stratagem figures as an essential link in the gods' plot. This complex and ironic view of divine aid in times of crisis is very like the sorts of analysis that will be applied to contemporary history by the biblical historians, and if Near Eastern chronicle rarely (if ever) approached this degree of subtlety, it was because the genres of prose chronicle had an ideological stake in minimizing both divine complexity and human ignorance. When Shalmaneser goes to war, Nergal gives him weapons and Shamash strengthens his arm. Thutmose can take his wretched enemies by surprise but would never be shown to be caught unawares himself. Here, though, even Gilgamesh himself does not know the real story behind the appearance of Enkidu. He cannot know of the gods' purpose in creating Enkidu; further, there is not even any indication that either he or the shepherds anticipate that Enkidu will be brought to the city, a development that is presented purely as the harlot's own initiative. Such a degree of ignorance on the part of a king, and such a degree of dominance by unforeseen contingency, would be unthinkable in the prose chronicles, whereas the *Gilgamesh Epic* goes out of its way to emphasize these points; the only function of the scene in which the shepherds ask Gilgamesh to approve of their plan for quieting Enkidu down is to show Gilgamesh unwittingly setting the stage for his own reformation.

Unknown in the prose chronicles, such a scene has no direct equivalent in the older mythic epic tradition either. The Sumerian and Old Babylonian mythic epics were fully alive to paradoxical behavior on the part of the gods, but they focused on timeless patterns and showed relatively little interest in working through issues of divine behavior in response to specific crises in human historical experience. It was left for the confluence of poetic epic and prose history to produce such a scene as this, in which the interaction of different social groups and the very tangible political problem of an irresponsible ruler—the story's hero—are viewed from the perspective of the mysterious complexities of myth.

A corollary to the historicizing of the poetic epic is the beginning of divine withdrawal from direct action in the story, a process clearly visible in the Bible as well. The gods are perfectly able to talk directly, and even to engage in sexual relations, with extraordinary figures like Gilgamesh, but their preference is for indirect dealings. Thus, they create Enkidu rather than intervening in person; later, when Ishtar wishes to harm Gilgamesh, she sends down the Bull of Heaven, an intermediary figure presented almost as a kind of robot. Indirect action is matched by a new emphasis on indirect communication: the epic contains numerous dreams, for which the human recipients must seek interpretations. Even though the gods can talk directly to Gilgamesh, they more often communicate even with him in this indirect fashion, a manner clearly resembling people's historical experience of communication with the gods.

The new emphasis on history within the epic tradition has a further corollary in a new interest in the idea of nature. In part, a highlighted nature begins to replace the presence of the withdrawing gods, and in part nature assumes a new authority as the locus of the hidden divine presence. Thus Gilgamesh will provide a substitute for the world of nature Enkidu has lost: in place of his former animal friends, the harlot tells him, he will have a new and better friend in Gilgamesh, who "like a wild bull lords over the folk." Thus the godlike Gilgamesh is also the animal-like Gilgamesh, and as a wild bull he will meet his greatest opponent in the Bull of Heaven sent down by Ishtar. The relation of civilization to the animal world is thus bivalent; it is essentially metaphoric, but the metaphor can move in either direction, and even, as in the example just given, in both directions at once. It can be said that Mesopotamian thought (like much "mythic" thought) sees the world not as a great chain of being but as a great circle. Humanity stands between the gods and the animal world on this circle, but at the same time, farther around the circle, the animal kingdom stands between humanity and the world of the divine, metaphorically representing the literal truths of the unseen world of the gods.

Interestingly, Enkidu's transition from the state of nature to life in the city is not direct, but requires an intermediate stage among the pastoralists. The harlot dresses Enkidu, dividing her clothing with him, and leads him to a community of shepherds: "Holding on to his hand, / She leads him like a child" (II, ii, 31–32). The next section (II, iii) describes how, like a baby, Enkidu must learn from the shepherds how to eat solid food, to wear clothing, and to take part in adult activities. Perhaps this is the earliest extant case of the trope, still common in recent times, of viewing primitive culture as childlike.

In opening with this movement away from the childlike state of nature, the epic gives an initial statement of the value of culture. The harlot, urging Enkidu to go to Uruk, praises the city in terms close to the barmaid's *carpe diem* philosophy in the Old Babylonian version. The harlot describes Uruk as a place

Where people are re[splend]ent in festal attire,
(Where) each day is made a holiday,

Where [. . .] lads . . .,
And la[ss]es [. .] . of figure.
Their ripeness [. . .] full of perfume.

(I, v, 7–11)

She then praises Gilgamesh's beauty ("He is radiant with man-
hood, vigor he has. / With ripeness gorgeous is the whole of
his body," I, v, 16–17) and describes him as even stronger than
Enkidu. A fitting friend—or a fitting husband; there are sexual
undertones running through the relationship of Gilgamesh and
Enkidu. In addition to hearing the praise of clothing, festivity,
and erotically charged friendship, Enkidu learns from the shepherds the pleasures of strong drink and of demonstrating his
prowess through capturing wolves and lions—a direct contrast
to his previous tearing up of traps (II, iii, 10–36).

Implicit in the comparison of primitive life to babyhood is
the suggestion that civilized life involves a loss of an uncon-
scious, direct relation to the natural/divine world, but also
brings about the gain of an adult, conscious, deliberate relation
to the gods. Enkidu now combs (or perhaps sheds) his hair
and no longer looks like the goddess of grain, but he can now
worship the gods and serve them in ways animals cannot. The
very first thing the harlot mentions, in fact, as awaiting Enkidu
in Uruk is "the holy temple, abode of Anu and Ishtar" (I, iv,
37). The essential duty of humanity, the reason for which humankind was created, is to serve the gods, supplying them
with ritual sacrifices, as we know from *Enuma elish* and the
Atrahasis Epic. In going to the city, then, Enkidu loses his un-
conscious similarity to the gods but gains the human consciousness of his duty to the gods that animals lack. In service
to the gods and to Gilgamesh, he can fulfill his humanity; he
becomes wise and godlike, in a change that has both similarities and differences with the Genesis story (on which more
below).

Enkidu goes to Uruk, where everyone is struck by his likeness to Gilgamesh:

The people were gathered,
Saying about him:
"He is like Gilgamesh in build!"

. . . .

The nobles rejoiced:
"A hero has appeared
For the man of proper mien!
For Gilgamesh, who is like a god,
His equal has come forth."

(II, v, 13–15, 23–27)

If Adam is created in God's image, Enkidu is the image of Gilgamesh, who is himself like a god, *kima ilim*, the same phrase used by the harlot to describe Enkidu after she sleeps with him. Barring Gilgamesh's way as he sallies out on one of his nocturnal expeditions, Enkidu wrestles with him.[9] For the first time, Gilgamesh has met his match, and they become fast friends. Enkidu turns Gilgamesh's thoughts toward legitimate exploits of valor, and they make an expedition to a distant mountain, slaying the monster Humbaba and cutting down his precious grove of cedar trees. The scene shows a close interweaving of mythic and historical elements. On the one hand, Humbaba is "a terror to mortals" (III, iv, 2), a divinely created guardian monster, full of elemental strength and mythic resonance; on the other hand, expeditions to cut down cedar trees in distant hill country were a common heroic (or heroic-economic) activity of Mesopotamian kings, described in several chronicles.[10]

In recounting this episode, the late version closely follows

---

[9] A further parallel to Genesis might be seen in the fact that Enkidu gains acceptance by wrestling with Gilgamesh, just as Israel does in the person of Jacob, renamed "Israel" (He who wrestles with God) after his match with God in the form of the angel (Genesis 32).

[10] For example, Tiglath-Pileser I records that Anu and Adad commanded him to journey to Lebanon in c. 1100 to cut cedar beams for their temple (*ANET*, 275). Another ruler, a Mesopotamian king named Yahdun-Lin, describes the journey to the Cedar Mountain as one of the greatest feats of his bold career (*ANET*, 556).

the plot of the old Sumerian version of this story, the adventure tale known as "Gilgamesh and the Land of the Living" (*ANET*, 47–50). The thematic development of the story, however, is quite different. The Sumerian story emphasizes heroic action as a means of gaining fame, which in turn eases the oppressiveness of the prospect of death. The story opens with Gilgamesh explaining to the sun god Utu his reasons for wishing to undertake the expedition:

O Utu, a word I would speak to you, give your ear to my word,
⌐I would have it reach you¬, give ear to it.
In my city man dies, oppressed is the heart,
Man perishes, heavy is the heart.
I ⌐peered over¬ the wall,
I saw the dead bodies . . . ⌐floating on¬ the river;
As for me, I too will be served thus; truly it is so.
The tallest man cannot reach to heaven,
The broadest man cannot ⌐cover¬ the earth.
Not ⌐(yet) have brick and stamp¬ brought forth ⌐the fated end¬;
I would enter the "land," I would set up my name,
In its places where the names have been raised up,
    I would raise up my name,
In its places where the names have not been raised up,
    I would raise up the names of the gods.

(lines 21–33)

Utu allows Gilgamesh to proceed, and he goes off, swearing an oath by his divine mother, Ninsun, and his mortal father, Lugalbanda, not to return without having fought Huwawa (the Sumerian version of "Humbaba"). The body of the tale describes Gilgamesh's fearless heroism and his successful struggle against the monster.

The late version carries on the themes of the fear of death and the virtue of heroism, but fills out these themes within its new preoccupation with the problems of knowledge and of the nature of human culture.[11] In place of Gilgamesh's passing ref-

[11]The issue of knowledge was first introduced in the Old Babylonian version,

erence to his parents in his oath, the late version gives an entire scene in which Gilgamesh and Enkidu go to Ninsun to ask her to pray to Shamash (the Akkadian name of the sun god) on their behalf. She does so, and her request for Shamash's protection begins with a personal reflection:

Why, having given me Gilgamesh for a son,
With a restless heart did you endow him?
And now you have moved him to go
On a far journey, to the place of Humbaba,
To face an uncertain battle,
To travel an uncertain road!   (III, ii, 10–15, Assyrian version)

Here the restlessness of mortals faced with the prospect of death is movingly presented through the sorrow of Gilgamesh's immortal mother. The scene is notably close to the scene early in the *Iliad* in which Achilles asks his divine mother, Thetis, to intercede with Zeus for aid in the battle against the Trojans. Thetis's reply to Achilles begins in terms not unlike the beginning of Ninsun's speech to Shamash:

Thetis answered him then, her tears falling:
"Oh, my own child; unhappy in childbirth, why did I raise you?
Could you but stay by your ships, without tears or sorrow,
since the span of your life will be brief, of no length."

(1.413–16)

The Homeric epic goes on to develop the scene much further than the Gilgamesh epic of five hundred years earlier, but the Akkadian epic already presents in an early form a characteristic aspect of the confluence of myth and history: an assessment of human culture from a viewpoint outside that culture.

---

in a speech of warning by the elders of Uruk: "You are still young, Gilgamesh, your heart has carried you away. / You do not know what you are attempting to achieve" (III, v, 10–11). Knowledge is an issue here, though not yet a problem, for Gilgamesh (foolhardy though he may be) proves to have no difficulty in overcoming Humbaba; it is the elders who are mistaken in believing that Gilgamesh is taking on more than he can handle.

The Rejection of Ishtar

If Ninsun's speech defines the restlessness of mortals from the perspective of the immortal, the scene that follows does the opposite: it presents a judgment of divine behavior from a human perspective. This is the newly added scene in which Ishtar tries, and fails, to seduce Gilgamesh. She is impressed by his splendid beauty when, home from slaying Humbaba, he bathes and dresses himself regally. If he will become her lover, she tells him, she will give him rich presents, and all other kings will be humbled before him.

Gilgamesh's reply is extraordinary. He begins diplomatically, asking what appropriate gifts he could possibly give to such a bride (VI, 22–8). Then he gets to the point, and criticizes Ishtar's failings in a diatribe almost fifty lines long. The heart of his argument is the fickleness of the goddess of love: "Which lover did you love forever? / Which of your shepherds pleased [you for all time]?" (VI, 42–43). Immortality is no guarantee of constancy; on the contrary, Ishtar's eternal and unvarying trait is her inconstancy.

The speech can be read in two ways: as a rejection of the love of women in favor of the more solid and lasting male bonding seen between Gilgamesh and Enkidu, or else as a part of the process of self-definition of human culture against the surrounding natural and supernatural world. These two readings are not contradictory, and each has ramifications elsewhere in the epic. It is evident that Enkidu's coming has changed Gilgamesh's attitude toward his life. Enkidu's first act on his arrival, in fact, is to block Gilgamesh's way as he is going in to sleep with a woman. This episode itself has both human and divine implications. Just before Enkidu's arrival, we are told ·that Gilgamesh is practicing the *ius primae noctis*, mating "with engaged women . . . / He is the first, / The ⌈husband⌉ comes after" (II, iv, 34–36). The specific nuptial scene Enkidu interrupts is, however, described in somewhat different terms: "For Ishhara the bed [of marria]ge is laid out. / For Gilgamesh, as a god, a (or the) . . . is set up" (II, ii, 44–45).[12] "Ishhara" is an appellation of Ishtar, and the scene has been read as depicting a *hieros gamos*, a sacred marriage rite in which the king sleeps with a woman who ritually represents the goddess.[13]

Whether the context is sacred or secular, we hear no more of involvement with women once Gilgamesh meets Enkidu, and indeed on Enkidu's death Gilgamesh mourns him "like a wailing woman." "He touched his heart, but it does not beat. / Then he veiled (his) friend like a bride" (VIII, ii, 3, 16–7). In this respect, then, Gilgamesh's discovery of Enkidu can be said to replace the love of women, hence the service of Ishtar, in his heart. The thematic significance of this rejection of women has to do with the harlot's and the shepherds' initial view of culture as valuable for wine, women, and song: Gilgamesh has begun to perceive larger and more lasting values than the transitory physical pleasures which the author symbolizes by the fickle Ishtar.

At the same time, Gilgamesh is rejecting the advances not simply of a mortal woman but of the goddess of love herself. Her effect on mortals is very different from the acculturating effect of the harlot on Enkidu: Gilgamesh sees Ishtar as the destroyer of culture. His speech has two parts, hinging on the central question "Which lover did you love forever?" The first part of the speech describes Ishtar in general terms in a remarkable series of metaphors, all of them comparing Ishtar to human artifacts. Gilgamesh compares her to the most mundane everyday objects (a back door, a waterskin, a shoe) and to larger constructions for the defense of society: a palace wall, a siege engine. In almost every case, however, Gilgamesh sees Ishtar

---

[12]The lines are lacking in *ANET*, but have been supplied by Tigay, *Evolution*, 91.

[13]The passage just quoted abbreviates a somewhat fuller description in the Old Babylonian version, which contains lines that may make the *hieros gamos* explicit, though the text is corrupt. Schott (in his German translation) conjecturally renders the lines as: "Gilgamesh is to come together at night with the goddess," though Tigay translates this line more secularly: "Gilgamesh wi[th the y]ou[ng wom]an / (Is to) jo[in] at night."

as the perversion of the proper function of the thing in question: she is "A back door [which does not] keep out blast and windstorm; / A palace which crushes (its) garrison . . . / A waterskin which ⌐cuts⌐ its bearer . . . / A shoe which pinches [the foot] of its owner!" (VI, 34–41).

The second part of Gilgamesh's diatribe goes on to list several of Ishtar's lovers, all of whom have suffered evil fates, in every case involving the direct reversal of their natures. First he lists several animals she has loved: a bird, whose wing is now broken; a lion, fallen into the pits she dug for him; a wild stallion, now brought under lash and spur. Having surveyed Ishtar in terms of human artifacts, then in terms of the animal kingdom, Gilgamesh concludes with examples of human lovers, whom Ishtar has turned into animals: a gardener is turned into a mole, trapped in his own garden (VI, 64–78), and a shepherd suffers an equally violent reversal:

Then you loved the keeper of the herd,
Who offered you loaf after loaf of bread baked in ashes;
Who daily slaughtered kids for you;
Yet you struck him, turning him into a wolf,
So that his own herd boys drive him off,
And his dogs bite his thighs.   (VI, 58–63)

This example forms an interesting mirror image to the effect of the harlot's love on Enkidu, who was brought away from the company of wild animals to become the shepherds' chief protector. Here, Ishtar's love has the opposite result, driving the shepherd away from his home, turning him into his own hereditary enemy.

Coming directly after Ninsun's sorrowful speech concerning the shortness of Gilgamesh's restless life, Gilgamesh's speech advances a counterclaim for the independent value of human culture: mortals can be more constant than fickle gods. The epic is not by any means advocating a complete separation of the divine and human realms, but rather a mutual support and tolerance that are possible only if each group keeps its place.

For Ishtar to intervene too directly in the world is likely to have consequences hostile to human culture, a point made not only in the metaphors of reversal just quoted, but also in the sequel to Gilgamesh's diatribe. When an enraged Ishtar determines to send down the Bull of Heaven to destroy Gilgamesh, her father Anu warns her that her methods will spread havoc far beyond her immediate purpose: the Bull will also destroy the country's crops, and the damage will be so great that the land will require seven years to recover. Ishtar replies that she has put aside enough grain to tide her people over during the famine, but it is clear that her people's well-being is secondary to her personal desire to punish Gilgamesh.

Indeed, Ishtar is quite prepared to upset the entire earthly order in her quest for revenge. She threatens Anu: if he does not give her the Bull of Heaven,

I will smash [the doors of the nether world],
I will ⌜pla[ce those above]⌝ below,
I will raise up the dead, and they will devour the living,
I will make the dead outnumber the living!

(VI, 97–100)[14]

Here the epic again foreshadows the *Iliad*, which questions the loyalty of the gods to humanity through the heartless readiness of Hera to betray the chief cities of which she is the patron goddess in her eagerness to pursue her own schemes of revenge (*Iliad*, 4.50–54). More directly, the scene is reminiscent of the *Descent of Ishtar*, where Ishtar makes the same threat, in the same words, to the gatekeeper who wishes to bar her entry to Ereshkigal's underworld palace (*ANET*, 107). A similar threat, more briefly phrased, also appears in *Nergal and Ereshkigal*, where it is Ereshkigal who threatens to raise the dead if

---

[14]In the translation of these last two lines I follow Tigay (173) in adopting the improved reading given by R. Frankena in "Nouveaux fragments de la sixième tablette de l'Épopée de Gilgamesh," in Garelli, ed., *Gilgameš et sa légende*, 121.

the heavenly gods refuse to give her Nergal as husband (*ANET*, 511). In both instances, what is at issue is the improper or unstable mixing of cosmic realms, which threatens to break down the fundamental distinctions between the worlds of the living and the dead.

As Tigay notes, the threat most logically issues from Ereshkigal, who controls the dead and can threaten the world of the living; this suggests that the *Descent of Ishtar* took the threat over from *Nergal and Ereshkigal*, transferring it to Ishtar since she is now the aggressor in the new tale. The *Gilgamesh Epic* in turn makes new use of the motif of the threat, and perhaps Gilgamesh's rejection of Ishtar's dangerous attractions carries with it something of Nergal's reluctance to become the husband of the queen of the underworld. The kinship between sexuality and death previously implied through the sisterhood of Ishtar and Ereshkigal is here represented through the single figure of the fatally attractive Ishtar.[15] So prominent is the violence of desire, in Gilgamesh's view, that in order to compare Ishtar to human artifacts he must portray each one in a violent reversal of its proper function: the wall crushes the garrison, the shoe hurts the foot, and so on. The only term in Gilgamesh's series of comparisons that does not reverse its normal operation in being likened to Ishtar is the siege engine, which pursues its customary destructive action.

In its play on Ishtar's epic background, the *Gilgamesh Epic* brings these mythic elements into its historical frame and into the earthly world. In this newly independent sphere, Gilgamesh succeeds in breaking the mythic pattern, as even the divine Nergal could not do. He rejects Ishtar's advances, opting

---

[15]Ishtar has a direct descendant in the Aphrodite of the *Iliad*. We may recall the scene in which Aphrodite orders Helen to seduce Paris away from defending Troy. When Helen tries to protest this betrayal of her adoptive city, Aphrodite replies, "Do not annoy me, perverse woman, lest in anger I give up on you, / and come to hate you as terribly as now I love you / . . . and you perish in misery" (3.414–17).

in effect for human relations over direct erotic relations with
the gods, and he and Enkidu defeat the death-dealing Bull of
Heaven that the enraged Ishtar sends to destroy them.

The Bull is an interesting figure, part living creature and part
artifact. Though it snorts and bellows and is finally killed, its
magnificent horns are those of a statue, and Gilgamesh even
calls his craftsmen over to give their professional judgment:

> Gilgamesh called the craftsmen, the armorers,
> All (of them).
> The artisans admire the thickness of his horns:
> Each is cast from thirty minas of lapis;
> The coating on each is two fingers (thick).
>
> (VI, 166–70)

By this depiction, the Bull becomes something between a living
mythic creature and an animated carved idol, a good emblem
for the transitional status of much of the epic between mythic
and historicist representation.[16]

With the human and divine worlds defined and set largely
apart, mortals can no more violate the boundary than the gods
can. It appears that in the late version the death of Enkidu
results from his hubristic attempt to strike too directly back at
Ishtar. On killing the Bull, Enkidu sees Ishtar up on the ramparts of Uruk and taunts her, acknowledging the gap between
them but foolishly asserting his own superiority:

> He threw the right thigh of the Bull of Heaven,
>   tossing it in her face:
> "Could I but get to you,
> I would do to you as to him.

---

[16]Lapis lazuli accessories are not unknown among well-dressed divinities; the
Serpent in the Egyptian "Story of the Shipwrecked Sailor" wears a lapis lazuli
beard. The Serpent, however, wears the beard as an emblem of kingship, as
even Queen Hatshepsut does in some portrayals; the Bull's horns are presumably a more integral part of his body. In any event the text introduces
Gilgamesh's admiring craftsmen to emphasize the constructed character of
the Bull's horns. In a Sumerian hymn, the moon god Nanna-Suen is called
a "fierce calf with powerful horns . . . who is adorned with a lapis lazuli
beard" (Åke Sjöberg, *Der Mondgott Nanna-Suen*, 174).

I would hang his entrails at your side!"

(VI, 159–62)

Enkidu thus falls into the fatal error of taunting the gods and of believing his strength as great as theirs. His folly is comparable to Diomedes' insane desire to defeat Apollo on the Trojan battlefield, in the fifth book of the *Iliad*. Diomedes is saved by the patience of Apollo, who warns him off, but Ishtar, for whom Enkidu's taunt is the last straw, determines to destroy him.[17]

The gods decree his death, and a moving scene follows in which the dying Enkidu dreams of the underworld and describes his vision to Gilgamesh. In his dream, Enkidu is overpowered by "a young man whose face was dark" (VII, iv, 17). This is Humuttabal (whose name means "Take Away Quickly"), the boatman who ferries souls across the underworld river. He takes Enkidu to the House of Dust, where the dead, clothed like birds, reside in darkness, eating dust and clay. The description parallels that in the *Descent of Ishtar* (quoted above, p. 67); the major change is the addition of several lines emphasizing the collapse of social distinction: rulers have lost their crowns, and princes wait on tables.

One mortal is mentioned by name: Etana, an early king of

---

[17]Despite Diomedes' good fortune in surviving the episode, a related point is being made: "poor fool, the heart of Tydeus' son does not see / that he who fights the immortals does not live long"(5.406–7). It should be said that it is not certain that Ishtar is the one who brings about Enkidu's death in the late version, though this seems likely in view of the taunting scene. Unfortunately, we lack the relevant columns in the late version where the gods have discussed the question (VII, i–ii). We do have, however, an earlier version of this passage, in Hittite. In this text, Anu wishes to kill Enkidu in retaliation for his slaying of Humbaba/Huwawa and the Bull of Heaven. In the late version, the newly prominent Ishtar would be taking Anu's place in this resolve. In the Hittite version, when Shamash tries to intercede, saying that Enkidu killed Huwawa only on his orders, Enlil angrily retorts that Shamash's close involvement only worsened the offensiveness of Enkidu's act: "Because [much like] / One of their comrades, you daily went down to them" (VII:15–16, *ANET*, 86). Thus the Hittite version also shows the theme of the fatal consequences of too intimate a mingling of the human and divine realms, a theme the late version develops through the new use of Ishtar.

Kish who was said to have flown to heaven on the back of an eagle in search of a plant that would bring his wife fertility. Etana's journey was the subject of a popular Akkadian epic, fragments of which survive from several periods (*ANET,* 114–18). Regrettably, we lack the end of the epic and do not know whether Etana's quest for this form of immortality was successful, though the Sumerian King List does show Etana's successor as his son. Whatever his fate in his own epic, his presence in Enkidu's underworld vision implies generally that his great adventures have only concluded with the common death awaiting everyone. Specifically, moreover, as Gilgamesh's most popular counterpart in epic stories of a quest after immortality, Etana serves to foreshadow the inevitable end of Gilgamesh's own journey.

In later epic, from the *Odyssey* onward, the encounter with famous heroes of the past is a central element in the underworld descent. Indeed, both the antiheroic and the monitory functions implicit in Etana's presence have explicit counterparts in the *Odyssey,* in Odysseus's underworld encounters with Achilles and Agamemnon. When Odysseus wishes Achilles joy in his Elysian Fields existence, Achilles' retort questions the value of heroism; he says it is "better to be on earth, hired out / to a tenant farmer, with little to eat, / than to rule over all the disembodied dead" (11.489–91). Secondly, Agamemnon's brooding presence warns Odysseus of the possibility that his own journey may end unhappily, and Agamemnon pointedly remarks that "there are no more faithful wives" (11.456).

The Flood and the End of the Age of Myth

The *Gilgamesh Epic*'s concern with the nature and limits of culture finds its climax in the longest addition to the earlier version: the detailed account of the Flood, given to Gilgamesh by his ancestor Utnapishtim. In the Old Babylonian version, Gilgamesh had sought out Utnapishtim as a mortal who had achieved immortality through the gods' special favor. It was the inspiration of the author of the late version to expand this scene greatly, having Utnapishtim retell the entire story of the Flood, which occupies some two hundred lines, two thirds of the final tablet of the epic. The framing visit still serves the earlier function of describing Gilgamesh's unsuccessful attempt to find an antidote to death, but the inserted flood story gives the quest a universal dimension. Having come to Utnapishtim in search of a force to counteract the fragility of individual human life, Gilgamesh instead receives a lesson in the fragility of human culture as a whole.

Far from being an inorganic appendage to the story, the flood account gathers up themes and imagery that have been active from the very beginning of the epic. Indeed, flood imagery is widespread in Mesopotamian writing, both epic and chronicle, as a pervasive metaphor for political and social dissolution. Even now, we speak of an army "storming" a town, or of a blitzkrieg; the flood-storm image was no dead metaphor in ancient Mesopotamia, where cities were built of baked clay and floods were a very live recurrent threat. To take one example of the metaphor in a chronicle, Shalmaneser III, in the ninth century, says that he "swept over Hatti, in its full extent (making it look) like ruin-hills (left) by the flood" (*ANET*, 277); see above, page 55, for the account of a later campaign in which Shalmaneser descends like the storm god "Adad when he makes a rainstorm pour down."

In the epic itself, the metaphoric comparison of battle to flood has already been introduced in the struggle against the monster Humbaba: "Humbaba—his roaring is the storm-flood, / His mouth is fire, his breath is death!"[18] The Old Babylonian, which

---

[18]Quoted from the Assyrian version (II, v, 3–4); compare the parallel Old Babylonian text in III, iii, 18–20 (both in *ANET*, 79). In view of this double comparison of Humbaba to a flood and a siege engine, his role as a guardian of the cedar forest is appropriate: cedar was the preferred material for construction of the siege engines or battering rams known as "floodstorm weapons." Indeed, at least one heroic journey to cut down cedar trees, made by Gudea of Lagash, was undertaken specifically for the purpose of making a "flood-storm weapon" (*ANET*, 268).

has the same lines, also adds: "An unequal struggle / Is (tangling with) the siege engine, Huwawa" (III, iii, 23–24). These themes have a long history in Gilgamesh stories, as can be seen in these lines from the Sumerian "Death of Gilgamesh":

Man's day of darkness has arrived for you,
the place of (sounding) the war-cry against man
   has arrived for you,
the wave of blackness that one cannot breast
   has arrived for you,
the unequal fight
   has arrived for you,
the skirmish, from which there is no escape,
   has arrived for you.[19]

In Utnapishtim's description, the Flood descends like an attacking army (XI, 110, 130), to drastic effect: "all mankind had returned to clay" (XI, 133). "Returning to clay" was a common term for a person's death; here, the Flood has literally melted the world's cities down to clay. This return to clay repeats on a worldwide scale the earlier fate of Enkidu; as Gilgamesh had said in lamenting him, "My friend, whom I loved, has turned to clay!" (X, ii, 13; X, iii, 30). Clay functions as a powerful image for the common elemental substance both of human life and of human artifacts, since it was not only the usual building material, but also the substance out of which the gods originally formed human beings (Atrahasis I, 190–260). Appropriately, in Enkidu's vision of the underworld, dust and clay are at once the building materials of the House of Dust and the food of the dead who reside there (VII, iv, 37). Further linking the convulsion of nature and the deaths of mortals, Utnapishtim sees in the oncoming flood not only the figure of the storm god Adad but also the figure of Erragal (= Erra or Nergal), god of the underworld (XI, 98–101).

---

[19]Quoted from Jacobsen, "Death in Mesopotamia," 20. Similarly, in the Sumerian tale "Gilgamesh and the Land of the Living," Huwawa is already compared to "the onrushing floodwater" (ANET, 49, line 102).

Two questions present themselves: How has the old mythic epic story of the Flood been altered in the process of including it in the late historicized epic of Gilgamesh, and how has the story of Gilgamesh in turn been affected by the insertion? In a sense, these questions apply to all of the late version's efforts to assimilate the story of Gilgamesh to the mythic creation-flood narratives, the process that culminates in the wholesale importation of the flood narrative from the *Atrahasis Epic*.[20]

The most radical change in the flood account is in voice: in bringing the flood hero into the story of Gilgamesh, the author has Utnapishtim recount the story in his own words, in the first person. This change leads toward a marked development of vivid eyewitness detail. Already in the *Atrahasis Epic*, as noted earlier, there were some early indications of historicizing interest in the sorts of details an eyewitness observer might have noted. In Utnapishtim's account, this tendency becomes pronounced, with realistic description, for example, of the practical difficulties people might encounter in trying to launch the largest and heaviest ship ever built: "[⌜The launching⌝] was very difficult, / So that they had to shift the floor planks above and below, / [⌜Until⌝] two-thirds of ⌜[the structure] [had g]one [into the water]⌝" (XI, 77–79). In addition to giving new descriptive detail, Utnapishtim's version shifts the emotional focus, abbreviating the gods' laments and stressing his own reactions. The gods' distress on seeing the consequences of the Flood had been given fifty-five lines in the *Atrahasis Epic*, but are only given fourteen in the *Epic of Gilgamesh*, which then devotes twice that amount of space to Utnapishtim's experiences in the aftermath of the Flood: seeing the waters subside, landing the ark, sending out the birds to test for dry land, and sacrificing to the gods. The description of the view after the Flood is particularly powerful:

---

[20]Tigay (214–18) has shown that the *Atrahasis Epic* is likely to be the direct model for the flood story as given in the *Gilgamesh Epic*; Utnapishtim is even called "Atrahasis" at the end of the account (XI, 187).

I looked at the weather: stillness had set in,
And all of mankind had returned to clay.
The landscape was as level as a flat roof.
I opened a hatch, and light fell on my face.
Bowing low, I sat and wept,
Tears running down my face.

(XI, 132–37)

Mourning his world as Gilgamesh mourns Enkidu, Utnapish-tim becomes Gilgamesh's double, experiencing on a larger scale what Gilgamesh experiences in the loss of his friend. The unifying of the story through the doubling of Utnapishtim and Gilgamesh is explicitly introduced in Gilgamesh's opening words to him: "As I look upon you, Utnapishtim, / Your features are not strange, for you are like me [ki iatima atta]. / You are not strange at all; you are like me" (XI, 2–4). Further linking Utnapishtim's troubles to Gilgamesh's, the author gives them the same cause: Ishtar. Enlil, the motivating force behind the Flood in the *Atrahasis Epic,* still appears but is now upstaged by Ishtar, who becomes the chief instigator of the Flood and the one who relents in the end and promises never to repeat the Flood (XI, 115–23, 162–69).[21]

Through these various adaptations, the old mythic story is both historicized and closely linked to the plot and themes of the story of Gilgamesh. Even so, it remains an intrusion in the epic's narrative flow, and in fact it is meant to be, for the author uses this episode to crystallize and heighten the process of defining human culture in historical terms. When Gilgamesh visits Utnapishtim, history visits myth. The epic has earlier tested human nature against both the natural world and the world of the gods; by comparing Gilgamesh to Utnapishtim, who even more than Etana faced natural cataclysm and divine hostility in their harshest form, the author sees an opportunity to meditate on the limits of modern, historical human life, in contrast to the possibilities suggested in older, mythic stories. Thus the

---

[21]Following Speiser in identifying the speaker in XI, 162–69 as Ishtar.

links between Utnapishtim and Gilgamesh do not merely double the themes of the rest of the epic. Rather, the flood story is included for the sake of its *difference* from the story of Gilgamesh. Utnapishtim not only survives his adventures but achieves immortality, and this is what Gilgamesh cannot do: for the times are past when the gods acted as they do in myth.

This theme forms the climax and conclusion to Utnapishtim's account. Utnapishtim closes his story by describing Enlil's accepting of his survival of the Flood:

Thereupon Enlil went aboard the ship.
Holding me by the hand, he took me aboard.
He took my wife aboard and made her kneel by my side.
Standing between us, he touched our foreheads to bless us:
"Hitherto Utnapishtim has been but human.
Henceforth Utnapishtim and his wife shall be like us gods.
Utnapishtim shall reside far away,
    at the mouth of the rivers!"
Thus they took me and made me reside far away,
    at the mouth of the rivers.
But now, who will for your sake call the gods to Assembly
    that you may find the life you seek?

(XI, 189–97)

The gods no longer take people by the hand and bless them, and the Assembly of the Gods no longer suspends the fundamental laws of nature on behalf of favored heroes.

What does the author of the late version think of the world of myth? In later times, thinkers of a historicizing and secularizing bent began to doubt the truth of the stories of the gods, or to euhemerize them, interpreting myths as old stories of human heroes. There is no need to suppose that this process has yet begun here, but we can see a process of rationalizing at work in a quite different way. Rather than calling the historical reality of Utnapishtim's experience into question, our author does something different: he renders it inaccessible. Utnapishtim's very dwelling place is not even reachable by any ordinary mortal: Gilgamesh is the first to have passed through the many dangers and obstacles described at length in the ninth and tenth tablets. His journey includes a dangerous underground passage through a twelve-league tunnel in a mountain range and culminates with the unprecedented feat of navigating through the "Waters of Death" that surround Utnapishtim's island.

In effect, the journey to Utnapishtim has been developed as an underworld descent. Utnapishtim's immortality would be hard to distinguish from an afterlife in the Elysian Fields; the major difference, indeed, is its greater isolation. Although the meeting between Gilgamesh and Utnapishtim plays on their similarity, it also notes their separation; the flood hero is first named as *Utnapištim rūqu:* "Utnapishtim the Faraway" (XI, 1).

Myth and history, then, are not to be contrasted in terms of fictional versus literal, but in terms of an irretrievable early history as against a more circumscribed modern world. The Flood was seen as the turning point in the shift from ancient history to modern history. Though modern history continues to have mythic overtones, it no longer shows the intimate direct contact with the gods and their world that was believed to have existed earlier. In Utnapishtim's account, in fact, the idea that the Flood marks a radical break with past time is enunciated by no less a figure than Ishtar, on seeing the destruction wrought by the Flood: "Alas," she cries, "the old days are turned to clay" (XI, 118). If the old times are dying, the new era is being born, and so it is appropriate that as Ishtar bewails the loss of the old world, we are told that she cries out "like a woman in labor" (XI, 116).

Gilgamesh began the epic in the form of an all-powerful hero, a man "like the gods," *kima ilim.* By the end, despite his resemblance to Utnapishtim, he is not like the gods in the way that Utnapishtim is. Yet the restlessness of mortality is quieted by new wisdom, an acceptance of the value of culture despite its limits, which have been displayed so synoptically over the course of his adventures. He has not gained a literal immortality on surviving a literal flood, but he has gained a deeper perspective and the stilling of the flood-storm of his own heart. It is in fact Gilgamesh, well before Humbaba appears, who is the first character in the epic whose spirit and actions are compared to a flood-storm. The prologue describes him as "the furious [f]lood-wave, who destroys (even) stone walls" (I, i, 32; in Tigay, 141), and the gods create Enkidu to quiet *ûmum libbishu*, "the storm of his heart" (I, ii, 31).

At the end of the epic, far from destroying walls, he returns home and gives his new companion, Utnapishtim's boatman Urshanabi, a tour of the city walls he has built.[22] Further, he engraves his story on a stone stela, and buries in the walls a lapis lazuli tablet containing his story. Utnapishtim, called Exceedingly Wise (Atrahasis), showed his wisdom in his ability to speak intimately with the gods and foresee the coming Flood. In contrast to these feats of wisdom, characteristic of ancient times, the wisdom of Gilgamesh is described in different terms in the prologue of the epic (in Tigay, 141):

[Him who] saw everything, let me [make kn]own to the land,
[Who all thing]s experienced, [let me tea]ch i[t] ful[ly].
[He ⌜searche]d⌝ the ⌜l[ands]⌝ entirely,
[⌜Was granted al]l⌝ wisdom, ⌜ex[perienced]⌝ all things.
[The hi]dden he saw, the undisclosed he discov[ered].
He brought back information from before the flood,
Achieved a long [j]ourney, exhausted, but at peace.
All his toil he [engra]ved on a (stone) stela.
He had the wall of Uruk (of?) the sheepfold built,
Of hallowed Eanna, the holy storehouse.
Behold its outer wall, which (or whose) . . . is like bronze.
Peer at its inner wall, which none can equal!   (I, i, 1–12)

Gilgamesh's visionary abilities do not reveal the future but reflect on his own experience, as summarized in the poem's opening lines, whose first words give the epic its Akkadian

---

[22]The magnificence of Uruk's walls is also stressed in the Sumerian epic of Lugalbanda, third king of Uruk, who is identified as Gilgamesh's father in the *Gilgamesh Epic*; we are told that "Uruk's city wall is spread out across the steppe like a net for birds" (Wilcke, ed., *Das Lugalbandaepos*, line 371).

title, *Ša nagba imuru,* "He Who Saw Everything." His unique communication is not with the gods but with Utnapishtim, from whom he learns of the past rather than of the future. Such immortality as he has achieved rests in the memory of posterity; he builds city walls and engraves his story on a stela, linking his life story and his public works. The adventures that have stilled the flood-storm of his heart and left him "exhausted, but at peace" have simultaneously lost and gained him immortality, and have won Uruk a constructive ruler in place of a destructive one.

In the late version, the *Gilgamesh Epic* becomes the story of the loss of myth and the gain of history. The history that is gained is the record of human constructions. The emphasis on the engraving of Gilgamesh's story does not represent a triumph of aestheticism, as though the beauty of his story were now the source of his immortality; rather, the epic champions what might be called artifactualism: the vitality of that which is made by human hands. The stela is one such artifact, walls are another; a third is clothing, which becomes a unifying element through the entire epic. The harlot welcomes Enkidu into civilization by dividing her cloak with him; Gilgamesh's elegant clothes attract Ishtar's admiration and desire; Gilgamesh even sails through the treacherous Waters of Death by stripping himself when his oars fail him and using his clothing for a sail (X, iv, 9–11). He loses the root of rejuvenation, but retains Utnapishtim's other gift: a spotless new cloak. The serpent can now shed its skin, which mortals cannot do; but they can cast off the old skins they wear and clothe themselves freshly, finding a substitute rejuvenation in the works of their own hands.

Myth as History in Genesis 1–11

In its transformation of the genre of poetic epic in light of its concern with historical cultural experience, the *Gilgamesh Epic* provides a valuable counterpart to the Bible's transformation of historical chronicle in the light of the transhistorical concerns of epic. If the *Gilgamesh Epic* gives the best extant case of historicized poetic epic, the story of King David is the fullest example of historical prose written from a poetic perspective. Yet this masterpiece of early Hebrew historiography remains a more decisive transformation of epic and chronicle than anything seen earlier. The late version of the *Gilgamesh Epic* is a major innovation within an established form, whereas the David story blends the two forms so fully as to produce what is in effect a new genre, that of an epic history, written in a poetic prose.

In contrast to the single shift toward history in the case of the *Gilgamesh Epic*, the production of the David story resulted from a double transformation of genre: first, the historicizing of poetic epic; secondly, the applying of historical-epic perspectives to contemporary history. Theoretically, it might have been possible for both these changes to occur at once, though that would have required a great deal of sudden development. The evidence suggests, however, that these changes in fact took place in two stages. The first stage, in which poetic epic was historicized within the Hebrew tradition, and also given prose form, is clearly seen in the opening chapters of Genesis. Only the second stage was specific to the David story: the application of the new form of historicized prose epic to the depiction of modern history.

The opening chapters of Genesis provide the clearest example of the transformation of epic form in Hebrew prose, as the nucleus of Genesis 1–11 is a clear version of a creation-flood epic. It is these chapters, indeed, to which the term "Yahwistic epic" can most properly be applied. Like the *Gilgamesh Epic*, the opening section of Genesis transforms the old stories of creation and flood in order to reflect on the nature of culture. The parallel to *Gilgamesh* is quite close: every incident in the opening chapters of Genesis has direct corollaries in the story of Gilgamesh. Thus the loss of Eden and immortality through the joint temptations of the serpent and Eve are comparable to the incident in which the harlot seduces Enkidu away from the steppe and the later episode in which the serpent steals Gilgamesh's root of immortality; the rivalry of Cain and Abel has an analogue in the (more harmonious) struggle of Gilgamesh and Enkidu, with both stories having roots in the struggles of Ishtar and her sister Ereshkigal; the flood story of Utnapishtim shares very many details with the flood story of Noah; and the building of Babel at the close of the Genesis epic corresponds to the evocation of the walls of Uruk at the close of the *Gilgamesh Epic*, recalling the *Atrahasis Epic*'s closing with the establishment of Babylon as offering-site after the Flood. Even the small incident of the sons of God mating with mortals (Gen. 6:1–4) can be compared to the scene in which Ishtar tries to seduce Gilgamesh.

Each of these parallels shows considerable differences as well as similarity (though the flood story shows a particularly close resemblance), and there is no need to suppose a direct dependence of Genesis on the *Gilgamesh Epic*; but it is evident that the two texts are parallel efforts, from roughly the same period, to rework the old mythic material of the creation and flood.[23] The many similarities between these texts, and their far-reaching differences both in form and theme, will, I believe, suggest much about the theological and literary forces at work in the early phase of the composition of biblical literature and will set the stage for a better understanding of the relations of the Yahwistic legendary material to the fully developed epic historiography of the story of King David.

A word should be said here about the extent of the Yahwistic version of this material. It is clear that the opening chapters of

---

[23]The very wide distribution of fragments of the *Gilgamesh Epic*, including findings in Palestine itself, does admit of the possibility that the text may well have found its way to Jerusalem. It could then have served as an example of the possibilities of extended narration and could have inspired the Hebrew writers to see what they could do with their own early traditions. Further, the flood traditions are so close that some direct transmission can be assumed, either in the form of the *Gilgamesh Epic* or through circulation of the *Atrahasis Epic* itself; this latter possibility is argued by Clark, "The Flood and the Structure of the Pre-patriarchal History," 184–88.

Genesis have undergone extensive revision from the time of their original composition as an independent text. The opening and closing portions of the section are of late composition by the Priestly writers, who added the creation story in Genesis 1:1–2:4a and inserted the long genealogy in Genesis 11:10–32 to strengthen the linkage of the unit to the following stories of the patriarchs. This leaves Genesis 2:4b through 11:9, the Eden story through the story of Babel, as the surviving nucleus of the Yahwistic account. Most of this material is Yahwistic, though there have been some alterations and additions, notably in the flood episode.

Though the Yahwistic account as we have it only begins in 2:4, it is worth noting that the full paradigm of creation-flood epics suggests that the Yahwistic account, too, originally began with at least a brief account of the creation of the world. Both *Enuma elish* and the *Atrahasis Epic* begin by linking the creation of human beings to the previous establishment of the universal order through the subduing and ordering of conflicting heavenly forces. It is reasonable to suppose that the Yahwistic creation-flood epic began similarly, but that the later Priestly writers found it necessary to suppress this account and replace it with one of their own. In the creation account, if anywhere, the elements of monolatry still often visible in the Yahwistic stories would have been much too close to outright polytheism for Priestly comfort. This suggests that the Priestly writers, in their clearly polemical arrangement of the creation story to exclude any active presence other than the Lord God, were arguing not only against pagan Canaanite beliefs but also against the less strict monotheism of earlier Yahwism.

One advantage of recognizing the presence of the paradigm of the creation-flood epic in Genesis 1–11 is to help in doing justice to the thematic shape of the text, which has long been obscured in the Christian tradition by the emphasis on the Eden story. Starting as early as Paul, who turned to Adam and Eve as types of the universal human experience, the Eden story has taken a pronounced priority in most readings of Genesis

2–11, which has been seen as an account of the "Fall" of humanity as a result of human pride. What is lost in this emphasis is the prominence the text gives to the Flood, which is the longest and most developed episode in the story. As Claus Westermann says, "the flood narrative . . . forms the center piece" of the primordial history, both in its Yahwistic and in its Priestly editions (*Genesis 1–11*, 590).

In this, the Genesis account follows its Old Babylonian models, in which the creation story is more of a prologue to the flood story than the major focus of interest. In the *Gilgamesh Epic* as well, the added creation story of Enkidu is given less weight than the much longer addition of the flood story, which introduces the dramatic climax of the epic. Certainly the Eden story receives new attention in Genesis, but it still leads toward the flood story, which receives half again as much space and ought to receive at least equal weight in our reading. The centrality of the flood story will prove to have important consequences for the understanding of Genesis 2–11 overall, and indeed for understanding the Eden story in particular, in relation to the epic tradition.

To begin with the most general contrasts, the Genesis creation-flood epic is unusual in several ways: it is in prose; scenes in heaven are largely, though not altogether, undeveloped; the problem of mortality is de-emphasized; and there is no equivalent at all to the underworld descent that was so integral to Akkadian epic. Further, whereas the introduction of mortality is closely linked to the flood story in the *Atrahasis Epic,* and indeed seems to follow the Flood, here the loss of immortality is placed long before, at the time of creation.

These are different aspects of the text: stylistic, structural, thematic; they are related, however, for they are all narrative consequences of monotheism. To begin with the most direct of these consequences, it is monotheism that accounts for the eclipse of the underworld here and throughout biblical narrative. It is not that the Hebrews ceased to be concerned with the problem of death, nor that the underworld had begun to look different; the frequent passing references to Sheol in Psalms and elsewhere paint a picture very like the Mesopotamian concept of the House of Dust. Rather, the underworld nowhere appears as a setting for scenes in Hebrew narrative because it has lost its dramatic interest. The change is that the House of Dust is a poor setting if no one is at home. The dead themselves are passive, not up to much activity of any sort; the real drama always involved conflicts among the gods or between visiting humans and the resident underworld deities. With these deities either banished or relegated to the status of minor demons, they cease to be effective opponents for God or impressive interlocutors for humans. Perhaps the underworld divinities made a final appearance in the suppressed initial chapter of the Yahwistic creation-flood account, but if so, their defeat was so spectacular as to rule them out of the narrative ring thereafter. Given the downplaying of independent, chthonic forces in the underworld, the human dead ceased to enjoy the degree of narrative interest they had formerly possessed. The Egyptians, for example, used to write letters to their deceased relatives and deposit them at their tombs, asking for assistance in dealing with the gods and with ongoing earthly affairs. In some instances, the letter-writers go so far as to chastise their departed loved ones for meddling in current matters, and one correspondent even threatens to bring an underworld lawsuit against the addressee.[24] No trace of a comparably vivid picture of underworld activity is found in the Bible, where the world of the dead has lost much of its symmetry with the world of the living, the old homology that had made the Mesopotamian afterlife an image of earthly life "prefixed with a negative sign."[25]

Actually characters like Maweth, Death, continue to exist and

---

[24]A collection and discussion of these remarkable letters may be found in Gardiner, *Egyptian Letters to the Dead.*

[25]Bottéro, "La Mythologie de la mort en Mésopotamie ancienne," 33. Bottéro has an interesting discussion of the dead as simultaneously "ex-vivants" and "anti-vivants."

to receive attention, but their sphere is now largely lyric: it is in the Psalms and in hymns in Job that God treads down the forces of Abaddon, and it is in the Song of Songs that love is called as powerful as Death. Narrative requires conflict; foregone conclusions have no narrative interest. They may still make an appearance as a secondary element within lyrical celebrations of the immensity of God's power, however; hence the continuing references in the Psalms to the old mythic struggles. Here it is possible to develop further the analogy made in chapter 2 between Near Eastern chronicle and the Psalms. Deities opposed to the God of Israel have much the same status that the vile Retenu and the miserable Asiatics have in the Egyptian historical texts. The pharaoh's divine omniscience and omnipotence preclude the sorts of complications that would have enabled the chronicles to move out of their fundamentally lyric mode into more developed historiographic narratives, and the same is true of the wars of Yahweh against the underworld powers: they are an ideal subject for celebration, but a poor subject for extended or independent narration.

A comparable process limits the narrative usefulness of heaven as well, and I might equally have begun there, except that this case is actually more complicated. Heaven still contains God and his heavenly court, and it will need some further consideration to show why the biblical writers should have so neglected the important scenes in heaven in the received flood tradition. Overall, however, it remains true that the Yahwistic underworld and heaven share the similarity of their absence of real conflict. This change has major implications for the development of an enriched historiography, for the social conflicts hitherto explored through heavenly rivalries are now displaced to earthly settings. Abundant examples could be traced in the patriarchal narratives, but the pattern is already clear in Genesis 2–11. The familial rivalry of Cain and Abel is developed on earth, between human actors, and not, as previously, either in the underworld (Nergal-Ereshkigal-Ishtar) or in heaven, as in the Egyptian tale "The Contendings of Horus and Seth."[26] Mesopotamian chronicle could also represent fraternal conflicts, but in the chronicles the problem is a local, practical one of power politics, with no moral ambiguity or depth of character evinced on any side.[27]

A still more direct case of displacement from heaven to earth can be seen in the birth of Noah, which closely parallels the creation of humankind in the *Atrahasis Epic*. In that text, human beings are created in response to the agonized protests of the secondary gods, the Igigi, who are oppressed by all the work they have to do for the major gods. When the Igigi go on strike and threaten to attack Enlil's temple, the major gods agree to provide a work force. The birth goddess creates seven pairs of humans, out of clay, and announces: "I have removed your heavy work, / I have imposed your toil on man" (I, 240–41).

It is this scene that surely underlies the naming of Noah:

When Lamech had lived a hundred and eighty-two years, he became the father of a son, and called his name Noah, saying, "Out of the ground which the Lord has cursed this one shall bring us relief from our work and from the toil of our hands." (5:28–29)

The parallel is so close as to have a verbal echo in the pairing of the Hebrew terms for "work" and "toil," *ma'aseh* (work) and *'itzvon* (hardship, pain, distress) in parallel to comparable Akkadian terms (*dullu* and *shupshikku*).

The first point to note here is that this speech has been given to a human character, Lamech; the earlier struggle of the divine Igigi for relief from toil is here translated into earthly, human terms. The emphasis shifts from the petulance of the overworked immortals to the weariness of the human farmer strug-

---

[26]Text in Simpson, *Literature of Ancient Egypt*, 108–26.

[27]See, e.g., Esarhaddon's account of his struggle for supremacy against his evil brothers, who "went out of their senses, doing everything that is wicked (in the eyes of) the gods and mankind," *ANET*, 289; complete text in Borger, *Die Inschriften Asarhaddons König von Assyrien*.

gling with the earth, whose cultivation became laborious as part of the limiting of human power that came with mortality.

Equally significant is the shift from timeless patterns of social relations toward the development of historical sequence. In the *Atrahasis Epic*, the Igigi and the humans created to assist them were related as masters and servants. The Bible could have reproduced this atemporal pattern, but instead chose a generational model: the aging father welcomes the strength of the young son. The difference here is one of degree and not an absolute break; generational sequence is also represented in the myths of the gods. It is, however, a secondary aspect of the gods' eternal relations, and indeed the heavily incestuous process of divine procreation creates a generational simultaneity among all the gods.[28]

In giving an earthly setting to the mythic pattern of the conflicts between two, or at most three, heavenly generations,[29] the story of Lamech and Noah sets the stage for the historicizing multigenerational sequences seen in the patriarchal stories and for the complex dynastic problems of Saul and of David. The new generational emphasis is evident in the Yahwistic genealogy (4:17 ff.) linking Cain to Lamech, and presumably originally also to Noah, now named by a new Lamech in the Priestly account in 5:28 ff.[30] The Priestly writers built on this Yahwistic will to historical connection as they revised Genesis 2–11, supplying the extended genealogies that now cement the links between the stories within Genesis 2–11 and between the entire unit and the story of Abraham.

The new generational emphasis is also evident in the thematic linkage of Noah to his ancestor Adam. As Lamech's

---

[28]See the "Babylonian Theogony," *ANET*, 517–18, in which the successive generations of gods are created through incest and murder.

[29]See *Enuma elish*, where the fundamental divine conflict is between the primordial generation of gods and the younger generation led by Marduk. One can speak of three generations involved here, but the myth has no need for any longer genealogical developments; three generations are sufficient to display the timeless patterns it wishes to explore.

[30]See Westermann, *Genesis 1–11*, 347–54, on the identity of the two Lamechs.

speech already indicates, Noah and Adam are parallel and complementary figures, and the heritage of Christian typology will perhaps incline us to say that Noah is a second Adam. In literary-historical terms, however, it would be more accurate to say that Adam is a proto-Noah, for the Bible has separated into two different figures the double character functions of the hero of the Babylonian flood stories.

Both the Sumerian and the Akkadian stories give their hero two dominant qualities: wisdom and immortality. In the Mesopotamian tradition, it is clear that the hero's two aspects are causally connected: the hero's wisdom leads to his uniquely close relation to his patron god Enki/Ea, who grants him immortality. The Babylonian hero has in fact different names that emphasize the different components of this pair of qualities: in Sumerian, he is called Ziusudra, "He Who Found Life," while in Akkadian he is traditionally called Atrahasis, "Exceedingly Wise." The *Gilgamesh Epic* preserves both, naming its flood hero Utnapishtim, evidently a translation of the Sumerian "Ziusudra," but also giving Utnapishtim the epithet "Atrahasis," which is how the god Ea names him in describing his forewarning Utnapishtim of the coming flood (XI, 187).

In the biblical account, the theme of wisdom is lacking in the account of the flood hero, and instead is associated with Adam and Eve, who become wise by eating the fruit (2:6). Noah, on the other hand, becomes the figure of ongoing life.[31] There is no question of personal immortality as in the Babylonian stories, but instead the issue is one of cultural survival. Here the biblical account shows far-reaching differences from its Babylonian predecessors, differences based on the biblical writers' very different attitudes toward the relations between human culture and the divine world. The *Atrahasis Epic* used the flood story as a way of exploring the gods' need of humanity. Humanity is saved from destruction because the gods realize that

---

[31]Similarly, Clark argues that the theme of revolt has been transferred from its place in the old flood tradition to its new location in Eden ("The Flood," 192).

they need the temple sacrifices by which they receive their chief nourishment. The usefulness of human beings in general, and of city culture in particular, as necessary for the building and maintenance of temples provides a check to the gods' natural capriciousness and will to evil.

The situation is reversed in the Bible, where a good God's dealings with Adam and Noah bring him to a tempered acceptance of a morally flawed humanity. Noah's reversal of the estrangement between God and Adam is made clear by the text in various ways, in close association with the two characters' names. When Lamech, in naming his son, predicts that Noah "shall bring us relief . . . out of the ground ['adamah] which the Lord has cursed," the cursed 'adamah certainly recalls Adam; and so too does Noah's name. Lamech's naming creates a somewhat indirect folk etymology for "Noah" (written with the consonants nwḥ in Hebrew), as it ignores the obvious choice of the root nwḥ, "to rest." Instead Lamech uses the verb naḥam, "to be consoled," a root that would better apply to a name like Menachem. By deriving the name from naḥam, however, the author of the story brings to bear a very specific set of associations, which are further played on as the story progresses.[32]

These associations are obscured in translation, as the verb is most often rendered in two very different ways in different settings: "to repent" or "to be comforted." The link between these senses can be clarified by a look at the contexts in which the word is used. It appears twenty-five times in the narrative books of the Bible, and in every case it is associated with death. In family settings, it is applied in instances involving the death of an immediate family member (parent, sibling, or child); in national settings, it has to do with the survival or impending extermination of an entire people. At heart, naḥam means "to mourn," to come to terms with a death; these usages are usually translated (e.g., in the RSV) by the verb "to comfort," as

---

[32]In his commentary on this issue, Cassuto notes that the derivation of "Noah" from naḥam may reflect a version of the Gilgamesh story, in which Gilgamesh is called Naḥmūlel (Commentary, Part 1, 288).

when Jacob's children try to comfort their father after the reported death of Joseph (Gen. 37:35). The word can take on a quasi-technical sense of the observation of a period of mourning, as when David sends ambassadors to "comfort" the Ammonites after the death of their king, that is, to help them observe the official period of mourning (2 Sam. 10:2, 3). Similarly, the end of a period of mourning is signified when Isaac is comforted after his mother's death (Gen. 24:67) and when Judah is comforted after his wife's death, at which point he can again engage in sexual relations (Gen. 38:12).[33]

From this basic meaning of the regret following the death of a family member, the term becomes applied to other cases of regret or change of heart ("repentance" in the RSV), almost always used when the repenter is meditating murder. "Repentance" then involves either the decision to kill or, conversely, the decision to stop killing. The term can be used in quite ignoble circumstances, as when Esau comforts himself for the loss of his birthright by deciding to kill Jacob (Gen. 27:42), but usually it is God who repents, either negatively or positively: negatively, by deciding to destroy his people; positively, by commuting a sentence of destruction (of Israel as a whole, Exod. 32:12, Deut. 32:36; of Jerusalem alone, 2 Sam. 24:16). There are two scenes in the Bible in which the term is used repeatedly, thematically, in this sense: in God's decision to destroy Saul (1 Samuel 15, a scene I will discuss in chapter 5) and in God's decision to unleash the Flood.

The inauguration of the Flood is nothing less than a worldwide repetition of the cursing of Adam, not only wider in scope but also more drastic: Adam merely lost immortality, but now all living creatures will violently lose their lives. God's language in announcing his repentance for having created life uses terms

---

[33]Similarly 2 Sam. 12:24 (David comforts Bathsheba after the death of their first child) and 2 Sam. 13:39 (David is comforted after the death of Amnon). The usage receives an interesting variation when Joseph proleptically comforts his brothers concerning his own death, assuring them that their children will be taken care of in Egypt even after he is dead (Gen. 50:21).

that directly recall the creation of Adam. Instead of using any of a variety of terms for humanity, or even using a plural form of "man," the text tells us that God repented (*yinnaḥem*) having created "the man" (*ha-'adam*, using the collective singular to signify "mankind"). God then announces that "I will blot out the man [*ha-'adam*] from the face of the earth [*ha-'adamah*]," cementing the earlier reference, in Lamech's speech, to the creation and naming of Adam.

Noah's name is played on here as directly as Adam's, with both senses of *naḥam* used in close proximity: Lamech will be comforted by Noah; a few verses later, God regrets having created "man." The introduction to the flood account ends by juxtaposing these double senses still more directly: God announces the impending destruction, and closes his speech by repeating, "For I repent that I have made them" (6:7), to which the text adds, "But Noah found favor in the eyes of the Lord." The text places "repent" and "Noah" in close proximity, the same distance apart, in fact, as "he will comfort" and "Noah" appear in Lamech's speech naming him.[34] Out of regret comes consolation, just as out of the earth comes Noah to ease the burden of Adam. For God as well as for humanity, Noah is the consolation for the fall of Adam.

The play on the double sense of *naḥam* reflects God's recognition that he will gain nothing by a truly universal destruction of his creation: he may as well continue to work with the same materials he began with. This sort of wordplay is not uncommon in the Yahwistic material (J); specifically relevant here is the playing on Adam's name in Genesis 2–3, which I will discuss shortly. Before turning to Adam, however, I wish to pursue the question of how the flood story has contributed to the Eden story. If the theme of wisdom has been displaced, how and why was this change made?

This displacement is one of several changes that can be seen

---

[34]There is virtually a poetic parallelism, of the inverted form, in the two lines with *Noaḥ x x yenaḥamenu* paralleled by *niḥamti x x we-Noaḥ*.

if the biblical flood story is compared with its Babylonian predecessors. In contrast to Enlil's reluctant acceptance of Utnapishtim after he has survived the Flood, God's recognition of
Noah as the saving remnant of the people comes at the beginning of the story, though the blessing of Noah still comes after
the Flood, in parallel to Enlil's blessing of Utnapishtim. A still
more major change is the almost total eclipse of any scenes in
heaven. The debates among the gods were a major feature of
the *Atrahasis* flood story; they are abridged in Utnapishtim's
account but still count as important. The Bible tells us of the
sons of God, members of his heavenly court, who descend to
earth and take mortal wives; this account is actually inserted
between the birth of Noah and the onset of the Flood, and may
suggest a human striving to reach beyond proper boundaries,
a sinful action that brings the Flood in punishment. Yet the
heavenly court never serves as a developed scene setting, even
though it is presupposed at various points when God is evidently speaking to his heavenly circle (in the flood story, in
6:7; in the Eden story, 3:22; in the Babel story, 11:6–7). Understanding the reasons behind these changes will not only
clarify the focus of the biblical flood story, but can also go far
toward accounting for the new emphasis on Adam and the
separation of the creation story from the flood story.

The absence of an inclination to portray any heavenly opposition to God's will is certainly an important factor in the
downplaying of the heavenly court: if everyone instantly agrees
with God, there's little to tell. Also involved, however, is the
suppression of the major theme of the heavenly scenes in the
Babylonian flood accounts: the shock and anguish the gods feel
when they see the terrible consequences of their decision to
destroy life on earth. In the biblical account, God repents having made human beings, but never repents ordering the Flood,
even though, like the Babylonian gods, he promises at the end
of the story that he will never do it again.

In the Atrahasis and Gilgamesh epics, this promise involves
an admission of wrongdoing on the part of the gods; they have

learned that they must show a better sense of proportion in the future. As we are told in the *Gilgamesh Epic*, Enlil brought about the Flood in a fit of "unreasoning" (XI, 168), and Ea delivers a sharp speech urging that in the future Enlil employ less drastic remedies, like famine and pestilence, when he wishes to chastise humanity (XI, 178–85). Clearly this theme holds no attraction for the Yahwists, so the problem of evil must be addressed in earthly terms. Noah himself, as the one man worth saving on earth, is hardly a suitable subject for the exploration of evil, so the issue is placed earlier, with Adam, still closely linked to Noah but separately developed. This is not to say that the figures of Adam and Eve were directly invented out of the figure of Noah; it is enough to observe that their story has been shaped by concerns displaced from the Noah story, to which the Eden story now serves as a prelude.

Along with the new emphasis on a pre-Noah figure goes the displacement of the introduction of mortality on earth. In his encounter with Utnapishtim, the godlike Gilgamesh learns the limits of his resemblance to the gods; he must accept wisdom as the godlike quality he can possess, but immortality is denied him. The Bible develops the relationship between wisdom and immortality quite differently. No longer the consolation for the loss of immortality, the acquisition of wisdom (in the form of the knowledge of good and evil) now precipitates the loss. What is involved here is a reordering of attitudes toward human culture and the world of the divine. The Babylonians typically saw much that was negative in their gods, and conversely exalted what was positive in human culture; the Bible could be said to do the reverse. In the Babylonian flood accounts, it is human wisdom that in some sense makes up for the faults of the gods. This view can be presented altogether affirmatively, as in the climax of the *Atrahasis Epic*, where the founding of Babylon cements the harmonious relationship between the divine and human realms. It can also be presented in a more muted context, as in the *Gilgamesh Epic*, where the return to the walls of Uruk provides a qualified compensation for the rather more limited relations mortals can productively have with the gods.

This affirmation of the absolute value of culture does not require a blindness to human wickedness or to the abuse of culture; instead, these faults can be directly laid to the gods themselves. This is the conclusion reached, for example, in the text known as "The Babylonian Theodicy":

Narru, king of the gods, who created mankind,
And majestic Zulummar, who dug out their clay,
And mistress Mami, the queen who fashioned them,
Gave perverse speech to the human race.
With lies, and not truth, they endowed them for ever.

> (Text in Lambert, ed., *Babylonian Wisdom Literature*, 63–91, lines 276–80)

As significant as the divine origin of evil, and a corollary of that origin, is the eternal nature of the evil in human culture. Culture is as it is, and cannot be changed. At most, the intervention of one's personal god can act locally to counter injustice in an individual case.[35] But in general, the presence of evil is acknowledged in the context of a highly positive sense of the overall value of human culture.

The Bible directly disputes this view, as Herbert Schneidau has argued at length in *Sacred Discontent*. The Bible's questioning of human culture and of cultural institutions will find

---

[35]This is the message of the remarkable text *Ludlul bel nemeqi* (Lambert, *Babylonian Wisdom Literature*, 21–62). The first half of the text paints a powerful picture of widespread social injustice and a whole host of evils besetting the speaker, whose eloquent laments foreshadow those of Job. The second half of the text is a hymn of praise of Marduk, who has heard the speaker's prayers and saved him from all his enemies and miseries. This denouement is in some ways the opposite of the pessimistic conclusion about the immutability of evil reached at the end of "The Babylonian Theodicy," but the two texts provide alternatives within the same overall worldview; in both cases, no human intervention can change the flaws within culture, and at the same time neither text questions the absolute rightness of the normative cultural order.

expression in the suspicion of the monarchy in the stories of Saul and David. In Genesis 2–11, this fundamentally anti-epic perspective leads to the dramatic reversal of the traditional ending of the creation-flood epics, in which the city is evoked as the center and validator of culture. As in *Enuma elish*, the text ends with the establishment of Babylon, but the view of the city is diametrically opposed. In *Enuma elish*, it is the gods who establish Babylon as their earthly seat after Marduk's defeat of the floodwaters of the primordial Tiamat.[36] The Anunnaki enthusiastically build the temple for Marduk, Enlil, and Ea, raising its tower to an immense height, as high as the depth of the primordial waters so recently subdued. The text then describes the gods settling down to a royal feast and closes with an incantatory recounting of fifty names of Marduk.

In Genesis, Babel is not constructed as a home for God and a place to name him but, on the contrary, is built by mortals in a vain effort to protect themselves on their own account. They hope to make a name not for God but for themselves ("let us make a name for ourselves, lest we be scattered abroad on the face of the whole earth," 11:4). The text concludes by travestying the city's name, ignoring the obvious derivation of *bab-'el*, "Gate of God," and asserting that the city was named from the verb *balal*, "to confuse," after God stopped the project by confusing the builders' language and scattering them over the face of the earth—the very fate they had been trying to avoid.

In reworking the old creation-flood epic, then, Genesis 2–11 creates an anti-epic that questions the achievements of the peoples of the past, even as it moves the locus of discussion decisively away from the divine sphere and into the human realm.

---

[36]Among other echoes of the flood story proper, the story of the defeat of Tiamat concludes with Marduk displaying his rainbow. He gives it three names: "Longwood is the first, the second is Accurate; / Its third name is Bow-Star, in heaven I have made it shine" (*VI, 89–90; ANET*, 69). The weapon that Marduk employs against the floodlike Tiamat will remain in Genesis simply as the reminder to God never to bring another flood.

The story of Adam and Eve is enriched with motifs transferred from the flood story, in order to provide an earthly setting for the problematics of evil previously explored in the heavenly scenes of *Enuma elish* and the *Atrahasis Epic*. The linkage of Adam to Noah introduces into the epic the characteristically Hebrew concern with genealogy, thus uniting the ordinary genealogical material of king lists and chronicles with the thematic concerns of poetic epic now cast into prose. Finally, the Yahwistic creation-flood epic closes with a parody of the establishment of Babylon, opening the way for the probing of earthly institutions that is central to Hebrew historiography.

From Yahwist Epic to Court History

If the Yahwistic reworking of old epic materials sets the stage in various ways for the development of Hebrew historiography proper, it remains the case that there is a considerable gap between these materials. The David story is highly rationalistic, with a pronounced downplaying of miraculous elements and a newly clear portrayal of causal relations, even a surplus of explanation, as in the different accounts of David's introduction to Saul. Indeed, the more important the event, the more causes are adduced, in a reflective manner hitherto found only in historical epic texts like the *Erra Epic*. Absalom's rebellion, for example, is shown as the result of an interlocking series of events: God's punishment for David's sin with Bathsheba; the natural result of the estrangement between David and Absalom following David's refusal to avenge the rape of Tamar; the consequence of Absalom's personal ambition. These multiple factors give a new, indeed a unique, depth and richness to the analysis of historical process, and stand in sharp contrast to the old Yahwistic stories, which, as von Rad has said, "seem like tightly closed mussels in their lack of any interpretation at all."[37]

---

[37]He continues: "And what do we understand of the life of Isaac? We read only

These differences have not been resolved by efforts to read a Davidic political ideology/theology into the Yahwistic materials. The stories in Genesis are not without a political aspect, but it is difficult to link the varied political outlooks of the different Yahwistic texts specifically to the needs of the early monarchy. To take the example of Genesis 2–11, the Noah story concludes on a directly political note, with the strange incident of Noah's drunkenness and his exposure to the eyes of his middle son, variously identified as either Ham or Canaan.[38] The episode provides the occasion for the cursing of Canaan, the ancestor of the peoples in whose lands the Hebrews would settle, and its seems clear that Canaan has been inserted into the story, and loosely identified with Ham, in order to provide theological support for the Hebrew dominance of the region.

Noah's curse, however, is phrased in terms that reflect the period of nomadic settlement in Canaan rather than the later period of the monarchy: "Cursed be Canaan," Noah says, "a slave of slaves shall he be to his brothers. . . . God enlarge Japheth, and let him dwell in the tents of Shem; and let Canaan be his slave" (9:25–27). The talk here is of masters and slaves, not subjects and rulers, dwelling in tents and not in cities. It is possible that an unusually subtle monarchic apologist had carefully anachronized this prophecy, but the simpler explanation is at least as likely: that the curse reflects Hebrew concerns from the premonarchic period of settlement.[39]

There are important thematic links between the two bodies

---

a few stories . . . he who had been laid by his father on God's altar carried the secret of his life with him to the grave" ("Typological Interpretation of the OT," 29).

[38]It is often said that Lamech's naming of Noah looks ahead to his discovery of viticulture, with wine symbolizing comfort and completing Noah's mitigating of the labor of agriculture laid upon the sinning Adam. It is difficult, however, to agree with Westermann (487–89) that there is no element of ironic reversal in the scene of drunkenness and disgrace when Noah first exercises this new skill.

[39]As Speiser says, the purpose of the curse "is not so much to justify an accomplished political fact, as it is to stigmatize distasteful practices on the part of the older inhabitants of the land" (Genesis, 62).

of material, however, though not necessarily expressed primarily in political or even in ethical terms. The older creation-flood epics were notably unconcerned with the problem of evil. Evil was not directly attributed to the hapless mortals who were swept away by the Flood, and even with the gods the thematic focus was not on accounting for their will to evil. Rather, the overall purpose of the story was to describe the process of accommodation of the gods to humankind. In developing the old stories, Genesis 2–11 gives a new prominence to ethical issues, as has been noted ever since the Mesopotamian parallels were first discovered. It has less often been remarked, however, that the problem of evil does not serve as a consistent leitmotif in the overall epic of Genesis 2–11. Prominent as the problem of evil is in the Eden account, it is treated almost casually in the flood story, where God first decides to destroy the world because of its universal corruption (6:5,11–3), and then simply reverses himself after the Flood, apparently deciding that the human tendency toward evil is too deep to reform (8:21). The story nowhere attempts to account for God's transition from rage to resignation, nor does it suggest that the facts have changed in any way. Even the possibility that the exemplary Noah marks a turning point in human nature is sharply undercut by the episode of his drunkenness and the cursing of his own son.

The problem of evil is pervasively present in these chapters, but it is not the subject of explanation; rather, it is part of the context in which a related but distinct subject is explored: the theme of separation of God from his creation. It is this process of separation that Genesis 2–11 chronicles with care and steady development. The spread of evil is closely involved in this process, though not in a consistent way: it can be the consequence of a stage of separation (Eden), a cause of a new stage (the Flood), a mixture of cause and consequence (Cain and Abel), or a kind of implicit corollary (Babel). The difference between the theme of evil and the theme of separation can be described as the difference between an ethical narrative basis and an ex-

istential basis. It is this existential basis that characterizes Yahwistic writing in general, as witness the relative unconcern of
the patriarchal narratives for the ethical status of the patriarchs;
as I hope to show, a similar existential emphasis is found in
the David story. The ethical issues are of major importance, but
they do not shape the narrative in any consistent way.

The Bible does not lack examples of the dominance of the
existential by the ethical, and the change in emphasis toward
a preponderance of ethical assessment is one way to describe
the difference between the pre-Deuteronomistic David story
and the Deuteronomistic history of the later monarchy. The
Deuteronomists are predominantly interested in organizing
their history through ethical assessments of the characters of
the monarchs; they play down the issues of character and personal interaction that accompany the earlier David story's exploration of the existential issues of continuity and separation
between Saul and David and between David and his sons. The
kinship of the David story with the Yahwistic writing is nowhere better seen than in the portrayal of character and event
in the development of the theme of separation.

The separation of Adam and Eve from God begins before the
serpent appears on the scene, hence before any discussion of
the problem of sin. Indeed, the whole Eden story is not so
much about the birth of sin as about the beginnings of a separation between God and Adam and Eve, a process that will
lead toward sin and more radical separation thereafter. The final stage of separation will occur with the disunity of humanity
that results from the multiplication of language in punishment
for the tower builders' attempt to make a name for themselves.
The first stage too is intimately associated with the problem of
naming, and with Adam's making a name first for Eve and
secondly for himself.

Adam is, of course, the great namer. No doubt his naming
of the animals indirectly signifies his dominion over them, but
this is not what the text actually says is the reason he is given

the task. Rather, God has realized that Adam ought to have "a helper ['*ezer*] fit for him" (2:18).

So out of the ground the Lord God formed every beast of the field and every bird of the air, and brought them to the man to see what he would call them; and whatever the man called every living creature, that was its name. . . . but for the man there was not found a helper fit for him. (2:19–20)

Apparently, in this version of creation, God creates all the animals in a fruitless attempt to find Adam a proper helpmate. Well before the appearance of the serpent, in other words, God has ceased to enjoy a full understanding of Adam and his needs. Had he truly understood Adam, after all, God would simply have created Eve directly, and when God finally hits on the idea of creating a woman, Adam reveals an impatience bred of the previous trial-and-error method: "This *at last* is bone of my bones and flesh of my flesh," he cries (2:23).

How could Adam and God already have drifted so far apart? The text offers no direct interpretation, but the order of events itself offers some clues. In setting about making Adam a "helper," God tries duplicating the method by which he had made Adam himself, creating the animals from the earth, the *'adamah*. Yet nothing he can create will do; he succeeds only when he takes a second step and creates Eve out of Adam himself. Made in the image of God, Adam is already different in kind from the earth from which he came: this is the first stage in the progressive separation of humanity from their native earth, and from God himself.

Further, what the creation of Eve shows is that God cannot simply breathe life into earth as he had done before; he must give life to a creation out of Adam's own substance. This places Eve at a step's remove from God's direct creation, a fact that prepares her role as the intermediary between the serpent and Adam. Now Adam's need for something God cannot directly imagine cannot stem from sin; Adam does not yet even know what evil is. Rather, it stems from his very likeness to God. In creating Adam, God sought to make an earthly representative, like himself but subordinate; and this is just what Adam himself proves to need. The problem for God here is that Adam is so much like God that he shares the lack that God had felt, and where God desired an Adam, Adam desires an Eve.

This understanding of the separation of Adam from God as a result of the similarity between them is not an arbitrary or even at heart a paradoxical move on the Yahwists' part; it is a logical way of dealing with the problem of evil in a monotheistic framework. If Adam cannot drift away from God through evil, as both he and God are good, and cannot drift away even though sheer unlikeness to God, as he is created in God's image (as the Priestly writers will put it), then he *must* drift away precisely through the consequences of his likeness to God.

This causal association is directly shown at the next stage, when Eve succumbs to the temptation of the serpent: she is tempted not through rebellion against God, but through a slightly skewed exercise of the very traits she shares with God: "When the woman saw that the tree was good for food, and that it was a delight to the eyes, and that the tree was to be desired to make one wise [lehaskil], she took of its fruit, and ate" (3:6). The first two of the three attractions of the tree are the very qualities God had bestowed on trees for human benefit: "Out of the ground the Lord God made to grow every tree that is pleasant to the sight and good for food" (2:9). Even the insight or understanding she desires from the fruit is a generally good quality; indeed, the same term is used in Proverbs to characterize a good wife: "A prudent wife ['ishshah maskalet] is from the Lord" (Prov. 19:14).

Thus Adam and Eve drift away from God to a large extent through a reapplication of the very qualities that made them similar to him. One could say that their guilt arises from their innocence itself. This is, in fact, the function of the serpent, to transform their innocence in a small but crucial degree, to turn it away from God and lead to a redefinition of identity. The serpent is not evil, as he cannot be, but subtle, 'arum. Just as it will play on the double sense of naḥam in viewing Noah as the consolation for the death of Adam, here the text introduces a pun between two similar words: 'arum, "subtle," and 'arom, "naked." These words stem from different roots, but their consonants are the same, and they can even be vocalized identically, as they are here. The two words are juxtaposed in neighboring sentences, as the text introduces the serpent directly after the creation of Eve: "And the man and his wife were both naked ['arumim], and were not ashamed. Now the serpent was more subtle ['arum] than any other wild creature that the Lord God had made" (2:25–3:1). Thus the nakedness that symbolizes the innocence of Adam and Eve, and their natural openness before God—which they cover up on their loss of innocence—is linked to the craftiness of the serpent. The serpent converts Adam and Eve from nakedness to subtlety through his ability to stand outside God's creative word and question it: "Did God say . . . ?" (3:1). As his questioning probes the divine language, Eve's reply shows a further drifting away from God's word. Asked if God has prohibited eating from any tree, Eve replies:

"We may eat the fruit of the trees of the garden; but God said, you shall not eat of the fruit of the tree which is in the midst of the garden, neither shall you touch it, lest you die." But the serpent said to the woman, "You will not die." (3:2–4)

The remarkable thing in Eve's reply is that she has the prohibition wrong. In ancient literature, long speeches are routinely repeated word for word, at times to the tedium of the modern reader. Here, however, God's simple prohibition has been altered, by the addition of the phrase "you shall not touch it." The surprise of this alteration was already felt in antiquity; according to the Talmud, "Eve said to the serpent that she was not even allowed to touch the fruit, although this was not part of the original prohibition. The Rabbis consider this (and any) embroidery of the truth to be the opening wedge of sin."[40] Eve's error of memory (or Adam's error in transmission) need not itself be viewed as an ethical lapse, but it opens the way for the moral problems that soon follow.

After Adam and Eve take the decisive step of transgressing the prohibition, they suddenly become aware of their nakedness and cover it up. When God appears and asks why Adam is hiding from him, Adam replies: "I was afraid, because I was naked; and I hid myself." "Who told you that you were naked?" God asks in surprise (3:10–11). Until now, the only living creature on earth whom Adam has not named is himself. Now he does so, identifying himself: "for I was naked," *ki-'erom 'anokhi*. The pun between "naked" and "subtle" is here doubled with a new pun, between *'arum* and *'Adam*.

Adam has made a name for himself; he is now subtle/naked, and like the serpent whom he newly resembles, he now dresses in clothing he can cast off. Once again the text inverts symbolism earlier seen in the Mesopotamian epic tradition. Whereas in the *Gilgamesh Epic* clothing was a symbol of maturity and the gifts of civilization, here it signifies only loss.

As Genesis 2–11 proceeds, it develops the theme that human culture is a product of the existential state of separation from God. Whereas the Babylonian flood epic takes care to tell us that Atrahasis saves not only his family but also a crew of artisans, in Genesis the artisans are descendants of Cain, whose son Enoch is the original builder of cities (4:17–22). After murdering his brother, Cain goes east of Eden to dwell in the land named "Wandering," Nod, and various forms of wandering and exile run through the Yahwistic material.

The theme of separation links the Eden and flood stories, and so too does their emblematic treatment of character and event. Over the course of time, this emblematic way of thinking evolved into the formal typological patterns emphasized in the

---

[40]San. 29a; quoted in Plant, *The Torah*, 41. On Eve's mistake, see Leibovitz, *The Form of the Book of Genesis*, 22–27.

New Testament, but already in Genesis's reworking of the old Mesopotamian creation-flood epic it is possible to see the emblematic function of character. The importance of the significations given to names, and the extended play on the names of both Adam and Noah, are signs of the degree to which these characters are treated as emblems of existential problems in the relation of humanity to God. Formerly the Mesopotamian gods would have carried out this exemplary function, and poetic mythic narrative would have been used to explore the basic constraints of human life and the tensions of society; now, through their simultaneous likeness to God and distance from him, mortals in history can become the subject of epic/mythic concerns.

Genesis 2–11 bequeathed a double lesson to the practitioners of historiography proper: the possibility of the emblematic treatment of characters in history, and the value of developing thematic patterns gradually across a succession of stories. The emblematic linking of characters like Adam and Noah, and of events like Eden and Babel, provided the means to develop broad themes across a series of generations. These lessons find their deepest expression in the David story, where it will be possible to see the gradual development of the emblematic treatment of character and event in the portrayal of historical process. Through its exploration of themes of separation, exile, and revolt, the David story produces the fullest transformation in the Bible of prose history into the mode of poetic epic.

4. Yahwist(s) and Deuteronomist(s)

In an earlier, happier time, a study of the influence of the Yahwist on the development of the David story, though a controversial topic, could at least have relied on generally accepted dates for the Yahwist, for the early components of the David story, and for the final assembly of the overall Deuteronomistic history of Joshua through 2 Kings. The topic would have been controversial for two reasons. First, it was believed that the Deuteronomistic historian had done little to shape the early materials he had inherited concerning David, materials that probably predated the Yahwist's composition of the first version of the Pentateuch. Secondly, the Yahwist and the court historians were considered to have worked separately with different kinds of material. This second assumption led not so much to a disputing of connections between the two bodies of texts as to a separation of study that simply left connections between them unexplored.

When connections have been observed, the belief in the priority of the David story has most often led to assertions of influence running from the David story to the Yahwistic material, though these assertions have not found widespread acceptance. Moreover, both the assumptions underlying such an understanding have been questioned in recent years: the Deuteronomistic historian is widely credited with a more creative role than that of a mere redactor, and the most extended component of the story of David's reign, the so-called Succession Narrative of 2 Samuel 9–20 and 1 Kings 1–2, is no longer assumed to be a virtual eyewitness account but one that may well come from a rather later time. These revisionary views create new problems of their own, as will be seen below, but they also make it easier to observe and account for parallels between the Yahwistic material and the early history of the monarchy.

The literary connections between the two bodies of material are in fact many and profound. They have often been neglected by historians, who have usually looked primarily at direct reuses of narrative material. In this case, the bodies of narrative are quite distinct, as the Yahwistic and Deuteronomistic sources deal with different periods, so direct connections are few. Literary analysis, however, can reveal and explore the indirect connections that abound, connections visible in the shaping of the different materials rather than in direct overlapping of stories.

Literary history ordinarily takes as a given a knowledge of the dates at which the materials in question were composed. Here the wide consensus of the past generation on the dating of the Yahwistic source (J) and the Deuteronomistic history can be of great value, though literary analysis may suggest some reordering of elements within the overall scheme. The problem is that in the past decade a number of scholars have advanced a variety of arguments that call the standard datings into question. The most basic challenges have been to the early dating of the Yahwist, who is now often displaced from his niche in the court of David and Solomon, in one of two ways. The Yahwistic material can be seen as not the product of a single figure at all, and not even of a single group working at one time, but instead as gradually developing over the course of four or five hundred years, from the time of David up to the time of the Babylonian Exile. Still more radically, the Yahwist can be seen as a single individual writing in the exilic period itself, partly reworking old material and partly inventing images of the patriarchal age and the history of the early monarchy in response to the needs of a much later time.

In a sense, these challenges to the early dating of the Yahwist do not so much alter as transpose the findings of the traditional view, as far as the relative dating of the materials is concerned. An early exilic Yahwist might still take priority over an exilic Deuteronomistic historian. But the problem is compounded by the fact that, whereas the Yahwist has been moving ahead, the Deuteronomistic historian has been moving backward, with several scholars arguing in various ways that the overall composition of the Deuteronomistic history occurred in two or more stages, with a crucial first edition written fifty or more years before the beginning of the Exile. This latter view would tend to rule out consideration of parallels with J altogether in discussion of the development of Hebrew narrative. Thus the search for a reasonably certain chronology has lost much of the sureness it enjoyed from the 1940s through the 1960s and increasingly resembles the bewildering croquet game in Wonderland: no sooner has the scholarly Alice straightened out the Yahwistic flamingo than she finds that the Deuteronomistic hedgehog has wandered away.

In the present state of our understanding, it is impossible to reach certain conclusions about the absolute dating of either the Yahwistic or the Deuteronomistic materials. It is for this reason that a casual glance at the historical situation usually results either in the literary critic's horrified recoil into "pure" literary study or else in the arbitrary plucking out of a convenient theory to support a preexisting literary judgment. As distressing as this situation is, however, it is not actually as difficult for the literary critic as for the historian of religion, since literary history is not at heart dependent upon absolute chronology. The literary historian will always be grateful for dates when they are available, but what really matters is not the absolute but the relative chronology of the materials under consideration. Each of the major possibilities for the dating of the texts raises problems of relative chronology, problems to whose discussion literary analysis can contribute, since most of the evidence is to be found in the literary relations among the texts, in the absence of much external historical information. To deal seriously with the historical problems does not preclude reaching some tentative assessment of the situation, however, and such an assessment can be of great value in grounding and guiding literary analysis. At the same time, however one comes out on the questions of dating, it is important to proceed with an eye open to the other possibilities as well.

My purpose in this chapter will be to describe some of the literary-historical implications of the major theories of dating that are currently under debate in historical scholarship. There are really almost as many theories as there are theorists, but I will group the possibilities under two headings: first, the view that the rise of Hebrew historiographic narrative was intimately linked to the establishment of the monarchy; second, the view that historiography arose instead during the monarchy's decline and fall. Within this second position, two principal theories should be distinguished: that historiography arose only during the Exile itself; or that it gradually developed during the course of the monarchy, reaching its full form during the Exile. I will try to suggest the ways in which literary study can help to refine the possibilities under each of these headings, and I will discuss the implications for literary analysis under each of them. To some extent, literary history can proceed while leaving all three options open, insofar as the differing possibilities permit a similar relative chronology; finally, though, it will be necessary to consider how one's analysis must be modified by following any one of the theories, to the extent that they ultimately conflict with each other. In conclusion, I will describe my own somewhat eclectic partial synthesis of the possibilities, both to show the assumptions underlying the analysis in the ensuing chapters and also to illustrate the kinds of text-historical issues that any effort at literary history must take into consideration. Sometimes conclusions can be reached with a fair degree of certainty; at other times, one can only clarify the possibilities. Even the tentative results that can be reached are, as I hope to show, of considerable value in gaining a sense of the growth of biblical narrative and in reading the resulting text.

These historical issues are important not only for the literary historian but also for the reader of the canonical form of the text, for each view of the rise of Hebrew narrative has direct consequences for the reading of the final form of the text. Each view has developed out of certain kinds of evidence within the text and in turn reinforces the importance of such evidence; as a result, each view inevitably guides our reading of the canonical text by highlighting some themes as against others, and by presenting a differing view of the historical reality to which the text seeks to respond. The Yahwist who arises in the triumphant moment of the establishment of the kingdom of Israel is a different figure from the Yahwist who writes at the time of the virtual destruction of Israel's national life; a Davidic-Solomonic Yahwist is to be seen as celebrating and consolidating a new religious and social order, whereas an exilic Yahwist would instead be trying to recreate a distant past as a way to understand what went wrong. Similarly, a Deuteronomistic historian whose goal is to support the religious and social reforms of Josiah in an uncertain but optimistic time produces a different text from an exilic Deuteronomistic historian who writes to denounce and condemn the whole history of the monarchy as a tragic series of rejections of God. The biblical texts provide evidence to support each of these views; the question is which is to be given priority and allowed to guide our overall reading.

The problem is familiar to any student of ambiguous texts, especially those from an earlier time; Shakespeare's attitudes toward English history, for example, are variously reconstructed, with differing implications for the reading of his histories. But the problem, if familiar, is sharper in the case of the Bible; at least we know that Shakespeare's Queen Elizabeth is the one who reigned from 1558 to 1603 and not the one whose reign began in 1952. Yet just this degree of chronological uncertainty is found in the span of four hundred or more years separating the early and late datings of the Yahwist. It is as if the Pierre Menard of Borges's story really had written *Don Quixote* anew in the nineteenth century, or rather as if we did not know whether he or Cervantes was the author of the book in the first place. This is the uncertainty that gives such urgency to the exploration of the problem of dating for any reader of the Bible, and that makes the reconstruction of the Bible's literary history so unusually important at that same time that it renders it unusually difficult to achieve.

Historiography and the Early Monarchy

In his essay, "The Beginnings of Historical Writing in Ancient Israel," Gerhard von Rad described the founding of the united kingdom as the necessary prerequisite for the development of historiography. Only with an established court, with its attendant group of court historians and its new sense of the nation as an entity, could history have been written. A further impetus was provided by the need of David and Solomon to consolidate the power of the new monarchy and to justify the transition from the traditional charismatic leadership to a strong, centralized, and dynastic form of government. To fill this need, the Yahwist assembled and shaped the old traditions about the origins of the people in order to present a series of promises and covenants that would lead up to the covenant with the house of David that established the monarchy on a permanent basis. Von Rad's views have been developed by many subsequent scholars. In one recent assessment,

there are many indications that the mind of the collector(s) [of J] was directed towards the empire of David and Solomon, which they considered to be the logical conclusion to the prehistory of their people and of the ancient oracles (or those oracles which were thought to be ancient).

We may therefore consider the J collection to be something like an apologetic writing intended to justify and legitimate the monarchy in Israel, a form of government which was certainly new and the subject of lively debate, if we consider the sources; this legitimation was achieved by means of an extremely shrewd choice from ancient material enriched by early prophecies which were probably *ex eventu*.[1]

This point of view has been developed at length by R. E. Clements, who argues, in *Abraham and David*, that the covenant with Abraham was advanced as the model for David's effort to unify Israel.[2] Similarly, in his article on "The Kerygma of the Yahwist," Hans Walter Wolff studies the political background of the Genesis stories, and concludes: "At no time except during the reigns of David and Solomon does this political outlook obtain" (Brueggemann and Wolff, *Vitality of OT Traditions*, 44). Quite apart from direct political reference, moreover, it is often thought that the stories about the patriarchs would most likely have been edited into a unified whole under the influence of the new nationalism of the young state.[3] Under this view, the Yahwist or Yahwists were less interested in bolstering the monarchy than in taking advantage of the political situation for their own theological purposes.[4]

If the political climate of the early monarchy was a crucial factor in the collecting of the old patriarchal legends by the

---

[1] J. Alberto Soggin, *Introduction to the Old Testament*, 102. Soggin focuses his discussion on political elements in Genesis, such as the promises of a kingdom to Abraham and to Judah (12:2; 49:10), with parallels in Nathan's promises to David (2 Sam. 7:9 and 7:12 ff.).

[2] See also Delbert R. Hillers, *Covenant: The History of a Biblical Idea*, who sees this activity as an extension of the premonarchic union between the tribes of Israel, the "amphictyony" postulated by Martin Noth. The idea of an amphictyony is itself widely debated, with many scholars following Noth and others arguing that the picture of a tribal league centered at Shechem is a fictional creation of later biblical writers. A fresh account of the tribal league, however, has been given by Norman Gottwald in *The Hebrew Bible: A Socio-Literary Introduction*.

[3] To quote one example: "We cannot really speak of the traditional concept of Israel before David's time. Not until then were the conditions created under which the Pentateuchal Yahwist (J) could make a first effort at unifying the tribal traditions" (Vink, "Date and Origin of the Priestly Code," 130). See further Herrmann, "Das Werden Israels."

[4] Thus Peter Weimar and Erich Zenger propose a Solomonic date for the Yahwist, who sought "to appropriate (not to legitimate!) the intellectual and political situation which had arisen with David and Solomon" (*Exodus*, 20).

Yahwist, still more was it the inspiration for the growth of the history of the monarchy, and those scholars who date J to the reigns of David or Solomon generally see most of the David story as having been composed at the same time, with relatively little reworking by the Deuteronomistic historian who later incorporated the story of David into his overall history of the monarchy. Modern discussion of the dating of the David story grows out of Leonhard Rost's path-breaking study of 1926, *Die Überlieferung von der Thronnachfolge Davids*. Rost argued that two blocks of material within the present David story were originally unrelated narratives, of separate origin and point of view: the "Ark Narrative" of 1 Samuel 4:1b–7:1 plus 2 Samuel 6, and the "Succession Narrative" of 2 Samuel 9–20 and 1 Kings 1–2. The Ark Narrative described the loss of the Ark to the Philistines, its recovery by David, and its triumphal installation in his new royal city, Jerusalem. The Succession Narrative dealt with David's later reign, with an emphasis on justifying Solomon's accession to the throne over the heads of his older brothers. The specific boundaries of Rost's early sources have been modified in subsequent discussion, but there is near unanimity concerning the validity of the overall reconstructions. The Ark Narrative can plausibly be dated to the reign of David, whereas the basic Succession Narrative is often considered to date from the reign of Solomon, though there is disagreement on whether the date should be early in Solomon's reign (c. 960) or toward the end of his reign (in the 920s).

Following Rost, subsequent scholars have analyzed other reconstructed early sources, notably a loose collection of materials about Saul's early career, worked into the present 1 Samuel 9–14, and a history of David's rise (approximately 1 Sam. 16:14 through 2 Sam. 15). The History of David's Rise is often considered to show signs of two or even three major stages of development, originating in the reign of David or Solomon as a political justification for the overthrow of Saul's house, then undergoing a later prophetically oriented revision, then receiving a final revision by the Deuteronomistic historian.

Assessments of the Davidic-Solomonic origins of historical writing usually give definite priority to the David story over the Yahwistic corpus. Von Rad actually postulates the dependence of J on the Succession Narrative. He sees J's emphasis on God's action in history as a consequence of the rise of interest in, and recording of, the political history of the monarchy:

> This new way of seeing God's activity in history was set in train by the figure of David, and the historical experiences of Israel under him as king; consequently we must on literary grounds assign to the Yahwist a date later than that of the account of the succession to the throne of David. It is at once obvious that this new perspective of the faith must be directed first of all to what is most immediate—the historical situation in which Israel found itself at the time.[5]

In keeping with this view, several attempts have been made to show a dependence of Yahwistic material on the David story. Joseph Blenkinsopp has sketched several general parallels between the opening chapters of Genesis and the David story, most notably stressing the similarities in Cain's murder of Abel and Absalom's murder of Amnon.[6] More ambitiously, in "David and His Theologian," Walter Brueggemann argues that

---

[5]Von Rad, "Form-Critical Problem of the Hexateuch," 71. This thesis was first advanced in the 1880s and 1890s by Karl Budde, who argued that historical writing in Israel began with the contemporary situation and then gradually worked backward to treat early times. The problem with this view lies in von Rad's immediate transition from consideration of "the perspective of faith" to conclusions about the literary composition of historical work. In many periods, after all, contemporary upheavals have inspired writers more directly toward a searching reexamination of their past than to an immediate turn to detailed recording of the present. As for the general growth of developed historiography, it might also be useful to consider the case of Greece, where the stages from the Halicarnassan chroniclers to Thucydides are definitely known to us. Here it is notable that Herodotus preceded Thucydides, rather than following him: it was Herodotus's brilliant history of events of one and two generations before him that inspired Thucydides to write the history of his own time.

[6]"Theme and Motif in the Succession History (2 Sam. xi 2 ff.) and the Yahwist Corpus." Less plausibly, he views Bathsheba first as parallel to Eve (a motif of the Woman who brings Death), and then as parallel to Rebekah, and he compares David's beauty and godlike wisdom to Adam's, though he notes in this instance that direct references to Adam's beauty and wisdom are developed more in Psalms, Isaiah, and other texts than in Genesis itself.

the old mythic materials in Genesis 2–11 have been collected and shaped with a direct political purpose: they represent "an attempt to create theological legitimacy for the monarchy and speak a warning in the context of covenant to the ambitions of the Davidic house." This ideological purpose has far-reaching literary consequences: "The particular order of the Genesis materials is dependent upon the career of the sons of David in their quest for the throne." Finally, if Genesis 2–11 speaks a warning to the Davidic monarchy it also, conversely, reinterprets ancient history under the influence of modern experience:

In Gn. 2–11, just below the surface of the mythological materials and affirmations about "the human predicament" lies the story of David's family and the God of the Davidic house. What Israel in the tenth century knew about sin and grace, curse and blessing, she knew because she had seen it happen in the current royal establishment. The theologian had the task of extending the experience of this representative man and his family to the experience of all men.[7]

To illustrate this, Brueggemann draws the parallel between the story of Cain and Abel and the story of Absalom and Amnon, compares David to Adam (and Bathsheba, this time, not to Eve but to the forbidden fruit itself), and suggests parallels between Noah and Absalom and between the builders of the Tower of Babel and Solomon as builder of the Temple.

Quite apart from the vagueness of most of these parallels, and the fact that the ordering of Genesis 2–11 is best understood as a reflection of the old traditions of creation-flood stories, to the extent that parallels can be seen in these materials it seems to me that they run in the other direction. The one really close parallel discussed by Blenkinsopp and Brueggemann is that between the slayings of Abel and of Amnon. Absalom's killing of his brother has both situational and verbal parallels to the story of Cain and Abel. The situational parallel

---

[7]"David and His Theologian," 157–59. Surely Brueggemann is having things both ways in claiming that the Yahwist is both using the old myths to criticize the Davidic house and using the Davidic house as the exemplum of all history and the model for faith.

is loose, though suggestive, as in both instances the fratricidal murderer flees and is later spared. What makes the parallel direct, however, are the echoes in the parable that the wise woman of Tekoa tells David preparatory to urging him to pardon Absalom and recall him from exile: "Your handmaid had two sons, and they quarreled with one another in the field; there was no one to part them, and one struck the other and killed him" (2 Sam. 14:6). She needs her surviving son spared, she says, lest her deceased husband have "neither name nor remnant upon the face of the earth" (v. 7). The sons in her parable quarrel "in the field," *bassadeh*, also the location of Cain's murder of Abel, and the father will have no heir upon the face of the earth, in an echo of Cain's punishment as a wanderer on the face of the earth. Thus it is the wise woman's fiction that builds directly on the old legend of Cain and Abel. The whole parable would lose much of its force if the author of the Succession Narrative (and his audience) had not had the Yahwistic legend as a frame of reference. Conversely, moreover, it is difficult to imagine the Yahwistic writer fabricating the story of Cain and Abel at a late date as a pseudo-archaic legend, under the inspiration of the parable within the Succession Narrative.

In this instance it seems clear that the Succession Narrative, at any rate, shows the influence of the Yahwistic material of Genesis 2–11, and this is not the only such instance in 1–2 Samuel. At a variety of points modern events are understood against the frame of reference provided by the emblematic stories both of creation-flood and of the patriarchs, in ways comparable to the echoes of the Flood in the *Erra Epic*. The stories of the fall of Saul and his house from divine favor, for example, have clear echoes of the story of Adam and Eve. There are three stories most directly involved in the loss of the kingdom by Saul and Jonathan. One of these is a late addition describing Saul's folly in not waiting for the arrival of the prophet Samuel before making an offering to God (1 Sam. 13:2–15); the other two episodes, original to the account, both have echoes of the

story of Adam and Eve. In the first incident, Jonathan falls
under his father's curse by eating forbidden food; he is con-
demned to death but then spared (1 Sam. 14:23–46).[8] In the
second and climactic scene, Saul himself disobeys a divine prohibition, letting himself be led by his people as Adam was led
astray by Eve, and then lying about his actions when Samuel
calls him to account (15:1–34).

Throughout biblical narrative, the king represents the people
before God and stands as a godlike figure before his people;
in both these incidents, Saul fails to live up to the task. In
consequence, he falls, and drags Jonathan, into repetitions of
the Fall itself. In these cases, and in others to be discussed in
the next chapter, it seems likely that the modern history of the
monarchy is assessed and understood in conjunction with the
Yahwistic stories of the foundations of society as a whole and
of Hebrew history in particular in the time of the patriarchs.
These stories may have been circulating in purely oral form,
but there are enough direct verbal echoes to suggest that at
least the traditional materials in Genesis 2–11 and 12–36 had
been brought together by the time of the composition of much
of the David story. If the Yahwist is to be seen as a single figure
working during the early monarchy, his work should be seen
as antedating the composition of the major elements of the
David story.

The picture that results gives a certain priority to the Yahwist
as the first to attempt an overall synthesis of a variety of materials. This is not to suggest that there was no contemporary
historical writing going on at the same time, but rather that
the first historians of David's and Solomon's reigns probably
produced nothing more ambitious than the spare annals and
chronicles typical of court historians everywhere in the Near
East. It was the Yahwist who first brought into Hebrew prose
the old epic concerns with cultural development and personal

---

[8]On the parallel between this episode and Eden, see Blenkinsopp, "Jonathan's
Sacrilege."

and national character. Gradually, these concerns were then taken over into the developing historiography of the monarchy. As will be seen in the next chapter, Yahwistic parallels are used in a simple and direct fashion in the early Ark Narrative and then in a more indirect and complex way in the several stages of the development of the History of David's Rise.

Though the Yahwist looks less like an apologist for the Davidic monarchy in this view, he (or they) can still be seen as acting under the inspiration of the dramatic unification of the country under David, which has often been supposed to have produced "an atmosphere of national exaltation, which was very congenial to the composition of historical works."[9] The Yahwist's success in the initial effort of constructing his theologically oriented history would have inspired subsequent court historians to increase the thematic and compositional density of their accounts of more recent times. This assessment would accord well with the common view of J as a first attempt at seeing large historical patterns, created through the assembly and reworking of traditional materials.[10]

The major problem for literary analysis that remains under this view is the suddenness with which we must imagine the transition from unrelated and loosely related groups of oral tradition to the very extended and comprehensive prose epic that the Yahwistic material presents. This problem is compounded by the arguments now being raised on various sides that the Yahwistic material is largely the product of a much later time than the early monarchy, and these views must be assessed

---

[9]Eissfeldt, *The OT: An Introduction,* 140. Stopping short of von Rad's claim of a textual dependence of J on the Succession Narrative, Eissfeldt suggests that "it was David's deeds or the recollection of them which first led a particular individual to set out a presentation of Israel's history linking it with the history of humanity" (140).

[10]"Notwithstanding the ingenuous and sometimes simplistic character of this vision of history, it cannot be denied that it is a first attempt at a synthesis, at seeing history as the causal and consistent development of interconnected events which are conditioned by one another and lead to a single goal. J thus constitutes the point of departure from a legendary and popular cycle of history to more advanced literary history" (Soggin, *Introduction to the OT,* 101).

before any conclusions can be drawn about the extent and nature of Yahwistic activity during the reigns of David and Solomon.

The Yahwists and the Exile

As early as the 1940s, questions were raised concerning the grounds for dating the Yahwist to the early tenth century. In 1949, in the course of a major attack on the identification of an Elohistic source in the Moses story, F. V. Winnett undercut the customary picture of the Elohistic document as added to an existing tenth-century Yahwistic history by arguing that J shows too many close links to concerns of the ninth century to have been composed in the tenth.[11] Winnett went further in his presidential address to the Society of Biblical Literature in 1964, "Re-examining the Foundations." He argues that Genesis was first assembled during the Exile itself, by an author whom he calls Late J. "Late J" had before him an old collection of patriarchal stories, originally composed for religious use, and already revised once by the Elohistic hand. To this document Late J added the new framework of promises to the patriarchs. References to "Ur of the Chaldaeans" in Genesis 11 make sense only after the rise of the Chaldaean empire in the late seventh century, and the listing of Japhethite peoples in 10:1–5 would most logically reflect the first Hebrew contacts with the Japhethite peoples during the exilic period.[12] To the revised pa-

---

[11]*The Mosaic Tradition*, 166–68. A late ninth-century date for J is also suggested by Gustav Hölscher, in his *Geschichtsschreibung in Israel;* he postulates this date in connection with an effort to see the Yahwist's material as continuing into the history of the monarchy itself, a view rarely advanced today. His student Hannelis Schulte, however, has recently made an ambitious effort to create a workable version of his thesis. Schulte argues that the Yahwist was a historian active around 910 or 900 who used materials by different authors to create the first unified history, including the stories both of the patriarchs and of the early monarchy (*Die Entstehung der Geschichtsschreibung im Alten Israel*).

[12]Winnett adduces these items in the course of his discussion of the primeval history, but as they form part of the genealogies that link the primeval history to the patriarchal stories, what they directly testify to is the period at which

triarchal collection Late J appended the Elohistic Joseph novella, with some editorial modifications, and he prefaced the whole with the primeval history, which Winnett views as having been composed by Late J himself, though using existing source materials, "mainly oral but possibly some written" (18).

Winnett argues persuasively that the recurrent promises to Abraham are closely associated with late ideas, and he suggests that the references to the Exodus in Genesis 15 actually point to the problems of the Exile. He asks: "May we not see in Late J's concern with the divine promises to the patriarchs an historian's way of conveying a message of comfort and hope to his people in a time of gloom and despair? If Late J be of postexilic date, the whole matter becomes readily intelligible" (13). An exilic setting gives new point to episodes such as the story of Sodom, whose destruction Lot and his family must flee without looking back in longing for their old life.

Winnett's brief discussion of the primeval history is less persuasive, as it rests on a very selective sense of Near Eastern and Hebrew intellectual history:

The strongest argument for an exilic, or even a postexilic, date is the author's universalistic and monotheistic outlook. He views the universe as the creation of a one and only God, YHWH. . . . Sin to him is not a nationalistic affair, the apostasy of the nation from YHWH, as it was to the eighth-century prophets; it is a universal, human phenomenon. There is an innate tendency to evil in the hearts of all men from their youth. While it is always possible that a writer is far ahead of his time . . . either the exilic or the postexilic period provides the most natural *milieu* for the author of the primeval history. (4)

It is difficult to see how this argument can point decisively to the exilic period; all it really does is suggest that the primeval history did not stem from the eighth century. The view of sin as innate and universal is, after all, widely found within second-millennium Mesopotamian literature and may well be sup-

Genesis as a whole was created, rather than indicating the date of the original composition of Genesis 2–11.

posed to have antedated the development of a nationalistic conception of sin in eighth-century Hebrew thought. In view of the close ties of the primeval history to Mesopotamian literary productions of the late second millennium, one may plausibly suppose that the primeval history was originally composed at an early date and attached as a whole, with some additions, to the patriarchal stories whenever the overall book of Genesis was created.[13]

Building on Winnett's work, several scholars have recently gone further in cutting the links traditionally envisaged as uniting the Yahwist to the early monarchy. In an article entitled "Abraham and David?" published in a *Festschrift* for Winnett, N. E. Wagner disputes the supposed association of the promises to Abraham with those to David, noting that the patriarchs are never mentioned in the David story at all, which instead draws parallels to the quite different (and later) conception of the covenant at Sinai. He argues that all of the material in Genesis was originally separate from the rest of the Yahwistic material and thinks that the overall collection of the patriarchal stories may well date from exilic times, when Abraham first became an important figure. Seconding these arguments is the conclusion of Lothar Perlitt that the theology of covenant is a Deuteronomic invention and hence hardly likely to be a unifying literary element much before the time of the exile.[14]

---

[13]If an exilic date for the composition of Genesis 2–11 were to be accepted, then it is clear that my discussion in the previous chapter would need to be phrased in different terms. Genesis 2–11 would need to be seen as a late expression of the reworking of epic norms, well after the rise of prose historiography, rather than as an indication of an initial shift in the direction of history. This could perhaps be maintained, but the many references to events of the primeval history in the David story (see further in this chapter and the next) strongly suggest that a version of the primeval history rather like the Yahwistic material in Genesis 2–11 must have been known to the writers of the early accounts of David's reign.

[14]*Bundestheologie im Alten Testament.* He stresses the significance of the absence of the formal concept of covenant in the eighth-century prophets; see esp. 129–55. Martin Rose has argued further that the Yahwistic theological program is an outgrowth of Deuteronomy and particularly of the historical perspective of Deut. 1–3 (*Deuteronomist und Jahwist*).

A more extended argument concerning the late importance of Abraham is John Van Seters's *Abraham in History and Tradition*. Van Seters disputes the general view of biblical archaeologists that the patriarchal narratives reflect conditions of the second millennium B.C. He argues that the archaeologists' own biases have prevented them from seeing that the evidence more closely reflects much later conditions well into the first millennium. He argues further that story variants in the patriarchal narratives are created by a purely literary process of interpretive rewriting and not by the collation of old traditions, and he argues that the patriarchal narratives show thematic emphases parallel to those in the exilic prophecy of Deutero-Isaiah.[15] He concludes: "The 'Abraham of history' can no longer be recovered from the traditions as we now have them, even to the limited extent of reconstructing his 'life and times' " (121).

The arguments for a late dating of J lead in two different directions. On the one hand, the Yahwistic and Deuteronomistic corpuses can both be seen as gradually developing over the course of several centuries. This view works against any effort to see unified themes at all in the Yahwistic material per se, with overall linkages like the covenant theme merely being secondary additions to essentially disparate materials. This is the conclusion of Rolf Rendtorff, whose 1977 study *Das überlieferungsgeschichtliche Problem des Pentateuch* argues that the real collection and harmonizing of the "Yahwistic" materials was undertaken by the Deuteronomistic and Priestly schools. In a recent article, Rendtorff writes, "I cannot assign any comprehensive redaction of the Pentateuch to the pre-Deuteronomistic

---

[15]Like Winnett, but in greater detail, Van Seters argues against the existence of a separate Elohistic collection of patriarchal stories, viewing the Elohistic elements in Genesis as reflecting a stage of revision of the Yahwistic text. I will not discuss the problem of the Elohist here, as the texts I am concerned with are chiefly Yahwistic, but my own belief is that the Elohistic patriarchal material, if it ever did exist as an independent collection, has been edited so thoroughly (and so selectively) into its present context as to render highly problematic any efforts to recover its earlier identity or its particular emphases.

period" ("Pentateuchal Studies on the Move," 43). As for the earlier activities of the Yahwist, in a 1975 article titled "The 'Yahwist' as Theologian?" Rendtorff flatly states that "there is no room here for the idea of the 'Yahwist' as a theologian. There is no such person" (10).

On the other hand, the Yahwist can still be seen as a single historian, but one working during the exilic period, probably integrating and reshaping a proto-Yahwistic body of traditions. The earlier traditions collected and revised by this historian (or these historians) can be regarded as possessing a definite degree of inner coherence and unity, distinct from later editorial additions by the Deuteronomistic and Priestly writers, though probably showing some influence from the Deuteronomistic material.

A good example of this viewpoint is H. H. Schmid's study *Der sogenannte Jahwist* ("The Putative Yahwist"), whose title already suggests the skepticism with which he approaches the idea of a single Yahwist. He does, however, allow for a defined body of material, showing Deuteronomistic and prophetic influences but separately formed:

Under the rubric "Yahwist" we will investigate that layer of the Pentateuch which evidently first brought the traditional material into connection across various pericopes and groups of pericopes, stretching from the primeval history at least up to the beginning of the Conquest, creating editorial linkages and thereby theologically reworking and reinterpreting the tradition, both implicitly and through new contributions. (17)

Like Winnett, Schmid believes that the differing materials in Genesis (the primeval history of Genesis 2–11, the patriarchal narratives of 12–36, and the Joseph story of 37–50) were separately composed at different times, and then brought together during the Exile. At that time, the Yahwistic writer reworked the patriarchal narratives to develop the theme of the promises to the patriarchs and to bring this material into a chronological union with the primeval history. Also during the Exile the

Moses story was reworked and greatly developed. Now, under the influence of eighth-century and exilic prophecy, Moses becomes a prophet, and prominence is given to Sinai, ignored by earlier tradition.

Schmid argues that the Yahwistic material as we have it is *mehrschichtig*, composed of several strata. "Thus, instead of speaking of the Yahwist as a single collector, author and theologian, one should rather speak of an (inner-)Yahwistic process of editing and interpretation" (167); "the 'Yahwist' is to be understood as a process of interpretation" (168). Schmid thus takes a middle position within the arguments for a late dating of the Yahwist. Unlike Rendtorff, he believes that the unification of the Yahwistic material was not purely a product of Deuteronomistic and Priestly editorial activity; unlike Van Seters, he argues for the recoverability of pre-exilic layers of material even though he agrees that the whole was only shaped in the Exile itself. In Schmid's view, the relations between the Yahwistic and Deuteronomistic materials must be viewed in the context of a long development of both sources. "Historically, theologically, and in terms of intellectual history, it no longer seems possible to apportion the connection between 'Yahwist' and Deuteronomy/Deuteronomistic according to alternatives of 'before,' 'at the same time,' or 'after' " (169).

The views of Winnett, Rendtorff, Van Seters, and Schmid have both thematic and literary-historical consequences. Thematically, the Exile is to be seen as the decisive period for the creation of the overall patterns in the two great bodies of biblical narrative, the Pentateuch and the Deuteronomistic history. All the writers just discussed view the crisis of the destruction of the Israelite state as the real impetus for historical reflection. Before the troubled times of the eighth century, which saw the downfall of the Northern Kingdom and the growing weakness of the South, history had simply been seen as the stage where God's power is manifested, a view common in earlier Near Eastern historiography. With the increasing troubles of the eighth and seventh centuries, culminating in the catastrophe of the Exile, God's activity had to be examined in deeper and less direct manifestations. "The crisis of history provided the impetus to become aware of history, both in itself and in its relevance for theology."[16] To make an analogy to Mesopotamian literature, biblical history writing would be seen as more closely resembling the *Erra Epic* than the *Tukulti-Ninurta Epic* both in origin and in purpose.

These new views are controversial, and various scholars have felt that the reports of the death of the Yahwist have been greatly exaggerated.[17] All the same, there is much to be said for the view that the Pentateuch as a whole, and even the Yahwistic narratives within it, received their decisive formulation during the period around the Exile. In this view, the impetus toward a general history of the nation, prefaced by the larger history of the world as a whole, would have come not from the establishment of the unified nation but from its dissolution.

The importance of the exilic period has been stressed in several recent studies, most notably Peter R. Ackroyd's *Exile and Restoration*. Ackroyd sees Deuteronomy as a call to new life amid the loss of the accustomed securities of national institutions:

Warnings are there in plenty, but the stress is much more upon the appeal to choose the way of life and so to receive the divine blessing. This is the more impressive when it is remembered that the final setting of these appeals is not a moment of success, not even a moment in which a prosperous outcome to the present situation seemed probable, but the moment when the people has suffered almost total loss

---

[16]Schmid, 182; similarly Van Seters: "It is to the despairing community of the exile that the unbreakable promises of the patriarchs are addressed, and Abraham becomes the focus of corporate identity and the lifeline of their hope and destiny" (*Abraham*, 311).

[17]See, for example, R. E. Clements's review of Rendtorff: "It is hard to become convinced that the very isolation and self-sufficiency of the 'larger units' of tradition, particularly of the exodus and wilderness, could have survived for so long without the existence of a framework with which to hold them in place in relation to each other. . . . That there was a pre-exilic, early monarchic framework such as the Yahwist has usually been thought to have established still appears a perfectly reasonable assumption" (53–54).

and destruction, and when little or nothing points to a new life ahead.   (76–77)[18]

The value of this observation will be apparent at various points in the chapters to follow, and there is little disagreement concerning its relevance to the composition of the Deuteronomistic history and the Priestly version of the Pentateuch. Indeed, over a century ago, Julius Wellhausen stressed the importance of the Exile, and it is worth recalling that in his view the Exile proved to be a time of creative ferment:

The new generation had no natural, but only an artificial relation to the times of old; the firmly rooted growths of the old soil, regarded as thorns by the pious, were extirpated, and the freshly ploughed fallows ready for a new sowing. . . . From the exile there returned, not the nation, but a religious sect—those, namely, who had given themselves up body and soul to the reformation ideas.   (*Prolegomena*, 28)

What is new in recent scholarship is the suggestion that the Yahwistic corpus might only have assumed a unified form as part of this same process.

In the context of Near Eastern historiography, these new views have an analogy in the only other extant example of a synoptic history, the *Babyloniaca* of Berossus. Described by its most recent editor as "the only known attempt by a Babylonian intellectual to survey his own culture" (Burstein, 10), the work was created in about 281 by Berossus in an attempt to persuade the new Hellenistic rulers of Mesopotamia of the importance and viability of traditional Mesopotamian culture. He sought to do this by showing the antiquity of Babylonian culture and the centrality of Babylon within world history. So far as can be told from the surviving fragments of the work, Berossus combined several different bodies of information, including texts that do not appear ever to have been joined together before

[18]See also Richard Elliott Friedman, *The Exile and Biblical Narrative: The Formation of the Deuteronomistic and Priestly Works*. Harvard Semitic Monographs 22 (Chico: Scholars Press, 1981).

him in Babylonian tradition: a listing of antediluvian kings, a record of ancient sages, and records of later kings.

As an effort to explain his culture to a foreign audience, Berossus's work is most directly analogous to later works like Josephus's *Jewish Antiquities*, but the sorts of material combined also have a definite similarity to those found in Genesis. It is not at all implausible that, three or four hundred years before Berossus, the prolonged crisis that began with the fall of the North and culminated in the Exile would have provided the impetus for the joining together of the different Yahwistic materials, as the Hebrews struggled to hold on to their endangered traditions and use them to make sense of the disaster that had befallen them.

A late dating of the assembling of the Yahwistic material creates certain difficulties for an effort to create a linear literary-historical development between the pentateuchal and the Deuteronomistic historical materials (on which more below), but it has certain advantages as well. To begin with, it is no longer necessary to suppose that Hebrew historiographic narrative sprang full-blown from the Solomonic court. If, at the same time, we allow for a gradual development during the centuries preceding the Exile, then we can do justice to the evident disparity of materials within the Yahwistic corpus while still allowing for their eventual combination and interrelation.

It is possible that the common conclusion that "the Yahwistic epic" received its full form in the first generations of literacy is, in part, an extension of the modern tendency to imagine first J, then JE, and finally the Pentateuch itself, as a book. James Barr offers a useful caution on this point, in the course of his argument that there was no defined scriptural canon during the period of the texts' composition and reediting:

In biblical times the books were separate individual scrolls. A "Bible" was not a volume one could hold in the hand, but a cupboard or chest with pigeonholes, or a room or a cave with a lot of individual scrolls. The boundary between what was scripture, and what were other holy books, was thus more difficult to locate, and so was the order of the books and the organization (if any) of the canon. (*Holy Scripture*, 57)

The Yahwistic corpus itself could similarly have taken the form of several separate scrolls, written and in some cases rewritten as separate manuscripts until an exilic editor brought them together into a unified narrative. The matter is clearest with the JE material in Genesis, which, as has long been recognized, divides naturally into three sections: the primeval history of chapters 1–11, the patriarchal sagas of 12–36, and the "Joseph novella" of 37–50. The stories of the Exodus and Sinai may have been heavily reworked during the Exile, as Schmid argues, but a basic form of the Yahwistic Exodus account appears to have been composed at an early date, as I will argue further in the next chapter.

Seeing the disparateness of the materials grouped under the heading of "J" has several advantages. It frees us from the unrewarding task of seeking a unified perspective or kerygma of the "Yahwist," a problematic effort if the major overarching links in the material are of late (and perhaps of Deuteronomistic and Priestly) origin. Further, it enables us to do justice to the early date of the separate materials, several of which may well have come from the time of David and Solomon. Finally, viewing the situation in this way yields a credible picture in terms of genre. In different ways, the separate materials of Genesis 1–11, 12–36, and 37–50 each make sense as transformations of known Near Eastern genres, and it is only reasonable to suppose that an initial period in which these forms were perfected should precede a rather later time at which quite different historical and theological pressures forced the merging of these established forms into the quite bizarre *Gesamtkunstwerk* that became the Pentateuch.[19]

---

[19]Here it may be appropriate to recall that the very name of Genesis, *Bereshit*, is a product of the late reworking of the material by the Priestly school, who added the initial chapter, whose opening phrase gives the book its title. Whatever name the book had in its original form is now lost to us, unless it hap-

A major factor in scholarly reluctance to clearly separate the periods of the composition and the assembly of the materials of Genesis has been the realization that these materials, taken in themselves, reveal great literary subtlety and refinement, qualities rather less in evidence in the compositions known to have later been produced by the Deuteronomists and the Priestly school. It has been natural to suppose that the same people who recorded the Genesis material also formed it into a sweeping and unified salvation history, in the "first lusty and creative impulse" of Yahwism, to borrow a phrase from Cross (*Canaanite Myth,* 190). The later contributions of the manifestly less literary Deuteronomists and Priestly writers served to elaborate and schematize what had been given its essential and decisive form by the Yahwist(s).

This argument should be reversed. It is precisely the literary refinement of the court of Solomon that casts doubt on the likelihood of the assembly of a connected proto-Pentateuch at that time. In the separate materials of Genesis and in the early units of the David story, the writers of the tenth century produced creative reworkings of established forms, and this is precisely what a refined and innovative literary sensibility would attempt in the ancient Near East. The Pentateuch, on the other hand, even in its Yahwistic form, cannot be viewed as the product of an innovative reworking of genre at all. On the contrary, it is the product of a general disregarding and even dissolution of traditional generic forms. This is just what one might expect from historians in the exilic period, when literary interests were heavily subordinated to theological concerns, concerns that included a manifest and urgent need to produce an integrated history in response to the social (and theological) crisis that confronted them.

The radical mixing of genres in the Pentateuch is a very different matter from the interest in and respect for form clearly

---

pened that the Priestly school preserved the opening words of an initial chapter they were replacing with their own composition.

visible in the individual Yahwistic/Davidic productions. Indeed, all the evidence of the cultural aspirations of the court of David and Solomon shows a cosmopolitan desire to share in, exploit, and adapt the forms of the older and wealthier societies around Israel. The Succession Narrative and units like Genesis 2–11 or 12–36, in other words, can be understood as parallel constructions to the Solomonic Temple or the Davidic-Solomonic national administrative structure, both of which were creative adaptations of closely observed foreign forms. The later construction of the Tetrateuch/Pentateuch involves an entirely different sort of cultural enterprise, one more readily to be associated with a period like the seventh or even the sixth century, and in any event unlikely to have coexisted with the very different principles underlying the initial composition of the different bodies of material that would later become the "J" elements of the Pentateuch.

Considerations of genre add further weight to the argument against the early composition of a unified Yahwistic epic history, for the Yahwistic corpus is not and never was an epic, oral or written, in poetry or prose. It is fair to use the term *epic* as an analogy, and the genre of Near Eastern epic can also be seen as a direct model for a specific unit like Genesis 2–11, but to the extent that the whole Yahwistic corpus does form a kind of epic, it is not a kind of epic that can readily be associated with the tenth century. At times the argument is directly made that an old poetic epic underlies the Yahwistic material, a claim forcefully made by W. F. Albright (see esp. *Yahweh and the Gods of Canaan*). In a recent restatement of this argument, Frank Cross writes that

Israel's religion emerged from a mythopoetic past under the impact of certain historical experiences which stimulated the creation of an epic cycle and its associated covenant rites of the early time. . . . The epic form, designed to recreate and give meaning to the historical experiences of a people or nation, is not merely or simply historical. In epic narrative, a people and their god or gods interact in the temporal course of events. . . . Israel's choice of the epic form to express religious reality, and the evolution of this form to centrality in their cultic drama, illustrates both the linkage of the religion of Israel to its Canaanite past and the appearance of novelty in Israel's peculiar religious concern with the "historical." (*Canaanite Myth*, viii–ix)

Cross seeks to account in this way for the sudden appearance of the Yahwistic corpus in the early monarchy, but the poetic elements in the Pentateuch cannot persuasively be shown to reflect a Hebrew poetic epic tradition.[20] Further uncertainty resides in his effort to identify Hebrew prose narrative as taking the place of Ugaritic mythic epic in religious ritual or "cultic drama." Cross's argument represents a welcome assertion of the importance of continuities with the earlier epic traditions, but it is difficult to feel that the linkage is so direct as he proposes, or applicable to the large scale of the whole Yahwistic corpus.

Short of this claim, it is often proposed that various collections of sagas and saga cycles lay ready to the Yahwist's hand and simply needed to be stitched together into a kind of prose epic. The Yahwistic corpus, however, is a sprawling work that includes some saga cycles but much other material as well, most of which is far removed from any immediate roots in oral tradition. This is not to say that the problems with any easy analogy of the Yahwistic corpus to the epic tradition should lead to the opposite extreme of rejecting epic as a contributing factor in the rise of Hebrew narrative. As I have argued in the last two chapters, Mesopotamian epic had a pronounced influence on the early Hebrew tradition, directly visible in the opening section of Genesis; it is also indirectly visible in epic elements in the David story, as will be seen in the next chapter.

To say that Genesis 2–11 is a historicized and prosaic reworking of the older epic traditions is, however, very far from claiming that the entire Yahwistic corpus can meaningfully be viewed as a direct translation into prose of the norms of epic.

---

[20] For a detailed discussion of this point, see Conroy, "Hebrew Epic: Historical Notes and Critical Reflections."

The confusion on this important point stems from a combination of two factors: first, the fact that one can rightly speak of Near Eastern epics, and second, the fact that the epics we have all grown up on are not the Akkadian epics but those of Homer and Virgil and their successors. Once we begin to speak of the epic aspects of J, we naturally begin to think of it by analogy to the Homeric epics. These analogies can be very useful, and are historically grounded in the clear development of many characteristics of epic from second-millennium Mesopotamia into first-millennium Greece. At the same time, it is necessary to use great care in analogizing to such a different time and place, as the Homeric epics show as many differences as similarities vis-à-vis Akkadian epics like *Atrahasis* or *Gilgamesh.*

As early as the Old Babylonian period, and certainly by the Middle Babylonian, the Akkadian epics had left the realm of oral composition and moved into a largely if not purely literary sphere. The Homeric epics were not only produced differently, but over the course of the centuries they attained a scale and elaboration far beyond anything found in Sumerian or Akkadian epic. In thematic development, characterization, dialogue, and imagery, the Homeric epics are the products of a different world. A major problem here is a very simple one: that of scale. We are so used to the length of the *Iliad*, which runs to over fifteen thousand lines, that we have no difficulty imagining the Yahwistic corpus as a single epic as well. Yet the Akkadian epics typically are only a few hundred lines long, and even the longest do not begin to approach the scale of the Yahwistic materials taken as a whole.

An analogy can still be made to Homer, but not to either of the epics alone. To take the example of Genesis, within its Near Eastern context it reads less like a single epic than like a combination of several different epics. It is as if an editor had attached the *Iliad* and the *Odyssey*, with the broad canvas of the stories of the patriarchs corresponding to the *Iliad*, and the Joseph novella corresponding to the *Odyssey*. Even this analogy only yields a rough thematic equivalent to Genesis 12–36 plus

37–50, so we will need to tack on Hesiod's *Theogony* at the beginning as an equivalent to the primeval history in Genesis 2–11. Some narrative transitions would need to be added and some of the thematic similarities developed, but the job could be done.

The problem of scale is significant, though not decisive; one might imagine a hypertrophy of Mesopotamian form, but for the fact that the Yahwistic materials are so disparate. To take Genesis alone, the text actually contains not three epics but three very distinct literary forms: a creation-flood epic, a collection of oral sagas and saga cycles, a wisdom-oriented novella. To unite these materials would have seemed even stranger to a tenth-century audience than the amalgamation of Hesiod and Homer would have seemed to eighth-century Greece. It is possible to imagine a later Alexandrian editor who might have tried to unify and harmonize the old Greek epics in such a manner. The result, however, would certainly have looked shapeless and unwieldy to the poets who crafted the original texts, and this is how "the Yahwistic epic" would have looked to any practitioner of Near Eastern epic. Here I am speaking only of the material in Genesis; the whole body of Yahwistic material in the Pentateuch would have presented an even stranger violation of known narrative forms. An editor who would force such disparate material together into such a vast and bulky form would most probably work in a later era, after the period in which epic was actively being created and reworked. This editor would have been someone no longer concerned with carrying on the literary tradition in the sense of creative authorship, but rather a compiler and harmonizer of old materials that were in danger of being lost or left behind by changing circumstances.[21]

---

[21]This issue can be pursued by considering the example we do have of the reworking of the two Homeric epics within a single text, namely the *Aeneid*. Virgil's creative adaptation of a living epic tradition led him to produce an "Odyssean" first half and an "Iliadic" second half of his epic, but the contrast to Genesis is immediately apparent. Far from stitching together versions of

Allowing for the long independent existence of the separate units that eventually became Genesis argues against the search for a single authorial intention, but still admits of (and even assumes) a single community in which they were created and transmitted. The existence of a common tradition amply accounts for the observable interplay between, for example, the stories of the patriarchs and the Joseph story, just as the *Odyssey* presupposes an Iliadic account of the Trojan war, though it is a separate composition and indeed never refers directly to the *Iliad*. Undoubtedly as works of Hebrew narrative were produced and transmitted they came to the attention of the composers of other works, and the recurrence of patterns like the triumph of the younger brother is a clear indication of a common tradition, even while the many differences between the two texts show their independence as compositions.[22]

It remains perfectly appropriate to speak of the Yahwistic school, but the achievement of these writers was both less and more than was supposed by a scholar like von Rad. Von Rad saw not only the Pentateuch but also the Book of Joshua as forming a united Hexateuch already complete in its essence by the time of Solomon, with the later additions by the Elohist and the Priestly sources contributing "no more than variations upon the massive theme of the Yahwist's conception, despite their admittedly great theological originality" ("Form-Critical Problem of the Hexateuch," 74). If the Yahwists' productions now seem less monumental, the gain is a much clearer, and

---

the two Homeric epics to produce a forty-eight-book mega-epic, Virgil blended elements from both into a shapely twelve-book epic not quite ten thousand lines long, less than two thirds the length of the *Iliad* alone.

[22]Thus, against R. E. Clements's objection to Rendtorff (see note 17), the self-sufficiency of the individual compositions does not require us to assume the hermetic isolation of the traditions, or indeed of the texts, from one another. To pursue the analogy of separate compositions to the Homeric epics, we can recognize both Homeric poems as stemming from the same milieu, possibly even from the same poet in their present form; but we would err in considering the two epics to be meant to form a unified whole, a view that could lead toward unprofitable efforts to harmonize the two epics' very different attitudes toward the heroic tradition they both rework.

more plausible, picture of a time of great cultural ferment, a period of tremendous and creative experimentation in a wide variety of directions.

The Yahwists can be credited with the production of an entire library of varied works. They took up the form of Akkadian epic in producing their own version of the story of the creation and Flood; they wrote down their oral traditions of the patriarchs; they (and/or the Elohists) composed a novella of Joseph; they wrote down versions of the Exodus and the more recent stories of the conquest of Canaan. Indeed, there is no reason to suppose that other, similar works were not also produced by the early Yahwists and their contemporaries, both the first of the chronicles to which the Deuteronomists allude and quite likely other literary compositions as well, texts that have passed into oblivion simply because they were not included in the eventual compilation of the unified Yahwistic corpus.

The two overall options for the dating of J, early and late, both present the possibility of literary relations with the Deuteronomistic historical material. The nature of these relations, however, is dependent as much upon the development of the Deuteronomistic history as on the dating of J, and it is now necessary to consider the less drastic but still major shifts in recent views of the dating of the Deuteronomistic history.

The Yahwists and the Deuteronomists

The fundamental questions at issue in the dating of the Deuteronomistic history are two: when did it reach its basic overall form, and how freely were earlier materials treated in the composition of the overall history? The questions are parallel to those concerning the Yahwist: was there a single Deuteronomistic historian, or was there only a Deuteronomistic redactor who combined fully formed source materials with no more than an occasional editorial clarification or expansion? Secondly, whether the Deuteronomistic history was the creation of a single historian or of a broad "traditio-historical" process, did the overall collection reach its basic form during the later years of the monarchy or only during the Exile?

As the Deuteronomistic history closes with the freeing from prison of Jehoiachin, king of Judah, by the Babylonian king Evil-merodach in 550 (2 Kings 25:27 ff.), it has usually been supposed that the Deuteronomistic historian composed his history at about that time. As his account of the early monarchy, the historian was thought by Wellhausen and his followers to have put together two sources with quite different perspectives: the "Early Source," highly favorable to the monarchy and dating from the time of Solomon, and the "Late Source," influenced by eighth-century prophecy and skeptical of the monarchy, written sometime between 750 and 650. Recently, however, several scholars have argued that the divergent views of the monarchy do not reflect conflicts in two old sources but instead are the results of two editions of the overall Deuteronomistic history itself.

In this view, though the Deuteronomistic historian presumably used specific documents like those identified by Rost, there was no overall source apart from some possible use of court chronicles. The basic history was composed in the later years of the monarchy, and then reedited during the Exile. Frank Cross, for example, has argued that a two-edition theory best accounts for the odd juxtapositions of promonarchy and antimonarchy passages. A promonarchic first edition was produced at the time of Josiah's reform, which began in about 621. In its political aspect, "The Deuteronomistic history . . . may be described as a propaganda work of the Josianic reformation and imperial program" (*Canaanite Myth,* 284). The history was addressed not only to Josiah's subjects in Judah but also to the North, calling for the tribes in what remained of the Northern Kingdom to return to Judah and to God's sole legitimate shrine in Jerusalem.

Josiah's reforms were advanced in a period of political as well as religious ferment, at a time when Assyria's dominance in the region was waning. Judah's period of relative independence was followed, however, by the ascendancy of Babylon, the end of the monarchy, and the deportations of many of the people's leaders to Babylon. Faced with this situation, an exilic historian reedited the Deuteronomistic history, adding the antimonarchic passages that now exist there and bringing the chronology down to 550, forty years into the Exile. In Cross's view, the basic Deuteronomistic history (Dtr$_1$) reflects the qualified optimism of the age of Josiah, laying great stress on the faithfulness of David as the cause of God's willingness to sustain the monarchy, and the nation, in later times. The second edition (Dtr$_2$) reflects exilic times in its scattered additions, which are to be seen as secondary to the work as a whole.

Other scholars have argued for no fewer than three editions of the Deuteronomistic history. Following suggestions put forward by the younger Rudolph Smend,[23] Timo Veijola postulates a promonarchic first edition, DtrG, in which even Saul is seen purely positively, posing the unresolved riddle as to why God should have rejected him. A second, law-oriented or nomistic, edition (DtrN) took up DtrG and "rendered it almost unrecognizable through a far-reaching revision" (*Das Königtum*, 119). In an analysis of the David story, Veijola sees another, prophetically oriented, edition of the work, which would have been produced sometime between the composition of DtrG in around 580 and the final edition, DtrN, in around 560.[24]

These new theories have significant literary consequences. There is a general assumption that the negative assessments of the monarchy in the text do not accurately reflect early opposition to the establishment of the monarchy but instead are closely related to changes in perception following the fall of the monarchy and the onset of the Exile. In these views, the antimonarchic passages are to be seen as revisionist commentary on a previously positive story. Within these views, priority can

---

[23]"Das Gesetz und die Völker," in Wolff, ed., *Probleme biblischer Theologie*. The volume contains several other important essays as well.

[24]Timo Veijola, *Die ewige Dynastie*. In both books, he develops the theory of three editions advanced by Walter Dietrich in *Prophetie und Geschichte*.

be given to the Josianic reform fifty years before the Exile (Cross) or to the Exile itself as the essential locus of the origin of the history and the central problem to which it is addressed (Veijola, Smend, Dietrich).[25]

The second area of literary consequence is to be found in the weight given to whatever earlier sources were used by the Deuteronomistic historian or historians. The effect of these arguments is to propose the basic formation of Deuteronomistic historical writing in the late seventh century or later, and to deemphasize the independent importance, and the sheer extent, of earlier materials within it. This corollary of a late dating is carried to its furthest extent by John Van Seters, whose recent book *In Search of History* is concerned to argue that biblical historiography developed out of roots in Near Eastern historiography of the middle first millennium, and not the later second millennium as generally supposed. Van Seters compares the Deuteronomistic historian to Herodotus and argues that Bible scholarship is perpetuating the naive assessments of ancient historiography common to the nineteenth century, when Herodotus was viewed as the careful compiler of earlier written sources and legends. Herodotus has long since been recognized as a creative reworker, and at times the free inventer, of his material, and the Deuteronomistic historian should be seen similarly. Van Seters locates the production of the Deuteronomistic history squarely within the Exile, dismissing theories of a pre-exilic first edition. So enthusiastic is Van Seters in his desire to give full credit to this exilic historian that he denies the importance, and perhaps even the existence, of court annals and chronicles that would have served as detailed written sources; he prefers to postulate that the Deuteronomistic his-

---

[25]Hans-Detlef Hoffmann has argued that the whole theme of reform is a late exilic or even postexilic concern; the mentions of reforms like that by Josiah do not indicate a full-fledged historical program at that date but are simply illustrations of the theme of the importance of reform. Thus the Deuteronomistic history was composed during or even at the end of the Exile, under prophetic inspiration (*Reform und Reformen*).

torian could have reconstructed his chronology from examination of monumental inscriptions (301). Throughout his discussion, Van Seters heavily discounts the importance of earlier sources within the Deuteronomistic history:

The tendency to separate Dtr's framework from the transmitted materials, as if Dtr's work was to be found only in the former, must also be given up. There is, in fact, a reciprocal relationship between the thematic framework and the received material such that Dtr left very little of it as it was. (320)

He denies outright that the "Ark Narrative" identified by Rost, and often studied since then, was ever an independent text (350); the only certain independent document is the Succession Narrative, but this should be dated *after* the composition of the Deuteronomistic history, to which it is a late, polemical, anti-Davidic addition.

It is unlikely that Van Seters will find much agreement on the bolder aspects of his thesis, and initial reaction in reviews of his book has been guarded at best. The analogy to Herodotus, however, is very suggestive, and it is remarkable that it has never been seriously advanced before. If one corrects for Van Seters's drive to attribute total control and free creativity to the Deuteronomistic historian, his views do present a more than usually coherent picture of how the Deuteronomistic history might have developed as an essentially exilic document.

A Working Hypothesis

In the foregoing survey of current debate, I have indicated where my personal sympathies lie, but it would be premature to attempt a definite conclusion in favor of one of the competing positions as against the others. To call such a decision premature is, indeed, to speak optimistically; in a pessimistic vein, one may well wonder whether any certain or even probable decisions can ever be reached. All the same, one can make considerable progress in literary analysis even within the constraints imposed by the existing uncertainties. My purpose in concluding will be to sketch out my own assessment of the possibilities, which will guide the discussion in the following chapters. In general, the analyses in the next chapters do not stand or fall upon acceptance of this assessment, though often they would need significant modification if the questions of composition and dating are weighed differently. The problem of the hermeneutic circle also arises, as the ensuing discussion is simultaneously shaped by and shapes the assessment of dating, since textual analysis provides much of the evidence on which any conclusion is to be reached. The following assessment is thus a working hypothesis to be both illustrated by, and tested against, the evidence brought forward in the next two chapters.

Like most of the writers discussed above, I tend to view the formation of the Yahwistic and Deuteronomistic corpuses in parallel terms. In both cases, one may well be skeptical of claims for the sudden creation of such extended prose narratives, so generically mixed, at a single time, whether Solomonic or exilic. If both bodies of material are the product of gradual growth, the result would seem to be a long period of mutual influence among the separate materials eventually united in the Pentateuch and in Joshua through 2 Kings. The precise outlines of the original materials must remain obscure in many places, but they can largely be recovered in others. In working with the David story, it appears that the different literary patterns observable in the text can often be closely associated with the separate units isolated by Rost and others after him. These literary patterns thus support the theory of the originally independent existence of the Ark Narrative and of the History of David's Rise; the latter text appears to have gone through two quite different versions before its incorporation into the Deuteronomistic history.

The resulting picture of the Deuteronomistic historian is a mixed one. I agree with Van Seters that this historian was probably the first to create an overall history, and in so doing he interwove his sources with great skill and with more literary sensitivity than he is often credited with having possessed. Against Van Seters, I believe that earlier scholars are correct in accounting for the wide variety of materials, particularly in the David story, as stemming from pre-Deuteronomistic sources. The Deuteronomistic historian altered these sources in places, but usually by expansion rather than by outright suppression; as for oral material, such as the early stories about Saul, this appears to have been treated with rather greater freedom.

It is not impossible that some of the tensions in the material result from two editions of the overall history, but the arguments for two (or three) editions often lack literary depth; they assume a remarkable purity in the sources used by the first edition, a univocality of theme that is more plausible in simple chronicle-writing than in developed historiography—or in developed epic, for that matter. Thus the two-edition hypotheses remain rather close to the literary methods of an older generation, in which almost any thematic complexity was taken to reflect the presence of one of the several separate sources of the classic documentary hypothesis. A two-edition hypothesis remains plausible, but if a single edition is to be favored, then certainly the Exile is its home, both in view of its ending and in view of the importance of exilic themes throughout.

The late dating of both the Yahwist and the Deuteronomistic historian does not require us to take all credit away from the Solomonic era. On the contrary, great weight can be given to the literary and historiographic advances of the end of David's reign and of Solomon's reign. It is perfectly plausible that Genesis 2–11 arose at that time as a historicizing translation of late-second-millennium creation-flood epic, and that, at the same time, the first efforts were made to expand historical chronicle along epic lines; a good example of this latter effort will be seen in the next chapter, in the Ark Narrative. Under the double influence of early Yahwistic narrative and of Davidic-Solomonic expanded chronicle, the History of David's Rise was written and then reworked into an early but highly developed version of epic historiography.

Thus, before the time of the Deuteronomistic historian or of the overall collection and integration of the Yahwistic corpus, Hebrew narrative had reached a full flowering, most strikingly seen in the Succession Narrative, which was probably not an eyewitness narrative from Solomon's reign but a rather later, wisdom-oriented composition. As the Deuteronomistic historical texts developed against the background of the Yahwistic stories, they exerted reciprocal influence on the Yahwistic corpus. If the materials of Genesis 12–36 were reworked by an exilic Yahwistic author in the course of assembling a unified history of early times, then one may well see Deuteronomistic influence in the presentation of the themes of memory and of exile. It is perfectly possible, on the other hand, that the unified Yahwistic corpus antedates the Deuteronomistic history; in this event, the lines of influence on these themes would presumably run the other way. Even supposing a late assembly of J, however, the early materials of the David story already seem to presuppose something rather like the Yahwistic form of Genesis 2–11, of at least a version of the patriarchal narratives,[26] and of the Exodus story.

These are the assumptions that govern the discussion to follow. If Genesis 2–11 has shown epic materials being treated in a quasi-historical way, the next step in tracing the growth of Hebrew narrative is to show the converse: the growth of epic themes, techniques, and perspectives within prose narrative of historical events. I will focus on the David story, whose several stages of recoverable growth show the whole process with un-

---

[26]See Wagner, *A Literary Analysis of Genesis 12–36,* for arguments in favor of a Yahwistic nucleus of the patriarchal narratives dating to around 1000; Wagner envisions this early collection as undergoing an Elohistic revision in around 750, and finally being reedited and joined to the primeval material and the Joseph story in the sixth century.

usual clarity. In so doing, I will seek to answer the question to which this study owes its genesis: How did the David story, that astonishing masterpiece of historical narrative, come into being?

5. The Growth of the David Story

Epic and Saga in the Ark Narrative

The several stages of the growth of the David story show a gradual integration of the narrative values of poetic epic and prose history. As perhaps the earliest extended narrative unit within 1–2 Samuel, the Ark Narrative early in 1 Samuel provides an exemplary case of an early attempt to construct an extended historical narrative out of a sequence of incidents. This narrative, which takes up less than four chapters (2:12–17, 22–25 plus 4:1b–7:1), is simply constructed, with a single plot-line and a clearly discernible and fundamentally single purpose: to account for the scandal of the Philistine capture of the Ark of the Covenant and its subsequent return to Hebrew possession. How could Yahweh have allowed this disaster to befall his Ark, the symbol and locus of his presence in Israel?

In contrast to later developments in the David story, the Ark Narrative is marked in general by a univocality of conception and presentation that rapidly disappears in the evolution of 1–2 Samuel. Here there is scarcely any ambiguity of character or complexity of motive, no interweaving of plot and subplot, and little developed dialogue between characters. Within these constraints, however, many features of fully developed Hebrew historiography already begin to appear, providing a good opportunity to observe the first development of Hebrew chronicle in the direction of poetic and epic values. In its overall structure, the Ark Narrative shows an ambitious mingling of genres, and if these genres are not so much blended as juxtaposed, this very juxtaposition can serve to show the beginnings of the process by which later Hebrew historiography transcended existing categories of genre in a more far-reaching way. The story approaches the problem of the loss of the Ark through a doubling of genres: through a family saga of Eli and his sons, and through a historicized mythic-epic encounter between Yahweh and Dagon, chief god of the Philistines. These two aspects of the story are essentially joined sequentially; the family saga explains the origins of the crisis; the combat between God and Dagon provides its resolution. These two elements flesh out a chronicle of the defeat of the Israelites in battle, the loss of the Ark, and its return after a plague breaks out among the Philistines.

The result is somewhat uneven in narrative terms, as the emphases and narrative techniques change markedly as the story moves from the family saga to the balance of the account. In the family saga, the focus is on human characters, the aging Eli and his wicked sons Hophni and Phinehas; in the balance of the story, there are no named human characters at all, and events in Philistine territory, such as the plague, are secondary results of the divine battle between Yahweh and Dagon.

The family saga begins by painting a vivid picture of the criminal behavior of Eli's sons, who subvert the system of temple sacrifice through their own greed. They send their servants to take the best portions of meat, by force if necessary, before the meat has even been burnt in sacrifice (2:12–17). The style of the episode is lively and ironic from the very start: "Now the sons of Eli were scoundrels and had no regard for the Lord." A literal translation of this line can make clearer the themes that are being introduced here: "Now the sons of Eli were sons of worthlessness; they did not know Yahweh." Two themes are central here: the theme of sonship and the theme of knowledge, both of which are important to the Ark Narrative that follows, and indeed to the David story as a whole.

"Sons of worthlessness" is a relatively common term in 1–2 Samuel, less often in other books of the Bible, for "good-for-nothings." Here, the direct juxtaposition of "sons of Eli" and "sons of worthlessness" creates an ironic tension between lineage and character, a tension reinforced by an echo of Eli's own name in the second phrase: *beney 'Eli, beney beli-ya'al.*[1] Along with the sons' separation from the upright character of their father goes their denial of their relationship to Yahweh, and here, as often, the verb "to know," *yada'*, can best be considered in its technical sense in treaty language: "to be loyal; to uphold a treaty."[2] From the start, the story of the family's failings has overtones of a general disruption of relations between God and his people. The passage ends by stressing that "the sin of the young men was very great in the eyes of the Lord; for the men treated the offering of the Lord with contempt" (2:17). The verb *na'atz*, "to treat with contempt, despise, condemn, reject, blaspheme," almost always describes a radical breakdown in relations between God and his people.[3]

As the people's representatives before God, Eli's sons bear a primary responsibility in maintaining the covenantal relationship through the obedience and service embodied in the system of sacrifice. Consequently, a judgment visited on them will appropriately take the form of a punishment affecting the people

---

[1] The parallelism may be closer still, if we treat *beliya'al* as a proper name; the KJV in fact translates the phrase as "sons of Belial." Modern dictionaries view the word purely as a common noun (a compound of *beli*, "without," and *ya'al*, "profit"), but the usage of the phrase "sons of X" in 1–2 Samuel rather strongly argues in favor of reading *beliya'al* as a symbolic proper name. Of some three hundred occurrences of the phrase "son(s) of . . ." in 1–2 Samuel, all but twenty-one are followed by a proper name. Of these twenty-one, nine are forms of "sons of *beliya'al*." The remaining dozen occurrences are found in three phrases: "son of valor," "son of death," and "son of (x) years." These phrases occur at least as often in 1–2 Samuel alone as they do in the entire rest of the Bible. "Son of death," which occurs three times, and is usually translated as "sure to die," is clearly in origin a reference to Maweth/Mot, the Canaanite god of death. Whether or not "son of valor" and "son of worthlessness" have so direct a personal referent, the phrase "son of worthlessness" must be regarded as a live metaphor, rather than a merely conventional phrase. See the discussion of Kiel, *The Book of Samuel*, 23.

[2] See Huffmon, "The Treaty Background of Hebrew Yada'," which discusses the Hebrew usage in light of Hittite and Akkadian parallels.

[3] Interestingly, on the two occasions when the verb is used for a purely human relation, it describes the wickedness of sons who reject their father's counsel (Prov. 5:12; 15:5).

as a whole, and the sin of Eli's sons provides the basis for understanding the loss of the Ark.

The punishment comes quickly. Hearing of his sons' wickedness, Eli reproves them, but they pay no attention (2:22–25); then comes the war with the Philistines. After an initial defeat, the Israelite elders ask for the Ark to be brought into the battle. Hophni and Phinehas accompany it, only to be slain and have the Ark captured by the Philistines (4:1–11). Hearing this news, Eli dies, in a scene doubled with an account of the hearing of the news by his pregnant daughter-in-law; the news brings on premature labor, and she dies soon after the child's birth. The text stresses that both Eli and his daughter-in-law die of shock and grief at the news of the capture of the Ark rather than at the news of the deaths of Hophni and Phinehas (4:12–22).

Then follows the great battle between Yahweh and Dagon. The Philistines place the Ark in Dagon's temple, and the next day the statue of Dagon is found prostrated before the Ark. They set the statue back in its place, but on the following day, matters have gone further: Dagon is again prostrate, but now his head and hands have been cut off. The story is told entirely from a human point of view, with no direct representation of the struggle between Yahweh and Dagon, but the scene is very clearly a prosaic and historicist representation of a divine battle, as Patrick Miller and J. J. M. Roberts have shown in their recent study of the Ark Narrative.[4]

This episode may be regarded as a secondary elaboration of the historical events that now follow this scene, in which a plague breaks out in each Philistine city where the Ark is kept. The Philistines are forced to return the Ark to Israel, along with golden effigies of five tumors and five mice, representing the plague and the accompanying rodent infestation in the five Philistine cities. The story ends with an account of the joyful reception of the Ark in Israelite territory, an initial disaster

---

[4]*The Hand of the Lord: A Reassessment of the "Ark Narrative" of 1 Samuel;* for example, the cutting off of the "palms of the hands" of Dagon (5:4) has direct parallels in Ugaritic poetic narratives of battles between gods.

when seventy Israelites perish through improper handling of the Ark,[5] and the final establishment of a duly consecrated priest, Eleazar the son of Abinadab, to tend the Ark.

The Ark Narrative gives a decidedly archaic impression, with its simplicity of narrative line and action, and even at times a certain crudeness, as when it dwells gleefully on the five golden tumors by which the hapless Philistines represent their affliction. Characterizations are largely absolute, where they appear at all; the scope of the action is modest; a single cause is presented for the disaster of the capture of the Ark. The story still moves well within the orbit of traditional chronicle, and in some ways the narrative is less developed than the most extended Mesopotamian accounts discussed above in chapter 2.

At the same time, however, the story has been expanded significantly, and the elements of family saga and the reworking of poetic epic in the struggle of Yahweh against Dagon are part of a far-reaching development toward a genuine merging of epic and chronicle. A variety of elements appear prominently here that are commonly found in epic but rarely if ever in the historical prose of other countries. We might begin with the story's basic structure. Though it is reasonable to suppose that the saga of Eli and his sons was attached to the story of the capture of the Ark as a way of accounting for that disaster, the text naturally presents the issue the other way around: the capture of the Ark is a result of God's response to the wickedness of Hophni and Phinehas.

What is involved in this conception may be compared to the ironic pitting of evil against evil in the *Gilgamesh Epic*. As an answer to Gilgamesh's oppression of his people, the gods create Enkidu, who oppresses the people still further; only grad-

---

[5]The Hebrew text presents this episode in what is probably a garbled form, with the seventy killed by looking into the Ark; it is likely that the story originally saw the problem as a lack of qualified priests in the town of Bethshemesh, where the Ark is first brought; this leads to the moving of the Ark to Kiriath-jearim, where it is properly attended. See McCarter, *1 Samuel*, 128 ff.

ually, and without the conscious participation of the earthly characters themselves, does this combination of evils resolve into good, as the gods' plan works itself out. The situation is similar in the Ark Narrative: Hophni and Phinehas oppress the people whose sacrifices they should be assisting and sin against God, who rectifies the situation with what at first appears to be a greater evil, the loss of the Ark. This evil proves to be a good, in two ways. First, it provides a decisive testimony to the power of God over Dagon and his people; secondly, and equally importantly, it eventually leads to the restoration of an honest priesthood for the Ark, in the person of Eleazar ben Abinadab.

If an element of epic irony is now to be seen in historical process, so too are elements of epic characterization. One index of this shift is the symbolic naming of characters. Both in epic and in historiography, to be sure, characters could have names of symbolic importance. The difference lay in the nature and function of these names. Typically, a historical king's name signified his eternal relation with his patron god, as in the many names built around a divine name. Even when a name was changed, as when Amenhotep changed his name to Akhnaton, the change signified a realignment toward the eternal forces of the mythic world. By contrast, an epic hero's name could be tied more closely to his particular story, as in Ziusudra, "He Who Found Life," or the *Gilgamesh Epic*'s folk etymology of Enkidu from *enqata*, "wise," at the point in the story when he is seduced.

In the Ark Narrative, there is the striking instance of the naming of Phinehas's newborn son by his dying wife. She names him Ichabod, which can be translated as "Alas for the Glory": "And she said, 'The glory [*kabod*] has been exiled from Israel' " (4:21–22). Ichabod is named, not for any personal quality in himself or even in his family, but as a reflection on the historical events being recounted. The symbolism behind the name actually becomes a framing device around the "exile" of the Ark. Late in the story, arguing that the Ark must be returned to Israel along with golden offerings, the Philistine priests tell their people that they must "give glory [*kabod*] to the God of Israel" (6:5). These are the only occurrences of the word in the Ark Narrative, and indeed the only occurrences in 1–2 Samuel, apart from a use in the Song of Hannah. Thus the loss and return of the *kabod* to Israel frame the story.

Further expanding the thematic reach of prose narrative, the disparate elements that make up the story are linked together through a variety of overall themes, comparable to the clothing motif in the *Gilgamesh Epic*. There is the theme of the hand of the Lord, which lies heavily on the Philistines and leads to the cutting off of Dagon's hands—a displaced punishment for the greedy hands that thrust forks into the sacrificial pots at the start of the story.[6] There is also the theme of sight. The narrative begins with the half-blind Eli, whose weakness of sight certainly symbolizes his inability to oversee his sons effectively, and it progresses to the public witnessing of the power of God by the Philistines, concluding with the joy of the Israelites when "they lifted up their eyes and saw the Ark and rejoiced to see it"—a tripling of expressions for seeing (6:13). These themes function as unifying leitmotifs across the elements of saga, chronicle, and mythic epic that have been woven together to form the story.

Perhaps the most basic unifying element, however, is the use of the Yahwistic Exodus story. The comparison appears at each stage of the Ark Narrative: in the initial account of the wickedness of Hophni and Phinehas, in the story of the battle, and in the preparations for the return of the Ark. The various uses of this older story show subtle direct and indirect shaping of the representation of contemporary history in the light of the emblematic early history of the people.

Two recurrences of language associated with the departure from Egypt frame the initial description of the wickedness of Hophni and Phinehas in 2:12–17, 22–25. We are first told of

---

[6]See Miller and Roberts, *Hand of the Lord*, for a full exposition of this theme.

the brothers that "they did not know the Lord" (*lo' yad'u 'et-YHWH*); this theme is a hallmark of the story of the freeing of the Hebrews from bondage in Egypt. Specifically, it is Pharaoh who declares, "I do not know the Lord" (*lo' yada'ti 'et-YHWH*, Exod. 5:2).[7] The echo of Pharaoh is strengthened at the end of the introductory section of the story, when the brothers refuse to listen to Eli's warnings: "But they would not listen to the voice of their father; for it was the desire of the Lord to slay them" (2:25). Thus the sons' refusal to listen to the voice of their father stems from God's desire to punish them, just as Pharaoh's refusal to listen to the voice of the Lord (Exod. 5:2, etc.) ultimately results from God's hardening of his heart in order to make an example of the Egyptians (Exod. 10:1–2, etc.).

These echoes of the Exodus story are developed explicitly as the story progresses. When the Philistines learn that the Ark has been brought into battle, they are thrown into consternation:

The Philistines were afraid; for they said, "A god has come into the camp." And they said, "Woe to us! For nothing like this has happened before. Woe to us! Who can deliver us from the power of these mighty gods? These are the gods who smote the Egyptians with every sort of plague in the wilderness. Take courage, and acquit yourselves like men, O Philistines, lest you become slaves to the Hebrews as they have been to you; acquit yourselves like men and fight." (4:7–9)

The confusion of the Philistines is comically shown by their conflicting cries and their garbled version of the Exodus story. Unable to understand the unitary nature of Israel's God, they imagine (in their second speech) that Israel has a whole panoply of gods, and along with this theological misconception goes their historical confusion, as they conflate the Egyptian plagues with the Hebrews' wandering in the wilderness. A significant point is reflected in this speech: that an accurate sense

---

[7]The phrase is then used several times of the Egyptians in general, and of the Hebrews themselves (they will know the Lord once he delivers them). These are the only occurrences of this phrase in Genesis through Judges, apart from one reference to the apostate Hebrew generation described in Judg. 2:10.

of history follows from a proper understanding of the divine nature; along with unbelief comes a tendency (witting or unwitting) to distortion, falsehood, and misperception.[8]

The Philistines' confused sense of the past is further seen in their vacillating conception of the historical moment in which they find themselves: in the same breath, they view the appearance of the Ark as a unique event ("nothing like this has happened before") and as a repetition of the history of the Exodus. Indeed, their sense of the unprecedented nature of their troubles is itself an unwitting expression of their resemblance to the Egyptians. As Moses tells Pharaoh, the plagues will be such "as neither your fathers nor your grandfathers have seen, from the day they came on earth to this day" (Exod. 10:6). Ironically, the Philistines' perception of the parallel to the Exodus inspires them to new valor and to their victory in battle, though they little realize that they are setting themselves up for a far worse defeat at Yahweh's hands. By their very attempt to resist the Exodus parallel they fulfill it, since their capturing of the Ark brings on the plague that devastates their land.

The Exodus parallel is further discussed by the Philistine priests, as they recommend returning the Ark: "Why should you harden your hearts as the Egyptians and Pharaoh hardened their hearts? After he had made sport of them, did they not let the people go, and they departed?" (6:6). These lines, which closely follow the Yahwistic language in Exodus

---

[8]Compositional questions could be raised by the doubled cry ("they said . . . and they said"), with the initial, simple perception of "a god" having come into the camp followed by the more elaborate and more comically confused description of the "gods" who smote the Egyptians in the wilderness. Was there originally only the simple first cry, with the second, more elaborate and sophisticated speech added later? In any case, there is no reason to smooth out the differences between the passages as some commentators do, still less to alter "smote with plagues in the wilderness" to "smote with plagues and pestilence." The readings of both the Hebrew text and the Septuagint should not be altered simply because the Philistines' account "is contrary to biblical tradition" (McCarter, 1 Samuel, 104)—that is just the point here, and should no more be excised from the text than the Philistines' mistaken belief that the Hebrews have many gods.

10:1–2, explicitly show the symbolic structuring of the story, in which the Ark plays the role of the Hebrew people in their enslavement in Egypt. Further, just as the Hebrews despoiled the Egyptians in departing, taking the Egyptians' golden jewelry (*keley zahav*, Exod. 3:22, etc.), so too the Ark returns with the five golden tumors and the five golden mice, which are also described as *keley zahav* (6:8).[9]

For all its brevity and the simplicity of many of its elements, the Ark Narrative shows an ambitious expansion of historical prose through introduction of elements both from saga and from mythic epic. Further, it shows a strong influence from the Yahwistic account of the legendary history of early times, seen as a model for the understanding of contemporary history. The time of the Exodus serves as a backdrop for modern history in ways comparable to those in which the flood story is used in the *Erra Epic* and the early adventures of Utnapishtim and Etana serve as reference points for the epic story of Gilgamesh. The shocking modern event is both understood and tamed through the comparison: by portraying the Philistines' golden tumors as parodies of the Egyptians' jewelry, the Ark Narrative presents the Philistines as comically reduced doubles of the greater enemies overcome in the past.

The Ark Narrative's triumphant assertions of continuity with the old times do not preclude an awareness that God's activity in history is no longer quite as direct and spectacular as it used to be. A great battle takes place between Yahweh and Dagon, but no one sees or hears it; the only evidence is the fallen and damaged statue. When Yahweh's power is demonstrated more widely in the land, the result is a single plague, and an ordinary bubonic plague at that, not the multiple and bizarre plagues of blood, darkness, and deaths of firstborn children known from the Exodus story. The demonstration of God's majestic power is sufficiently muted that the Philistines actually

---

[9]See Miller and Roberts, *Hand of the Lord*, 55–56 and notes, for a discussion of this parallel. For further parallels between the Ark Narrative and the Exodus, see Garsiel, *The First Book of Samuel*, 51–4.

need to construct an experiment to test the hypothesis that it is Yahweh who has caused the plague: they put the Ark in a cart drawn by two untrained cows, and see if the cows head for Israelite territory without prompting, as in fact they do (6:7–12). Miracle thus seeks support from hard science, as a result of the increasing orientation of narrative toward earthly settings and observable phenomena. This is a further intensifying of the historicist pressure toward the withdrawal of God from direct action, already visible in the later epic tradition, a withdrawal that will be still more pronounced in the later stages of the David story.

The Ark Narrative remains as willing to distort and even suppress uncomfortable facts as the Assyrian chronicles were: only from scattered references elsewhere in the Bible do we learn that the Philistines destroyed the important shrine at Shiloh at the same time that they captured the Ark. If historical objectivity remains subordinated to theological concerns, the story nevertheless shows a new sense of historical perspective, as seen both in the overall use of the Exodus model and in the particular differences between the Philistine troops' confused idea of the precedent, the Philistine priests' more accurate though belated recognition of the parallel, and the narrator's own construction of his account through a flexible use of direct and indirect allusions to the Exodus. These elements are all developed further in later stages of the composition of the David story. Although the masterly Succession Narrative has received the greatest attention from literary scholars, the very perfection of that narrative renders it somewhat atypical. A less developed and probably earlier unit of material, the History of David's Rise, already shows a fully "poetic" reworking of historical material. Its transformation of the story of David and Goliath provides an unusually good opportunity to observe the flowering of Hebrew narrative after the tentative early experiments represented by the Ark Narrative.

Goliath in the History of David's Rise

The History of David's Rise was first postulated as a once-independent unit by Leonhard Rost, who saw the material in 1 Samuel 16:14 through 2 Samuel 2:5 as forming an account of David's early career and a defense of his overthrow of Saul and Saul's household. Parallels can be found for histories whose purpose is to justify the establishment of a new dynasty, and in particular a Hittite text known as "The Apology of Hattu-šiliš" has many parallels to the story of David's rise.[10] Like David a youngest child, Hattušiliš was a loyal subject of his king (in his case, his nephew) and served as his general; he only began to seek power when the king grew jealous of him and sought to destroy him. Hattušiliš is aided by his patroness, the goddess Ishtar of Šamuha, who had previously resolved to abandon his predecessor and had promised the throne to him. Throughout his account, Hattušiliš emphasizes his loyalty and his moderation, his desire to deal fairly with his king, and his obedience to Ishtar.

Hattušiliš's narrative appears to have been used as a sort of brief before the Hittite senate to justify and consolidate his claim to rule, though the text may additionally have been used by the priests of Ishtar of Šamuha, to whom we may owe its preservation; the text closes by stressing the priority of her cult and the necessity of supporting it fully in the future. Many scholars have supposed that David had a similar need to justify and consolidate his power, at a time when the new monarchy was only beginning to achieve a strong and centralized position of power in the country. Given the divine anointing of Saul, it was necessary for David to show how he could legitimately inherit (and extend) the theological and political mantle of his predecessor, after the civil war that brought him to power.[11]

[10] Otten, ed., *Die Apologie Hattusilis III*. An English translation is in Sturtevant and Bechtel, *A Hittite Chrestomathy*, 42–99.
[11] For a full listing of parallels between the two texts, see the appendix to Herbert Wolf, *The "Apology of Hattušiliš,"* 176–78. Wolf goes too far, though, in

It is reasonable to suppose that an apologetic document of this nature underlies the account of David's introduction to Saul's court, Saul's increasing madness and jealous fear of David, his attempts to destroy his former protégé, and David's reluctant rise to power, culminating in the destruction of Saul's household, the people's choosing of David as king, and his establishment of Jerusalem as his capital. After its initial composition in the early 900s, the text appears to have undergone an extensive reworking, perhaps under prophetic influence, in about the eighth century. The final Deuteronomistic editing of this narrative is generally agreed to have been quite light, largely consisting of expansions to a few speeches in order to bring out Deuteronomistic themes.

Having examined early narrative practices in the Ark Narrative, I would like now to concentrate on the middle stage of the growth of the History of David's Rise, the stage at which it lost its largely apologetic focus and became a broader and richer narrative. A particularly clear intrusion into the original History of David's Rise is the pre-Deuteronomistic story of David and Goliath in 1 Samuel 17. The tale not only doubles the very different account in the previous chapter of Saul's introduction to David but actually causes unusual narrative difficulties. In chapter 16, David enters Saul's court to play the lyre and soothe Saul's depressions, leading Saul to love him greatly and appoint him his armor-bearer (16:21). In the Goliath episode, however, Saul has never even seen David before; he asks his general Abner who David is; Abner also doesn't know (17:55). Why has this incompatible story been inserted here? As I hope to show, this is not a matter of the simple insertion of a charming folktale that a later editor could not resist in-

arguing for a direct dependency of the History of David's Rise on the "Apology." Quite apart from the three hundred years separating the texts, a period during which the Hittite empire ceased to exist, there are major differences between the texts, differences that Wolf chooses not to discuss. All the same, the parallels are extensive, and it is perfectly plausible that comparable circumstances called forth comparable justifying texts in the two cases.

cluding even though it disrupted the story. Rather, the Goliath story is a key element in the reshaping of the History of David's Rise. Furthermore, the Goliath motif is reworked by the Deuteronomistic historian when he joins the History of David's Rise to the other material now around it. The development of the Goliath story thus provides an unusually good opportunity to observe the generic and thematic shaping involved in the creation of the overall story of the rise of the monarchy.

The matter is complicated by the fact that the Goliath story itself appears to be a conflation of two quite different Goliath stories, and there is no general agreement as to the process by which these two stories came into the text. The literary critic should not despair, however, for the very complexity of compositional history will provide us with valuable clues concerning the evolution of biblical narrative. Furthermore, a close literary study of the use of the Goliath story in 1 Samuel will prove to yield important evidence to help establish the relative chronology of the growth of the story and its surrounding narrative.

The Goliath story as it now appears in 1 Samuel 17 is a disruption of its context not only in terms of narrative flow but also in terms of genre. Amid the realistic descriptions of Saul's introduction to David in chapter 16 and David's early military successes in chapter 18, we are suddenly confronted with the story of the Giant-Killer. Goliath, ten feet tall, his breastplate alone weighing a hundred and fifty pounds, taunts the Israelites with the classic threat of all invading monsters: unless a single hero can be found to slay him, the entire people of Israel must become slaves of the Philistines. The young lad David, visiting from the country, wearing no armor, kills the giant with a stone from his sling and wins fame and fortune at the court of King Saul. All that is lacking is that he should be rewarded with marriage to the king's daughter, which in fact is what Saul's troops tell him will be his reward (17:25), though nothing more is said of this idea at the end of the episode; Saul does, however, take David into his service.

The insertion of this episode is all the more surprising as it is not the only version of the slaying of Goliath. A far more historically credible account is preserved in a group of miscellaneous materials at the end of 2 Samuel. There, four different Philistine warriors are killed. The first battle involves David directly; David personally accompanies his army into battle against the Philistines, and grows exhausted.

> Then Ishbibenob, one of the descendants of the giants, whose spear weighed three hundred shekels of bronze, and who was girded with a new sword, thought to kill David. But Abishai the son of Zeruiah came to his aid, and attacked the Philistine and killed him. Then David's men adjured him, "You shall no more go out with us to battle, lest you quench the lamp of Israel." (21:15–17)

The scene here makes sense: David is no mere youth visiting his brothers but the king going into battle. Ishbibenob is only one of many warriors involved in the struggle, rather than a lone, archetypal figure, and at issue is the real-life question of whether a king ought to go personally into the forefront of battle. This episode is followed by accounts of three other skirmishes. In the second of these, one of David's soldiers kills "Goliath the Gittite, the shaft of whose spear was like a weaver's beam" (21:19)—a description also applied to Goliath's spear in the David and Goliath episode. In the final skirmish, David's *brother* slays a Gittite giant who taunts Israel. The whole account concludes, "These four were descended from the giants in Gath; and they fell by the hand of David and by the hand of his servants" (21:22). It may be that the folktale of David and Goliath developed in oral tradition out of memories of the battles here described in sober annalistic style, or the story may be a purely literary composition based directly on the written record. In either case, the story as it now stands in 1 Samuel 17 has taken over specific details from the historical account now preserved in 2 Samuel 21.

Historical criticism adds powerful evidence for the hypothesis of a literary relation between these accounts, one that would go beyond a simple independent development of parallel traditions, for it seems probable that the annalistic account of the defeat of the four Philistine warriors has not always stood at the end of 2 Samuel, which is an unlikely point for the story to appear as the Philistines have long been defeated by then. It is generally agreed that the account of the four battles with the giants belongs instead in 2 Samuel 5, along with the full account of the wars of Saul and David against the Philistines, the wars that cost Saul his life and began the independent career of David. A second such series of anecdotes from the Philistine wars (2 Sam. 23:8–39), originally following directly from the story of the four giants (now divided from it by the hymn in 22:1–23:7), is actually preserved in the parallel account in 1 Chronicles at the appropriate place (11:11 ff.), corresponding to 2 Samuel 5.

Now 2 Samuel 5 is the very end of the History of David's Rise as it is delineated by most scholars, and 5:17–25 still preserves the general account of David's battles against the Philistines.[12] It can be supposed, then, that the historical account of the slayings of Ishbibenob and Goliath originally formed part of the conclusion to the History of David's Rise, but were later displaced, probably by the Deuteronomistic historian; reasons for this displacement will be suggested below.

The introduction of a version of the Goliath story in 1 Samuel 17, then, created a frame in which David's rise begins with an

---

[12]There is no certainty as to the precise end-point of the History of David's Rise. Some scholars include elements beyond chapter 5, pointing particularly to the reappearance of Michal in 6:20–23 and postulating that the text concluded with a version of the permanent establishment of David's dynasty, now described in chapter 7. Others prefer Rost's original suggestion that the document proper ends in 5:10; the material in the balance of chapter 5 could then be viewed as an appendix or a mixture of original material and later additions. As for 5:17–25, the verses relevant to the present discussion, it is clear that they are thematically linked to the preceding account; compare the oracle in 5:19 to those in 1 Sam. 23:2 and 2 Sam. 2:1. Either 5:17–25 originally came somewhat before the present 5:10, or they formed part of an appendix after the formal ending, or else the History of David's Rise extended somewhat beyond the ending proposed by Rost.

initial skirmish against the Philistines and concludes with the decisive vanquishing of the enemy in 2 Samuel 5. Yet the prominence of the Goliath story in its new location, and its intrusiveness there, suggests that most scholars are correct in seeing chapter 17 as an addition made after the initial composition of the History of David's Rise. An exploration of the literary ramifications of the story will suggest why this was done. I have earlier noted that two quite different stories of David and Goliath have been interwoven in chapter 17. One of these, in many ways more expansive and more explicitly theological, seems likely to stem from the late, Deuteronomistic reworking of 1–2 Samuel. This later version, together with the complicated compositional problems raised both by it and by the textual history of the entire chapter, will be discussed in due course. At this point, I wish to take up the other version, which appears to be the original addition to the story, an addition made when the History of David's Rise was originally adapted for theological use and redirected from its original annalistic and apologetic functions.

In seeking to understand the reason for the interpolation of the earlier version of the story of David and Goliath, we may begin by considering what follows from it. As a narrative intrusion, it has no direct consequence at all. This is surprising, as the single combat against Goliath is presented as a decisive struggle. In the later version of the story, indeed, Goliath issues an explicit challenge: that the entire war would be decided by single combat; the loser's people would become the slaves of the winner's people. This does not happen; in chapter 18, hostilities continue as usual. Further, as noted above, Saul does not offer his daughter in marriage to the young hero. Near the end of the interpolation, he makes David general over all his armies (18:5), but when the older story resumes, Saul is shown giving him only the rank of commander of a thousand (18:13), an event perfectly imaginable as a promotion from the rank of armor-bearer bestowed on him in 16:21, before the insertion of the Goliath episode.

The Goliath episode is not without a slightly less direct result, however, for the troops' idea that Goliath's vanquisher should receive the hand of the king's daughter in marriage finds a response later in the interpolation: Saul offers his daughter Merab to David. Yet this offer is very far from being a reward for David's defeat of Goliath; it comes some time later, after David's ongoing successes in battle have made Saul jealous and fearful of his young commander. The offer of Merab is not a reward but a trap: "Then Saul said to David, 'Here is my elder daughter Merab; I will give her to you for a wife; only be valiant for me and fight the Lord's battles.' For Saul thought, 'Let not my hand be upon him, but let the hand of the Philistines be upon him' " (18:17).

Saul's plan is foiled by the modesty (or caution?) of David: protesting that his family is too lowly to deserve to marry the king's daughter, he declines the offer, and Merab is given away to another man.[13] Foiled for the moment, Saul finds a better opportunity with his second daughter, Michal, when he learns that she has fallen in love with David. Saul makes a new offer, carefully improving on the first: now he doubles his approach to David, both making the offer directly and also instructing his attendants to reinforce the offer in private through flattery (18:21–22). When David repeats his objection that he has no wealth with which to make an appropriate marriage present, Saul has a proposal ready, a refinement of his earlier general request that David fight his battles. This proposal is again transmitted through intermediaries:

Then Saul said, "Thus shall you say to David, 'The king desires no marriage present except a hundred foreskins of the Philistines, that he may be avenged of the king's enemies.' " Now Saul thought to make David fall by the hand of the Philistines. And when his servants told David these words, it pleased David well to be the king's son-in-

---

[13]The end of the episode should be read: "And at the time when Merab, Saul's daughter, would have been given to David, she was given to Adriel." The KJV and RSV miss the point here, and translate the initial *w-* as "but" rather than "and."

law. Before the time had expired, David arose and went, along with
his men, and killed two hundred of the Philistines; and David brought
their foreskins, which were given in full number to the king, that he
might become the king's son-in-law. And Saul gave him his daughter
Michal for a wife. (18:25–27)

In the Ark Narrative, the wicked Philistines prepared their own
ruin by their efforts to harm the good. Here too Saul, attempting to destroy David, succeeds only in giving him new status
as a member of the royal household.

Though this reuse of the Goliath story resembles the Ark
Narrative in its use of narrative irony, it also shows a newly
subtle relation to earlier narrative tradition. The Ark Narrative
was structured directly around the Yahwistic Exodus story; the
transformations of the Goliath story show a broader, and
stranger, relation to Yahwistic narrative and thematic patterns.
The truly bizarre detail that enters into Saul's second effort at
seducing David through the offer of a daughter is the nature
of the proof he requests that David has killed the hundred Philistines: a hundred foreskins. As the lines quoted show, this
surprising request is fulfilled twofold by David, and the text
stresses his presentation of the full two hundred foreskins to
the king. What are we to make of this strange evidentiary proceeding?

Most directly, Saul's stratagem recalls the tactic employed by
the sons of Jacob in Genesis 34. Shechem, son of the Hivite
king Hamor, rapes Jacob's daughter Dinah and then proposes
marriage. Seeking a chance for vengeance, Dinah's brothers
agree to the marriage, but only on condition that the Hivites
be circumcised. Here too the request for circumcisions as pre-
condition for marriage is a trap: while the Hivites are still sore
from the operation, Jacob's sons attack their town, slaying Hamor and Shechem and plundering the city. The parallel is clear,
and there may even be an echo of Hamor's reaction to the
brothers' proposal when David receives Saul's offer: their reactions of pleasure at the proposals are described in similar

terms (*wayyitevu divreyhem be'eyney Hamor*, Gen. 34:18; *wayyishar haddavar be'eyney Dawid*, 1 Sam. 18:26).

In contrast to the direct use of Yahwistic models in the Ark Narrative, here the plot is turned around, a ruse of the malevolent king against the young hero. Further, the circumcision plot takes on new overtones. Often in 1–2 Samuel, the new institution of the monarchy stands in a somewhat uneasy relation to the traditional covenantal relationship between God and the people. As God tells Samuel when instructing him to give in to the people's request for a king, "They have not rejected you, but they have rejected me from being king over them" (1 Sam. 8:7). If the king is chosen by the people as a more visible and tangible king than the Lord God, then a bad king will quickly come to resemble a kind of anti-God.

When Saul befriends David after the defeat of Goliath, Saul's son Jonathan is explicitly described as making a covenant (*berit*) with David (18:3). Now Saul seeks to dissolve this covenant, and in his madness and jealousy he becomes a grim parody of the God he is supposed to represent on earth. The covenant with Abraham had established circumcision as the sign of God's promise of fertility and land. Now circumcision becomes the sign of death between the fallen king and his loyal subject, and the promise of wealth and fertility implied in the offer of Michal is only a lure by which Saul hopes to destroy his erstwhile protégé.

The rapidly growing distance between Saul and David, emphasized by Saul's new reliance on intermediaries when he communicates with David, begins to take on overtones of the gulf between a people and a distant, silent God. Soon David is asking Jonathan what has gone wrong, in terms that could be used unchanged by the stricken Job: "What have I done? What is my guilt? And what is my sin before your father, that he seeks my life? . . . truly, as the Lord lives and as your soul lives, there is but a step between me and death" (20:1–3). As David talks with Jonathan, the comparison to the sacred covenant between God and Israel is made explicit: "Deal kindly with your servant," David asks Jonathan, "for you have brought your servant into a sacred covenant [*berit YHWH*] with you."[14]

A ratio is established whereby the relation between king and subject is like the covenantal relationship between God and Israel. With the king as a metaphoric God, the narrative can engage in deep exploration, in earthly, historical narrative, of formerly legendary and mythic-epic existential themes. The shift already under way in the historicized epic elements of the Ark Narrative is now complete; where Yahweh fought Dagon, now David fights Goliath. As the Goliath theme is developed through the History of David's Rise, the elements of political apologetic that have often been noted in the narrative, and that we may suppose to have dominated it at the text's inception, are subordinated to existential concerns of the sort traditionally found in Mesopotamian epic.

From Saga to Epic: The Theme of Marriage

The confluence of saga and epic elements within the History of David's Rise is furthered through the relationship of David and Jonathan. As the story now stands, this relationship has been developed far beyond anything that would have been required simply to assure the audience that David and Jonathan were close friends and that David did not wish to deny the succession to Saul's heir. Hattušiliš makes these claims concerning his brother and nephew, but his "Apology" never tries to show any inner picture of intimacy, even to the limited extent that it portrays the close relationship of Hattušiliš and his wife. The History of David's Rise both takes up and goes beyond the Yahwistic dynamics of brotherly relations, and it does

---

[14]Perhaps through the influence of Rost's highly secularizing and political reading of 1–2 Samuel, commentaries often play down the startlingly direct theological language here. Thus, for example, the Oxford Annotated Bible notes for this verse: "*Sacred covenant* is a reference to the deep friendship of David and Jonathan" (!).

so in a fundamentally epic manner. The relationship of David and Jonathan is in fact developed in terms very similar to those used in the *Gilgamesh Epic* to describe the friendship of Gilgamesh and Enkidu.

In both texts, the relationship between the friends has clear overtones of a relationship of husband and wife. It will be recalled that Enkidu first meets Gilgamesh by preventing him from going in to a woman, and thereafter takes the place of women in Gilgamesh's heart. On Enkidu's death, Gilgamesh mourns for his friend "as for a bride." Later poetic epic tradition develops this theme further, notably in the relation of Achilles and Patroklos, and a parallel line of development can be observed in the story of David and Jonathan. If anything, indeed, the parallels to the *Gilgamesh Epic* are closer in the History of David's Rise than in Homer, not surprisingly in view of the greater proximity of the texts both in time and in space.

The meeting of Jonathan and David, in the aftermath to the slaying of Goliath, is described as love at first sight. Saul and David have a brief conversation, in which David identifies himself.

When he had finished speaking to Saul, the soul of Jonathan was knit to the soul of David, and Jonathan loved him as his own soul. And Saul took him that day, and would not let him return to his father's house. Then Jonathan made a covenant with David, because he loved him as his own soul. And Jonathan stripped himself of the robe that was upon him, and gave it to David, and his armor, and even his sword and his bow and his belt. And David went out and was successful wherever Saul sent him. (18:1–5)

Here the language is simultaneously familial, political, and erotic. The knitting of the souls of Jonathan and David expresses a bond of kinship (compare the parallel phrase used to describe the love of Jacob for his favorite son Benjamin, in Gen. 44:30–31). This kinship has both a political expression and erotic overtones. The political union of the two, and the subordination of Jonathan in the relationship, is symbolized by Jonathan's gift of his royal robe and his armor, after which David assumes Jonathan's role as Saul's commander in chief.

At the same time, the language of love is repeatedly used here, and although this language has a political aspect (Near Eastern vassals are often described as "loving" their rulers, i.e., showing proper loyalty), the scene equally suggests a quasi-marriage. Marriage is, after all, the way in which a kinship tie is forged between adults, and the language here would be appropriate to a betrothal. Indeed, very similar language is used in Genesis 34 in the story of Hamor, Shechem, and Dinah, earlier alluded to as a parallel and likely model for Saul's circumcision ruse. Shechem's "soul was drawn to Dinah the daughter of Jacob and he loved the maiden" (34:3); here, "Jonathan's soul was bound to the soul of David, and Jonathan loved him as his own soul."

Where Hamor seconds his son's passion by making a formal offer of marriage, hoping to induce Dinah and her clan to give up their independence and move into his city (34:10), here Saul takes David and does not allow him to return to his father's house. Hamor is an altogether appropriate prototype for Saul. He is a wicked king and a threat to the survival of the bearers of the true covenant with God; even his personal failings find an echo in Saul, as Hamor is characterized by greed, the failing for which Samuel condemns Saul in 1 Samuel 15. The language used for Saul's "taking" of David is also suggestive (the verb, *laqaḥ*, figuring in the common locution "to take a wife"), and the motif of (not) returning to the parental house is elsewhere always associated with marriage or the end of a marriage.[15] In the next chapter, we are told that Jonathan "delighted in"

---

[15]Compare the language of love and possession in the Song of Songs; here the speaker, a woman, is acting the part of the man: "I found him whom my soul loves. / I held him, and would not let him go / until I had brought him into my mother's house" (Song of Songs 3:4). Elsewhere, a widow "returns to her father's house" (Lev. 22:13), and Naomi urges her widowed daughters-in-law to "return to your mother's house" (Ruth 1:8); this theme is also reflected in the mournful return of Jephthah's daughter to her father, where her sacrifice will take the place of a marriage (Judg. 11:39).

David, using the verb (*haphetz*) earlier used to describe Shechem's desire for Dinah (1 Sam. 19:1; Gen. 34:19).

The relationship between the story of Dinah and the David story goes beyond the points mentioned here, as the rape of Dinah has clear parallels in Amnon's rape of Tamar. Yair Zakovitch has argued that this latter set of parallels results from revision of the Dinah story on analogy to the story of Tamar ("Assimilation in Biblical Narratives," 185-92). Zakovitch believes that this revision was undertaken in order to worsen the portrayal of Shechem, thereby strengthening the moral justification for the violent retribution carried out by Dinah's brothers. A further exploration would be required to unfold the full relationships among these three episodes, but it seem likely that together they provide a notable instance of reciprocal influence, with an early Yahwistic story influencing the History of David's Rise and then in turn being revised in light of the later Succession Narrative account of Amnon and Tamar.

To return to the relationship of David and Jonathan, just as the marriage theme in the *Gilgamesh Epic* reaches its most direct expression at the close of the relationship, in Gilgamesh's lament for Enkidu, here it is developed most explicitly in David's lament after Saul and Jonathan die in battle. David praises them as "beloved and lovely," gives a somewhat formal lament for Saul, and then concludes with a moving apostrophe to Jonathan: "very pleasant have you been to me; / your love to me was wonderful, passing the love of women" (2 Sam. 1:26). This comparison crystallizes the metaphor and goes beyond it in the same breath. If the story of Hamor and Shechem has helped to shape the story of Saul and Jonathan, the theme of marriage, like the theme of circumcision, has undergone a change from the literal to the metaphoric; the historical narrative of David's introduction to Saul and Jonathan has been developed through a confluence of the plotting of a legendary, sagalike episode and the thematic resonances of poetic epic.

Having said this much, it remains to show the use to which the friendship-as-marriage motif is put in this new context. As

David prepared to fight Goliath, the troops speculated that the slayer of Goliath would surely receive the hand of the king's daughter in marriage. In his meeting with Saul and Jonathan after the battle, David does not yet get the king's daughter; but he does get the king's son. Jonathan's narrative role in the chapters that follow is closely parallel to that of David's wife, Saul's daughter Michal; just as she aids his escape by a timely ploy, so too does Jonathan. Indeed, Michal's efforts to protect David from Saul (19:8–17) are neatly framed by Jonathan's, in 19:1–7 and in chapter 20 (with one interpolated incident, 19:18–24, coming between Michal's ruse and Jonathan's second effort).

A shift has occurred here: David comes into Saul's household like a bride but then takes on the role of the young husband, metaphorically in relation to Jonathan, literally in relation to Michal. A variability in the terms of the friendship-as-marriage metaphor is in fact characteristic of its use from *Gilgamesh* to the *Iliad*.[16] In part, the nature of friendship is such that either friend can at times take on echoes of husband or wife; in part, too, in the particular case of David and Jonathan, the shift in the metaphor traces David's rapid rise from a position of youth, weakness, and poverty to his commanding status as the king's most successful general.

This shift is already figured in the initial encounter of David and Jonathan, in Jonathan's symbolic gift of his royal robe and armor to David. This gesture can be compared to the woman's acculturating gift of the cloak to Enkidu as he makes the transition from the state of nature to life in the city. Throughout the History of David's Rise, clothing serves as a symbolic motif in ways comparable to its use in the *Gilgamesh Epic*. As in that

---

[16]On Enkidu's death, Gilgamesh acts both roles simultaneously, veiling his dead friend "like a bride" and also mourning him as women mourn the death of a husband. In the *Iliad*, Achilles is clearly the "lover" and Patroklos the "beloved," yet it is Patroklos who is the older man, in a reversal of the Greek custom.

epic, clothing appears at a series of turning points in the story, and serves to crystallize basic issues of cultural definition. In *Gilgamesh,* clothing symbolized the products of human culture and ultimately stood as a metonymic representation of human culture as a whole. As a result, it figured prominently at every point at which human culture clashed with its boundaries: the state of nature (Enkidu's nakedness covered by the harlot's cloak); the world of the gods (Ishtar's attraction to Gilgamesh's gorgeous robes); the underworld (Gilgamesh's cloak serving as a sail to navigate the Waters of Death).

In the reworking of the History of David's Rise, clothing is closely associated with the theological issue of the definition of kingship, the problem of the relation of human authority to divine authority. Of several words for outer garments, one particular word is several times used: *me'il,* a word rarely found outside 1 Samuel, except in Exodus, where it describes the priestly/royal robe worn by the High Priest. At the start of the History of David's Rise, when Samuel informs Saul of his rejection by God, the kingship is symbolized by Samuel's robe: "Then when Samuel turned to go, Saul caught hold of the skirt of his robe, and it tore away. Samuel said to him, 'The Lord has torn the kingship of Israel away from you this day and has given it to your neighbor, who is more worthy than you' " (15:27). This scene is echoed when Saul's son unwittingly fulfills this symbolism by giving his robe (again, *me'il*) to David (18:4). Further, once Saul has driven David into exile, on the first occasion when David catches Saul unawares he cuts off the hem of Saul's *me'il* as proof that he could have harmed him but did not. The potency of the symbolism of the royal robe is seen by David's remorse after he has taken this piece of evidence: "Afterward David's heart smote him, because he had cut off the hem of Saul's robe" (24:5 [6 in Hebrew]). Here too there is a further ironic reversal of the language involving the divine covenant, already suggested by Samuel's speech about the tearing of the kingdom away from Saul; David's "cutting" (*karat*) of the hem is the same word used for the making (lit., "cutting") of a covenant, a phrase stemming from the cutting up of a sacrifice used to ratify a covenant.

The History of David's Rise develops the story of David and Jonathan through narrative incidents and symbolic motifs as a part of its meditation on the nature and meaning of the divine covenant in human history. The struggle over the kingship is less a political matter than an issue of finding the proper balance between historical pressures and divine imperatives, and the development of the Goliath theme through the balance of the History of David's Rise shows very clearly the subordination of political/theological apologetic to the exploration of more general existential issues. After the failure of Jonathan's efforts at mediating between Saul and David, David flees into exile and has a variety of strange adventures. These have their tendentious aspect, showing, for example, how David becomes the protector of the Yahwistic priesthood after Saul turns on his priests and slaughters most of them at Nob. At the same time, however, David's own character and actions are developed with a complexity far exceeding the requirements, and even the generic proprieties, of apologetic historiography. The "Apology of Hattušiliš" and several other texts describe parallel situations of the early struggles of a king (or future king) against powerful enemies, but I cannot think of any earlier Near Eastern historical text that describes its hero's first supporters in these terms: "To him there gathered every man in difficulties and every man sought by a creditor and every man with a bitter spirit, and he became their commander" (22:2). This is not exactly Robin Hood and his merry band! But the story contains stranger passages than this, such as the scene just before it, in which David tries to enlist as a mercenary in the service of the Philistines; when they reject his offer and things look dangerous, he escapes harm by feigning madness, drooling in his beard and spitting on the gateposts at the entrance to Gath (21:13).

Clearly more is at issue here than a drive to justify David's overthrow of Saul. If the historian had to account for the uncomfortable fact that David had been a Philistine mercenary and an outlaw, a purely apologetic work could easily have cast these episodes in a better light. The chapters that follow, which evidently stem from the original account, are much closer to the Robin Hood paradigm, with David and his men aiding the oppressed, delivering the town of Keilah from the Philistines (23:1–6), their actions guided by the will of Yahweh as revealed through the priest Abiathar, who functions here as David's Friar Tuck. Later, David actually does go to work for the Philistines (chaps. 27–29), in a version of the story that is at pains to stress David's honorable behavior in a difficult time; why then was the strange anecdote of chapter 21 added to the account?

Here the issue can be sharpened by taking note of the events of the first half of the chapter. Fleeing into exile, David and a few men pause at Nob and beg for food from Ahimelech, the chief priest there. David lies to Ahimelech, claiming that he is on a secret errand for Saul, and asks for bread to feed his men. Ahimelech gives him holy bread from the altar, and then David asks him if perhaps he has a weapon to lend.

And the priest said, "The sword of Goliath the Philistine, whom you killed in the valley of Elah, behold, it is here behind the ephod; if you will take that, take it, for there is none but that here." And David said, "There is none like that; give it to me." And David arose and fled that day from Saul, and went to Achish the king of Gath. (21:9–10)

Carrying Goliath's sword, then, David flees to Goliath's own city. Has David become Goliath?

Goliath, David, and Saul

The meaning of this remarkable transformation is shown in the episodes that follow. Most directly, David has been forced into the role of Goliath through Saul's actions; more generally, David's exile becomes emblematic of Israel's struggle to survive in a hostile world. To begin with the more immediate of these aspects, the transformation of David into Goliath shows a classic biblical symmetry: by persecuting David, Saul turns his protégé into his own enemy. Where David first came into Saul's service as his defender against the Philistines generally and Goliath in particular, Saul has turned the tables, not on his young hero, as planned, but on himself. Saul's dereliction is not so much political as moral and theological; by turning from God, Saul has made himself into an ersatz anti-God, perverting his covenant with the people into a covenant of death. In his attempt to destroy his most loyal subject, Saul recreates David in the image of his monstrous double, Goliath.

This theme reaches its fullest development in David's encounters with Saul in the wilderness. Twice David has Saul in his power, twice he lets him go, in a doubling that reaches a dramatic climax in the antagonists' second encounter. The second encounter appears to have been the original one, with the first encounter later added to the text. The two stories together now serve as vehicles for David's moral development. In the interpolated first episode, David cuts off the hem of Saul's robe as the king is relieving himself in a cave. In taking only this token, David resists further violence, hoping that this evidence of his restraint will bring him back into Saul's good graces. The specific method of proof here, the cutting of Saul's hem—occurring when Saul has exposed himself in order to relieve himself—serves as a redemptive inversion of the cutting off of the hundred foreskins to prove David's worthiness as a son-in-law. Now, for the first time since their falling-out, Saul and David affirm a father-son relationship. David follows Saul out of the cave and calls to him; he begins formally ("My lord the king!"), but soon shifts to familial terms: "See, my father, see the skirt of your robe in my hand" (24:11 [12]). Though David is standing in front of him, Saul responds to his voice: "Saul said, 'Is this your voice, my son David?' And Saul lifted up his voice and wept" (24:16–17 [17–18]).

Saul's response to David's voice makes sense in the original encounter in chapter 26, where David calls across to Saul from the opposite side of the valley; there, he might well be heard more clearly than seen. Brought back into this interpolated encounter, the hesitant recognition makes Saul seem blind, only able to recognize David by his voice. The language of fatherhood and sonship so prominent here may remind us of an earlier scene of a blind father's uncertainty at his son's identity, the scene in which Isaac bestows his blessing on his second son Jacob, mistaking him for Esau. In a variety of ways, that episode appears to stand behind the shaping of the encounter of Saul and David. The confrontation ends, like that in Genesis, with the father's bestowal of his blessing, here formulated in terms of an acknowledgment that David will inherit Saul's throne: "I know that you will surely become king and that the kingship of Israel will be established in your hand" (24:20[21]); in the original version of the story, after Saul recognizes David's voice, the encounter ends with a still more direct blessing: "Then Saul said to David, 'You are blessed, my son! In whatever you undertake you will surely succeed!' " (26:25).

David here supplants Saul's firstborn son Jonathan, as Jacob supplants Esau. At the same time, however, this repetition of the theme of the triumph of the younger brother has been transformed, through the immediate and intimate friendship of the two and Jonathan's willing subordination to David, itself reaffirmed in a wilderness encounter shortly before this (23:15–18). Now the motif of the loss of the birthright is transferred to Saul himself, since, if Saul stands in the role of Isaac in relation to David's Jacob, at the same time this pattern is doubled in relation to God: God is the father bestowing the kingship, and Saul, like Esau, loses this right through his malfeasance and must see it transferred to God's younger favorite, David. For this reason, Saul simultaneously acts the roles of Isaac and of Esau, as the text shows in Saul's double reaction of speech and weeping: "Saul said, 'Is this your voice, my son David?' And Saul lifted up his voice and wept." Whereas the first sentence echoes Isaac, the second echoes Esau's reaction to the loss of his blessing, at the close of the scene: "And Esau lifted up his voice and wept" (Gen. 27:38).[17]

Saul has been brought to acknowledge the justice of the coming transfer of the kingship, but David, though not harming Saul himself, still speaks in the language of vengeance: "May Yahweh judge between me and you! For Yahweh will give me vengeance upon you, though I shall not touch you" (24:12[13]). The next step in David's moral development comes in the next incident, the self-contained story of Abigail and Nabal (chap. 25). It has often been observed that this story parallels the sparings of Saul that frame it, since in this instance too David refrains from exacting vengeance against someone who has denied him his due. The scene is, in fact, more than merely analogous; within the frame of the sparings of Saul, it serves to inaugurate the decisive transformation of the Goliath motif, which will be completed in the second encounter with Saul.

Nabal is a debased and parodic version of Saul, a rich miser who refuses to aid David with supplies, instead using his food and drink to feast "like a king" (25:36). David decides to raid Nabal's household and sack it, but Nabal's prudent wife Abigail secretly takes food to David and dissuades him. She points out that Nabal, whose name means "fool," is not worth becoming angry over: "Let not my lord regard this ill-natured fellow, Nabal, for as his name is, so is he" (25:25).[18] Further, she urges David to consider that justice lies in God's hands, and she expresses her trust in God in terms that directly recall David's victory over Goliath by faith rather than force of arms:

---

[17]The phrase "to lift up the voice and weep" is often associated with scenes of dispossession. Examples include Hagar's abandonment by Abraham (Gen. 21:16), the people of Israel learning that the Canaanites look too powerful for an entry into the Promised Land to be possible (Num. 14:1), and the people mourning after an angel announces that God will punish them for breaking their covenant with him (Judg. 2:4).

[18]See Garsiel, *The First Book of Samuel*, 122–33, for an extended discussion of relevant associations to the name of Nabal, including comparisons to Jacob's father-in-law, Laban (whose name, as was already observed in antiquity, is "Nabal" in reverse). See also his *Kingdom of David*, 87–126, on the wider thematic relevance of the lessons David learns from Abigail.

"If men rise up to pursue you and seek your life, the life of my lord shall be bound up in the Book of the Living in the keeping of Yahweh, your god; but the lives of your enemies he will sling away in the pocket of a sling" (25:29).

If Goliath was killed by a stone from a sling, here Abigail envisions Nabal himself as becoming that stone, and this in fact is what happens. Abigail goes home, and the sheer recounting of her prophecy of harm to David's enemies lays her husband low: "In the morning, when the wine had gone out of Nabal, his wife told him these things, and his heart died within him, and he became a stone. And about ten days later the Lord struck Nabal, and he died" (25:37–38). With Nabal a cross between Saul and Goliath, here it is Abigail who acts the role of the young hero David. David thanks Abigail for her lesson: "Blessed be you for preventing me this day from entering into bloodguilt and gaining my victory by my own hand!" (25:33). As David won the love of the king's son through his exploit against Goliath, here Abigail wins David, the new heir to Saul: on Nabal's death, David sends for her and marries her (25:39–42). Thus Abigail has brought out the moral meaning of the initial encounter of David and Goliath, which was told in the spare form of an adventure story. There is no theological commentary (in the first version of the story), and David's use of the slingshot could simply testify to his own cleverness in catching Goliath off guard with an unexpected weapon. Now, in the discourse of the wise Abigail, David is brought to a moral understanding of his own past and is guided to a more openly faithful future behavior.

David applies this lesson in his second encounter with Saul. David and a companion creep into Saul's camp at night. Standing before the sleeping Saul, David rejects his companion's plea to be allowed to kill the king. Instead, David merely takes Saul's spear and water jar, and leaves. David then taunts the Israelites from a distance:

Then David went over to the other side, and stood afar off on the top

of the mountain, with a great space between them; and David called
to the army, and to Abner the son of Ner, saying, "Will you not answer, Abner?" Then Abner answered, "Who are you who calls the
king?" And David said to Abner, "Are you not a man? Who is like
you in Israel? Why then have you not kept watch over your lord the
king? For one of the people came in to destroy the king your lord. . . .
As the Lord lives, you deserve to die, because you have not kept
watch over your lord, the Lord's anointed. And now see where the
king's spear is, and the jar of water that was at his head." (26:13–
16)

Here Saul's general Abner, the very man who did not know
who David was in the interpolated episode of David and Goliath (17:55), once again does not recognize him. Though the
reappearance of Abner serves as a specific linking device to
associate the two scenes, David's confrontation with Saul and
Abner more broadly parallels the taunting of Israel by Goliath,
as it is preserved in the late version of the Goliath episode.[19]

And the Philistines stood on the mountain on the one side, and the
Israelites stood on the mountain on the other side, with a valley between them. And there came out from the camp of the Philistines a
champion named Goliath. . . . He stood and shouted to the ranks of
Israel, "Why have you come out to draw up for battle? Am I not a
Philistine, and are you not servants of Saul? Choose a man for yourselves, and let him come down to me. . . . I defy the ranks of Israel
this day; give me a man, that we may fight together." (17:3–10)

The parallel between the scenes does not lead to the logical
denouement, combat between David and Abner, even though
David begins by mockingly singling out Abner as a champion:

---

[19]In general, the two stories of David and Goliath in chap. 17 seem to be preserved intact; each one can be read coherently without the other. In the matter
of the introduction of Goliath and his challenge to Israel, however, there
seems to have been enough direct overlap for the later version to have actually
replaced the corresponding passage in the earlier version. As it stands, the
earlier version alone lacks any introduction of Goliath or discussion of how
he emerges as a single figure who must be defeated. In order to have functioned as a coherent story, the early version must have had some passage
corresponding to 17:1–11.

"Are you not a man? And who in Israel is your equal?" (26:15; compare Goliath's "Am I not a Philistine, and are you not servants of Saul? Choose a man for yourselves"). The parallel goes no further because David, who has renounced vengeance against Saul, prefers to seek a public reconciliation. Following Abigail's lesson, he demonstrates a new trust in God. Where in the first scene David showed a desire for vengeance at the Lord's hand, now he is prepared to leave matters entirely to God, who will deal with Saul however he pleases: "As the Lord lives, the Lord will smite him; or his day shall come to die; or he shall go down into battle and perish" (26:10). By this change the story of David and Goliath is turned inside out. David, who fled into exile armed with Goliath's sword, now rejects vengeance altogether. The image of Goliath is transformed from that of invading monster to that of a trusting but mistrusted son. Though David continues to be forced into the outward role of Goliath, it is Saul, like Nabal, who is the true Goliath who will find his punishment at God's hands.

In acknowledging that God may choose to punish Saul directly by smiting him, or indirectly by having him die in battle, or simply by leaving him to drag out his life until a natural death overtakes him, David's speech shows a new theological openness to the presence of contingency in history. The History of David's Rise thus fully allows the awareness of chance events that the Ark Narrative partially admitted but largely repressed through the story of the experiment with the Philistine cows. There, the plague's direct connection to God's will was proven by the movements of the cows, whose remarkably direct and purposive march to Israelite territory dramatized and demonstrated the hidden order behind the breaking out of the plague. In a related but more radical way, David's speech asserts that any possible result must be seen as the expression of God's just and benevolent will. No miracle or spectacular scientific proof will be needed; rather, history fully merges with the ethical imperatives of the divine order. It does so not through the absolute power and knowledge of the heroic king,

as in earlier historiography, but through the poetic mystery of
the limitations on human strength and wisdom formerly emphasized in the epic tradition, and now extended to the study
of modern history. As Garsiel says, these stories serve to blunt
the originally sharp contrast between Saul and David: "One is
not a complete villain knowing nothing of humanity or con-
trition, and the other is not an angel of light on whom anger,
vindictiveness and the love of power have no hold" (*First Book
of Samuel*, 124).

Thus developed, the stories of David's struggles with Saul
still serve an apologetic purpose, establishing a sympathetic
context in which to view David's sojourn in Philistine territory,
which follows directly after the second sparing of Saul. At the
same time, the complexity of the reworking of the Goliath motif, with its echoes of the story of Jacob and Esau, extends the
story well beyond the requirements of this apologetic purpose,
making David into an emblematic figure of the struggle of the
faithful minority within a hostile and unbelieving world. This
is the existential reorientation that accompanies the political development of Saul's reuse of the Goliath plot: though David is
forced into the role of Goliath, in the transformation of that
role he becomes an emblem for the power of faith even in exile
in a hostile land. This theme was central to the Ark Narrative
as well, where the capture of the Ark by the Philistines was
mourned as an experience of exile: Eli's daughter-in-law "called
the child Ichabod . . . for she said, 'Glory was exiled [*galah*]
when the ark of God was captured' " (4:21). In condensing the
story of David's skirmishes with Philistine champions into the
single encounter of David and Goliath, the recomposer of the
History of David's Rise has developed the theme of exile metaphorically, through the emblematic treatment of character and
event. But why did he not develop the story of David and
Ishbibenob instead, retaining the name of the giant with whom
David was most directly involved? In a text in which, as Abigail
says of her husband, a man resembles his name, "Goliath" is

the ideal emblem for David in this phase of his life: for the meaning of "Goliath" is "Exile."[20]

The Third Goliath

After the historical Goliath merged with his comrade Ishbi-benob to become the folkloristic Goliath of the pre-Deuteronomistic reworking of the History of David's Rise, a further transformation awaited this new Goliath. Interwoven in 1 Samuel 17 are two quite distinct Goliath stories. Until now, I have been discussing only one of these; it remains to discuss the other, a version that appears to be a product of the Deuteronomistic historian himself. Like many of the Deuteronomistic historian's elaborations on received material, this final version of the Goliath story serves both a theological and a narrative function, developing his favorite themes and also strengthening connections between sections of the composite history of the early monarchy.

The two Goliath stories have been skillfully intertwined, and their separate identities might never have been fully perceived but for an unusual quirk of textual history: only one of the two stories is preserved in the Codex Vaticanus, an important manuscript of the Septuagint. Although other Septuagint manuscripts include the verses, the Codex Vaticanus is distinctive in its freedom from correction toward the later Hebrew (Masoretic) tradition, and consequently seems closest of surviving manuscripts to the Old Greek of the initial Septuagint. It appears, then, that the Septuagint originally lacked 17:12–31, 41, 48b, 50, 55–58, and 18:1–5, 10–11, 17–19, 29b–30. These verses contain the Goliath story in the form I have been discussing, together with the beginning of the friendship of David and Jonathan and the first reuse of the Goliath story, Saul's

---

[20]To the Hebrew author, "Goliath" would most readily derive from *galah*, though the actual derivation of the name is probably not Hebrew at all.

offer of his daughter Merab. These verses form a virtually complete and coherent narrative, lacking only an initial setting of the scene, which can be supposed to have been replaced with the beginning of the second version (see note 19). The remaining verses in chapter 17, the verses common to both the received Masoretic text and the Septuagint, also form a coherent and unified version of the Goliath story, one with clear Deuteronomistic emphases (17:1–11, 32–40, 42–48a, 49, 51–54).[21]

Although this textual evidence brings a certain clarity to the confused course of events in 17:1–18:30, it also introduces enormous uncertainties of a different sort. How did the "earlier" story of Goliath not find its place in the Codex Vaticanus? Several solutions have been proposed, but no general agreement has been reached to date. The problem here is that each solution has a different consequence for the understanding of the evolution of the text as we have it now. One commonly suggested explanation, for example, is that the missing version simply never existed in the Hebrew text, up until some time after the fourth-century establishment of the textual tradition that underlay the third-century Old Greek translation. This basic hypothesis continues in one of two variants: that the missing version was invented out of whole cloth sometime between the fourth century and the fixing of the Hebrew text of 1–2 Samuel in around the second century; or that the missing variant is indeed older than the Deuteronomistic version, but circulated separately, in purely oral form or as a separate document, until its eventual inclusion in the Hebrew text during the fourth or third century.

If the "early" version of the Goliath story was only added to the Hebrew text at such a late date, however, then it can hardly have served as a structuring device for the pre-Deuteronomistic version of the History of David's Rise, as I have been sug-

---

[21]The two versions may be found conveniently printed separately in McCarter's commentary.

gesting. At the same time, however, the many and close links observable between this version of the Goliath story and the balance of the History of David's Rise argue strongly in favor of an early connection. Against the theory of a late addition of the story it must also be objected that there is no visible reason for such an extended late addition of primitive material that would have been largely superseded by the Deuteronomistic Goliath story. Further, the attractive simplicity of the hypothesis of a late addition has the unfortunate consequence of marginalizing the entire episode. Thus, to take one recent discussion as an example, McCarter concludes that the missing version "is, at least from the perspective of the textual critic, properly *excursus* material," and consequently he makes no effort to explore its relations to its context; he simply suggests vaguely that the story was "attracted" to this context by the presence of the Deuteronomistic Goliath story (*1 Samuel*, 307–9).

This unsatisfactory solution is, however, not the only one available. Many scholars have followed or adapted the early hypothesis of Wellhausen that the two stories were indeed both present in the text from Deuteronomistic times onward, but that the more primitive story was then removed by a later editor who objected to the contradictions between the two versions. Against this solution it is apparent that this hypothetical later editor would have been both unusually sensitive to contradiction, in this one instance, and unusually inconsistent in ignoring all the other doublings throughout the text. Further, once the two versions had been woven together, it is difficult to suppose that a later editor would so perceptively have disentangled them again and restored the two freestanding versions, retaining one and discarding the other. Finally, as Emanuel Tov has shown through a close examination of the Septuagint version, it bears many signs of being a faithful translation of a Hebrew original, and furthermore differs in significant details from the generally parallel verses in the canonical Masoretic text; thus it is almost certainly not an abridgement of the canonical text but a translation of a distinct Hebrew original ("Composition of 1 Samuel 16–18").

The possibilities are not yet exhausted, however. The Deuteronomistic version, as will be seen below, is essentially an expansion and commentary on the earlier ("missing") version. In developing the older story, the Deuteronomistic historian did not simply embellish the existing story, but recomposed it altogether, adding speeches to clarify and develop his themes and also adding further details from the very first Goliath story. By this means, the new, Deuteronomistic Goliath story came to include several vivid details from the old chronicle of the skirmishes with the four giants, which we may suppose to have still been retained at the end of the History of David's Rise by the author who drew more sparingly on it to begin with. Thus the Deuteronomistic Goliath story took over the vivid details of the weight of Goliath's armor and his enormous height.

Having plundered the old historical account of the skirmishes, the Deuteronomistic historian moved it to the end of the story of David's life. This was not done to obscure the now increased appearance of contradiction between the differing accounts of the defeat of the Philistine giant(s); this sort of contradiction was allowed to stand in many places in Samuel, and if it had been troublesome in this instance, then surely the expanded Goliath story in 1 Samuel 17 would have been advanced as the true story and the first version would simply have been dropped from the text altogether. Rather, the displacement of the first version from its proper place in what is now 1 Samuel 5 served to extend its use as a framing device. Where the Goliath figure(s) had come at the beginning and the end of the revised History of David's Rise, now they come at the beginning and end of the new, complete story of David's life.

Once the Deuteronomistic historian had made his new version of the story, he had two choices: to fold it into the existing Goliath story at the start of the History of David's Rise, or to replace the older interpolation outright with his new version. The inconsistency between Codex Vaticanus and the Masoretic text suggests that both options were tried, either at the same time or within a fairly brief period. In one edition, the older story was simply thrown out, and this edition survived to become the basis of the Old Greek translation underlying Codex Vaticanus. In another, more conservative edition, the older material was retained and the new story carefully inserted; this conservative edition survived to become the basis of the Masoretic text.[22]

It should be stressed that this hypothesis, like both the others, lacks any external corroboration, and no certain conclusions can be drawn from the limited parallels to be found elsewhere when the Septuagint is compared to the canonical text. Among the narrative books of the Bible, 1–2 Samuel are almost uniquely corrupt, and discrepancies between the versions are rarely so extensive as in this instance. In some cases, a shorter Septuagint version can be shown to reflect the original Hebrew text, later subjected to editorial expansion by Deuteronomistic hands, as Alexander Rofé has argued in the case of a story in Joshua ("Joshua 20"). Emanuel Tov has advanced similar arguments concerning Jeremiah ("Literary History of the Book of Jeremiah"). As Tov himself has elsewhere noted, however, the Septuagint is no unified creation but "a heterogeneous collection of translations, original and revised, early and late, free and literal" (*Septuagint Translations*, 168). Consequently, lessons learned from the Septuagint version of one book cannot necessarily be applied to problems in other books. This would seem to be particularly true in this instance, where it is the Septuagint version, and not the canonical text, which is exclusively Deuteronomistic in character; hence, this does not

---

[22]For an extended development of this hypothesis, see de Vries, "David's Victory over the Philistine as Saga and as Legend." I am in full agreement with de Vries on this overall approach, though I am not sure that it is possible to follow his confident reconstruction of no fewer than six redactional levels in 1 Samuel 17.

appear to be a case of a Septuagint version free from later Deuteronomistic expansion. In the absence of determinative external evidence, then, literary judgments become a crucial factor in reaching a decision,[23] and biblical scholars, never having observed the literary connections between the "missing" Goliath story and the balance of the History of David's Rise, have often drifted to one of the other hypotheses than the one adopted here.

If I have analyzed the textual history correctly, the story of David and Goliath provides a good example of the mutually beneficial interplay of historical and literary study. Text history pointed the way to reconstruction of the two Goliath stories, an important step preliminary to studying the role of Goliath in the pre-Deuteronomistic and the Deuteronomistic stages of the text. This analysis, in turn, provides valuable evidence in favor of one hypothesis of textual history as against the others, thus providing a new vantage point from which to survey the conflicting claims of these hypotheses.

The importance of the Goliath motif depends, of course, on its having been deliberately chosen as a structuring device, and this assumption could be challenged. Perhaps Goliath stories were stock tales, so common that nothing should be concluded from their appearance in a given context? Here the certainty of analysis is limited by the lack of any Hebrew literature from the period apart from what has been preserved in the Bible. It is noteworthy, however, that the only significant echo of the Goliath story in 1–2 Samuel outside the History of David's Rise is the ruse by which David sends Uriah to his death, in 2 Samuel 11. Here, however, the analogy is noticeably looser and can best be seen as a secondary elaboration of the motif, with the *subject's* wife being sought by the *king*. Goliath stories, then, are very far from being stock elements in 1–2 Samuel (or in

---

[23]See the thoughtful discussion by Johan Lust, who concludes that the relative merits of the Goliath stories in the Septuagint and the Masoretic text can only be adjudicated on the basis of broader literary analysis ("Story of David and Goliath in Hebrew and Greek").

biblical narrative at large) but are markedly concentrated in this one section of the text; and the previous section of this chapter will have suggested their importance to each context in which they appear. Taken together, they form a structuring leitmotif throughout the History of David's Rise.

I have presented the evolution of the Goliath motif in the way that seems to me to account best for the evidence in the text. Nevertheless, the evidence could be read differently. If, for example, the centrality of the Goliath motif were granted but the pre-Deuteronomistic inclusion of the "early" Goliath story were denied, then it might be possible to argue that the entire Goliath motif came into the text at the hand of the Deuteronomistic writer who created the "late" version of the Goliath story in 1 Samuel 17. This would presumably be the approach of a critic with the viewpoint of Van Seters, who sees the Deuteronomistic historian as the great creative and shaping force behind almost the whole of the Deuteronomistic history. Such an interpretation would also have the advantage of bolstering Rofé and Tov's arguments in favor of the priority of several Septuagint variants.

A case could be made along those lines, though it would be a question whether such a reading could account for as much in the text as the view advanced in this chapter. It is the "early" version, after all, that contains the crucial elements of the troops' speculation about Saul's offer of his daughter in marriage and the important scene in which David and Jonathan establish their loving covenant. In my view, the interests of the Deuteronomistic Goliath story are quite different from the existential focus of the History of David's Rise, a focus shared in the "early" Goliath story and in the various transformations of the motif that follow it. Taking the Deuteronomistic Goliath story, then, as a homiletical rewriting of the earlier Goliath story, I would now like to discuss the contribution that the third Goliath makes to the Deuteronomistic historian's creation of the overall story of the early monarchy.

The emphases of the Deuteronomistic Goliath story can be

described in two categories: thematic and narrative. The thematic interest is straightforwardly theological; the centerpiece of the story is a speech—that favorite Deuteronomistic vehicle for theological commentary—in which David stresses that it is not he but God who will win the battle. In the earlier version, David defeated Goliath by his agility and through the element of surprise. Considering this aspect of the story, Moshe Dayan has written that David's "greatness did not consist of his willingness to go out into battle against someone much stronger than he, but in his knowing how to use a weapon by which someone weak could take the advantage and become strong" ("The Spirit of the Warriors," 52). The Deuteronomistic version alters this emphasis altogether. Both Goliath's strength and David's weakness are increased, and now only God can save the day. The earlier focus on David's personal struggle is thus replaced by the emphasis on God, as announced by the human protagonist himself. Now, indeed, the entire point of the battle is instructional: God will defeat Goliath in order to teach a lesson whose ultimate audience is the Hebrew people themselves. "This day the Lord will deliver you into my hand," David now tells Goliath, "that all the earth may know that there is a God in Israel, and that all this assembly may know that the Lord saves not with sword and spear" (17:46–47). The political realities of the struggle between Philistia and Israel had already been overlaid in the revision of the History of David's Rise by the existential emphasis on the figure of David. Now secular political issues are wholly eclipsed by the didactic message that the Deuteronomistic historian sees at the heart of the story.

Students of the Deuteronomistic contributions to 1–2 Samuel have often been content to discuss the theological contributions of the historian, who has generally been given little credit for creative literary activity. Even though the historian's concerns are primarily schematic and didactic, however, his shaping activity is by no means divorced from creative employment of narrative artistry. In developing the Goliath motif, for example, the Deuteronomistic historian elaborates a variety of themes already present in the History of David's Rise, and does so in a variety of ways. In the remainder of this section, I would like to look at two examples: the themes of clothing and of sight. Both these themes had reached their basic development in the earlier Ark Narrative and History of David's Rise, but the remarkable success of the Deuteronomistic unification of these older materials stemmed to a significant degree from the historian's sensitivity to these and comparable themes, and to the care with which they have been reworked and aligned in their new, larger context.

Where the revised History of David's Rise developed the theme of the royal robe, now the Deuteronomistic historian goes a step further, elaborating a theme of the nakedness of faith. This new theme first appears in the revised Goliath story, in the new description of David's refusal of Saul's armor. David has no need for the royal accoutrements since, as he tells Goliath, "you come at me with sword and spear and scimitar, but I come against you in [or: with] the name of YHWH Sabaoth, god of the ranks of Israel, whom you have defied this very day!" (17:45; the Hebrew proposition *b-* can mean both "in" and "with," giving David's antithesis a nice rhetorical flourish).[24]

This motif is used a second time in 2 Samuel 6, a chapter that serves as a bridge between the History of David's Rise and the story of David's reign that now follows it. In the first instance, David had refused Saul's royal armor and weapons; now, David outrages his wife Michal—Saul's daughter—by his state of undress when he brings the Ark into Jerusalem. He dances before the Ark, wearing only a linen ephod, and Michal is scandalized: "How the King of Israel honored himself today, uncovering himself today before the eyes of his servants' maids, as a dancer shamelessly uncovers himself!" (6:20). In this brief scene, the symbolism first seen in Jonathan's giving of his royal robe to David finds a profound completion in Da-

---

[24]The theme of forgoing armor has roots in Mesopotamian epic. In the *Tukulti-Ninurta Epic*, the Assyrians remove their armor, though not so much through trust in the gods as to give freer reign to their own ferocity (V, 46'–49').

vid's nakedness. What Michal does not see is that David for-
goes his royal robe because he is dancing before the true King
of Israel: "It was before the Lord," he replies (v. 21).

Although it strives to make its theological themes clear, the
Deuteronomistic Goliath story is also geared—unlike the Goliath story of the historian of David's rise—toward establishing
links to the wider story of the early monarchy. It looks forward,
in the example just noted, to the story of the return of the Ark
to Jerusalem; it also looks back to the Ark Narrative itself, and
its Goliath explicitly echoes Dagon: he now falls on his face to
the ground (*wayyipol 'al-panaw 'artzah*, 17:49) just as Dagon fell
on his face to the ground before the Ark (5:3). The climax is
also closer to that of the battle in the Ark Narrative; though
David has already felled Goliath with his sling (which killed
him, according to the earlier version, 17:50), now he actually
kills Goliath by cutting off his head (17:51), as God had cut off
Dagon's head (5:4).[25]

In this instance, the Deuteronomistic historian has brought
out an implicit similarity between the struggles of God against
Dagon and of David against Goliath. The two episodes, already
present in the existing Ark Narrative and History of David's
Rise, described parallel scenes of Philistine defeat; to bring
them into direct linkage, it was merely necessary to identify
David with God, as is done by the speech in which David asserts that God is the real combatant. At the same time that the
Ark Narrative is recalled, it is also transformed, as the emphasis shifts away from warfare and slaughter to a direct testing
of faith. There is no new scene of the slaughter of thousands
of Hebrews and thousands of Philistines through battle and

_____

[25]Is there a further echo of the Ark Narrative in the oddly specific detail of the
"five smooth stones" that David picks up to hurl against Goliath? The plot
makes no use of any but the first stone, but perhaps there is a recollection
involved of the five golden tumors, which symbolize the five cities of the
Philistines, as the Ark Narrative stressed. The stone motif could have a further
grounding in the Ark Narrative in the location of the Israelites' crushing defeat: Ebenezer, which means "Stone of Help." Now, armed with five true
stones of help, David defeats the champion of the five Philistine cities.

plague, though a history of the Philistine wars along the lines of an expanded version of the brief account in 2 Samuel 5 could easily have served as a direct continuation of such a narrative. Had it done so, it would have remained close to Assyrian and Babylonian chronicles, with their interest in recording numbers of troops slaughtered and amounts of tribute received. A vivid narrative incident like the defeat of Goliath could well have appeared in such a chronicle, but it would have remained subordinated to the historical impulse, or the historical-theological impulse, to record the campaign as a whole.

The Deuteronomistic historian's interest in the Goliath episode does not differ in kind from the concerns motivating many Mesopotamian battle accounts: theologically, to show the power and majesty of the king's patron god(s); politically, to bolster the king's image as the gods' trusting (and hence undefeatable) servant. The narrative emphasis differs, however, in that the faith of the hero and his people is actively tested by historical events, which have the power to transform people's understanding of God and their relationship to him. In echoing the Ark Narrative, the Deuteronomistic Goliath story creates a progression away from the theology of holy war found in earlier Near Eastern chronicle, and in so doing it introduces narrative elements that would have been unthinkable to the historians of Egypt or Mesopotamia.

The Ark Narrative had itself initiated this change, beginning with a shocking reversal of the type-scene of the overwhelming of the enemy through the bringing of the divine image onto the battlefield; an example of this motif has been discussed in chapter 2, in Thutmose's victorious march into battle "accompanied by my father Amon." The Philistines are duly terrified at the apparition of the Ark, but find to their own surprise that their force of arms is more than sufficient to produce a stunning victory, at least on the battlefield. The Ark Narrative goes on to show the weakness of their reliance on force of arms, but it does not dispute the underlying principle that victory by force is the key to political relations and the ultimate sign of divine favor. God by no means abandons force; he simply has greater power than Dagon and better weapons than the Philistines, whom he traumatizes through the biological warfare of the bubonic plague.

In contrast, the Deuteronomistic Goliath story asserts that victory through force of arms is a side issue at best. Right still makes might, but the theme of force is now used primarily to characterize the perspective of the pagan Philistines as against the Hebrews (or Hebrews as they *ought* to be, as represented by the lone figure of David). Goliath's taunt is an expression of the Deuteronomistic search for cultural self-definition in the midst of peoples whose cultural norms are seen as very real and seductive alternatives. Goliath shouts to the Israelites: "Why have you come out to draw up for battle? Am I not a Philistine, and are you not servants of Saul?" (17:8). To be a Philistine is to trust in force; to be an Israelite, David tells his countrymen, is to trust in God.

This revisionist echoing of the Philistine wars of the Ark Narrative provides a bridge between that old material and David's climactic renunciation of vengeance against Saul late in the History of David's Rise. I have previously argued that the sparing of Saul had been brought into essentially its current form in the course of the pre-Deuteronomistic reworking of the History of David's Rise; in this event, the Deuteronomistic historian was able to develop an implicit connection—in other words, one already lying to hand in the separate materials. I have presented the matter in this way in keeping with the traditional view, still generally held, that the materials of 1 Samuel show little substantial Deuteronomistic reworking. It is possible, however, that it was the Deuteronomistic historian who introduced the theme of the renunciation of vengeance into the second scene of the sparing of Saul, and one might go further and credit him with the creation of the first sparing of Saul as well.

In the current state of scholarship, this matter must be left open. It may be that no resolution will prove to be achievable on this issue at all, but it may well be that further, comprehensive study of the literary relations between the Deuteronomistic historian and the earlier stages of the development of the material will in time produce a more certain picture of the Deuteronomistic historian's creative contribution. Although few scholars seem prepared, at least at present, to accept Van Seters's broad claims for the fundamental compositional activity of the Deuteronomistic historian at virtually every point in Joshua through 2 Kings, the example of the different versions of the Goliath story suggests that this historian was actively concerned in the narrative as well as the theological shaping of his material.[26]

The difficulty of establishing the precise relations in many cases between the Deuteronomistic historian and his predecessors is related to the variety of ways in which patterns of meaning could be established across the material of 1–2 Samuel. The progressive renunciation of violence, as I have suggested, could have been built by the Deuteronomistic historian out of existing materials. With elements of the theme already present in less developed form, the Deuteronomistic historian merely needed to rework his sources to a limited extent and add the explicit emphases of the revised Goliath story. Alternatively, on a more activist interpretation of the Deuteronomistic historian's role, the theme could have been created by the historian himself and planted in 1 Samuel 24–26 as well as in chapter 17.

In other instances, a third possibility presents itself, when there is no clear indication of active creation or reworking by the Deuteronomistic historian: themes could be "found themes." By this I mean similar themes independently present in the separate materials that begin to take on a wider significance simply by the fact of the joining of these materials together. The product of the common cultural milieu rather than

---

[26]If one were to pursue a revisionist exploration of Deuteronomistic contributions to the older materials, perhaps the doubled reactions to the deaths of Hophni and Phinehas in the Ark Narrative should be examined. Might it be that the second speech, by Phinehas's wife, with its explicit theme of exile, is a Deuteronomistic creation?

of any direct interplay of texts, such elements can begin to take on shape and meaning as a result of their new context, with or without direct elaboration by the historian who joined the material together. As with the first two forms of patterning just described, here too the dividing line is not always clear; it is not always possible to say whether a theme or narrative element is part of a pattern deliberately created by the historian or whether it is a "found" pattern produced as a secondary consequence of the joining of material for other reasons.

An example can be found in the motif of the blind father. Saul's seeming blindness when David first spares him has a number of verbal echoes to the story of Jacob and Esau, as discussed above; these echoes are numerous and specific enough to suggest a deliberate analogy to the Yahwistic story. At the same time, however, there is also a degree of analogy to the first failed father in 1 Samuel itself: the blind Eli, who must hear (what he cannot see) that the Ark has been taken from Israel and his sons have been killed. The literally blind Eli and the metaphorically blind Saul appear to be the products of independent creation in the separate narratives in which they figure. It is possible that the Deuteronomistic historian did actively rework the descriptions in order to bolster this parallelism, but it is likelier that this parallel served as a "found" imagistic motif that fortuitously bolstered the theological connections that the Deuteronomistic historian wished to draw between the fates of Saul and Eli.

In one of the longest clearly Deuteronomistic interpolations to 1 Samuel, the connection between Eli and Saul is made through a long speech. An unnamed "man of God" abruptly comes to Eli and condemns him for his greedy appropriation of sacrifices—a crime that the Ark Narrative had attributed only to his sons. The man of God then prophesies that Eli's house will be punished for this sin:

The days are coming when I shall cut off your descendants and the descendants of your father's house. . . . One man shall I spare you at my altar to wear out his eyes and use up his strength, but all the rest of your house will fall by the swords of men. And this, which will happen to your two sons, Hophni and Phinehas, will be a sign to you: both of them will die on a single day. Then I shall raise up for myself a faithful priest who will do as I intend and desire. I shall build for him a secure house, and he will walk before my anointed forever. (2:31–36)

This oracle looks ahead to the slaughter of the house of Eli by Saul at Nob, the slaughter that only Abiathar survives. Though Abiathar becomes David's high priest, he is banished by Solomon after supporting Solomon's rival Adonijah. "So Solomon expelled Abiathar from being priest to the Lord, thus fulfilling the word of the Lord which he had spoken concerning the house of Eli in Shiloh" (1 Kings 2:27). Although the primary force of the oracle of the man of God is directed to this priestly history, the oracle is strongly suggestive of Saul's fate as well. Like Eli, Saul will see his house destroyed as a result of his greed; he and Jonathan will die on the same day; a single man of his family, the crippled Mephibosheth, will survive to beg at David's table. This parallelism fits in directly with the Deuteronomistic view of the monarchy as heir to the institution of prophet-judges, and the destruction of Saul's house follows the logic, and even many of the details, of the destruction of Eli's line.

The motif of blindness provides a natural seconding element in the implicit parallel between Eli and Saul (rather than in the explicit linking of Eli's sin to Abiathar's banishing; the theme of sight does not enter into the portrayal of Abiathar). Was it deliberately developed as a theme by the Deuteronomistic historian, or is it simply an appropriate coincidence? If the latter, is it one of which the historian was at any rate aware, or is it the product purely of a modern close reading, perhaps influenced less by emphases important to the Bible itself than to the modern fascination with themes of blindness and insight?

No certain resolution of these questions is possible, but there is evidence that favors the view that this found theme was elsewhere exploited by the Deuteronomistic historian and is not purely the construction of a modern reading. Sight imagery appears prominently within the "man of God" episode itself. In accusing Eli of greed, the man of God uses an interesting phrase: Eli looks at the sacrifice with a selfish (lit., narrow) eye (2:29).[27] This phrase, moreover, has an echo at the close of the Deuteronomistic Goliath story, in Saul's jealous gaze after David begins to gain popularity and to raise Saul's fear of being overthrown: "And Saul eyed David from that day forward" (18:9).

Further, the theme of blindness or false sight as a corollary of wickedness is developed in the body of the Deuteronomistic Goliath story as well. Whereas the older Goliath story gave no indication of Goliath's opinion of David, the Deuteronomistic version stresses Goliath's reaction to David's appearance: "And when the Philistine looked, and saw David, he disdained him; for he was but a youth, ruddy and comely in appearance. And the Philistine said to David, 'Am I a dog, that you come at me with sticks?' " (17:42–43). Most directly, this speech creates a contrast between the seeming weakness of the unarmed David and the bulk and power of Goliath; secondarily, it also develops the theme that "God sees not as man sees," as God had told Samuel when ordering him to anoint David rather than any of his older and more impressive brothers (16:7)—in direct contrast to the superficially imposing stature and strength of Saul (10:23).

Goliath's visual misinterpretation reinforces the implicit link between Saul and Eli, whom we first meet when Hannah comes to the temple to pray for a son: Eli sees her lips move as she prays silently, and mistakes her praying for drunkenness (1:13). In this scene, Eli is not portrayed in the highly negative terms of the interpolated speech by the man of God, though there is a certain irony in Hannah's parting supplication: "Let

---

[27]Following Cross and McCarter in restoring the text on the basis of the Septuagint; see McCarter's textual note ad loc.

your maidservant find favor in your eyes" (1:18). At the same time, the scene begins the preparation for the downfall of Eli and his house. Once Hannah has corrected Eli's mistake and explained that she is praying, he genially tells her, "Go in peace, and the God of Israel grant your petition" (1:17). Not bothering to inquire what she is praying for, he has no way to know that he is seconding her petition for a son; even if he knew that, he could not know that this son will become his own protégé Samuel—the protégé whom God will choose to supplant him, giving Samuel the same relation to Eli that David will have to Saul.[28]

In developing this and other themes, the Deuteronomistic historian took advantage of "found" themes, developed implicit connections explicitly, and created themes of his own. As in the case of his reworking of the Goliath story, he was concerned to clarify (and to modify) the theological implications of the stories and also to develop their coherence as a unified narrative. Yet his success in this endeavor was achieved at a cost: the doublings of event that create internal contradictions both small and large. Was Goliath killed by the stone or by the sword? Was Eli a weak but good man or as wicked as his sons? An important question is to what extent the Deuteronomistic historian perceived this problem. Further, to what extent *should* he have perceived it? In the balance of this chapter, I would like to discuss the nature and meaning of narrative doubling, its roots in oral tradition and its literary consequences both as an issue in a modern reading of 1–2 Samuel and as a theme that is developed within the text itself.

Oral Variants and Literary Doublings

The first thing to observe is that the doublings in 1–2 Samuel occur both on the level of content and on the level of form.

---

[28]See Garsiel, *First Book of Samuel*, 99–106, for further analogies between Saul and Eli.

The thematic linkages I have been discussing characteristically take the form of doublings of character and event: Saul becomes a new Isaac, a new Eli, a new Goliath. Along with this thematic doubling go the many narrative doublings in the story: Goliath is joined by a second Goliath; Saul is rejected twice by God, meets David twice, is spared by him twice. Often these repetitions seem contradictory to a modern reader, and even in late antiquity the rabbis were at pains to justify (and if necessary to explain away) the more pronounced contradictions. Yet these repetitions were clearly not shunned but relished by the Deuteronomistic historian. During the period of the growth of these texts, a complex interplay must have developed between theme and form. On the one hand, a metaphoric view of character and history inspired the seeking out of such analogies and bred a tolerance for narrative doublings; on the other hand, the compositional pressures inherent in combining disparate sources and traditions would in turn have reinforced a metaphoric and ironic view of history as a series of repetitive transformations of earlier events.

In 1–2 Samuel, these themes and compositional techniques reach their fullest development in the Succession Narrative and in the work of the Deuteronomistic historian, but they find expression in the earlier units of material as well. Indeed, the real roots of the technique must stretch back to oral tradition well before the period of the monarchy, when patterns of thought and modes of narration were developed that profoundly affected the transmission and then the shaping of the historical material in literary form.[29]

---

[29]The study of oral tradition, long a staple of traditional form criticism, has lately begun to take new directions, making use of comparative folklore studies and Homeric studies in a sophisticated way; see the special issue on orality of *Semeia* (vol. 5, 1976), and see Alexander Rofé, *The Book of Balaam*, on the literary adaptation of oral techniques. In the case of 1–2 Samuel, David Gunn has vigorously championed the cause of the importance of oral tradition, and discusses the issue at length in *The Story of King David: Genre and Interpretation*. It must be said, however, that his theoretical discussion of the importance of oral tradition has little observable effect on the reading of the David story

The distinctness of biblical prose certainly is intimately related to its debt to the living oral tradition, even in the case of purely literary composition. There is no reason to suppose that the Israelites were unique in their possession of a vital oral tradition; later Arabic cultures showed it as well, and indeed provide valuable analogies to biblical narrative. The Israelites' contemporaries, however, very rarely engaged in extended literary reformulation of oral methods, at least in texts that have survived. Other nomadic groups may well have had very similar saga traditions, but any literary productions that may have followed from these have disappeared, just as the Hebrews' own literary activity would have vanished without a trace if their religious tradition had not kept it alive long after the disappearance of their world.

It is also possible that the Hebrews, like the pre-Islamic Arabs, had a more vital oral tradition than most, a tradition bred and sustained in their nomadic life. The Hebrews were unusual in achieving a settled, city-oriented life (complete with literacy) very soon after the long period of the clans' existence as nomadic pastoralists, and their literary records commence unusually quickly after this period. In contrast, the older Mesopotamian societies had long been settled in agrarian societies before the development of writing. As the city-states arose, a scribal culture grew up to manage administrative and religious affairs, long before the gradual adaptation of writing to literary purposes late in the third millennium. Whatever role oral tradition played in those cultures in their own preliterate phases, literacy had taken on an independent life of its own by the time of the composition of the major extant literary works. Pronounced traces of oral influence are found in Sumerian literature of the third millennium, but the Akkadian literature of the Old Babylonian period early in the second millennium is al-

___

that it introduces. Van Seters has questioned whether Gunn has found firm evidence of independent oral tradition recoverable from the literary form the story now takes ("Problems of Orality in the Literary Analysis of the Court History of David").

ready moving within a largely literary sphere. Oral tradition certainly continued after this period, but exerted less of a shaping influence on literary tradition.[30]

No doubt various doublets in the Yahwistic and Deuteronomistic material result from the collection of variant traditions. Some of these will have been included essentially as received; in other cases editorial revisions have been undertaken, either to harmonize the variants or to distinguish them, using their differences to create narrative progressions.[31] A good example of this process can be seen in the accounts in Genesis of "the ancestress of Israel in danger," the three different occasions on which Abraham or Isaac claims that his wife is his sister. Though it has often been supposed that these variants represent received traditions included despite their evident repetitiveness, it can also be maintained that the second of the variants builds on the first, and the third builds on the first two. John Van Seters, who has devoted an extended analysis to these variants, goes so far as to argue that the latter two variants were freely composed by later writers as correctives to the first (and then, the first and second) variants (*Abraham*, 161 ff.). This may well be overstating the case; a middle position would be that independent variants were brought together and then edited into a progressive relation.

Two stages can be seen here: simple collection, and literary revision of oral material. The vitality of oral tradition in Israel had less direct results as well. A third stage of literary adaptation of orality can often be seen in the far-reaching doublings in 1–2 Samuel: purely literary composition on *analogy* to oral

---

[30]I am much indebted in this part of my discussion to conversations with my colleague Robert Tannenbaum.

[31]Tigay (*Evolution of the Gilgamesh Epic*, 85 ff.) has shown a striking case in which identical and repetitive scenes of dreams in the Sumerian poems were rewritten in the Old Babylonian epic to differentiate them and create a narrative progression. This provides a useful counter to the usual practice of biblical scholars in assuming that story variants must have been mechanically collected from divergent sources. See Zakovitch, "Assimilation in Biblical Narrative," for a discussion of several examples of assimilative creation of story variants in the Bible.

composition. This analogy need not have been deliberately or self-consciously pursued; rather, in a culture in which oral narrative was still the norm and literary composition the exception, literary creation would naturally borrow heavily from the methods of oral story telling. In pre-Islamic Arabic literature, for which the evidence is fuller, the same process can be observed as purely literary narratives come to be composed on the basis of old oral techniques.[32]

This oral habit of composition can be seen in cases where a unified oral tradition is certainly not present. An interesting example is the arrangement of material in the miscellany at the close of the story of David. As they now stand, the disparate materials in 2 Samuel 21–24 are organized in a form remarkably close to the ring composition so often seen in Homer. An outer frame is formed by accounts of Saul's sin against the Gibeonites (21:1–14) and David's sin in taking a census (24:8–39). Nested within these narratives are two summaries of the adventures of David's heroes (21:15–22; 23:8–39). In between these two summaries are two psalms of David (22:1–51 and 23:1–7). Thus the entire "unit" shows a symmetrical ring composition of the form *a b c c b a*.

As Meir Sternberg notes, what is most striking about the use of this literary device here is its lack of any literary function (*Poetics*, 40). It is a kind of appendix to the account of David's life, in which disparate blocks of material are assembled in a convenient manner. In oral narrative, ring composition was an important technique aiding the singer's memory and providing suspense and resolution within speeches and episodes; here, however, the technique survives as the natural organizational method even though literacy has replaced the need for aids to oral memory and even though no special dramatic movement is being created. Indeed, this elegant ring composition was not even the result of a single artistic act, but was gradually

---

[32]See J. R. Porter, "Pre-Islamic Arabic Historical Traditions and the Early Historical Narratives of the Old Testament."

produced in a series of stages, with the introduction of the two "framing" narratives separately for different reasons, and then a later addition of the summaries of the deeds of the heroes, itself later divided by the addition of the psalms.[33]

As oral techniques became literary, the biblical historians found in oral variants a powerful compositional tool. Along with a healthy skepticism concerning the reliability of oral tradition went a growing awareness of the literary exploitability of oral form. The result in 1–2 Samuel is a narrative whose structure is built out of variants of individual stories, and out of different stories reworked into variants of each other. At the same time, the text thematizes the doubling of narrative in a variety of ways, providing within its narration a virtual taxonomy of the possible motives and consequences of variation in reporting of events. It is in this theme of doubled reports that the Deuteronomistic historian comes closest to the methodological reflection in Herodotus. Where Herodotus openly discusses the problems he faces in sorting through differing accounts and in distinguishing true from false and probable from improbable, the Deuteronomistic historian gives this problem to his characters.[34]

Already in the Ark Narrative, the theme of the variability of oral tradition was seen in the garbled Exodus story recounted by the terrified Philistine troops. Here the theme is treated straightforwardly: pagans lack a true understanding of history. The revised History of David's Rise takes the theme further, once again focusing on tales told by unbelieving troops, but the earlier sharp distinction between pagan and Israelite no longer appears. Now the troops are Saul's own men, not outright pagans but certainly imperfect believers, the representa-

---

[33]The basic description of this process was worked out at the turn of the century by Budde, *Die Bücher Samuel erklärt* ad loc. See also McCarter, *II Samuel*, 18–19. For further discussion of the transitional status of much biblical narrative between oral and literary techniques, see Robert C. Culley, *Studies in the Structure of Hebrew Narrative*.

[34]Compare Polzin's discussion of hermeneutical themes in the book of Deuteronomy in *Moses and the Deuteronomist*.

tives of the ideology of force that has been stymied by the superior power of Goliath.

All the men of Israel, when they saw the man, fled from him, and were much afraid. Then a man of Israel said, "Have you seen this man who comes up, coming to defy Israel? If there were a man who could kill him, the king would give him great riches, and his daughter, and would make his father's house free in Israel." (17:24–25)

Lacking David's knowledge of the true dynamics of history, namely the need for total and direct dependence on God, one of the soldiers tells a story about their difficulty. Forgetting God altogether, he casts the conflict in terms of a folktale, whose characters are the king, the giant, a hero, and the king's daughter. This rumor spreads, and when David inquires whether a reward has been offered for the slaying of Goliath, the people pass on the rumor as fact.[35] This fiction is an expression of the people's unbelief, their need to imagine an earthly solution to the crisis that faces them, and their fantasy of vast earthly rewards for the *homo ex machina* who would save them. Saul has, of course, offered no such reward, and no more is heard of riches and the offer of a daughter until his self-destructive jealousy leads him to put forward the same tale, now a conscious fiction on his part.

In its present form, then, this Goliath story shows the dangerous connection between fiction and unbelief, worked out through the portrayal of the genesis of rumor and its reappearance in Saul's grim parody of the tale.[36] It is possible that

---

[35]The RSV and some other translations make this story a collective rumor from its inception, translating the initial report of the rumor, *wayy'omer 'ish yisra'el*, as "and the men of Israel said." Both the verb and the noun are in the singular, however, and there is no reason to read a collective plural here. Rather, there is a progression from the initial speculation by the single man to its general acceptance by "the people" (*ha'am*).

[36]The text creates its theme by direct juxtaposition of the man's rumor and Saul's ruse. It is not a matter of concern to the author to explore Saul's state of mind to a sufficient extent to show whether he has deliberately exploited the rumor or simply hit on a parallel ruse by chance. Throughout the narratives in the Deuteronomistic history, unbelievers regularly fall into repetitive patterns of self-destructive behavior, consciously or otherwise.

the author of the revised History of David's Rise adapted the general folktale of the slaying of a giant for use here, with no direct source apart from the chronicle of the skirmishes between David's men and the giants in Gath. It is also possible that there had actually been a folktale in circulation in which David *was* rewarded with the hand of Saul's daughter upon the slaying of the Philistine champion. In either event, the result is a deliberate transformation of a common folktale motif, motivated by a new understanding of the ironies of the interaction of character in human history under God's rule.

The pre-Deuteronomistic and Deuteronomistic interest in reworking old folk patterns has a parallel, and probably a model, in the Yahwistic material of Genesis. Using Vladimir Propp's schematic analysis of folk motifs, Roland Barthes has shown that the episode of Jacob's struggle with the angel (Genesis 32) takes much of its power from an uncanny reversal of the folk pattern it revises. The kingly figure of God sets Jacob a task, but to accomplish it he must overcome a blocking figure, the angel who bars his way as he tries to cross over into his brother's territory. At the climax of the story, the blocking figure is revealed to be God himself.[37]

Similarly, in Saul's ruse, the Philistine opponents are in reality his own tools. The motif has been developed further, however, in several ways. The focus is no longer on a literal wrestling match, but on the moral struggle between David and Saul in which military exploits increasingly take second place; characteristically, it is only Saul who is concerned with the physical struggle, fearing David's success in battle and attempting to hit him with spears. Further, the folktale is now presented *as* a folktale; the transformations implicit in the Yahwistic account become part of the theme in 1 Samuel. A third level of development can be seen as well, as the Yahwistic saga material itself

---

[37]Barthes, "Struggle with the Angel." See also John Barton's discussion of the essay in *Reading the OT*, 117–19. As Barton says, "If the meaning of a folktale is a function of the conventions of the genre, then the meaning of *this* tale is a function of the flouting of those conventions" (119).

becomes malleable tradition suitable for metaphoric revision: the capture of the Ark recalls the sojourn in Egypt; Saul variously plays the roles of Hamor, Isaac, and Esau, and perhaps also of Pharaoh as well, in his tyrannical and self-destructive opposition to God's will.

Truth and Fiction in the Succession Narrative

The theme of doubled reporting, and the corresponding practice of doubling incidents, are thus already associated with each other in the History of David's Rise; they reach their furthest development within the Succession Narrative (2 Sam. 9–20 plus 1 Kings 1–2). Oral techniques are still used, but less directly; symmetrical framing now provides purely thematic resonances with no necessary link to story variants. Thus the beginning of David's sin is unwittingly recalled by Absalom at the height of his rebellion, when he goes in to his father's concubines. In order to make his assumption of his father's role as public (and as humiliating) as possible, he has a tent set up on the roof of the palace—the very spot from which David had first seen Bathsheba (11:2; 16:22).

In the History of David's Rise, the folktale of David and Goliath was used to structure the history that followed it through an extended series of direct doublings of incidents on analogy to oral variants. Now, David struggles not with an emblematic giant but with his own children. Echoes of the Goliath story may still be seen, both at the beginning of David's sin, with Uriah sent out as Saul had sent David, and at the end: Absalom is caught in a tree as he tries to flee from David's men. The tree is an oak, 'elah, a detail that may serve to recall David's first great victory, against Goliath, in the Valley of Elah. These echoes are indirect, however, and add resonance to a story now primarily shaped by ambiguities of human character and motivation.

In the Succession Narrative, the earlier connection between faith and truthful reporting is extended and broadened into an exploration of problematics of knowledge and judgment. Now, oral variants are presented in terms of truth and fiction, or are collapsed into parables. In this narrative, doubled reports are characteristically produced not by the collection or composition of variant scenes, but by pressures on characters within a given scene. From motives honorable or dishonorable, characters are as likely to lie as to tell the truth; one recent study discusses no fewer than eighteen separate instances of deception within the fifteen chapters of the Succession Narrative (Hagan, "Deception"). Not all false reports are even deliberate; rumor serves as a free agent, unmotivated within the story. The most striking example of a false rumor occurs when Absalom kills his brother Amnon in vengeance for the rape of their sister Tamar. In order to catch his brother off guard, he invites all his siblings to a feast at his residence. Once Amnon is drunk, Absalom's servants kill him, and David's other sons flee.

While they were on the way, tidings came to David, "Absalom has slain all the king's sons, and not one of them is left." Then the king arose, and rent his garments, and lay on the earth. . . . But Jonadab the son of Shimeah, David's brother, said, "Let not my lord suppose that they have killed all the young men the king's sons, for Amnon alone is dead, for by the command of Absalom this has been determined from the day he forced his sister Tamar. Now therefore let not my lord the king so take it to heart as to suppose that all the king's sons are dead; for Amnon alone is dead." (2 Sam. 13:30–33)

The false report of the death of all of David's sons is unmotivated within the story, evidently an example of the exaggeration customary in times of crisis. At the same time, however, the author exploits the rumor in various ways. The immediate focus of the false report is on the reassuring speech given by David's nephew Jonadab, whose role continues after his speech: he announces to David that his surviving sons have been sighted approaching Jerusalem (v. 35). But Jonadab's role is more complicated than that of purveyor of reassurance, for his knowledge of the truth stems from his complicity in the original rape of Tamar—an aspect of the story he does not choose to mention to the king in explaining Absalom's motive for slaying Amnon. It was in fact Jonadab himself who had counseled Amnon in the deception by which Amnon would be able to get his sister alone.

The object of the deception had not been Tamar as much as David himself. "Lie down on your bed," Jonadab tells Amnon, "and pretend to be ill; and when your father comes to see you, say to him, 'Let my sister Tamar come and give me bread to eat. . .' " (13:5). The story goes on to show in detail that Amnon carried out the conversation with David, who then ordered Tamar to attend to her brother. Thus David, having been deceived by Jonadab's plot, is now reassured that Absalom is only retaliating for the consequences of the plot—not knowing that its very instigator is the bearer of this reassurance. David is caught up in a world where good and evil, truth and falsehood, are subtly intertwined, a world in which the king is under a constant obligation to exercise judgment in difficult cases.

The false report and Jonadab's speech also serve to establish or to reinforce echoes between the story and other events, both legendary and modern. Most directly, the presence of Jonadab as the counselor of his cousin Amnon is a debased version of the role that Jonathan had played for David; "Jonadab" and "Jonathan" are semantically parallel, and may even have the same meaning, "The Lord Gives."[38] Whereas Jonathan helped David to deal with his malevolent father Saul, Jonadab helps Amnon to thwart his benevolent father's watchful eye. Amnon's lust for his sister parallels the lust for the kingdom that Saul had imagined David to feel.[39]

David is caught up in a tragic situation that is outside the scope of his knowledge and beyond his control, but at the same

---

[38]*Nathan* is the customary verb meaning "to give"; the root of "Jonadab," the verb *nadav*, means "to offer freely," "to volunteer," or also, interestingly, "to urge on, prompt." It is notable too that some manuscripts give "Jonathan" as the name of Amnon's cousin, in place of "Jonadab."

[39]Hagan ("Deception") notes that almost every deception in the Succession Narrative has as its object the acquisition of either a woman or the kingdom.

time it is a situation of his own creation, since the sexual transgressions that precipitate Absalom's disaffection and later rebellion are a punishment for David's own adultery with Bathsheba. The death of Amnon is the second of three deaths of David's sons that help to structure the narrative, and at this middle point the presence of Jonadab as a trusted counselor at David's side provides a commentary on David's entrapment within the consequences of his earlier misdeeds.

The force of this commentary is sharpened by the content of the false report: that *all* of David's sons have been killed. Within the story, we are shown a David who is helpless in the face of a wild rumor, needing Jonadab's sober recollection of past history to scale things down to reality. David seems to have forgotten (a modern reader might say, to have repressed) his awareness of Absalom's motives for hostility to the defiler of his sister—though the living memory of this crime is seen in the fact that Absalom has taken Tamar into his household (13:20); indeed, he actually names his own daughter after her (14:27).

If David's paralysis in the face of the rumor provides a commentary within the story, it has resonances outside the story as well, as the rumor that all of his sons have been killed points toward a famous instance in which all of a king's sons *were* slain. In 2 Kings 9–10, the prophet Elisha anoints Jehu the son of Jehoshaphat as king; Jehu is commanded to strike down the reigning king, Joram the son of Ahab, and his brothers, Ahab's seventy other sons. When the princes' guardians submit in terror to his authority, Jehu privately orders them to kill their wards. Once they do so, he publicly denounces them and slaughters them as well. He then heads toward Samaria, where he will destroy the remnants of Ahab's house there; on his way, he meets a man—Jehonadab, leader of a group of zealous servants of God. Jehu and Jehonadab affirm their mutual friendship and loyalty, and Jehonadab accompanies Jehu as he completes the destruction of Ahab's house.

"Jehonadab" is a variant of "Jonadab," and in fact Jehonadab is called Jonadab when Jeremiah goes to visit his followers (Jeremiah 35). He and Amnon's cousin are the only people of that name in the Bible, and these are their only appearances. In 2 Kings 10, Jehu is in the midst of avenging the religious transgressions of Ahab, who had been incited by his wife Jezebel to slay the prophets of God and substitute the worship of Baal (1 Kings 16 ff.). When David meets Jonadab, he is a passive spectator learning of Absalom's avenging of the breaking of the incest taboo by Amnon. If the cunning Jonadab is an ironic echo of the zealous Jonadab/Jehonadab, David is a reduced Jehu, failing to carry out justice on his own wicked son. The matter is more complicated here than in the black-and-white portrayals in 1–2 Kings, however: David ought to be enforcing justice, like Jehu, but at the same time, it is his own sons who are the criminals, and he is the sinning father whose crimes reecho in the younger generation. In this respect David is parallel to Ahab as much as to Jehu, and he is paralyzed by reluctance to exercise judgment against his own household.[40] In a further thematic development, wickedness is not absolute and immutable (as with the evil Jezebel and the irrevocably weak Ahab), but is fostered by David's own inaction: his failure to deal with Amnon breeds new crime, as Absalom—after two years in which David has done nothing—turns to fratricide, the first step on his road to rebellion.

This reading of the parallel between the two Jonadabs assumes, of course, that the Succession Narrative was written after the events described in 2 Kings 10, which occurred in 842, some eighty years after the end of Solomon's reign. This parallel adds evidence to support those recent scholars who have disputed the older supposition that the Succession Narrative

---

[40]The parallel between David and Ahab is reinforced by the fact that, apart from David, Ahab is the only recipient of a parable of judgment in biblical narrative: a prophet tells a parable by which Ahab is unwittingly led to pronounce judgment against himself for a dereliction of duty (1 Kings 20:35–43); compare Nathan's famous parable of the poor man and his lamb (2 Sam. 12:1–15) and see the discussion by Uriel Simon, "The Poor Man's Ewe Lamb."

was a virtual eyewitness account written in the time of Solomon himself. If the Succession Narrative is a product of a later time, it does not necessarily follow, however, that it was written after the composition of the Deuteronomistic history as a whole, in which the story of Jehu and Jehonadab is now found.[41] If the Succession Narrative predates the composition of the Deuteronomistic history, as most believe, the story of Jehu's meeting with Jehonadab may have been circulating in oral tradition. On the other hand, it may well have existed in written form in a source later used by the Deuteronomistic historian, the "Book of the Chronicles of the Kings of Israel," to which the reader of 2 Kings is referred for further information on Jehu's life (2 Kings 10:34). In either case, the earlier event of Absalom's vengeance is evaluated against the example of recent history, in a manner that complements the older practice of shaping historical representation against the emblematic patterns of primordial history.

The theme of the importance of just judgment in the face of conflicting reports also points to the story of Solomon, who will exercise judgment far more effectively than David. This foreshadowing is particularly clear in the case of the dispute between Mephibosheth and Ziba. After Saul's death, his sole surviving son, Mephibosheth, is treated kindly by David. When Absalom's rebellion forces David to flee Jerusalem, Mephibosheth's servant Ziba comes to David with supplies, saying that he has stolen them away from his master, who hopes to

---

[41]Van Seters has advanced this argument in his recent book, but initial reactions, at any rate, have ranged from skepticism to disbelief. See the reviews by R. A. Oden, B. Halpern, and D. L. Petersen. Like Petersen, I find it difficult to credit Van Seters's underlying claim that the Succession Narrative is a bitter denunciation of the monarchic ideal as embodied in the figure of David, a denunciation he sees as arising in response to the disaster of the fall of the monarchy and the deportations to Babylon. The Succession Narrative is no more an antimonarchic polemic than it is a *pro*monarchic polemic. Though the portrayal of David is at its most complex here, there is much that is sympathetic to him, and the negative aspects are hardly, if at all, worse than the negative aspects already found in the History of David's Rise.

regain power by supporting Absalom. After David defeats Absalom and returns to Jerusalem, Mephibosheth comes to David:

The king said to him, "Why did you not go with me, Mephibosheth?" He answered, "My lord, O king, my servant deceived me; for your servant said to him, 'Saddle an ass for me, that I may ride upon it and go with the king.' For your servant is lame. He has slandered your servant to my lord the king." (2 Sam. 19:25–27 [26–28])

A direct conflict is presented between the stories of Ziba and Mephibosheth, a conflict that the narrator interprets for us by relating that Mephibosheth has gone in mourning for the entire duration of the rebellion (v. 24 [25]). In any event, either Ziba or his master must be lying, but David cannot be bothered to sort out the truth: "And the king said to him, 'Why speak any more of your affairs? I have decided: you and Ziba shall divide the land.' And Mephibosheth said to the king, 'Oh, let him take it all, since my lord the king has come safely home' " (vv. 29–30 [30–31]).

This scene is directly modeled on the most famous story of Solomon's wisdom: the conflict between the two women who both claim to be the mother of one child. Solomon resolves the question by ordering the child cut in two; he knows that the true mother will be the one who would rather give up her child than see it cut apart (1 Kings 3:16–28). But where Solomon is supremely ingenious, the impatient David merely happens to stumble on the device of ordering the division of the contested property, and then he misses the point when the true owner gives up his claim rather than insist on a division.

The irony of this missed opportunity is increased by Mephibosheth's trust in David and willingness to accept any judgment as just. He expresses his trust and gratitude in a speech that clarifies the issues at play here and in other scenes of judgment: "My lord the king is like the angel of God," he says after pleading that Ziba has deceived him; "do therefore what seems good to you. For all my father's house were but men doomed to death before my lord the king; but you set your servant among those who eat at your table. What further right have I, then, to cry to the king?" (19:27–28 [19:28–29]).

On hearing of Solomon's judgment concerning the disputed child, the people of Israel are in awe, "because they perceived that the wisdom of God was within him [*ki-ḥokmat 'Elohim beqirbo*], to render justice" (1 Kings 3:28). Mephibosheth has the same opinion of David, but he expresses it in heightened terms: he says that his lord the king is "like the angel of God," *kemal'ak ha'Elohim*. By this praise, Mephibosheth unwittingly echoes the flattering terms used by the wise woman of Tekoa in urging David to forgive Absalom for the murder of Amnon: "Your handmaid thought, 'The word of my lord the king will set me at rest,' " she tells him, " 'for my lord the king is like the angel of God, discerning good and evil' " (14:17). If the content of her parable of fratricide recalls the story of Cain and Abel, the flattery following it recalls the tempting of Eve by the serpent. The woman is wise, *ḥakam*, ironically the term also used for the wisdom that enables Solomon to dispense justice. The same term was also used for Amnon's friend Jonadab when he counseled Amnon in furthering the sexual transgression he desired (13:3). In that scene, the beginning of the troubles in the younger generation echoed the story of the Fall; now, as the consequences of Amnon's transgression are worked out, David too is drawn in. Like Eve, he is tempted to be like God, knowing good and evil. The temptation is actually strengthened by the addition of the phrase "like *the angel of* God," as it deflects an impious assertion of direct likeness to God while at the same time flattering the king (*melek*) as God's angel (*mal'ak*).

A parable is a kind of collapsed double report: a fiction that shields a true story. Not content with one such double story, the Succession Narrative doubles its parables, in a further linking of the story of the rebellion to the earlier story of David's sin with Bathsheba. The parable that Nathan tells to bring David to his senses is an example of a constructive use of parable, to restore the king to self-knowledge. When David angrily condemns the rich man of Nathan's parable, who has stolen a poor man's sheep to feed a guest, Nathan replies, "You are the man," and goes on to deliver God's judgment against him. David is brought to repentance and self-understanding through this parable, but the same cannot be said for the parable told by the woman of Tekoa. In this case, the king, who consistently fails to distinguish true from false, is led into allowing the return of the estranged and criminal Absalom; and Absalom, as he begins to build a base of general popularity, does so by exploiting popular awareness of the uncertainty of judgment at David's court. He stands at the city gate and intercepts anyone who comes to seek judgment from David. "Absalom would say to him, 'See, your claims are good and right; but there is no man deputed by the king to hear you.' Absalom said moreover, 'Oh that I were judge in the land! Then every man with a suit or cause might come to me, and I would give him justice' " (15:3–4). The former vigilante puts himself forward as the exponent of formal legal procedure, as a ruse to build a political base for parricidal rebellion.

The Succession Narrative displays many more such moments of tension between speech and thought, appearance and truth. The examples discussed above will suffice, however, to show the close connection between narrative doublings and the theme of duplicity. The issues of knowledge, judgment, and understanding are developed into a searching exploration of the nature of kingship, not in the interests of bolstering or attacking the Davidic line, but as a locus for exploring the problematics of human relations with God. In this, it can be compared to the *Gilgamesh Epic's* concern with defining the meaning and value of human culture in light of the limitations on both human power and human knowledge. Where Gilgamesh was literally part human and part divine, struggling to discover the meaning of being like the gods, *kima ilim*, David as king is metaphorically godlike, but we are shown the limitations of God's earthly representative. David must come to terms with his inability to control history, even to control his own family, and at the same time we are shown the guiding power and wisdom of God underlying events but never overriding human initiative.

Type-Scenes and the Meaning of Repetition

What is the nature of the Succession Narrative, and why was it written? Leonhard Rost believed that it was composed in the reign of Solomon in order to justify his accession instead of his older brothers. In a recent statement of this position: "An un-expected candidate had succeeded to the throne, and his reign had started a minor bloodbath. What justification could there be for all this?" (Thornton, "Solomonic Apologetic," 161). Others have felt that this view overemphasizes the political di-mension of the story, and it has been argued that the title "Succession Narrative" gives too much prominence to the final chapters. Consequently, the text is now often referred to, more neutrally, as the Court History of David, and it is sometimes suggested that the final chapters dealing with Solomon's succession (1 Kings 1–2) are no more than an appendix, or perhaps a later addition, formulated roughly in the style of the Court History in order to orient the document toward a justi-fication of Solomon's accession. In this view, essentially pro-David accounts in 2 Samuel have been given a pro-Solomon and perhaps anti-David emphasis by the addition of 1 Kings 1–2.[42] On the other hand, several recent writers, agreeing that the focus of the Succession Narrative is largely on David but stressing the negative aspects of his story, have argued that the narrative was always anti-David and probably anti-Solomon as well, until it was later revised to look more positive.[43]

---

[42]Thus McCarter, *II Samuel*, 9–16, with a good summary of other views.
[43]See in particular Delekat, "Tendenz und Theologie der David-Salomo-Erzähl-ung." These views have been developed further by Veijola (in *Die ewige Dy-nastie*), who sees a subsequent pro-David revision by the Deuteronomistic historian; Würthwein sees a pre-Deuteronomistic revision toward a positive

In my view, 1 Kings 1–2 has been created by the Deuteronomistic historian as a bridge between the stories of David and of Solomon, and the historian has edited the David story to reinforce the connections. Thus the story of Ziba and Mephibosheth looks ahead to the judgment of Solomon in 1 Kings 3, and it looks back, as well, to the time of the judges before the establishment of the monarchy. Mephibosheth's praise of David as the angel of God echoes the people's wonder at Solomon's wisdom, but with a significant difference in wording. Solomon's wisdom enables him genuinely "to do justice," *la'asot mishpat*, also translatable as "to render legal decisions." In contrast, the too trusting Mephibosheth says that "my lord the king is like the angel of God; do therefore what seems good to you," literally, "do what is good in your eyes," *wa'aseh hattov be'eyneyka* (2 Sam. 19:27[28]).

By doing what is right in his own eyes, as opposed to doing justice, David endangers the kingdom, risking a return to the chaotic days before the monarchy. Mephibosheth's statement echoes, in fact, the closing words of the Book of Judges, the Deuteronomistic verse that provides the transition between the time before the monarchy and its establishment in 1 Samuel: "In those days there was no king in Israel; every man did what was right in his own eyes," *hayyashar be'eynaw ya'aseh* (Judg. 21:25, which is followed directly by 1 Samuel in the Hebrew Bible).

This phrase appears once in 1–2 Samuel as well: in the climactic speech by Joab after the death of Absalom. David, whose strength of character and faith in God have seen him through all his difficulties until now, breaks down, sitting by himself and weeping, "O my son Absalom, my son, my son Absalom! Would I had died instead of you, O Absalom, my son, my son!" (2 Sam. 18:33 [19:1]). "The victory that day was turned into mourning," the narrator says, "and the people stole

---

presentation (*Die Erzählung von der Thronfolge Davids*). Langlamet goes further, seeing three separate pre-Deuteronomistic editions ("Pour ou contre Salomon?").

into the city as people steal in who are ashamed when they flee in battle" (19:3[4]). Joab comes to David and urges him to pull himself together and return to his responsibilities. The heart of his speech is a stinging rebuke: "Today I perceive that if Absalom were alive and all of us were dead today, that would be right in your eyes," *yashar be'eyneyka* (19:6[7]). David gets up, and goes to sit at the gate of the city, which is the place where Absalom had stood, stirring discontent by questioning David's ability to dispense justice and hence his fitness to rule.

This scene reinforces the links between Mephibosheth's ambiguous praise of David, the coming story of Solomon, and the earlier stories of the time of the judges. It also doubles an episode found at the beginning of 1 Samuel, the scene in the Ark Narrative in which Eli learns that his sons have been killed and the Ark captured by the Philistines. Eli is also sitting at the gate, or perhaps on top of it (thus McCarter), the customary place where someone eager for news waits to learn the outcome of a battle. Hearing of the Israelite defeat, he falls over (or even, off the gate), breaks his neck, and dies. The narrator then adds a chronological note: "He had judged [*shaphat*] Israel forty years" (1 Sam. 4:18).

This scene provides a model for the portrayal of David at the moment at which he suffers the full consequences of his poor judgments in dealing first with Amnon and then with Absalom. This general observation raises questions, however, as it is not self-evident that the scenes involved can be discussed as elements in an overall literary structure. First of all, they presumably were both present in the separate compositions, the Ark Narrative and the Succession Narrative. Secondly, what is clearly involved here is what Robert Alter has called a type-scene (*Art of Biblical Narrative*, 47–62). Is it fair to assume a genuine literary relation between these two scenes if they not only stem from different sources but also represent different examples of a stock situation? Does their similarity only strike the modern eye as significant, given the loss of most of the literature of the time, so that we imagine a deliberate thematic connection where in reality there is only a chance repetition of a situational cliché?

As Alter has argued, the conventional nature of such scenes does not in itself divest them of thematic relevance in the contexts in which they are used. He shows, with witty examples from Genesis and from Hollywood westerns, that type-scenes depend for their effect both on adherence to conventions of presentation and on modification of those conventions: the sheriff must always be quicker on the draw than the villain, and any variation in the formula of the shoot-out at high noon immediately signals a problem that the audience can expect to see resolved within the rules of the type. Thus, if the sheriff appears on the scene with his right arm in a sling, the audience is immediately alerted to the question of how he will get to his gun with his left hand.

The type-scene of the announcement of battle news appears three times in 1–2 Samuel, and the middle instance forms a bridge between the two currently under discussion. This is the scene in which David learns of the death of Saul and Jonathan. The parallels are very close to the announcement of the Philistine victory and capture of the Ark. In both instances, a messenger appears, having fled from the battlefield with torn clothes; seeing him, Eli/David asks, "What is the news?" (*meh-hayah haddavar*, 1 Sam. 4:16; 2 Sam. 1:4). In reply, the messenger says that the army fled; a great many fell, and also Eli's sons (in the second case, Saul and Jonathan) are dead.

Neither of these scenes is the source of the other; rather, each plays in a different way on the underlying conventions of the type-scene involved.[44] The Ark Narrative's account of Eli already presupposes a basic type-scene in which the anxious father learns the tragic news of the death of his son(s) in battle, an element reinforced by the fact that Eli addresses the mes-

---

[44] Arguments for a direct dependency can be made, but not altogether persuasively, as in Zakovitch's argument that the story of the fall of Saul is actually dependent on the death of Eli (*For Three—For Four*, 300–6). His evidence more readily shows variations on an underlying type.

senger familiarly as *beni*, "my son." The scene strengthens this association in order to play against it, as we discover that Eli is killed with grief not at the report of his sons' death at all, but at the messenger's concluding statement that the Ark was captured as well.

The second scene, from the History of David's Rise, exploits the conventions of the type in a different way. Here David anxiously awaits news of the climactic battle between the Philistines and the forces of Saul. This battle has already been described by the narrator, complete with a scene of the death of Saul; the audience's interest in the scene of the report to David will be in his reaction. Will he mourn at the Philistine triumph over Israel and capture of several cities, or will he rejoice at the death of his mortal enemy? The account pursues this question through an extensive modification of the type-scene. When the messenger, an Amalekite from Saul's army, announces the deaths of Saul and Jonathan, David does not react either with joy or with grief, as the audience would expect, answering the central question raised by the scene; instead, he asks, "How do you know that Saul and his son Jonathan are dead?" (2 Sam. 1:5).

Suddenly, and surprisingly, the focus is neither on the dead king nor the king-to-be who has received the news but on the messenger himself. In reply, the Amalekite describes his personal involvement in the death of Saul. He says that he himself killed Saul, at Saul's request, after Saul had lost the battle, and he has brought along Saul's crown and armlet as proof. Thus the messenger, asked to prove the certainty of his report, is able to demonstrate not merely his direct observation of the battle but his own involvement in its climax. The Amalekite, however, is lying. The narrator has just told us that at the time of his death Saul was not with the Amalekite but with his armor-bearer. Saul asked his armor-bearer to kill him, but the armor-bearer feared to harm the Lord's anointed, and refused; Saul then killed himself by falling on his own sword, and his armor-bearer followed suit (1 Sam. 31:3–6). The discrepancy

between these accounts has sometimes been taken as evidence
of different sources incongruously combined, but as other commentators have noted, the scenes work perfectly together if the
messenger is inventing his account in hopes of currying favor
with David.

The Amalekite messenger thus embodies one of the two possibilities that the narrator would have expected to be present
in the minds of his audience: that David would rejoice at Saul's
death. On the contrary, as the Amalekite learns to his grief,
David is heartbroken and orders the Amalekite put to death
for having killed the Lord's anointed king (2 Sam. 1:14–16).
The audience's question is thus answered in a dramatic fashion, one that furthermore serves to exonerate David of any
charge of having sought to destroy Saul. In his lying account,
the Amalekite places himself in the position of Saul's armor-
bearer and claims to have done what the narrator has told us
the armor-bearer refused to do. By this detail, the History of
David's Rise portrays the Amalekite as the negative image of
David, who, it will be recalled, began his military service (at
the beginning of the History) precisely as Saul's armor-bearer
(1 Sam. 16:21). The audience, meanwhile, must credit David
with utmost generosity or else must see itself cast in the image
of the self-seeking Amalekite, who falsifies history for personal
gain. As a foreigner, a resident alien (ger), the Amalekite lacks
the instinctive sense of the sacredness of God's choice of the
king that a true Israelite should have, and by showing the fals-
ity of his perspective the author binds us to David at the very
moment when the way is cleared for him to take Saul's place.

There is no reason to suppose that the historian of David's
rise meant his audience to recall the death of Eli on hearing
the story of David's reaction to the death of Saul and Jonathan.
On the contrary, his purpose was very different, and the whole
force of the justification of the heroic, generous, and faithful
David would be weakened if his audience were to dwell on
analogies to the pitiful figure of the blind Eli. The two scenes
are separate examples of an underlying type-scene, which is

not found in "pure" form in either case but is modified and played on, in different ways and for different purposes, by the authors of the Ark Narrative and the History of Daivd's Rise.

The matter is somewhat different with the version of the type-scene in the Succession Narrative. Once again there is a modification of the underlying form, but in this case the scene appears to have been shaped in order to recall the earlier stories. Some of this shaping seems to have been undertaken by the author of the original Succession Narrative, in order to justify David's treatment of Absalom on analogy to his treatment of Saul. Further shaping, however, appears to have been contributed by the Deuteronomistic historian in the course of creating the overall history of the early monarchy.

In the first stage, it is evident that the author of the Succession Narrative has gone to some lengths to show that David did not seek the death of his son: David announces publicly his desire that Absalom be spared, and the whole army hears him (2 Sam. 18:5, 12). Presumably the author's purpose was to clear David of the imputation of bloodguilt against his own son. What better way for the author to bolster the credibility of this effort than to model David's reaction to Absalom's death on his reaction to the death of Saul, as reported in the History of David's Rise? It may be for this reason that the narrator uses a metaphor of military defeat, when the people see David's grief: they steal into the city "as people steal in who are ashamed when they flee in battle" (19:3). The victory over Absalom is thus made to resemble the defeat at the hands of the Philistines, when the Israelites did flee from battle on seeing Saul's death (1 Sam. 31:7).

When the Deuteronomistic historian came to create the overall story of Samuel, Saul, and David, the type-scene was present as a "found" element within each of the major existing narratives that would go into the new history. He then cemented the pattern, fortuitously present, through the addition of a culminating version of the type-scene, in his added account of the accession of Solomon. When Solomon is anointed as king on David's orders, his chief rival Adonijah hears tumult in the city—an emphasis on noise that makes the coronation resemble a battle—and asks what has happened. In comes a man, Jonathan ben Abiathar, who has been out in the city, and Adonijah greets him, saying, "Come in, for you are a worthy man and bring good news" (1 Kings 1:42). These words echo David's words on seeing the messenger who comes from the battle against Absalom: "He is a good man, and comes with good tidings" (2 Sam. 18:27). Adonijah is wrong, however, as David was wrong—or right in spite of himself, as David also was. The tidings are very good for the kingdom, but bitter to the recipients.

By structuring this account in the light of the type-scene of a battle report, the Deuteronomistic historian has created a density of instances of this type-scene that brings them into the foreground of the overall story, helping to link the once separate elements into a unified story and providing analogies by which any one scene can be assessed against the others. This unification could have been created simply by the assembling of the materials and the addition of the fourth scene; in addition, the historian may well have edited the earlier scenes in order to strengthen their similarity. Perhaps the close parallels in wording between the stories of the announcements of the deaths of Eli's sons and of Saul show not only the underlying type-scene but also a degree of editing to create an explicit comparison where none would have been intended by the original authors. Perhaps too the Deuteronomistic historian contributed, or expanded, the long speech of rebuke in the Succession Narrative scene, when Joab urges David to pull himself together after the death of Absalom. Speeches of rebuke are a favorite Deuteronomistic device for clarifying themes and linking stories, as in the addition of the speech by the "man of God" rebuking Eli. That speech has indeed a certain relevance to the present scene: the man of God accuses Eli of honoring his sons above God (1 Sam. 2:29), as Joab accuses David of preferring Absalom over his entire people (2 Sam. 19:6[7]). It is likely, too, that the notice that Eli had "judged" Israel for forty years is a Deuteronomistic insertion into the Ark Narrative, and by these insertions the historian has created a direct relation between Eli and David, one that looks back to the anarchy before the creation of the monarchy, and forward to the wise judgments of Solomon.

The wide range of opinion concerning the purposes of the author of the Succession Narrative and the Deuteronomistic assessment of the monarchy stems to a large degree from the fact that these writers often made their points not through explicit editorial commentary but through skillful manipulation and modulation of patterns within their material. What is most needed for the better understanding of this aspect of their work is careful and detailed study of the use of type-scenes and of the possibilities for creation of meaning through narrative juxtaposition. This is the area that structuralist biblical study has claimed as its own, but this structural study can best be pursued in conjunction with a close attention to the history of the text. The four versions of the type-scene just discussed were not created in an ideal nontime and nonspace, but have come into being in particular contexts and then have found new life in the new context of the overall story of the monarchy. In the preceding pages I have given a version of the dynamic of this development, though certainly the views presented here would require modification in various ways if aspects of the underlying text history were seen differently. Perhaps, for example, the stories in 1 Kings 1–2 were always part of the Succession Narrative and the Deuteronomistic contribution is less than I have supposed. To the extent that the process has been successfully outlined, however, the study of the use of this type-scene gives a clearer sense of the literary development of the text.

A further question remains: Does this reconstruction of the literary history give guidance in interpreting the resulting narrative? I believe it does, since the text preserves conflicting perspectives from the various stages of its development. In the

absence of a clear sense of the text's evolution, different interpreters are left picking out one emphasis at the expense of
others, a process that leads to radically divergent views of the
text as a glowing evocation of Israel's greatest hero (thus von
Rad) or a bitter denunciation of David and the entire Davidic
dynasty (Van Seters). A literary-historical analysis should,
ideally, lead to a sense of the nature of the dialogue still preserved in the canonical text. What seems clearest, in the present state of this analysis, is that the text shows a gradual movement away from a directly apologetic focus. The type-scene of
the battle report is used in the History of David's Rise for a
clearly apologetic purpose, to paint David's character and motives in the best possible light. This account presumably formed
part of the original edition of the History, whose purpose was
to justify David's replacing of the house of Saul. The highlighting of Saul's armor-bearer in the scene, with its reference back
to the early version of the introduction of David to Saul as lyre-
player and then armor-bearer, shows the original framing of
the History of David's Rise, with themes later disrupted and
to some extent overridden by the subsequent addition of the
Goliath story and its echoes.

The Succession Narrative was composed farther away in time
from the events it describes, if we assume that the first edition
of the History of David's Rise was written in David's own reign
and the Succession Narrative was written at least eighty years
after the death of Solomon, as argued above. The Succession
Narrative still justifies David in his treatment of Absalom, but
here, and throughout the narrative, David is shown in ambiguous terms. The text is neither pro-David nor anti-David. There
is much truth in R. N. Whybray's assessment: "There is, in fact,
no hero in the Succession Narrative" (*Succession Narrative*, 48).
Better, perhaps, one might say that there is no polemic. David
is the focus of intense interest, an interest simultaneously loving and questioning, in an account whose deepest concerns are
with issues of knowledge and understanding.

In integrating and refining his varied materials, the Deuteronomistic historian enhances the theological perspective, downplayed both by the reviser of the History of David's Rise and by the author or the Succession Narrative, but he is also sensitive to the value of the issues of knowledge and judgment, themes that he directs ahead to the figure of Solomon. Even the Deuteronomistic historian is not ultimately promonarchy or antimonarchy; rather, he is concerned to explore the ways in which the monarchy can be made to work well or badly. His own criteria, seen in the body of 1–2 Kings, are largely religious, but the more broadly existential concerns of the History of David's Rise and the Succession Narrative are allowed to stand, though now they may be seen as secondary filling out of the crucial early years of the monarchy rather than as the real focus of the story that they were to their authors. In the many-layered text that has resulted from these shifting modes of composition, prose history achieves the depth and beauty of poetic epic. David has become the most complex hero since Gilgamesh, and 1–2 Samuel has become the masterpiece of biblical narrative.

6. Law and Narrative in the Priestly Work

So compelling are the great Yahwistic and Deuteronomistic narratives that the work of the Priestly writers has often suffered by comparison. One problem is the writers' relative lack of interest in story telling. They greatly expanded and ordered the Pentateuch, creating the text in its canonical form; but though the structure is impressive, it is not an unmitigated pleasure to read.[1] A second and greater problem is the Priestly writers' intense interest in law. If their narratives often fare poorly in literary readings, the legal material does worse, characteristically treated with benign neglect by Jewish literary scholars and outright hostility by critics with Christian backgrounds. Examples have been quoted in chapter 1 of sweeping and almost automatic dismissals by scholars interested primarily in biblical narrative, but even scholars who stress the importance of the legal material for the surrounding narrative show a pervasive distress at the intractably nonliterary character of so much of the Priestly work. One writer on covenant and narrative is even driven to the rhetoric of deviant psychology: "The reader who tries to read the Bible like other books is apt to be confused or annoyed at the interruption of the story by bodies of laws—indeed it would be abnormal not to feel something approaching

---

[1] Even scholars who praise the Priestly work often do so with evident difficulty. In a recent assessment, Walter Brueggemann passes rather quickly over the legal material (the "bulk of detailed and tedious material" in Exodus 25-Numbers 10) and turns to the narratives for relief. Even here, all he can say is that the Priestly stories are "very carefully placed. These narratives, in contrast to the primitive power of the Yahwist's stories, generally have little dynamic or movement but are transparently vehicles of a message. . . . These narratives again reflect P's remarkable discipline and self-consciousness" ("The Kerygma of the Priestly Writers," 102).

262 / THE NARRATIVE COVENANT

a personal dislike for the author of Leviticus" (Hillers, *Covenant*, 87).

Leviticus customarily receives short shrift from literary analysts. Indeed, faced with such an unappetizing vein of gristle in the midst of the Pentateuch, the natural reaction of most readers is simply to push it quietly off the plate. Thus von Rad, in a summary of the narrative contents of the Pentateuch, can neglect to mention Leviticus altogether ("Form-Critical Problem," 2), and literary studies of the book are virtually nonexistent. More polemically, Harold Bloom dismisses the Priestly regulations in Leviticus and elsewhere as pitifully belated attempts at domesticating the numinous and uncanny (in short, truly poetic) essence of the Pentateuch, the Yahwistic narratives (" 'Before Moses Was, I Am' ").

Such neglect, whether benign or hostile, distorts the central literary concern of the Priestly writers who shaped the final form of the Pentateuch, which was precisely the interweaving of law and history. Far from interrupting the narrative, the laws complete it, and the story exists for the sake of the laws that it frames.[2] If the Yahwistic Moses was the giver of the Law, the Priestly Law is the giver of Moses, who becomes its embodiment. This new emphasis leads to a reciprocal influence between law and narrative, and this mutual influence will be the subject of this chapter. On the one hand, the narrative focus is altered, and the very representation of history is affected, by the prominence of ritual/legal material (and ritual/legal perspectives) in the Priestly Pentateuch. At the same time, on the other hand, the presentation of the Law is in turn affected by the great body of narrative around it, and the laws themselves are typically presented in narrative form.

Leviticus is a good place to begin in considering the literary activity of the Priestly writers, for here their particular interests are seen in their purest form. Rather than a sterile opposition

---

[2]As Sigmund Mowinckel argued twenty years ago, the Priestly writers' historical work was undertaken in order to provide the context for the law (*Erwägungen zur Pentateuch Quellenfrage*).

between law and narrative, Leviticus shows a complex but harmonious interplay between two *forms* of narrative. Law and history meet on a common ground composed of ritual, symbolic, and prophetic elements, in the most ambitious revolution in genre since the early Yahwistic merging of prose chronicle and poetic epic.

The Ritual Order

The opening chapters of Leviticus provide a clear illustration of the narrative quality of law in the Pentateuch overall. In the earlier stages of the Priestly composition, before the Torah was divided into separate books, the material of Leviticus 1–7 was not included. The great account of the construction of the tabernacle, which now closes Exodus, would have been directly followed by the anointing of the tabernacle and the investiture of Aaron and his sons, the material that now constitutes Leviticus 8–10. A decisive literary decision was taken, then, to open the new book, not with a direct continuation of the story from Exodus, but with seven chapters' worth of ritual prescriptions concerning sacrifices. Why was this done?

Historical criticism variously accounts for this material as an instruction manual for priests at Jerusalem or, more politically, as the result of priestly disputes at the time of the text's reformulation. On this reading, the priests from Jerusalem inserted this material in order to establish Sinaitic authority for their particular ritual practices, as against other practices at Shiloh or elsewhere in the country. The writing down of these laws may well have had the impetus of some such setting in life, but the choice to insert them here, at the start of the book, serves a literary purpose as well. Indeed, the theological meaning of the insertion is most clearly understood through the passage's narrative function.

The whole section has been constructed with care. The first three chapters show a consistent triadic form. Three kinds of sacrifice are described (burnt offerings, cereal offerings, and peace offerings). Each of these offerings is in turn divided into three variants, which describe different offerings that can be made to fulfill each type of sacrifice. This tripled threefold structure gives these chapters a certain lyrical aspect. Each subsection, a few verses in length, functions stanzaically, even ending with a refrain, some variation on the formulaic phrase "it is an offering by fire, of a sweet savor to the Lord."

The first chapter is the most consistent in this, giving its refrain identically each time, and furthermore giving the refrain a three-part form of its own: "it is a burnt sacrifice, an offering by fire, of a sweet savor to the Lord" (1:9, 13, 17). The quasi-repetition of "burnt sacrifice" and "offering by fire" is instructive. The first term is the technical term for this particular sacrifice, *'olah*, whereas the second is the generic term for offerings involving fire, *'isheh*. Clearly there is no real need to repeat both terms, as the first presupposes the second, but the phrasing strongly suggests the parallelism characteristic of Hebrew poetry. (In chapters 2 and 3, where the cereal offering and peace offering are also burnt, but where the poetic potential of two parallel terms for burning is lacking, the text simply concludes with "it is an offering by fire to the Lord.")

If the structure is lyric, the presentation is dramatic. Rather than simply prescribing the necessary details, the text stages the event, showing us a little ritual drama of interaction between the person offering the sacrifice, the priest, and God:

And if his gift for a burnt offering is from the flock, from the sheep or the goats, he shall offer a male without blemish. And he shall kill it on the north side of the altar before the Lord, and the priests, Aaron's sons, shall sprinkle its blood round about on the altar. And he shall cut it into pieces, with its head and its fat, and the priest shall lay them in order on the wood that is on the fire which is upon the altar; but he shall wash the entrails and the legs with water. And the priest shall bring it all, and burn it on the altar; it is a burnt offering, an offering by fire, a sweet savor to the Lord. (1:10–13)

The identity of the priest(s) has been specified as "the sons of Aaron" in order to emphasize the narrative setting at Sinai, though occasional lapses into the singular indicate the original general designation of "the priest" before these rules were put into their present context. The style, though simple, is unhurried, with occasional flourishes like "on the wood that is on the fire which is upon the altar" that emphasize the sense of ritual order and fill out the scene of ritual drama.

The presentation of the variants in each form of sacrifice has been handled with great skill. The burnt offering, for example, can be made in three ways: by offering a bull, a lamb or goat, or a dove or pigeon. Lambs and goats are sacrificed in essentially the same way as bulls, whereas birds require somewhat different treatment. The text could simply have mentioned the lambs and goats briefly as an alternative to bulls, but it gives them as much space as the birds, allotting to each variant a full scenic description, as in the example quoted above. These latter descriptions are slightly abbreviated from the first version, so the repetition does not become wearying, but they are full enough to impart an overall sense not so much of three choices as of a sequence of three sacrifices. Thus the text dramatizes the sense of orderly sequence at the heart of ritual. The singularity of the giving of the Law at Sinai is extended, through the rituals inaugurated at Sinai itself, to a narrative order of varied repetition.

The emphasis on the different forms of sacrifice gives a place for narrative contingency within the ritual order. The rites reflect different points in the ritual year and different problems that require the several different types of sacrifice. Equally importantly, the variant forms allow for different circumstances on the part of the people making the offerings. Lambs and goats are permitted for people who cannot afford a bull; birds are specified for people too poor to offer a lamb or a goat (as is stated later, in 12:8 and 14:21). The ritual order is not a millennarian order that would gloss over details of wealth and poverty; it remains linked to individual circumstances as well as to the cyclical order of the ritual calendar and the structural order of different kinds of sin.

At the same time, individual circumstance is delimited and ordered, in the implicit division of society into only three economic groups (wealthy, average, and poor). This is not an individualized narrative, or even an image of extended contingency with a multiplicity of categories (envisioning, for example, other groups of people too poor to buy even a bird, or so rich that even a bull would be too trivial a sacrifice). It remains a ritual order, but one in which narrative variety and narrative progression are both given a definite place.

History

Having established this ordered ritual narrative, however, the text immediately calls it into question, in the story of the investiture of Aaron and his sons (chaps. 8–10). This is the only extended passage of full-fledged narrative in the book. In it, Moses follows the instructions given him in Exodus 29 for the anointing of the tabernacle and the consecration of Aaron and his four sons as the chief priests. The initial preparation alone takes a full week and is intricate and difficult, even dangerous, given the immense divine power with which they are dealing. Aaron and his sons perform everything flawlessly:

And Moses said to Aaron and his sons, ". . . . Therefore you shall stay at the door of the tent of meeting day and night for seven days, and keep the instructions of the Lord, or you will die; for so I am commanded." So Aaron and his sons did all the things which the Lord commanded through Moses.   (8:31, 35–36)

So far so good, and on the eighth day Aaron offers the final series of sacrifices (chap. 9), which culminate in a direct response from God: "And fire came out from the Lord, and consumed on the altar the burnt offering and the fat; and when the people saw this, they shouted, and fell to the ground" (9:24).

No sooner is the ritual complete, though, than disaster strikes. Aaron's eldest sons make the mistake of improvising an offering of their own, not specifically requested by God:

And Nadab and Abihu, the sons of Aaron, each took his censer, and put fire in it, and added incense, and offered strange fire before the Lord, which he had not commanded. And fire came forth from the presence of the Lord and devoured them, and they died before the Lord. Then Moses said to Aaron, "This is what the Lord has said: 'I will be made holy in those who approach me, and before all the people I will be glorified.' " And Aaron held his peace. (10:1–3)

A strange inauguration of the ritual order! Here the officiants themselves go the way of the burnt offering just made by their father.

Clearly the episode serves, in part, a monitory purpose, to warn against the invention of new practices or the importation of practices external to the cultic order. ("Strange fire," *'esh zarah*, can also be translated as "foreign fire," and suggests something either lying outside the prescribed order or else literally coming from another people.) The purely ritual message here is the stress on the danger inherent in God's power. Like the fire that concretely expresses God's will in the scene, God's power is the basis of civilized life if handled properly but becomes a raging, destructive force if misused. This ritual moral is drawn by the passage in its description of the strange fire not actually as something forbidden but simply as something that God had not asked for. This is also the view taken in chapter 16, when the deaths are again alluded to and described as the result of Nadab and Abihu's having come too close to God: "they drew near to God and perished" (16:1).[3] Here the narrative details have dropped out as unimportant to the purely ritual message, which refers to the inherent structure of divine-human relations rather than to anything specific to the historical incident.

Yet the shocking quality of the event, both in its timing and in the stature of its victims, has a broadly disturbing effect. Indeed, within the text itself, the disaster shakes Aaron's own

---

[3] Some modern translations obscure this by assimilating this passage to the earlier one, adding in "when they offered illicit fire," but the Masoretic text simply uses the verb *qarav*, whose normal sense is "to approach."

faith in his ability to carry on with the ritual order. The chapter ends with Moses discovering that Aaron's surviving sons have failed to eat the goat of the sin offering, as they were supposed to do. He angrily reproaches them, but Aaron replies:

> "But see, today they have made their sin offering and their burnt offering before the Lord; and such things have befallen me! If I had eaten the sin offering today, would it have been acceptable in the sight of the Lord?" When Moses heard this, he was content. (10:19–20)

A clue to the wider meaning of the episode lies in the sudden shift from Aaron's sons to Aaron himself, and specifically in his sense that the death of his sons is something that has befallen *him*, a sign that he himself is not entirely worthy in God's sight. It is in fact Aaron who is the focus of this enigmatic episode, whose ramifications show a classic case of the biblical confrontation of the present in the form of the past.

Nadab and Abihu have no existence apart from Aaron; this is their one action in the Pentateuch, apart from accompanying their father on Sinai in Exodus 32. Their names, however, have a more extended life. In 1 Kings appear a pair of brothers, Nadab and Abijah, the sons of King Jeroboam I. These brothers die young, both because of their own misdeeds and because of their father's sins, which have determined God to destroy his lineage (1 Kings 14–15). Now Jeroboam's signal sin was his establishment of a cult of a golden calf, at Bethel and at Dan (1 Kings 13); at Bethel, he personally offers incense at the altar—just the kind of offering that brings about the death of Nadab and Abihu in Leviticus (see Gradwohl, "Das 'fremde Feuer' ").

The parallel to Aaron's great moral lapse, his forging of the golden calf at Sinai, is clear, and indeed the one alteration in the names of the brothers only serves to point to Aaron as the real focus of the Leviticus story. "Nadab" is unchanged, whereas "Abijah," which means "God is my father," is altered to the more general "Abihu," "He is my father." In the present context, the father is certainly Aaron, who here receives his punishment for the forging of the golden calf.

The meaning of the echo of Jeroboam's idolatry is much disputed, and the link is occasionally denied any real meaning at all.[4] Given the historical fact of Jeroboam's establishment (or reinstitution) of calf symbolism at Bethel, how did the Deuteronomistic historian alter the received story in Exodus 32? What purposes are served by showing Aaron participating in the shocking apostasy of the people? Finally, if Exodus 32 reached its basic form through a Deuteronomistic reworking of Yahwistic material, what did the story later mean for the Priestly writers, for whom Aaron had become the founding father of the entire cultic apparatus?

Behind both golden calf episodes there appears to lie an earlier stage of Yahwistic or proto-Yahwistic religion, later repudiated, in which God was syncretistically worshiped in the form of a calf or bull, which symbolized God's power and majesty. Traces of this old symbolism are still found elsewhere, in the epithet of God as "the Bull of Jacob" (Gen. 49:24, Isa. 1:24). When Jeroboam set up the calves at Bethel and at Dan, he would not have meant to inaugurate an idolatrous break with Yahwism—the later interpretation of the Deuteronomistic historian. Rather, his purpose was the reverse: to forestall faithful Yahwists from going to worship at Jerusalem by laying claim to an older and more "authentic" Yahwism than that being practiced in Jerusalem. To this end, he revived the old symbolism of the calves as images of God's power and authority, images on which God would be considered to be enthroned.[5]

---

[4]Walter Beyerlin limits the connection to a degree of historical linkage; both stories recall the calf cult at Bethel, but the textual traditions are to be seen as entirely distinct: "The connection certainly does not consist in the dependence of Exod. xxxii on the Deuteronomist, however. The description of the calf in Exod. xxxii.4 sounds [!] more ancient than that in 1 Kings xii.28 and the former can hardly have arisen from the latter" (*Origins and History of the Oldest Sinaitic Traditions*, 126).

[5]See Cross, *Canaanite Myth and Hebrew Epic*, 74–75. Cross views the calf as an aspect of pre-Yahwistic symbolism, dating from the pre-Israelite period, in

If the symbolism of the calf was originally legitimate early Yahwistic symbolism, then it is possible that underlying the story in Exodus is an old legend in which the making of the calf was viewed favorably. Various theories have been proposed, including the theory that Moses himself was originally the maker of the calf[6] and the theory that Aaron was the hero of the positive legend, formulated by the priests at Bethel as an etiological explanation for the origin and authority of their cultic practice (Cross, *Canaanite Myth*, 74).

In the received Yahwistic account, however, the forging of the calf is clearly a direct result of the weakness of the people's faith, their need for a tangible symbol to worship and follow. The focus of the conflict is largely on Moses and the vacillating people, with Aaron playing only a secondary role in carrying out the will of the people—assuming that he was present at all in the Yahwistic version of the story.[7] At the close of the Yahwistic account, God sends down a plague "upon the people because they had made the calf"; a later editor, more interested in Aaron than the original account was, has expanded the phrase into its present form, which reflects the new stress on Aaron at the expense of grammatical clarity: "because they had made the calf which Aaron made" (Exod. 32:35).

In the Deuteronomistic reworking of the story, the focus of blame is placed squarely on Aaron, who orchestrates the making of the calf and then lies to Moses about his role. The narrative describes Aaron's request for gold jewelry and his fashioning of the calf, evidently by a two-stage process of casting it and then engraving it, but when he recounts this episode to Moses, he pretends to have had no active role at all beyond

---

which "Yahweh" was a cultic name of the Canaanite god 'El. The calf symbolism became anathema as Yahwism began to differentiate itself definitively from the worship of 'El.

[6]So, for example, Heinrich Valentin, *Aaron*, who argues that Aaron was later substituted for Moses when the Yahwists came to condemn the cultic use of bull symbolism.

[7]See George Coats, *Rebellion in the Wilderness*, for a development of Noth's thesis that the people as a group were the original constructors of the calf.

collecting the gold: "I threw it into the fire, and out came this calf!" (32:24). Aaron's action is seen as closely parallel to Jeroboam's idolatrous currying of popular favor, and the people greet the making of the calf in words taken from the story of Jeroboam's calves: "Whereupon they exclaimed, 'These are your gods, O Israel, who brought you up out of the land of Egypt!' " (Exod. 32:4; 1 Kings 12:25). As many commentators have noted, the phrase must have originated in 1 Kings, where two calves are involved (hence the plural "your gods") and where the king is addressing the people (hence *"your* gods," not "our gods" as the people ought to say in the Exodus passage).

The Deuteronomistic Sinai story, then, is shaped directly by the experience of modern history. This shaping can be understood in various ways. One can say that the Exodus story has been reworked in order to strengthen the polemic against Jeroboam as the seminal villain in the *"Unheilsgeschichte"* of the divided monarchy.[8] In this connection one might also consider the interesting parallels between the early history of Jeroboam and that of Moses. In 1 Kings 12, Jeroboam is portrayed as a kind of anti-Moses. He waits in Egypt until he is called to lead the North in its separation from the South; as the people's new leader, completing the disintegration of the Promised Land to which Moses had led the people, he leads all Israel to sin with the golden calves he sets up.[9]

Conversely, if the Exodus is seen as the dominant term in the comparison, one can say that Jeroboam's sin is being worked into a larger pattern of apostasy and forgiveness, with the shocking modern example used to strengthen the drama of the people's near extermination just at the moment when they were about to receive the Law, their true hope for salvation.

---

[8]See Jörg Debus, *Die Sünde Jerobeams*, esp. part 3, "Die Unheilsgeschichte Israels."

[9]These parallels are noted in Rudolph Smend, *Yahweh War and Tribal Confederation*, 125–26.

The Priestly writers come to this story with new concerns of their own. Aaron, who had formerly been a secondary figure, with perhaps a purely political role as a kind of assistant commander under Moses,[10] is now identified as the first high priest, the establisher with Moses of the entire ritual and legal system at the heart of the Priestly writers' vision of the future of Israel. How then do they deal with Aaron's shocking behavior in the account they have received? To understand the Priestly use of the Aaron story, it is necessary to consider their view of the overall nature and role of history. Their legal and ritual focus leads them away from the Deuteronomistic political emphasis, but at the same time they retain much of the Deuteronomistic interest in history and historical sequence as the necessary ground of meaning in religious experience. As their drive to associate every law with Sinai shows, the ritual order is by no means divorced from history but, on the contrary, exists in an indissoluble bond with the historical process of the growth of the people and their relation to God.

The Priestly writers' deep interest in history is clearly seen in their impatience with the more purely emblematic Yahwistic/ Elohistic representation of Moses. The JE story of Moses' birth and his adoption by Pharaoh's daughter presents Moses in the most general way; his parents' role, and their very identities, are obscured in such a way as to remove Moses from a particularized history. His parents are not named at all in the early account: "Now a man from the house of Levi went and took to wife a daughter of Levi" (Exod. 2:1). The child of "a man" (*'ish*) and an unnamed woman, Moses is portrayed against the background of the primordial history of creation and flood. When his mother sets him afloat on the Nile, he relives the experience of the Flood, a point made through verbal echoes of the flood story. He is set afloat in "a *tevah* of papyrus." *Tevah* is a word that appears only here and in the flood story, where it is Noah's ark.[11] His mother carefully caulks the *tevah* to pre-

[10]Valentin calls him a *"komissarischen Volksführer"* (*Aaron*, 410).

[11]Modern translations, under the pressure of a realism not felt by the author of the story, invent translations for Moses' *tevah* like "papyrus basket."

pare it for the voyage, just as Noah was instructed to seal the ark.

Flood symbolism continues to appear in the Moses story, and the wandering in the wilderness is represented as a new experience of the Flood, with the entry into the Promised Land seen as parallel to the reestablishment of society after the receding of the floodwaters. The Priestly writers were by no means averse to the use of this symbolism, and built on it themselves, but though the Moses story could continue to echo the emblematic primordial history, it also had to be brought into relation to the particularities of modern historical experience. Where the Yahwistic/Elohistic birth story declines to establish a specific genealogy for Moses, leaving his parents unnamed and even giving the crucial task of naming Moses to Pharaoh's daughter, the Priestly writers specify Moses' lineage, in a long genealogical listing of the heads of the clans who will be leaving Egypt. Here we learn that Moses is a great-grandson of Levi, actually both a grandson and a great-grandson, as his mother, Jochebed, was his father's aunt, and we are given an indication of the period of Moses' birth via notices of the length of his ancestors' lives (6:20). The account ends by stressing the particularity of the identities established in this way: "These are the Aaron and Moses to whom the Lord said 'Bring out the people of Israel'. . . . this Moses and this Aaron" (6:26–27). In the absence of any indication of the existence of another Moses and Aaron who were competing for credit in the Exodus story, the doubled stress on *this* Moses and *this* Aaron shows a dissatisfaction with the purely emblematic presentation of the earlier birth story: the protagonists have not been fully identified, fully realized, until they have been brought into history through the establishment of their lineage, their offspring, and the period of their birth.

In the Deuteronomistic history, Jeroboam's sin in setting up the golden calves and offering incense before them results in the deaths of his sons Nadab and Abijah. In the Priestly story in Leviticus 10, Nadab and Abihu are struck down after offering their "strange fire" to God. The parallel could hardly be clearer, and yet the application to Aaron is not spelled out, as the Deuteronomistic historian would likely have done (and did in 1 Kings). At least, the moral is not spelled out directly at the time of the deaths of Nadab and Abihu, but it is their deaths that give a literal point to the initial cleansing of the people at the end of the golden calf episode. Moses calls together all the Levites, who fan out among the people and slay the three thousand ringleaders among the other clans. Since all the Levites have rallied around Moses, they are not slaying their own kinsmen, but Moses describes their feat in a striking metaphor: "And Moses said, 'Today you have ordained yourselves to the Lord's service, everyone at the cost of his son and of his brother, so that God may bless you this day' " (Exod. 32:29). In Leviticus 8–10 we have the literal ordination, and the literal death of sons and brothers.

It is often thought that the story of the Levites' bloody ordination in Exodus 32:25–29 was introduced into the text by the Deuteronomistic reworkers of the material in chapter 32, perhaps as part of a polemic by the Zadokite priests of Jerusalem against the Aaronite priesthood supported by Jeroboam.[12] In this event, Exodus 32:25–29 would not originally have pointed forward to the scene of the ordination of Aaron and his sons, a Priestly construction that did not yet exist. Instead, the accounts of Aaron's two rebellions against Moses, here and in Numbers 12, would originally have been followed by the direct punishment of Aaron.[13] As the text now stands, however, Aaron escapes any direct retaliation. In Numbers 12, where Aaron and Miriam speak out against Moses' authority, Miriam is punished with leprosy, but Aaron is untouched, and in Exodus 32, every guilty figure is punished except Aaron, seemingly the guiltiest of all.

---

[12]This explanation, or a variant of it, seems the likeliest, though it has also been suggested that 32:25–29 is itself a Priestly addition; see Herbert Schmid, *Mose*, 82–90.

[13]See Moses Aberbach and Leivy Smolar, "Aaron, Jeroboam, and the Golden Calves."

If the Priestly writers wished to adapt the received Deuteronomistic accounts of Aaron to suit his new prominence and his fundamentally positive role in their view, then the later deaths of Nadab and Abihu can be understood as a deliberate displacement of Aaron's punishment. Their deaths now appear within the context of the proper ritual that Aaron himself has been shown helping to establish. Further, they are brought into a new context through the stepping forward of Aaron's remaining sons, Eleazar and Ithamar, to take their place. This consequence has nothing to do with the political history of Jeroboam, but it does have a different relation to the Deuteronomistic history and further represents another step in the advancement of Aaron alongside his brother Moses. Of Aaron's surviving sons, the dominant one will be the elder, Eleazar, who becomes the new high priest and the founder of the later Aaronite priestly lineage. It has often been suspected that his name is more than coincidentally a variant of the name of Moses' son Eliezer, who has no role at all in the Pentateuch as we have it; it may well be that as Aaron's role grew, his family was given the priestly inheritance of Moses through the transfer of "Eliezer" to "Eleazar."[14]

In making this transfer, the Priestly writers brought the evolving story of Aaron and his sons into line with a pattern found in the Deuteronomistic history. It will be recalled that the opening chapters of 1 Samuel describe the downfall of the house of Eli after his wicked sons Hophni and Phinehas abuse the sacrificial system; after their deaths and the loss and recovery of the Ark, they are succeeded as keepers of the Ark by one Eleazar, the son of Abinadab. Not only is there the general pattern of a priestly father, two brothers who incur the divine wrath, and a new taking up of priestly duties; the final figure has the same name in both cases. The Eleazar of 1 Samuel is even the son of Abinadab, whose name can be read as

---

[14]The suggestion goes back to Wellhausen; a contemporary exponent of the view is Smend, in *Yahweh War and Tribal Confederation*, 130–31.

276 / THE NARRATIVE COVENANT

"My Father Is Nadab." In a further recurrence of names, Aaron's son Eleazar, like Eli, has a son named Phinehas.

The parallel is not precise, and it is not necessary to suppose that there has been a deliberate conflation of the families of Aaron and Eli; the Eleazar and Phinehas of 1 Samuel could well have had common priestly names whose popularity stemmed from old traditions about the origins of the priesthood. It is enough that the several similarities of names reinforce the echo of the story of Eli in the Priestly revising of the story of Aaron. Important to the Priestly account is the redirecting of the valuation of Aaron. If, as is widely supposed, the Deuteronomistic Exodus account had mounted a direct attack on Aaron, the analogy to Eli could give a valuable counterinterpretation. Aaron, like Eli, could be seen as a good but weak man, allowing himself to be led by the people but himself a committed proponent of true Yahwism. His weakness then receives a fitting punishment during the ordination, when he fails to control his sons and keep them within the precise and due measure of the ritual ordinances.

There may even be an echo in Leviticus of the Deuteronomistic language condemning Aaron in Exodus 32:25, where "Moses saw that the people had become unrestrained [*parua'*], for Aaron had let them become unrestrained to their shame." In Leviticus, immediately after the death of Nadab and Abihu, as the bodies are carried out of the camp, Moses warns that Aaron and his surviving sons cannot formally mourn the deaths, as this would render them unclean in the midst of the ordination, which would kill them in turn. The first thing Moses says is, "Do not let the hair of your heads hang unrestrained [*tiphra'u*], and do not rend your clothes, lest you die" (10:6). Thus the older polemic against Aaron is redirected to a message concerning the need for restraint and care within the ritual order.

This new ritual emphasis does not require the expunging of the negative acts of Aaron in the Exodus story, nor does it involve the rejection of the Deuteronomistic parallels to the history of the monarchy. As we have seen, these parallels are even strengthened, in the new relevance of the story of Eli, and the parallel to Jeroboam is still quite visible both in Exodus 32 and in the Priestly narrative of Leviticus 10. At the same time, the doubling of reference to monarchic history makes the parallel both broader and less sharp than the earlier polemical comparison to Jeroboam alone.

Four distinct layers of history are folded into the ritual order by the story of the offering of the strange fire by Nadab and Abihu. First, the complexity of the historical moment at Sinai is encapsulated, as the brothers in effect repeat the golden calf episode and their father is brought to face the consequences of his sin. Aaron's making of the golden calf is now seen as stemming from his moral weakness in the face of the people's demand for a tangible divinity, one that would serve to prop up their own spiritual weakness. Second, the proleptic reference to the history of Jeroboam brings the action forward into the time of the monarchy, strengthening the association between priest and king already implicit in the regal paraphernalia given to Aaron as high priest (Exodus 28). In contrast to the weakness behind Aaron's misdeed, Jeroboam's making of the calves is an act of cynical power politics, as he tries to keep the people from returning to worship in Jerusalem, where he fears that they will end up renewing their allegiance to the Davidic dynasty. The episode is typical of the history of the monarchic period, with politics as the central testing-ground of moral issues; the premonarchical period represented by the time of the Exodus stages moral issues more directly in terms of divine leadership and ethical demands. The secondary parallel to Eli combines aspects of both the political and the moral emphases.

Thirdly, the fact that it is Aaron's eldest sons who fail in their duty ties the scene into the family politics of the patriarchal period, when in case after case the younger brother takes the lead after the elder brother is shown to lack moral strength. On the death of Nadab and Abihu, the younger brothers Eleazar and Ithamar begin to play an active role for the first time, and become the forefathers of the divisions of Levites later organized by David. In its reference to Aaron, the episode of Nadab and Abihu also completes the logic of Aaron's subordination to *his* younger brother, Moses. On a deep symbolic level, this triumph of the younger over the older represents, as has long been noted, one aspect of Israel's self-understanding as the people chosen by God over the heads of the older and stronger cultures around them. At the same time, the pattern is subtly modified, insofar as it is the son of the older brother, Aaron, and not Moses' son Eliezer, who inherits the priestly role.

These three historical levels, patriarchal, Sinaitic, and monarchic, provide resonance for a fourth, that of contemporary history. Leviticus reached its final form during or soon after the period of the Babylonian Exile. Both the fickleness of the people and the misuse of royal and priestly power under the monarchy were seen as responsible for the nation's downfall. Nadab and Abihu serve as a warning of the importance of just leadership by the priestly class, in the absence of any formal government during the Exile. More generally, they are an image of the justified destruction already visited on a large part of the population and a threat of even further woe to the remnant if the survivers fail to reform. In this respect, the plaintive cry of Aaron concerning the sin offering acknowledges the shock of the Exile, even while the story also asserts the need to pick up the pieces and carry on.

The Symbolic Order

The fivefold interweaving of narrative orders (ritual, patriarchal, Sinaitic, monarchic, and contemporary) in Leviticus 10 forms a fitting conclusion to the first third of the book. Taken overall, Leviticus 1–10 serves as a narrative introduction to the symbolic order of moral laws and cultic regulations that make up the remaining two thirds of the book: the laws of purity and atonement in chapters 11–16, and the group of ordinances known as the Holiness Code (chaps. 17–26, with an appendix in chap. 27). After long neglect, these sections have begun to receive attention on several fronts, with path-breaking work in the 1960s by Paul Ricoeur and by the structural anthropologist Mary Douglas, followed by Julia Kristeva, and by René Girard's sustained attempt to explore the literary/social function of the sacrificial system. Historians of religion are also showing renewed interest, as seen in recent work by scholars such as Jacob Neusner.[15] As Douglas says, "Rites of purity and impurity create unity in experience. So far from being aberrations from the central project of religion, they are positive contributions to atonement. By their means, symbolic patterns are worked out and publicly displayed" (*Purity and Danger*, 2–3).

These symbolic structures can be deduced, though they are not explicit in the text. Once they have been observed, can they be shown to have any connection to the narratives around them? Readers who have come to see the literary value of the opening chapters of Leviticus are likely to view chapters 11–25 with dismay, as the assorted regulations and ethical statements given here largely lack the narrative form of the earlier chapters. In fact, we are presented not with a nonnarrative but with an *anti*narrative, whose purpose is to complete the transformation of history inaugurated in Leviticus 1–7.

If we return for a moment to prehistory as seen by the Pentateuch, we can say in rhetorical terms that the Eden story describes a scene of metaphorically based union with God, in whose image and likeness human beings are created, whereas the fall away from God and into history takes the form of a series of metonymic displacements illustrated in the several stages of prehistory (Eden, the story of Cain and Abel, the Flood, and the Tower of Babel). This world of metonymies, of cause-and-effect relations, parts standing in for inaccessible

---

[15]Ricoeur, *The Symbolism of Evil*; Douglas, *Purity and Danger*; Kristeva, *Powers of Horror*; Girard, *Violence and the Sacred*, with amplifications in his later books *Des Choses cachées depuis la fondation du monde* and *The Scapegoat*; Neusner, *The Idea of Purity in Ancient Judaism*.

wholeness, is the world of biblical narrative. In describing Leviticus as a book that uses literary methods for nonliterary
ends, I mean to describe an antinarrative process that reaches
its fullest form in chapters 11–25. The narrative patterns of
chapters 1–7 are still here—regulations are often still described
scenically, for example—but typically they are transformed in
strange ways. The narrative order is subordinated to a concep-
tual order, and the surviving fragments no longer show a progressive narrative development. Instead, we find disconcerting
moments such as the following:

Thus shall Aaron come into the holy place: with a young bull for a
sin offering and a ram for a burnt offering. He shall put on the holy
linen coat, and he shall have the linen breeches on his body, be girded
with the linen girdle, and wear the linen turban; these are the holy
garments. He shall bathe his body in water, and then put them
on. (16:3–4)

The narrative goes backward here, first describing the entry
into the inner part of the Temple, then describing how Aaron
is to have dressed, and finally describing his bath before he
dresses. In an extended series of variations of this rhetorical
movement, the sacrificial order creates a series of disjunctions
and substitutive displacements, by which Leviticus 11–25 seeks
to reconstruct a metaphoric wholeness from the pieces of the
metonymic narrative progressions it has taken apart.

In a certain sense, the goal of this symbolic order is the overcoming of time, as Blenkinsopp has argued (*Prophecy and Canon*,
73–79). It might be better to say that the text mixes together
past, present, and future in a variety of ways, complicating
temporal relations but also building on the tensions it preserves
and even fosters between different times. This interanimation
of temporal orders has consequences for the Exodus narrative
proper, as can be seen in the calling of Moses in Exodus 3.
Moses asks, "Who am I that I should go to Pharaoh and bring
the sons of Israel out of Egypt?" God replies with the announcement of a reassuring sign of his presence and support:

"I will be with you; and this shall be the sign for you, that I have sent you: when you have brought forth the people out of Egypt, you shall serve God upon this mountain" (3:11–12). The remarkable thing about this sign is its futurity: the reassuring sign will appear only after the successful escape has been completed. It seems likely that the narrative in its original Elohistic form had some clearer and more present sign; Brevard Childs has made the attractive suggestion that the burning bush functioned as this sign (*Exodus*, 56–60). In the long development of the tradition of the calling of Moses, however, the emphasis was placed on worship at Sinai, and the burning bush became a secondary element prefiguring the later events on Sinai. Though the original Elohistic story identifies the location of the call as Horeb (3:1), for the Priestly writers "this mountain" is Sinai, which is where Moses will worship God. The prefiguring function of the burning bush can then be understood as the inspiration for the unusual choice of vocabulary used here for "bush": *seneh*, a word used only of this bush, and strongly suggestive of "Sinai" itself.

The future orientation of the Priestly account may be contrasted to the use of the Exodus story in the Ark Narrative. There, the understanding of the contemporary history of the war against the Philistines was grounded in the past history of the struggle against the Egyptians. Here, within the story Moses is to take his assurance from the coming establishment of worship at Sinai. A parallel lesson is to be learned by the text's audience as well; with the Priestly reworking of the Pentateuch taking place at or somewhat after the close of the Babylonian Exile, the fulfillment of past history is to be anticipated in the coming restoration of full religious observance in Israel. Past and future merge in the iterative present of ritual. This reordering of time is heralded by the Priestly account of the establishment of Passover as the unique but infinitely repeatable beginning of time in the ritual calendar: "This month shall be for you the beginning of months. . . . This day shall be for you a memorial day, and you shall keep it as a feast to the

Lord; throughout your generations you shall observe it as an ordinance for ever" (12:14).

As Childs says, in "the dialectic between redemption as hope and redemption as memory. . . . Israel remains a people who has been redeemed, but who still awaits its redemption" (*Exodus*, 205). Perhaps a schematic dialectic could be constructed as follows: in a first stage, the Yahwistic writers grounded their narrative in the past; secondly, the Deuteronomistic historian redirected the narrative emphasis into the future as communicated by the many prophetic figures who carry forward the meaning of events; finally, the Priestly writers took up both modes into a narrative grounded in the ritual present.

Though such a dialectic has its merits, it might be better to put aside the division according to past, present, and future, a distinction corresponding to the basic tense structure of Indo-European languages; instead, we could adopt an analogy from the Semitic languages and speak of perfective and imperfective temporalities. This is the basic temporal distinction in Semitic verb systems: perfective forms are used for singular, one-time actions; imperfective forms are used for ongoing or habitual activities, whether past, present, or future. Distinct though these modes are, they are often combined in biblical Hebrew, with past-tense narration using a perfective form followed by an imperfective, and with the imperfective coming first when the context is future or habitual. Thus, a phrase that would translate into English as "He came up and said" would be formed with a perfective and an imperfective, literally, "He came up saying." Conversely, "Saul would call David and ask" would be written with an imperfective followed by a perfective.

On this analogy, the Yahwists concentrated their focus on perfective accounts of exemplary events, and the Deuteronomistic writers began to develop the perfective into a mixed mode with strong imperfective overtones. In the history of the monarchy, for example, the narrative is still structured around the perfective, singular, historically defined particularities of the individual monarchs, giving the dates and leading events of their reigns. At the same time, the events described are selectively chosen and developed to bring out the repetitive, "imperfective" patterns of apostasy, prophetic condemnation, punishment, and conditional restitution that the author sees as virtual constants over the whole course of the history of the monarchy.

The Priestly writers carry the mingling of perfective and imperfective a large step further. Nothing might seem more imperfective than ritual ordinances, and nothing might seem more perfective than the unique theophany on Sinai; but the Priestly writers give the presentation of the Law a strongly perfective aspect and the presentation of history an equally pronounced imperfective aspect. Thus, in the rituals of Leviticus 1–7, the iterative, imperfective regulations are not presented abstractly or as an exhaustive series. Rather, thanks to the fullness of scenic description, one envisions a specific, perfective scene that is then repeated with variations. Further, the perfective quality of the ritual repetitions is grounded in the frequent reminders that the ritual regulations are being delivered in a very singular manner in a very specific setting in time and space: over and over, a group of laws is introduced with briefer versions of the first verse of Leviticus, "The Lord called Moses, and spoke to him from the tent of meeting."

If the presentation of the Law is given a perfective specificity, the historical narrative around the blocks of law is conversely characterized by a high degree of imperfective iteration. This tendency is most clearly seen when the narrative describes ritualistic moments in the story of the Exodus, as in the description of the offerings brought by the twelve tribes when the tabernacle is set up in the wilderness (Numbers 7). Other biblical authors might simply note in one sentence that the people gathered and made offerings to God (as in, e.g., Judg. 20:26); the Priestly writers, however, devote eighty-nine verses to their historical account, whose form is comparable to the ritual prescriptions for offerings in the opening chapters of Leviticus. Each tribe makes its own presentation on its own day, and each

presentation is lovingly detailed in full, though the only significant changes in each section, one might say in each stanza,
are the names of the tribe and its representatives.

Along with such iterations go the formally structured repetitions that run through the Exodus and wilderness accounts.
Whereas the Deuteronomistic history had been characterized
by overall patterns of apostasy and its consequences, the Priestly writers create a more formal and schematic structure, most
notably through the parallel patterning of ten plagues in Egypt
and ten episodes of Israelite murmurings against Moses and
God in the wilderness, narrative apostasies set around the legal
and ethical ideals embodied in the Ten Commandments. This
temporal ordering is mirrored spatially, in the geometric precision with which the Israelites are ordered to encamp around
the tabernacle, with three tribes each on the north, south, east,
and west sides of the tabernacle and the Levites (here not identified as one of the twelve tribes) encamped in the center by
the tabernacle itself (Numbers 2).

Through these means, the perfective historical narrative is
brought into a close relation to the imperfective narratives of
the ritual order. They do not entirely merge, of course, a fact
all too evident to readers uninterested in the Law who find the
story so rudely interrupted by the blocks of ordinances scattered through it. The continuing distinctness of law and history
has thematic consequences, in the doubled theme concerning
the necessary response to God: the people must both hear and
remember. "Hearing" is the basic term for obedience to the Law
("Hear, O Israel: the Lord thy God is one God"), and remembrance is the essential bearer of past history. The Priestly writers take these themes from Deuteronomy and the Deutero-
omistic expansions of the Exodus story, and extend them both
through the Exodus story and in the presentation of the Law.

As an example of the earlier Deuteronomistic linking of hearing and remembrance, we can return to the story of the golden
calf. When God determines to destroy the Israelites after they
have forged the golden calf, the scene is developed into a re-

markable recapitulation of the Yahwistic story of Sodom. As in the earlier case, God ends his announcement of doom with the promise to create a great nation out of the faithful survivor, Moses (Exod. 32:10; compare Gen. 18:17). Just as Abraham pleaded with God to change his mind and spare the people of Sodom, so Moses pleads with God to spare the apostate Hebrews.

Parallel though the scenes are, however, Moses does not use anything resembling Abraham's argument that God ought to save the city if there were fifty righteous men to be found there, or forty-five, or forty, or even ten righteous men. Moses makes no attempt to appeal to the supposed virtue of the people, but takes a very different tack:

> But Moses besought the Lord his God, and said, "O Lord, why does your wrath burn hot against your people, whom you have brought forth out of the land of Egypt with great power and with a mighty hand? Why should the Egyptians say, 'With evil intent he brought them out, in order to slay them in the mountains, and to consume them from the face of the earth'? Turn from your fierce wrath, and repent of this evil against your people. Remember Abraham, Isaac, and Israel, your servants, to whom you did swear by your own self, and did say to them, 'I will multiply your descendants as the stars of heaven, and all this land that I have promised I will give to your descendants, and they shall inherit it for ever.' " And the Lord repented of the evil which he thought to do to his people. (32:11–14)

The heart of Moses' appeal is the doubled petition that God hear and that he remember: he is to hear what the Egyptians will say if he destroys the Israelites (words that Moses conveniently utters in full, so that God hears them now), and he is to remember his covenant with the patriarchs. The speech is closely parallel to the account in Deuteronomy 9, where Moses recalls the various occasions on which he has saved the people from God's just wrath. At the same time, several changes have been made. In Deuteronomy, the speech was placed at the climax of the series of Moses' intercessions, when the people refused to follow God's command and enter the

Promised Land (9:23–29); now, the Deuteronomistic editor of Exodus has preferred to associate the speech with the sacrilege of the golden calf. Rhetorically, the speech has been subtly developed as well. Where in Deuteronomy Moses begins and ends his speech with the plea that God not desert "your people and your heritage," now Moses makes no such claim for such an indissoluble union between God and the people. Indeed, the text in Exodus suggests that no such link can be assumed: Moses now makes his plea to "the Lord *his* God," YHWH '*Elo-haw*. This link is, however, just what Moses wants to restore, and his effort to do so is shown in another modulation of his speech. Whereas in Deuteronomy Moses centers his plea on God's remembering his covenant to "your servants Abraham, Isaac, and Jacob," now Moses gives the phrase a new form: "Remember Abraham, Isaac, and *Israel*, your servants," the only time in the Pentateuch in which Jacob's new name is used in this phrase.

Building on this Deuteronomistic theme, the Priestly writers identify the simultaneous activity of hearing and remembrance as an essential characteristic of God himself. This idea is now introduced at the very start of the story, in the Priestly gloss on God's response to the Egyptian oppression of the Hebrews: "And God heard their groaning and God remembered his covenant with Abraham and Isaac and Jacob. And God saw the sons of Israel and God understood" (2:24–25). The second sentence lyrically doubles the first, with God's seeing paralleled by his hearing, and his remembrance doubled by his understanding (lit., "knowing," *yada'*, which may signify his acknowledgment of his covenant).

If hearing and remembrance are the characteristic divine activities, their absence is typical of unbelievers and those of weak faith. In the symmetrical patterns of the ten plagues and the ten murmurings in the wilderness, Pharaoh and the Israelites resemble each other in their inability to hear or to remember. God tells Moses that he will have this problem with Pharaoh: "Pharaoh will not listen to you" (7:4). In refusing to listen to Moses, Pharaoh carries on the role of anti-God that the Yahwistic writers saw as his nature. Undoubtedly aware of the Egyptian kings' claim to literal divinity, they portray Pharaoh as a god manqué, a grim parody of true godlikeness. Where God established his covenant with his servants through the gifts of land and fertility, Pharaoh degrades service into slavery, keeps the people from their land, and tries to inhibit their fertility. He acts as though his power is absolute, in phrases that echo the Eden story; furious at Moses after eight plagues, he cries, "Get away from me; take heed to yourself; never see my face again; for in the day you see my face you shall die" (10:28). His order merges the divine prohibition against the eating of the fruit of the tree of the knowledge of good and evil and the fatal danger, since the Fall, of seeing God's face.

But Pharaoh is not divine, and his word has no creative power. Significantly, though his magicians can match Moses' initial miraculous signs, their powers fail when they try to duplicate the third plague. They cannot turn dust into gnats, and tell Pharaoh, "This is the finger of God" (8:19). Their failure at this point involves a telling irony, as throughout the history of Egyptian culture a fundamental symbol of rebirth through divine magic was the scarab, the insect believed to generate its young spontaneously from a ball of dust or dung.

The Priestly writers extend these Yahwistic motifs to the Hebrew people as well, in their murmurings against Moses. Like Pharaoh, they seem to suffer from a kind of amnesia, quickly forgetting the meaning of God's many miraculous acts. As Pharaoh demanded that Moses and Aaron prove themselves by working miracles (7:9), so too the Hebrews require a constant infusion of new signs of God's power and protection, and in their wavering faith they increasingly resemble the Egyptians. They even advance the hostile argument Moses warns God on Sinai that the Egyptians could make: the people fear that God has brought them out to die in the wilderness (14:11).

These failures to hear the Lord's word and remember his

mighty acts provide the context for the giving of the Law and the explanation for its importance in history. Ritual unites the memory of the historical constitution of the people with the hearing and obeying of the eternal Law. Further, ritual reinforces God's own memory of his covenant with his people. The high priest goes into the temple carrying on his garments the names of the twelve tribes: "So Aaron shall bear the names of the sons of Israel in the breastplate of judgment upon his heart, when he goes into the holy place, to bring them to continual remembrance before the Lord" (28:29).

Aaron's breastplate is thus similar to the sign of the rainbow at the close of the flood story. The difference is instructive: in place of a natural phenomenon the Priestly writers give a ritual object, the breastplate of judgment. Its efficacy is operative not in the course of the cycles of nature (with the rainbow appearing at the end of rainstorms that recall the Flood) but in the course of the ordered ceremonies of ritual.

A similar movement from the natural to the ritual can be seen in the metaphor of covenant as marriage. The Yahwists told of a literal marriage between Adam and Eve; the Deuteronomistic historian told of a metaphoric marriage between king and country, reflected at various points in the story and directly enunciated during the climactic events of Absalom's rebellion by his adviser Achithophel: "I will bring all the people back to you," he promises Absalom, "as a bride comes home to her husband" (2 Sam. 17:3).[16] Where the Yahwist shows a literal marriage and the Deuteronomistic historian uses metaphor, the Priestly writers turn to the symbolic mode of ritual. When the people betray God by making the golden calf, Moses takes the calf, burns it, grinds it to powder, scatters it on water, and makes the people drink it (Exod. 32:20). It has often been noted that this action resembles a trial by ordeal found in the Priestly regulations in Numbers 5, but against this analogy it has been observed that

---

[16]Following most contemporary commentators in restoring the corrupt Hebrew text of the verse (reflected in the KJV) on the basis of the Septuagint (so RSV, Hertzberg, McCarter, and others).

the scene in Exodus does not have the purpose of a trial, namely, to determine guilt or innocence, as the people's guilt is perfectly clear. The parallel does hold, but not for the proof value of the ordeal. Instead, what is relevant is its thematic value, for the ordeal in Numbers 5 is arranged for a particular category of criminal: women accused of adultery.

And the priest shall set the woman before the Lord, and let loose [once again, *para'*, as in Exod. 32:25] the hair of the woman's head, and place in her hands the cereal offering of remembrance, which is the cereal offering of jealousy. And in his hand the priest shall have the water of bitterness that brings the curse. . . . Then the priest shall write these curses in a book, and wash them off into the water of bitterness; and he shall make the woman drink the water of bitterness that brings the curse, and the water that brings the curse shall enter into her and cause bitter pain. (Num. 5:18–24)

By reflecting this law, Exodus 32:20 gives a symbolic expression to the analogy of people to spouse.

The words of the curse have a power that survives the destruction of their physical form: the curse is carried in the very ink after it has been washed off the page. In this the curse shares the quality of the Law as a whole, which survives the shattering of the tablets and is reinscribed on "tablets like the first" (34:1). The ideological importance of this assertion of identity is highlighted rather than undercut by the fact that the commandments listed in Exodus 34, the product of a complex process of collection and revision, do not in fact exactly duplicate the Decalogue written on the first set of tablets. The ideology of the Law, seen here in its pre-Priestly formulation,[17] is extended by the Priestly writers to the historical narrative as well.

---

[17]Exodus 34 is most often seen as stemming from a Yahwistic original, with substantial pre-Deuteronomistic and Deuteronomistic revision and perhaps some final Priestly shaping; see Childs, *Exodus*, ad loc., for a survey of theories.

The Law in Exile

A profound expression of the union of law and history is the relation now constructed between holiness and exile. In much of the Hebrew Bible, the rhetoric of displacement is presented through the theme of exile (see Ackroyd, *Exile and Restoration*). In the Priestly exposition of the Law, exile can fairly be said to be the very basis for the construction of the antinarrative ritual order. To be holy, *qadosh*, is to be set apart; the root means "separation, withdrawal, dedication." If a metaphoric union with God is no longer possible in a fallen world, the Law can instead create a life built around a principle of separation that will serve as a metaphor for the transcendent otherness of God. God himself repeatedly makes the point that the people's separateness is to mirror his own: "You shall be holy; for I the Lord your God am holy" (Lev. 19:2).

The separation from what is not holy creates a close spiritual connection not only between God and human beings but also between human beings and the material world. If the people must obey purity laws concerning physical disfigurements, these laws apply not only to their bodies but also to their clothing and even to their houses, with mold and mildew analogized to leprosy (Lev. 13–14). The people are to be separated not only from their neighbors but even, in a sense, from themselves: "Thus you shall keep the children of Israel separate from their impurity, so that they do not die in their impurity, when they would defile my tabernacle in their midst" (15:31).

The Priestly writers build the connection between holiness and exile as they go about creating a metaphoric wholeness of God, people, and land through the mechanisms of purity and avoidance. Even the people's ritual link to the land of Israel expresses not a sense of possession but a permanence of exile. The land itself must keep the Sabbath, and cannot be sold in perpetuity, for it belongs not to the people but to God: "The land shall not be sold for ever, for the land is mine, and you are strangers and sojourners with me" (25:23). The term *ger*, "stranger," might best be translated into modern English as "resident alien," and was the term for the Israelites when they were guest workers in Egypt. In taking up the term, the text transforms the lament of Moses, who named his eldest son in sorrow for a life of exile. In the eloquent phrasing of the King James Version, "He called his name Gershom: for he said, 'I have been a stranger [*ger*] in a strange land' " (Exod. 2:22). Leviticus expresses a desire for something closer than possession: a fellowship of shared exile, shared among the people, their servants, their cattle, their goods, and the land itself.

The transformation of exile makes alienation the basis for a renewed ethical closeness to one's neighbors and even to strangers: "you shall love your neighbor as yourself; I am the Lord. . . . the alien who lives with you shall be to you as one born among you, and you shall love him as yourself; for you were aliens in the land of Egypt; I am the Lord your God" (19:18, 34).[18]

The historical experience of exile is symbolically transformed into the basis of the ritual order, but exile retains its historical force as well. The historical and the symbolic orders are both prominent in the prophetic discourse with which Leviticus closes. Composed after the subjugation of the nation to Babylon, Leviticus presents a body of ritual that had never been fully observed and whose physical and spiritual focus, the Temple, had now been destroyed. Looking toward the future, the entire collection functions prophetically, and this aspect comes to the fore in the book's conclusion. In describing the good that will follow the keeping of the Law, and the evils that result from the failure to keep it, Leviticus 26 looks to the Babylonian Exile, and beyond.

And I will devastate the land, so that your enemies who settle in it will be astonished at it. And I will scatter you among the pagans, and I will unsheath the sword after you; and your land shall be a desolation, and your cities shall be a waste. Then the land will enjoy its

---

[18]See Schneidau, *Sacred Discontent,* esp. chap. 1, "In Praise of Alienation."

sabbaths. . . . As long as it lies desolate it shall have rest, the rest which it had not in your sabbaths, when you lived on it.   (26:32–35)

The devastation of the land of Israel is seen, with rich prophetic irony, as the earth's long-delayed chance to observe the fallow periods required by law but hitherto neglected by the greedy tenders of the land. The chapter deals throughout in imagery of journeying and promises that if the people walk in the Law, God will walk with them (as he had walked with Adam in the garden). "If you walk in my statutes, and keep [lit., "hear"] my commandments. . . . I will walk among you, and I will be your God, and you will be my people" (26:3, 12). In contrast to this orderly walking and hearing will be the disordered flight and confused hearing of the sinful in their new exile:

And as for those of you that are left, I will send faintness into their hearts in the lands of their enemies; the sound of a rustling leaf will put them to flight, and they will flee, as one flees from a sword; and they will fall when none pursues.   (26:36)

Even in the new exile, though, God will be prepared to remember his covenant if the people repent, as the conclusion of the chapter stresses (26:40–45). With faith and active repentance, the people can find a new Sinai even in Babylon.

Sinai, in turn, is a new Ararat. The Priestly writers were deeply interested in the flood story, and altered the flood narrative in Genesis to foreshadow the building of the Temple in Jerusalem. The Temple is anticipated in greater detail by the building of the tabernacle in the wilderness, which thus serves as the switch-point between the ark and the Temple. In the Priestly revisions to the flood story, Noah "did all that God commanded him" (Gen. 6:22), in parallel to Moses in constructing the tabernacle (Exod. 39:42), and in the Priestly chronology of the Flood, in which specific dates become important, the new world emerges from the floodwaters on the first day of the new year, the same day on which Moses sets up the sanctuary in the wilderness (Gen. 8:13, Exod. 40:2).[19] As for the construction of the tabernacle/Temple, in its shape, proportions, orientation, and furnishings it is a physical manifestation of the Law, an image of the order of the universe.[20]

Thus the Priestly writers orient the Yahwistic flood story toward the ideal order of ritual, and at the same time the Flood serves as a background for the history of the wanderings in the wilderness. Whereas the Yahwistic Moses recapitulated the primordial history in his youthful voyage on the Nile, now the people as a whole journey across the empty land in search of a place to come to rest. When they reach the border of the Promised Land, Moses sends out spies as Noah had sent the raven and the dove. Like the dove with its olive branch, the spies bring back not only information but also growing things:

And they came to the Valley of Eshcol, and cut down from there a branch with a single cluster of grapes, and they carried it on a pole between two of them; they brought also some pomegranates and figs. That place was called the Valley of Eshcol ["Cluster"], because of the cluster which the men of Israel cut down from there. At the end of forty days they returned from spying out the land.   (Num. 13:23–25)

Despite this evidence—evidence featuring grapes, the first crop planted by Noah after the Flood—the people fail to carry the analogy through. Afraid of the numbers of Canaanites reported in the land, the people insist on turning away. The etiological notice about the naming of the valley is noteworthy, since even as the land is presented as heavily populated with hostile Ca-

---

[19]"For P, then, the deluge serves a double function. It is a parable of judgment and salvation for those who had come through the flood waters of exile (cf. Ps. 124:4–5). It is also the celebration of the Israelite God's victory resulting in the building of a sanctuary infinitely greater than that of Marduk in the Babylon that had been left behind" (Blenkinsopp, *Prophecy and Canon,* 66). See also Fishbane, *Text and Texture,* chap. 1, for a sensitive summary of parallels between Priestly ritual and the Priestly account of the creation of the world in Genesis 1.

[20]See Haran, *Temples and Temple-Service in Ancient Israel,* for detailed discussions of the symbolic proportions and decorations of the Temple; see also Clements, *God and Temple,* on the Temple as "a microcosm of the macrocosm" (67).

naanites, it is also presented as virgin territory, nameless, awaiting inhabitants to give it definition.

In punishment for the people's weakness of faith, God sends them back into the wilderness for a full forty years, with the result that the period in the wilderness comes to serve the traditional temporal function of the Flood, marking the epochal change from premodern history to modern history. Like the Flood, this period of wandering sees the destruction of the old world and the creation of the new world order. In Numbers 26, a census is taken, rounding out the body of the book, which began with the census at Sinai in the first year of the Exodus. After forty years of wandering, the numbers of the people are almost identical, in both cases a little over six hundred thousand. The same, but different:

These were those numbered by Moses and Eleazar the priest, who numbered the people of Israel in the plains of Moab by the Jordan at Jericho. But among these there was not a man of those numbered by Moses and Aaron the priest, who had numbered the people of Israel in the wilderness of Sinai. For the Lord had said of them, "They shall die in the wilderness." There was not a man of them, except Caleb the son of Jephunneh and Joshua the son of Nun. (26:63–65)

Only Caleb and Joshua, who urged the people to proceed with the conquest of Canaan on their first arrival, are left alive to go into the Promised Land, into the history of Israel.

As a result of this punishment, the Ararat of the flood story is recreated as two separate mountains: Sinai, where the true order of worship is established, but from which the fearful people fail to go directly to reestablish their society; and Mount Pisgah, from which the people finally survey the Promised Land they are about to enter. To say that the functions of Ararat have thus been divided gives a negative explanation: the stop at Sinai should have been the penultimate event immediately preceding the entry into the Promised Land. A more positive explanation can be given as well. The flood story had nothing to say about the period of the Flood itself; God and Noah have extended dealings both before it and after it, but the time of flooding is simply an empty transitional space, in which there is no interaction to describe. In contrast, the Priestly writers see the wilderness as exemplifying the fullest potential of a life of exile: that the place where everything has been lost can be the place where everything is gained.

The stark landscape of the wilderness seems to the people to be a dead end, lacking all hope, one might say all narrative possibility: "and they said to Moses, 'Is it because there are no graves in Egypt that you have taken us away to die in the wilderness?' " (Exod. 14:11). For the Priestly writers, it is precisely this emptiness that gives the freedom for the fresh creation of a morally perfect society. If Mount Pisgah is the place from which Moses sees the land he will never enter, it is also the place from which Balaam will affirm the positive value of the ineluctable separateness of the children of Israel from the peoples around them, a solitude that will persist even in their possession of the Promised Land. Commanded by the hostile king Balak to curse the Hebrews, Balaam blesses them instead, and he stresses their separateness in his first blessing:

How can I curse whom God has not cursed?
How can I denounce whom the Lord has not denounced?
For from the top of the mountains I see him,
from the hills I behold him:
behold, a people dwelling alone,
not reckoning itself among the nations!

(Num. 23:8–9)

The wilderness is the physical expression of this spiritual state, a necessary lacuna between cultures and between past and future history. Here the people can receive the redemptive symbolic order of the Law, an order that will require their continuing separation from their past and future cultural contexts:

And the Lord said to Moses, "Speak to the children of Israel, and say to them: I am the Lord your God. You shall not act as they do in the land of Egypt, where you have lived, and you shall not act as they do in the land of Canaan, to which I am bringing you. You shall not walk in their statutes. You shall do my ordinances and keep my statutes and walk in them. I am the Lord your God." (Lev. 18:1–4)

The trackless wilderness offers no stray paths to tempt the people (though even here they can construct their own); here, if anywhere, they can learn to walk in the path of God's will. If they are not yet able to do this at Sinai, another forty years may teach them to walk in "the way which I commanded them" (Exod. 32:8); "the way" is *ha-derek*, and *derek* means both "path" and "custom, habit, usage." In their enforced wandering through the wilderness, the people historically enact the journey that will be ritually repeated on the people's behalf by the scapegoat in ages to come:

Aaron shall lay both his hands upon the head of the live goat, and confess over him all the iniquities of the people of Israel, and all their transgressions, all their sins; and he shall put them upon the head of the goat, and send him away into the wilderness by the hand of a man who is in readiness. The goat shall bear all their iniquities upon him to a solitary land; and he shall let the goat go in the wilderness. (Lev. 16:21–22)

Here it may be appropriate to note the root of the term *wilderness*, from which the Book of Numbers takes its Hebrew name, *Bemidbar*, "In the Wilderness." "Wilderness" is *midbar*, which has a second meaning, in the Song of Songs, of "mouth"; the open steppe may be seen as the "mouth" of the cultivated land. The root of *midbar* is *davar*: "word, speech, event." The Word of the Lord is literally folded within the wilderness. The Book of Numbers plays on this linkage in its opening phrase, from which its title comes: *waydaber YHWH 'el-Mosheh bemidbar Sinay*, "And the Lord spoke to Moses in the wilderness of Sinai."

Wilderness and Promised Land merge in the Priestly work. In the presentation of the Law within their vision of the redemptive power of exile, the Priestly writers have combined historical narrative and ritual ordinance into a mode of discourse at once perfective and imperfective, a unique combination of elements held within a majestic structure, the culmination of biblical narrative.

Conclusion: Deconstruction or Reconstruction?

Throughout this study, I have argued that a close conjunction of literary and historical criticism is needed for a full understanding of the origins and growth of biblical literature. If I have shown that genuinely literary-historical work is possible, however, I have not yet shown that it is desirable. For historical criticism poses a stark challenge to our reading of the text in its canonical form, and it is this challenge that has created the greatest difficulty for literary critics who have considered the problem of the unusual evolution of biblical narrative. Once the variegated and often self-contradictory nature of its many-layered texts has been explored, how then is the Bible to be read? Is it necessary to renounce the reading of the final form of the text as an innocent pleasure appropriate only to the Eden of naive reading or the Olympus of structuralist theory? Once one begins to wander in the wilderness of historical study, is there any way back to the wholeness of the unified text? This tension is, of course, nothing new; it inheres in the very name of the book. Is it "the Bible," a great code whose unity transcends its separate parts, or is it *ta biblia*, "the books" whose different forms and often contradictory viewpoints have been brought together by the pressures and accidents of cultural history? Historical criticism has not invented this issue, but it has extended it to the level of the individual books themselves.

Ordinarily, the literary history of a major text provides a ringing affirmation of the greatness of the text and its author; our appreciation of Shakespeare's creativity is only enhanced by the study of his sources, whose material seems to us to have been lying inertly, awaiting the quickening force of his art. Few historians, however, have given the Priestly writers a greater share of literary credit than the Yahwists. Scholars may well have often underrated the literary importance of the Deuteronomistic and Priestly contributions, but even if the later stages of the text are given equal consideration, it remains the case that the earlier stages of the text have a major presence in its received form, and a kind of literary power both specific to themselves and in some ways opposed to the literary and theological concerns of the later stages. The presence of several important and even competing layers in texts like Genesis or 1–2 Samuel clearly poses unusual problems for anyone who wishes to take them into account while focusing on the text as a whole.

Composite Artistry

Robert Alter has addressed this issue in a thoughtful chapter at the end of his influential *Art of Biblical Narrative*. His discussion is far more balanced than the dismissive polemics of Meir Sternberg, but like Sternberg he is finally fighting a holding action against what he sees as the corrosive effects of historical criticism. As he poses the problem, "What, then, are we to do with our literary notions of intricate design in reading these texts which the experts have invited us to view, at least in the more extreme instances, as a crazy quilt of ancient traditions?" (132).

If the question must be posed in this form, its answer is simple: we cannot do anything at all. If the historical approach indeed chops the text into a jumble of disparate traditions, we have only two alternatives: to give up our love of intricate design, or to dismiss historical criticism outright. This, however, is the sort of choice between Athens and the truth that it would be a great pity to be compelled to make. But is there any alternative?

The first thing to note is that the choice is not, after all, so very stark. Hard-core atomizers are few and far between these days, and within historical scholarship in the past two decades there has been a broad movement toward the rehabilitation of the later stages of the biblical texts and an increasing interest in relating source study to the context of the overall text. Even apart from special movements like canonical criticism, on a very general level the continuing erosion of the remnants of the classic documentary hypothesis has done much to bring the perspective of historical criticism closer to that of literary analysis. To Wellhausen and his followers, the pentateuchal sources had seemed complete in themselves, at least in origin. Worse still for analysis of the final form of the text, they were thought to be essentially independent of each other. The Yahwistic and the Elohistic sources were parallel but separate; the Priestly document was independent of both; and the whole of the pentateuchal traditions had developed without any direct relation to the Deuteronomistic historical material, except insofar as the classic J and E sources might extend partway into it. Aspects of this older view remained strong in the middle of the century, in the work of such influential scholars as Noth and von Rad, but these echoes are faint today. The independent existence of the "Elohist" is widely questioned, and in any event it is now often seen that the Elohistic material has been edited into its present contexts in ways that bring it into direct relation with the material around it. The Priestly writers are more often seen as reworking the earlier material than as having composed a separate document of their own, and it is no longer a surprising idea to give considerable weight to thematic and structural relations between pentateuchal and Deuteronomistic materials.

There remains historical criticism that will strike literary readers as atomistic and irrelevant, and such material simply *is* to be disregarded. But then, to paraphrase Eliot, if most historians are failed critics, so are most critics. The value of either approach is not to be assessed from its weaker or its more extreme manifestations, and the best historical criticism has much to teach the literary reader. Though the historians expose tensions within the text, they also outline the historical and theological pressures that lie behind these tensions, and this evidence is directly useful to the literary student of the final form of the text. Quite apart from invaluable historical information, historical criticism frequently yields subtle literary insights as well. Usually these insights appear by the way, as the historian's chief interests lie elsewhere, and it is natural that a literary critic will be likely to take up these perceptions more systematically and fully than the historian; but for historians as for literary critics, points of conflict within texts are often clues toward literary discoveries.

In assessing the productive possibilities of the tension between sources, Alter finds a suggestive approach in the idea of "composite artistry," which serves as the title for his chapter on the problem. He proposes that the authors of the final stage of the biblical texts were by no means blind to the contradictions raised by their sources. They were willing to accept these contradictions, however, for the sake of the advantages of perspectival complexity offered by their combinations of material. By introducing David to Saul first as a musician and then as the slayer of Goliath, the author of the canonical form of the text could create a kind of montage, giving two divergent but complementary views at once.

Alter's view has much to recommend it, and potentially the concept of composite artistry can encompass a full reading of the text in the light of its history. It is not, however, certain how far a composite reading in Alter's sense of the term is really possible; sometimes the author of the canonical text may well be exploiting tensions within his sources, but how often is this the case? Are the narrative practices behind such diverse texts as Genesis, Leviticus, 1–2 Samuel, and Isaiah really so consistent? Further, how far does a reading of the text's composite artistry involve a close attention to its history? In Alter's own exposition the insights of compositional history turn out to have only a very limited application, and this raises questions about the sureness of his assertion of the definitive shaping role of the text's final authors. These questions can be examined by looking at some of Alter's examples. He gives several extended readings of passages to show the operations of composite artistry in the Bible, including examples from the Joseph story (the conflicting accounts of the brothers' discovery that the money they have paid for grain has mysteriously reappeared in their sacks) and from the David story, the contradictory introductions of David to Saul in 1 Samuel 16 and 17, first as musician and then as warrior.

In the case of the Joseph story, it should be noted that Alter's analysis is in a way open to the very charge of atomization that he levels against historical critics. Here, the atomization is directed against the integrity of the older sources, which Alter treats by a policy of dividing and conquering. He begins by noting that one account of the finding of the silver stems from the Yahwists, whereas the other is Elohistic. He suggests that each contributes thematically to the composite picture that the author of the canonical text wishes to create. The Yahwistic version "is crucial for the writer because it ties in the discovery of the money with the theme of Joseph's knowledge opposed to the brothers' ignorance" (138–39). This thematic element contributes a moral and psychological aspect to the overall story, whereas the Elohistic version, less concerned to show the characters' reactions to their discovery, gives the story a theological-historical dimension.

In this way Alter gives a perceptive description of the thematic differences between the two accounts. Is it, however, a description with a more general validity, or is this distinction between moral-psychological and theological-historical accounts an ad hoc invention of the close reading of this particular episode? The hypothesis remains to be tested: Does the Yahwistic material characteristically stress the moral over the theological, or the psychological over the historical? Does the Elohistic material consistently do the opposite? These binary oppositions are a little too pure for comfort, but perhaps a difference in overall emphasis could be traced through the two bodies of material. Here, historical criticism, fully applied, could help to validate or refine the distinction observed in the particular instance. In the absence of any wider sense of the Yahwistic and Elohistic contexts, however, the Yahwistic source is effectively reduced to the Yahwistic anecdote, artfully manipulated by "the" author for the needs of the moment.

This view of composite artistry, then, virtually does away with historical criticism at the very moment that it acknowledges its value. The final irrelevance of modern historical criticism brings Alter's position squarely within the great tradition of rabbinical midrash. Long before the rise of historical criticism, or indeed of modern historical consciousness, the rabbis sought to account for contradictions in the text through the assertion of their thematic complementarity. These assertions could take an essentially syllogistic form, particularly in legal analysis, where apparently contradictory laws and ritual provisions had to be shown to apply to different cases or circumstances.

In nonlegal (haggadic) exegesis, the complementary reading of textual doublings usually took a homiletical turn. Thus, as recorded in the Midrash on Genesis, the rabbis pondered the meaning of the two common names for God, YHWH and Elohim, the same duplication that much later critics would use to identify and name the Yahwistic and Elohistic sources. A distinction according to separate sources was, of course, unthinkable, as Moses had written the entire text at the dictation of God himself, but the rabbis suggested a thematic solution: "YHWH" was used when the context wished to emphasize God's mercy; "Elohim" was used for the God of strict justice (Midrash on Genesis, 12, 15). This speculation opened a rich vein of theological reflection that is still productive in Jewish thought today.[1] Alter is well aware of his affinity for rabbinic thought, though he points out that his readings are more continuous and less didactically motivated than the classical midrashim (11). At the same time, in his rejection of "the contem-

---

[1] See the eloquent use of this distinction in the conclusion to the first volume of Abraham Heschel's *The Prophets*, 218–20.

porary agnosticism about all literary meaning" (179), he
extends to secular literary analysis the rabbinic drive toward
totalizing interpretation. In the process, historical analysis is
used only to the extent that it can confirm interpretations that
arise out of the final form of the text.

In view of its history, the Bible can well be read as the product of some kind of composite artistry, but it must be acknowledged that the elements of this composition do not always work
in a purely complementary fashion. Certainly it is not necessary to return to the old view, no longer widely held among
historians, that the later "redactors" did little to shape their
material, but it is reasonable to agree that the later composers
of the text did not have complete freedom in their appropriation of the older material. Sometimes the later authors do indeed find ways to build an additive complexity through the
assembling and creation of complementary parallels, but at
other times it seems clear that the later author really wishes to
suppress the earlier source, or at least to co-opt it and impose
on it a structure and emphasis that guide the reader toward a
new perspective in preference to the old.

The introduction of David to Saul gives a good example of
the revisionary process often visible in biblical narrative. In his
analysis of 1 Samuel 16 and 17, Alter persuasively shows the
complementary value of David's twin debuts as musician and
as warrior. Historical criticism can obviously explore the separate histories of these materials, but what can it contribute to
this elegant discussion of the canonical text?

To begin with, it is surprising to note that, though his theme
is the combining of disparate perspectives, Alter says nothing
at all about the two Goliath narratives that have been woven
together to form chapter 17. Treating the chapter as a unified
whole, a single tale that "the author" has juxtaposed entire to
the tale in chapter 16, Alter takes most of his image of the
conflict with Goliath from the Deuteronomistic version of the
story. Quoting David's great speech about his coming at Goliath with the name of the Lord rather than with sword and

spear, he concludes, "David's conquest by slingshot is a literal enactment of the monotheistic principle of 'not by the sword does the Lord give victory' which he announces to Goliath" (151).

What has happened in this reading is that the Deuteronomistic historian has won out over the earlier version in the History of David's Rise. In that earlier version, it will be recalled, David *does* win by the sword; the slingshot serves as a kind of secret weapon that triumphs over Goliath's clumsier armaments. The early version makes no mention of faith in God; rather, David is a folktale hero, really a trickster, who craftily takes the giant by surprise. For the historian of David's rise, this tale forms the beginning of a long moral journey that will encompass a wide range of experience and in which the theological message emerges only gradually, never dominating the action. The Deuteronomistic historian has not excised this adventure story. He did not need to; by folding in his longer and more explicitly theological account, he has simply overridden the earlier story. Thus Alter quotes the great Deuteronomistic speech by David in 17:45–46 and simply passes over the climax of the earlier version, still present in 17:55–18:5, in which David's prowess against Goliath leads to Jonathan's giving him his sword and bow so that David can become Saul's chief military hero.

The Deuteronomistic historian would be pleased. He would not be pleased at his narrative victory as such, as his interests were not primarily literary; rather, he would be pleased at his theological victory, clearly reflected in Alter's literary reading. For Alter sees the story as enacting "the monotheistic principle of 'not by the sword does the Lord give victory,' " and this is precisely the idea that the Deuteronomistic historian was intensely concerned to get across. What he wished to suppress was the older view of the conflict against the Philistines, the view advanced in the Ark Narrative and still retained in modified form by the historian of David's rise, that the Lord does indeed give victory by force of arms. Further, he wished his own view to be identified as *the* viewpoint of monotheism, and this is how the chapter has often, univocally, been read. There is, however, nothing unmonotheistic about the conception of the historian of David's rise, that the Lord rewards his faithful by making them unstoppable in battle. The difference from polytheism is clear: it is only the Lord who gives strength in battle, whereas a Shalmaneser would pray to, and expect aid from, an entire panoply of gods. The Deuteronomistic historian is not fighting polytheism at all here, but a different strain of monotheism than his own, one more appropriate to the period of Israel's expansion in Canaan than to his own era, a time of contraction and near extinction at the hands of pagan powers whose swords were very strong indeed.

Alter concludes his comparison of chapter 16 to chapter 17 by noting that "the joining of the two accounts leaves us swaying in the dynamic interplay between two theologies, two conceptions of kingship and history, two views of David the man" (152). Our reading will be enriched, rather than atomistically reduced, if historical criticism helps us to see that we are actually dealing with *three* theologies and three views of David the man in these chapters.

Further, such a realization can mitigate the internal contradictions into which readers may be led through an unawareness of the mixed nature of chapter 17. Thus Alter, having stressed the Deuteronomistic theology of the chapter, goes on to argue that the chapter is actually quite untheological: "the king's election is, one might say, ratified rather than initiated by God; instead of the spirit descending, we have a young man ascending through his own resourcefulness, cool courage, and quick reflexes, and also through his rhetorical skill" (153). What Alter is now describing is the portrayal of events in the earlier Goliath story; with this aspect of the chapter momentarily dominant, Alter concludes that chapter 17 shows the triumph of cool courage and quick reflexes, a conclusion that must have horrified the Deuteronomistic historian just when he thought he had won Alter over. Now all the Deuteronomistic redirection of emphasis in David's great speech is reduced to the afterthought that David possesses "rhetorical skill"—the very assertion of God's preeminence is thus reduced to grist for David's artful linguistic play.

The reason for Alter's sudden shift to the other side of the fence of chapter 17 is not a belated interest in the inner dynamics of the History of David's Rise, nor a wavering in any commitment to Deuteronomistic monotheism; rather, it is the rhetorical exigency of the moment by which he now wishes to draw a binary opposition between the activities of God in chapter 16 and in chapter 17. The opposed roles of David that he earlier focused on were very nicely presented in the contrast between the old portrayal of David as musician in the original story from the first edition of the History of David's Rise and the later Deuteronomistic story of David and Goliath; this kept Alter from looking further into chapter 17 at that point. There is, however, no clear binary contrast between the theology of the story of David the musician and the Deuteronomistic Goliath story, so Alter looked around some more in chapter 17 and came out with a very different reading of the dynamics of that chapter, not coincidentally the very reading inherent in the earlier Goliath story and suppressed by the later version.

By this point, Alter has almost uncovered the tension within chapter 17, but he goes no further, having constructed a pair of complementary oppositions between chapters 16 and 17, drawing their elements, under the needs of the moment, from the two different but undiscussed sources in chapter 17. As a result, the "composite artistry" seen in his reading of these chapters is as much his own creation as that of the Deuteronomistic historian who created the canonical text, running as it does against that final author's intentions as often as it follows them. In this case, then, the matter is more complex than meets the eye of close reading alone. Though at times historical criticism can help to guard against over-reading, here it helps keep us from under-reading the complex internal dialogue of the text.

Four Analogies

In seeking analogies to the composite biblical texts, literary critics have most readily turned to the paradoxical and self-questioning compositions of modernists like Henry James (or Sergei Eisenstein, whom Alter quotes in developing his analogy of montage). The problem with the creations of a James or an Eisenstein is that they are, if not always unified works, at least the product of a single creative mind in a single period of activity. But examples do exist of works that have evolved over a longer period of time, either in the work of a single author or through the activities of a series of authors. To show something of the range of possible comparison, I would like to suggest four analogies, all of which have been useful to me in thinking about different aspects of the Bible's composite artistry. Various other examples could be chosen, but these will provide a sufficient range for present purposes and together can serve as a useful reminder that we are by no means unable to read texts that do not let us forget their checkered compositional careers. Each of these examples can be viewed in a variety of ways, but as I am here using them to sketch a certain range of possibility, I will treat each example under one of four rubrics, each of which is relevant to the problem of reading the Bible: appropriation; the recovery of the past; dialogic evolution; perspectival assembly.

Appropriation in Mesopotamian Literature

The natural place to begin in drawing analogies is with Near Eastern literature. Chapter 3 will already have suggested ways in which the evolution of the *Gilgamesh Epic* can provide analogies to the growth of biblical literature, as well as providing specific thematic parallels. In this instance, modern readers have little difficulty in welcoming the changes by which the material transcended its early adventure-tale quality and *carpe diem* philosophy, and the older materials surviving in the final form of the text are heavily subordinated to the emphases of the final author. In other cases, however, material created for one context is not so much transformed as simply appropriated for use in a new situation. The "Apology of Hattušiliš" may well have survived the original moment of its production as a political justification through an act of appropriation by the priesthood of Ishtar of Šamuha, whose rights and privileges are stressed at the end of the text. Similarly, the detailed instructions for childbirth found in the *Atrahasis Epic* suggest that the flood epic, in the form in which it has been preserved, had been taken over into a ritual use.

Such instances of appropriation offer the modern reader a relatively free choice. Most commentators on the "Apology of Hattušiliš" have stressed the original, political use of the document, noting its religious aspects within the context of a political reading. Alternatively, one might choose to take the clue of the conclusion and view the text instead as a religious document. Few readers, however, are likely to be inspired to send in contributions to Ishtar of Šamuha, and to that extent we all ignore the intentions of the document's final editors. Similarly, we now read the *Atrahasis Epic* with less emphasis on its guidance in childbirth than its final author intended, though at the same time his contributions continue to give a particular weight to the scene of the creation of humanity.

In a very real sense, every reader of the Pentateuch who gives more emphasis to the great Yahwistic narratives than to the Priestly regulations is already reading the text selectively, and reading with a pronounced bias toward an earlier stage of the text. Historical criticism here serves a valuable function in enabling us to restore the integrity of the Yahwistic material when we do wish to emphasize that layer of material, and in helping us to observe the shaping that the Deuteronomists and the Priestly writers later gave to it.

The Recovery of the Past in the Icelandic Sagas

One major impetus for the evolution of biblical narrative, and particularly for the work of the Deuteronomistic historian, was the effort to recover or recuperate a rapidly vanishing past, and the literature of medieval Iceland provides a very interesting point of comparison. The analogy between biblical composition and the redaction of the Icelandic sagas was regularly made in the first half of this century, though usually the comparison was made to the activity of the Yahwist. That reconstructed figure or circle was compared with Snorri Sturluson and his fellow sagamen, all viewed as faithful transmitters of oral traditions handed down from the heroic age some centuries before them. The analogy has rightly come under heavy criticism in recent years, both because the historical fidelity of the Yahwist(s) seems less certain than it did to Gunkel and his contemporaries, and because Icelandic scholarship over the past several decades has shown that the sagamen of the thirteenth century were creative authors rather than simple recorders of stories from the tenth century.

These shifts have caused the Icelandic analogy to fall out of favor, but it need not be abandoned; rather, it should be redirected. The activity of the sagamen is comparable to the work of the Deuteronomistic historian in many ways. Like him, they recall, collect, and adapt stories from the age of the settling and founding of the nation. These events, which occurred in Iceland during the tenth and eleventh centuries A.D., are reworked and committed to writing during the thirteenth century, a time when Iceland was coming under increasing pressure from the expansionist court at Norway. The Icelanders, who had left Scandinavia in search of independence from monarchic rule, had created an anomaly in medieval Europe: a nation with no central government. The loose association of clans, with no armies and no state apparatus apart from the annual assembly or Althing, had survived for three hundred years, but was now inexorably being drawn into the orbit of Norway, a process that culminated in Norway's absorption of Iceland in the 1260s. In the face of this pressure, the authors of the family sagas sought to preserve and elaborate their heritage, looking back to the establishment of the country in the pagan times before the acceptance of Christianity in A.D. 1000.

Two texts are particularly interesting to consider as analogies to the reworking of old material by the Deuteronomistic historian. The author of *Njal's Saga* created the longest and most elaborate of all the family sagas by incorporating two separate saga traditions, one involving Gunnar of Hlidarend, the other, Njal. These two figures are portrayed in the new saga as best friends, giving the author an opportunity to connect their separate adventures through a number of linking scenes. Together, these saga materials are worked into a searching examination of the old heroic ideal, which Gunnar continues to represent, though he sees its destructive limitations, and that Njal's family finally transcends.

Woven into these materials is a formerly separate account of the conversion of Iceland to Christianity, inserted into the middle of the story of Njal, who is presented as one of the major proponents of the conversion. The author also adapts legal documents in constructing his accounts of the lawsuits that figure prominently in the saga. Through this interweaving of materials, the text builds up a complex portrait of Icelandic society that both preserves and questions the heroic past. *Njal's Saga* can serve as an exemplary model of the successful interpretive assembly of disparate materials, and the tensions between these materials are part of the text's power, as they are in different ways in the Succession Narrative and in the Priestly story of the Exodus. The author was well aware of these tensions and extends them to his portraits of his heroes: Gunnar, who wonders whether he is less manly than other men for disliking bloodshed, but who is finally destroyed by his insistence that "he would rather die than yield"; Njal, who utters a prophetic message for later Iceland, "With laws shall our land be built up but with lawlessness laid waste," but who also manipulates the legal system in order to further the marital ambitions of his foster son (*Njal's Saga*, 173, 159). Here indeed is a form of composite artistry that produces characters and scenes of great ambiguity that resist any univocal reading.

The ambiguities are rather differently presented in the *Prose Edda* of Snorri Sturluson. Himself a Christian, but one who wishes to commemorate the greatness of his pagan ancestors and to keep alive the memory of their world, Snorri retells the old stories of the gods, in the only comprehensive medieval collection of Germanic myth. He uses written sources and embroiders stories on his own account, describing the creation of the universe, the activities of the gods, and the coming destruction of the world, Ragnarök. As a Christian, Snorri does not accept these stories as literally true; he begins his work with a remarkable prologue in which he euhemerizes the myths, treating them as stories of human heroes. He traces the name of Thor to "Tror," his version of "Tros," from whom Troy took its name; the pagan gods as a group received their name (Aesir) by their origin in Asia.

This is the historical prologue to the *Edda*; in addition, in ironic awareness of his own *Sitz im Leben*, Snorri presents his whole survey within a framework of delusion: these are stories told by the Aesir to delude an inquisitive Swedish king, Gylfi. At the end of the mythological account, Gylfi's interlocutor concludes by telling him, "I've never heard anyone tell more of the story of the world. Make what use of it you can." He then vanishes, along with his entire castle (Sturluson, *Prose Edda*, 92–93).

Three narrative forms are juxtaposed, or opposed, here: myth, historiography, and fiction. It is left to the reader to decide what to make of it all, and the three narrative forms interact deconstructively, rather than constructively as in *Njal's Saga*. The most direct analogy in biblical narrative would perhaps be the tense relation of the verse body of the Book of Job to its prose frame tale, but throughout biblical narrative we may encounter additions whose purpose is to deconstruct what went before or what follows them, such as the sarcastic second version of the story of Saul among the prophets, 1 Sam. 19:18–24, which undermines the wholly positive version of 10:9–13.

The double analogy of the *Edda* and the *Saga* may also help to keep us aware of the varied relations to earlier tradition possible even in a single period. There is no more reason to posit a single poetics at work in every biblical narrative, or every stage of a given biblical narrative, than there is to equate the transformations of tradition in *Njal's Saga* with those in the *Prose Edda*.

Dialogic Evolution in Montaigne

As the analogy of Snorri Sturluson's *Edda* shows, a single writer can take up earlier material in ways comparable to aspects of biblical practice. This earlier material need not necessarily come from a previous source, however, and Montaigne's *Essais* presents a remarkable case of a text whose author revises it at later periods but chooses to make his changes additively, not erasing earlier paragraphs even when they may conflict with his additions. Though Montaigne did not go so far as to label his supplementary passages to distinguish them from the first edition's material, many scholars of the past century have been interested to keep these stages clearly in view, and modern editions often do actually enter sigla into the text to indicate with great precision what paragraphs, sentences, and even isolated phrases have been interpolated into the first edition. Thus the most widely used edition, the Pléiade, carefully labels every passage or subpassage with the letters *a*, *b*, or *c* to indicate its provenance from one of the three editions Montaigne prepared of his *Essais*.

Indisputably, this editorial reconstruction has a somewhat intrusive aspect, and Terrence Cave has recently questioned the absolute validity of markers that Montaigne did not choose to employ.[2] Even Cave, however, describes the modern recon-

---

[2]As he says in part, "Even the exercise of reconstituting (say) the 1580 text by

struction of the three layers as indispensable to understanding the text's inner dynamics, and his reading of Montaigne makes ample use of this evidence. Modern students of literature have no difficulty in taking advantage of their knowledge of Montaigne's revisions of his first edition, entered before their eyes into the text itself, in a way that has never happened with the Bible's reconstructed JE, D, and P.

The ease with which this aspect of the *Essais* has been accepted has, of course, something to do with its appropriateness to Montaigne's themes. As Cave says, "Supplementation governs the whole of the writing project, from its uncertain beginning to its inconclusive ending. The *Essais* always remain to be rewritten" (*Cornucopian Text*, 282). The homology between ideology and practice may make Montaigne's supplements easier to read than the Bible's, since in the latter case historical criticism requires us to read against the text's ideology in reconstructing its history. Still, modern readers are accustomed to exploring the differences between ideology and practice in many instances, and it is finally the narrative practices that build the text we have. Even Montaigne in the end is trying to reconstruct, or to construct, a picture of his self that will show some degree of unity amid its many shifts, in something like the ways in which successive biblical writers seek the unities hidden in the history of Israel.

This concern leads Montaigne occasionally to statements that the rabbis might have used of the Bible, a development that itself can be traced through the editions of the *Essais*. In the second edition, he added the great essay "De la vanité," and in that essay he describes his method of adding without altering the existing text: "J'adjouste, mais je ne corrige pas" (*Oeuvres complètes*, 941). In the third edition, he adds a para-

---

reading only the (a)-layer is contaminated by the awareness of what is 'left out'; and it is equally arguable that the making of layers fractures the complete version, reminding the reader that certain passages were inserted and thus inviting him to consider them as in some sense a supplementation" (*The Cornucopian Text*, 282).

graph that clarifies, or confuses, the matter further. He asserts, in almost mystical language, that "mon livre est tousjours un" through all its editions, despite the changes he has made in it. He is well aware that the text, if not altogether atomized, is at least broken up to some extent by his additions, and he calls his essays "une marqueterie mal jointe," a poorly constructed parquet floor, to which in later editions he adds new design elements, "quelque embleme supernuméraire." Thus Montaigne uses the image of renovation (and not deconstruction) in describing the growth of his narrative structures. As Constance Jordan says, "The *Essais* does not demonstrate a dialectic, in that Montaigne deliberately refrains from coordinating its parts, but rather a dialogic, in that each part is an answer and a new beginning" ("Montaigne's 'Chasse de Cognoissance,' " 275).

Much of biblical narrative could be described in similar terms, and the experience of reading a text like 1–2 Samuel often resembles the experience of reading Montaigne. The later additions occasionally flatly contradict the earlier stages, but more often they comment on them and guide our understanding. The value of historical criticism in engaging this aspect of the text is in clarifying our choices as we follow the later readings, ignore them, or fashion an amalgam of earlier and later stages.

Perspectival Assembly in the Thousand and One Nights

For all the many analogies made by biblical scholars to Bedouin social customs, living conditions, and linguistic usages, it is somewhat surprising that no serious use has ever been made, so far as I know, of the great resource of the *Thousand and One Nights*.[3] It comes, to be sure, from a later age, but much of it

---

[3]In his article "Pre-Islamic Arabic Historical Traditions," J. R. Porter notes that early Islamic literature is not markedly different in character from the pre-Islamic *ayyam* tales of everyday life he examines. Though the pre-Islamic material of the fourth to seventh centuries A.D. is somewhat closer in time to the Bible, in some respects the necessity of the later tradition to deal with the impact of Islam only increases the relevance of the later Arabic tradition for

is no later than the Icelandic sagas so often alluded to, and it is all well earlier than the modern Serbo-Croatian epic traditions so useful to Homeric scholarship in the wake of Milman Parry. Perhaps most people are accustomed to thinking of the *Thousand and One Nights* simply as children's stories, a misperception fostered by the expurgated editions so widely circulated even today, and perhaps too a degree of Eurocentrism leads readers to compare Hebrew narrative to Henry James sooner than to the other great body of Semitic prose literature.

Be that as it may, the *Thousand and One Nights,* in the two thousand pages of its unexpurgated length, offers a wealth of comparative material, both thematically and in its compositional techniques. These techniques are too many and too subtle to explore in any detail here, but I will examine one particularly striking tale, one in which historiography is mingled with religious discourse and fictive play in an extraordinary fashion. The penultimate tale in the collection is an extended account of the downfall of Haroun al-Rashid's grand vizier, Ja'afar the Barmakid. The story is told realistically, with reference to the work of several Arabic historians, as it describes the sudden fall from favor of Ja'afar, long Haroun's closest friend, followed by the death of the brokenhearted caliph himself thereafter.

In its stark realism, this story contrasts markedly with most of the tales in the collection, and it gives a very different portrait of Haroun al-Rashid than the idealized image of the magnificent master of the universe and patron of the arts that the rest of the collection sets forth. It draws on (and elaborates) vivid eye-witness accounts to show the troubled last days of an aging monarch, mortally ill, whose favorite sons are plotting

---

the comparison to Hebrew narrative. As for the pre-Islamic material, it too stands ready for literary comparison; discussion of it by biblical scholars has largely concentrated on questions of orality and literacy. See G. Widengren, "Oral and Written Literature among the Hebrews in the Light of Arabic Evidence, with Special Regard to Prose Narratives," and references in Porter's article, notes 8–11.

against him: "Though he remained all-powerful until his death, al-Rashid imagined that he was surrounded by traitors. He feared to be poisoned by his sons, who were indeed no cause for pride."[4] Al-Rashid demonstrates the plausibility of his fears in a conversation with al-Tabari, a court historian:

"Would you have proof of their plots? I have ordered a riding horse to be sent to me, and instead of choosing one with a strong and easy action, you will see them bring to me a worn beast, having a broken pace to aggravate my suffering."

This prophecy was fulfilled; al-Rashid was given such a horse as he described, and he accepted it with a look of sad understanding to al-Tabari. (520)

This moving historical narrative has been incorporated into the collection at the point at which Shahrazad is preparing to bid farewell to the world of her fictions. As she tells of the deaths of Ja'afar and Haroun al-Rashid, Shahrazad comes to the brink of her triumph over the sentence of death that has hung over her throughout the narrative, a triumph that will, however, spell the end of the book and of her existence in an ongoing story.

Her victory in the closing of the frame tale is thus muted by an awareness of the transience of the historical world, and even of the world of fiction itself. Following the realistic account of the deaths of Ja'afar and Haroun al-Rashid, Shahrazad's final story is an idealized fairy tale of the hopeless love of Prince Jasmine for Princess Almond, whose father condemns her to death when she refuses to marry another man. Jasmine braves death to win his beloved, and like Orpheus tames wild beasts with music. Princess Almond's father relents and revokes the sentence of death he had passed on his daughter (a story element with a clear moral for Shahrazad's husband), but Almond's brothers refuse to allow her to marry Jasmine. They

---

[4]*The Book of the Thousand Nights and One Night*, trans. Powys Mathers from the French translation of J. C. Mardrus, 520 (all references are to the fourth volume, except as noted).

arrange another marriage instead, but on the morning of her wedding Almond escapes with Jasmine. As the thousand and first night draws to a close, Shahrazad concludes: "Nothing has since been heard of them, or their abiding place. There are few upon this earth worthy of happiness, worthy to take the road which leads to happiness, worthy to draw near to the house of happiness" (530). Then there follows the closing of the frame tale, with Shahryar's admission that he loves Shahrazad far too much too kill her; he is cured of his jealous madness, and the frame tale ends with feasting, the marriage of Dunyazad to Shahzaman, and the king's order that his annalists "write out the tales of Shahrazad from beginning to end, without the omission of a single detail. So they sat down and wrote thirty volumes in gold letters, and called this sequence of marvels and astonishments: *The Book of the Thousand Nights and One Night*" (536). This "narratological" ending thus concludes the collection on the order of one of the characters within it.

In this way the book closes with three very different endings, which operate in ways both complementary and contradictory to take leave of the worlds of history and fiction. The closing of the frame tale incorporates a further ending as well. After Shahryar has had the book written, he and Shahrazad live happily ever after, until the appearance of the character who closes the volume, as he has closed many of the stories within it: "the Separator of friends, the Destroyer, the Builder of tombs, the Inexorable, the Inevitable" (536).

The story of Ja'afar and Haroun al-Rashid that begins the series of closures is, to be sure, not a simple historical chronicle but a masterpiece of historical fiction, freely composed on the basis of chronicles and poems about the end of Haroun al-Rashid's life. Even so, it retains its quality of marked difference from the sequences of marvels around it, and the question I wish to ask here is how our reading of this historical narrative is affected by its literary setting. This case of generic appropriation is particularly interesting as the surrounding context can itself be seen in different ways. Even as the historical narrative is enclosed within a fictive frame, the frame tale itself is enclosed (a fact rarely discussed) in a religious frame of its own. The first volume opens with the assertion, given "in the name of Allah, the Merciful, the Compassionate," that the stories to follow will serve as lessons for the moral betterment of the reader (I, xii); and the final volume closes with praise of "Him . . . Who, changing all things, yet Himself changes not," and with a prayer for "our Lord Muhammad, Prince of Messengers, Jewel of the World, our hope for an auspicious END!" (IV, 537).

One can choose to disregard this outer frame as an insincere gesture toward orthodoxy, but it is equally possible to give considerable weight to the presence of religious themes in the work. However strongly one emphasizes the heterodox quality of the stories' celebrations of wine, boys, and song, in a very real sense the book deals with narrative tensions inherent within Islamic orthodoxy itself. Allah enjoys an absolute knowledge of the world, frequently pictured as a text spread out before him, from which he reads or on which he writes, but mortals are not granted any easy access to such knowledge. The very theme of stories enclosed within doubled frames could take inspiration from the Koran's description of the human condition: "He created you from one being, and then from that being He made its mate. . . . He created you in the wombs of your mothers, creation after creation, in a threefold gloom."[5] Religious issues are often presented directly, in characters' references to Allah and to Fate. Indirectly, theological issues of knowledge and fidelity are often transposed to the representation of human passion, in ways comparable to the transformations of divine love seen in the Song of Songs. In any event, however we choose to read it, the religious frame encloses the narrative frame tale proper.

Thus the *Thousand and One Nights* actually has five endings—political, mythic/fictive, narratological, physical, and reli-

---

[5]Surah 39:6 in *The Meaning of the Glorious Koran*, trans. Mohammed Marmaduke Pickthall.

gious—and its readers are left to make of it what they can. As the text says just before its final prayer, "Allah knows all! He alone can distinguish between the true and the false. He knows all!" (537). Layers of stories and juxtapositions of genres have combined to created a mysterious and shifting compendium of no definable genre, one that resists assessment along any one of its many axes. As with the Bible, the complexity is fostered in part by the shifting cultural backgrounds of the material, some of which is pre-Islamic, some of which is heterodox Islamic, some of which is entirely orthodox. Theological and social tensions combine with the heritage of oral tradition to foster the story's reluctance to rest at any fixed referential point.

The text openly invites multiple readings in various places, among them at the conclusion to the story of the downfall of Ja'afar and his family. The story is constructed in such a way as to maximize the surprise and mystery of the event. Ja'afar is briefly separated from his beloved caliph, who sends frequent messages of friendship and regret for the separation. As Ja'afar rests in his tent one evening, his old friend Masrur, the caliph's executioner, suddenly bursts in and tells him to prepare for death on the instant. The only allowance he can make for their years of friendship is to give Ja'afar a few moments to record his last wishes. Ja'afar, however, has no final instructions to give, and wishes only that the caliph's years will be increased by the years taken from his own life. Masrur then cuts off his head.

So far the narrator has given us no direct information about Haroun al-Rashid's motives or frame of mind; we know no more than the command that Masrur says he has received to execute his vizier. On receiving Ja'afar's head, al-Rashid

looked at the head of his old friend and, leaning forward suddenly, spat upon it. But his resentment was stronger than death. He ordered the body to be crucified at one end of the bridge of Baghdad, and the head to be exposed at the other. The punishment was more degrading than any which had ever been inflicted upon even the worst of malefactors. At the end of six months he ordered that his wazir's remains should be burnt on cattle dung and scattered among the privies. (512)

The event is shocking, and it proves fatal to al-Rashid and his world. He mourns Ja'afar incessantly, ceases to be able to bear to live in Baghdad, and establishes a new capital, where he and his court sadly dwell until his death. Shahrazad knows only one story of any conversation in which al-Rashid ever alluded to his reasons for the destruction of his friend. Some years after the event, al-Rashid's young sister Aliyah plucked up her courage and asked why Ja'afar had to die. "Al-Rashid's face grew dark, and he pushed her away, saying: 'My child, my sole remaining happiness, how would it advantage you to know the reason? If I thought that my shirt knew, I would tear my shirt in pieces' " (512–13).

Within Shahrazad's story, no one ever learns the cause; but Shahrazad shares with Shahryar (and with us) the speculations of later historians. In an interesting doubling of the five endings of the *Thousand and One Nights* itself, Shahrazad has heard of five different explanations for the downfall of Ja'afar and the Barmakids, and she recounts these along with anecdotes that serve as supporting evidence. The first explanation is political: Ja'afar and his family became so powerful that Haroun al-Rashid came to fear that "they are the true power and I am only a figure" (513). The second explanation is moral: the Barmakids became so proud that they made many enemies, who fanned al-Rashid's jealousy, and when Ja'afar showed leniency to an enemy of the caliph's, al-Rashid determined to destroy his old friend. The third explanation is religious: generations earlier, the Barmakids had been slow to convert to Islam, and al-Rashid found Ja'afar supporting heretics.

The fourth explanation is sexual. This explanation lies closest to Shahrazad's heart, and she details it at the greatest length, describing it as the most probable explanation of all. The story goes that Haroun al-Rashid had developed "a strange and deep tenderness" for his own sister Abbasah and could not bear to be out of her company. At the same time, he could not do without the presence of Ja'afar, but religious law forbad Ja'afar and Abbasah to be together if they were neither related nor married. So al-Rashid ordered them to contract a white marriage, forbidding them to consummate it on pain of death. Gradually, Ja'afar and Abbasah fell in love, and finally, by a ruse, Abbasah contrived to spend a night with her "husband." When al-Rashid learned of this, he killed them and the child born of their night of passion.

Shahrazad concludes her account with a fifth explanation, one that undercuts all the rest:

It remains for me to say, O auspicious King, that other and quite worthy historians contend that Jafar and the Barmakids had done nothing to deserve their fate, and that it would not have come upon them if it had not been written in their Destiny.

But Allah knows all!   (518)

These five explanations encapsulate the orders of cause and effect that operate throughout the *Thousand and One Nights*. In taking the historical narrative into her story sequence, Shahrazad privileges the explanation closest to the book's own preference for tales of misdirected sexuality, but every other kind of explanation is retained as well. Perhaps too a sixth cause, one Shahrazad does not mention, should be adduced as well: the power of story telling itself. Running through Shahrazad's explanations is a pattern of story telling gone out of control and destroying those it touches. In the first explanation, the Barmakids are destroyed by their power and magnificence, "the tale of which became a weariness even in the ears of those who benefited, and which called forth rather envy and dislike than grateful friendship" (513). In the second account, al-Rashid's wrath at the Barmakids' pride is fanned by "anonymous detractors, who allowed unsigned bitter verses and perfidious prose to come to the ears of the Khalifah" (513). In the fourth account, Abbasah contrives to disguise herself as a slave girl and persuades Ja'afar's mother to stir his interest by advance praise of this new beauty. Finally, in the fifth explanation, the Barmakids' unmerited fate was "written in their Destiny."

Thus we must consider five or six different kinds of causality in assessing the story of the downfall of the Barmakids, and this perspectival multiplication of viewpoints provides a thematic analogue to the multiplication of frame tales, beginnings, and endings in the narrative structure. Like the Bible, the *Thousand and One Nights* is the product of an interplay between, on the one hand, the varied viewpoints of its disparate sources, and, on the other hand, a lively sense of the mysterious complexity of human character and divine will, which leads to the seeking out and conjoining of sources with varied viewpoints. This composite artistry is rather less coherent and consistent than the products of a single authorial consciousness usually are, and sometimes the text fosters a unified reading, other times not. Sometimes the stories are carefully arranged to create thematic progressions, and in other instances different versions of a story appear in different places without any visible literary purpose to the repetition: they are oral variants pure and simple.

The net result of the book's multiplication of compositional principles and causal explanations is that the reader is forced to attempt the difficult feat of viewing the story in several different ways at once. On analogy to historical criticism of the Bible, it would be possible to reconstruct, at least in a schematic fashion, the kinds of reading of Ja'afar's downfall appropriate to each kind of material found in the book. To the extent that the story does derive from old chronicles, one could posit that the political explanation with which Shahrazad begins her tour of causes is the explanation naturally inherent in the original story. One could then note that the sexual explanation is the one privileged by oral tradition (embodied in Shahrazad herself), whereas the story telling explanation fits most appropriately with the perspective of the author of the principal narrative frame, for whom a guiding motif is the life-giving and death-dealing power of story telling. Finally, the religious explanation is closely related to the outermost framework of the book, and the very multiplication of perspectives serves to underscore the point that only Allah knows the difference between truth and fiction.

Of the four analogies outlined in this chapter, that of the *Thousand and One Nights* gives the fullest example of a multifaceted composite artistry produced through a gradual growth of the text. At the same time, the genuinely composite character of the book casts doubt on a reading of the text as harmoniously dialogic. The political/historical, fictive, and religious viewpoints simultaneously complement and undermine each other, and at many points the reader is left with an uncertain shifting between levels. What can Shahryar, or we, learn from such mysterious events? Should the story's end, or ends, be read as comic or tragic? Different readers, and any given reader at different times, will construe the balance differently.

The Dynamics of Biblical Narrative

The Bible is more concerned to communicate truth than is the *Thousand and One Nights*, but it often creates a similar uncertainty, sometimes deliberately, at other times only of necessity. Certain sequences, like the Succession Narrative, do directly thematize the problem of multiple reports and highlight the complexity of motives, leaving the reader to be the judge. In some ways the entire Yahwistic source, perhaps through its relative closeness to oral tradition, achieves a parallel complexity, not through an open multiplication of motives but through its very refusal to give any explanations at all in so many instances—the reverse side of Shahrazad's expository technique. At other times, as often in the narrative expansions by the Deuteronomistic historian and the Priestly writers, the reader is given stories that serve as direct or indirect instructions in reading the surrounding text, and these instructions variously complement, redirect, deconstruct, or even effectively suppress the emphases of the material into which they are inserted.

The result is not a forced choice between the "confused textual patchwork" of historical criticism and the "purposeful pattern" to be sought by literary analysis.[6] Rather, the integration of literary and historical study reveals what might be called a purposeful patchwork, though the image lacks enough dimensions, since several different patchworks are variously interlaced and overlaid. In reconstructing this four-dimensional pattern, we read both with and against the intentions of the various authors involved in the text, and we are also brought to multiple readings of individual passages. To do full justice to the dynamics of biblical narrative, we must often read a passage three or even four ways at once.

This is not quite possible, of course, and at any given moment we may entertain the reading fostered by one of the authors at work in the text; then, in a reversal of figure and ground, another reading comes uppermost. It is difficult for Eli to be both kindly and evil; we can read him one way or the other, in each case following one of the authors of the text; or we can construct a temporary amalgam in which we correct each author in the light of the other, a solution that might be, but probably is not, what the later author intended us to do in this instance. Historical criticism both helps us to recover authorial intentionality and also forces us to see our distance from it, in the many cases where the intentions of the different authors do not easily harmonize. This may represent a loss of meaning for those readers who are committed to the ideology of tenth-century Yahwism, or fifth-century Priestly thought, but for most readers an awareness of the multiplicity of biblical narrative should enrich the reading process it destabilizes.

No sharp dichotomy can be sustained between deconstruction and reconstruction in the study of the biblical texts. The two activities proceed together, resulting in readings that are less stable but also more faithful to the complex historical pres-

---

[6]The opposition between these terms appears in Alter, *Art of Biblical Narrative*, 133.

sures that shaped the unique literary forms of biblical narrative. The close conjunction of literary and historical study gives us the perspective necessary to understand the process by which the biblical writers produced their great narratives, at once suppressing and revealing their own history, as they sought to refashion the narrative covenant between text and audience in order better to express the sacred covenant as they understood it. Their work is no longer transmitted through a serenely ahistorical tradition, a tradition which bred a kind of wholeness and certainty in reading that can no longer be taken for granted. What is gained, however, is a far clearer picture of the world in which the Bible was created and the ways in which it grew. With this new understanding we can refashion the narrative covenant with writers whose shaping activity we can now observe and assess. By recovering the work of authors whose greatest ambition was to disappear into their text, we recover not the poetics of biblical narrative but its dynamics, and in this way we can gain a new understanding of both the strangeness and the immediacy of that text which, more than any other, questions our lives even as we seek to reveal its own inner life.

Bibliography

Texts

Biblia Hebraica Stuttgartensia. 2d ed. Ed. K. Elliger and W. Rudolph. Stuttgart: Deutsche Bibelgesellschaft, 1983.

Borger, Riekele. *Die Inschriften Asarhaddons König von Assyrien.* Graz: 1956.

Burstein, Stanley Mayer. *The Babyloniaca of Berossus.* Sources from the Ancient Near East Ser. 1, vol 5. Malibu, CA: Undena, 1978.

Cagni, Luigi. *L'Epopea di Erra.* Studi Semitici 34. Rome: Istituto di Studi del Vicino Oriente, 1969. French trans. in René Labat, *Les Religions du Proche-Orient asiatique,* 114–37. Paris: Fayard-Denael, 1970.

Civil, M. "The Sumerian Flood Story." In Lambert and Millard, *Atra-Ḥasīs,* 138–45, 167–72.

Ebeling, Erich. *Tod und Leben nach den Vorstellungen der Babylonier.* 1. Teil: Texte. Berlin: de Gruyter, 1931.

Gardiner, Sir Alan H. *The Admonitions of an Egyptian Sage.* Leipzig, 1909; repr. Hildesheim: G. Olms Verlag, 1969.

———. *Egyptian Letters to the Dead.* London: The Egypt Exploration Society, 1928.

Götze, Albrecht. *Die Annalen des Muršiliš.* Mitteilungen der Vorderasiatisch-Aegyptischen Gesellschaft 38. Leipzig: Hinrich, 1933.

Grayson, A. K. *Babylonian Historical-Literary Texts.* Toronto: University of Toronto, 1975.

Gurney, O. R. "The Sultantepe Tablets: The Myth of Nergal and Ereshkigal." *Anatolian Studies* 10 (1960): 105–29.

Homer, *The Iliad.* Ed. A. T. Murray, 2 vols. Cambridge: Harvard University Press; London: Heinemann, 1978.

———. *The Odyssey.* Ed. W. B. Stanford, 2 vols. London: Macmillan; New York: St. Martin's, 2d ed., 1959.

Kramer, Samuel N. "Gilgamesh and the Land of the Living." *Journal of Cuneiform Studies* 1 (1947): 3–46.

Lambert, W. G., and A. R. Millard. *Atra-Ḥasīs: The Babylonian Story of the Flood.* Oxford: Clarendon, 1969.

_____. *Babylonian Wisdom Literature*. Oxford: Clarendon, 1960.

Lichtheim, Miriam. *Ancient Egyptian Literature*, 3 vols. Berkeley: University of California, 1973, 1976, 1980.

Machinist, Peter. *"The Epic of Tukulti-Ninurta I": A Study in Middle Assyrian Literature*. Ph.D. diss. Yale University, 1978.

Otten, Heinrich. *Die Apologie Hattusilis III: Das Bild der Überlieferung*. Studien zu den Boğazköy-Texten 24. Wiesbaden: Harrassowitz, 1981. English trans. in George Bechtel and Edgar Sturtevant, *A Hittite Chrestomathy*. Philadelphia: University of Pennsylvania, 1935.

Pritchard, James B. *Ancient Near Eastern Texts Relating to the Old Testament*, 3d ed. Princeton: Princeton University Press, 1969.

Simpson, W. K. *The Literature of Ancient Egypt*. New Haven: Yale University Press, 1972; 2d ed., 1973.

Speiser, E. A. "Akkadian Myths and Epics." Revised by A. K. Grayson. In Pritchard, *ANET*, 60–119, 501–18.

Wilcke, Claus. *Das Lugalbandaepos*. Wiesbaden: Harrassowitz, 1969.

Criticism

Aberbach, Moses, and Leivy Smolar. "Aaron, Jeroboam, and the Golden Calves." *Journal of Biblical Literature* 86 (1967): 129–40.

Ackerman, James. "The Literary Context of the Moses Birth Story (Exodus 1–2)." In Gros Louis, *Literary Interpretations*, vol. 1, 74–119.

Ackroyd, Peter. "The Chronicler as Exegete." *Journal for the Study of the Old Testament* 2 (1977): 2–32.

_____. *Exile and Restoration: A Study of Hebrew Thought of the Sixth Century B.C.* Philadelphia: Westminster, 1968.

Albrektson, Bertil. *History and the Gods: An Essay on the Idea of Historical Events as Divine Manifestations in the Ancient Near East and Israel*. Lund: Gleerup, 1967.

Albright, William Foxwell. *Yahweh and the Gods of Canaan*. The Jordan Lectures, 1965. London: Athlone Press, 1968.

Alonso Schöckel, Luis. *The Inspired Word: Scripture in the Light of Language and Literature*. Trans. Francis Martin. New York: Herder & Herder, 1965.

Alster, Bendt. *Death in Mesopotamia*. Mesopotamia 8; XXVIe Rencontre assyriologique internationale. Copenhagen: Akademisk Forlag, 1980.

Alter, Robert. *The Art of Biblical Narrative*. New York: Basic Books, 1981.

————. *The Art of Biblical Poetry*. New York: Basic Books, 1985.

Anderson, G. W., ed. *Tradition and Interpretation: Essays by Members of the Society for Old Testament Study*. Oxford: Clarendon, 1979.

Barr, James. *Holy Scripture: Canon, Authority, Criticism*. Philadelphia: Westminster, 1983.

————. "The Meaning of 'Mythology' in Relation to the Old Testament." *Vetus Testamentum* 9 (1959): 1–10.

Barthes, Roland. "The Struggle with the Angel: Textual Analysis of Genesis 32:23–33." In *Structural Analysis and Biblical Exegesis: Interpretational Essays*, 21–33. Ed. Roland Barthes et al. Pittsburgh: Pickwick, 1974.

Barton, John. *Reading the Old Testament: Method in Biblical Study*. Philadelphia: Westminster, 1984.

Barzel, Hillel. "Moses: Tragedy and Sublimity." In Gros Louis, *Literary Interpretations*, vol. 1, 120–40.

Baumgartner, Walter. *Zum Alten Testament und seiner Umwelt*. Leiden: Brill, 1959.

Beyerlin, Walter. *Origins and History of the Oldest Sinaitic Traditions*. Trans. S. Rudman. Oxford: Blackwell, 1965.

Blenkinsopp, Joseph. *Prophecy and Canon: A Contribution to the Study of Jewish Origins*. Notre Dame: University of Notre Dame Press, 1977.

————. "Jonathan's Sacrilege." *Catholic Biblical Quarterly* 26 (1964): 423–49.

Bloom, Harold. " 'Before Moses Was, I Am': The Original and the Belated Testaments." *Notebooks in Cultural Analysis* 1 (1984): 3–14.

The Book of the Thousand Nights and One Night. Trans. Powys Mathers from the French translation of J. C. Mardrus, 4 vols. New York: St. Martin's, 1972.

Borges, Jorge Luis. "Tlön, Uqbar, Orbis Tertius." In *Ficciones*, trans. Anthony Kerrigan, 17–35. New York: Grove, 1962.

Bottéro, Jean. "La mythologie de la mort en Mésopotamie ancienne." In Alster, *Death in Mesopotamia*, 25–52.

————. "Symptômes, signes, écritures en Mésopotamie ancienne." In *Divination et rationalité*, 70–197. Paris: Seuil, 1974.

Bowra, C. M. *Homer*. London: Duckworth, 1972.

Brueggemann, Walter. "David and His Theologian." *Catholic Biblical Quarterly* 30 (1968): 156–81.

————. *David's Truth in Israel's Imagination and Memory*. Philadelphia: Fortress, 1985.

————. "The Kerygma of the Priestly Writers." In Brueggemann and Wolff, *The Vitality of Old Testament Traditions*, 101–13.

Brueggeman, Walter, and Hans Walter Wolff. *The Vitality of Old Testament Traditions*. Atlanta: John Knox, 1975.

Budde, Karl. *Die Bücher Samuel erklärt*. Tübingen: Mohr, 1902.

Cancik, Hubert. *Grundzüge der hethitischer und alttestamentlicher Geschichtsschreibung*. Wiesbaden: Harrassowitz, 1976.

Cassuto, Umberto. *A Commentary on the Book of Genesis*. Part 1: *From Adam to Noah*; part 2: *From Noah to Abraham*. Trans. I. Abrahams. Jerusalem: Magnes, 1961, 1964.

Cave, Terrence. *The Cornucopian Text: Problems of Writing in the French Renaissance*. Oxford: Clarendon, 1979.

Childs, Brevard S. *The Book of Exodus: A Critical, Theological Commentary*. Old Testament Library. Philadelphia: Westminster, 1974.

————. *Introduction to the New Testament as Scripture*. Philadelphia: Fortress, 1985.

————. *Introduction to the Old Testament as Scripture*. Philadelphia: Fortress, 1979.

————. *Old Testament Theology in a Canonical Context*. Philadelphia: Fortress, 1986.

Clark, W. M. "The Flood and the Structure of the Pre-patriarchal History." *Zeitschrift für die alttestamentliche Wissenschaft* 83 (1971): 184–211.

Clements, R. E. *God and Temple*. Philadelphia: Fortress, 1965.

————. "Pentateuchal Problems." In Anderson, *Tradition and Interpretation*, 96–124.

————. Review of Rendtorff. *Journal for the Study of the Old Testament* 3 (July 1977): 46–56.

Coats, George W. *Rebellion in the Wilderness: The Murmuring Motif in the Wilderness Traditions of the Old Testament*. Nashville: Abingdon, 1968.

Conroy, C. "Hebrew Epic: Historical Notes and Critical Reflections." *Biblica* 61 (1980): 1–30.

Cornford, F. M. *Thucydides Mythistoricus*. London: Edward Arnold, 1970.

Cross, Frank Moore. *Canaanite Myth and Hebrew Epic: Essays in the History of the Religion of Israel*. Cambridge: Harvard University Press, 1973.

Culley, Robert C. "Oral Tradition and Historicity." In Wevers and Redford, *Studies*, 102–16.

————. *Studies in the Structure of Hebrew Narrative*. Philadelphia: Fortress, 1976.

Dahl, Nils A. "Contradictions in Scripture." In *Studies in Paul: Theology for the Early Christian Mission*, 159–77. Minneapolis: Augsburg, 1977.

David, M. "Le Récit du Déluge et l'Épopée de Gilgameš." In Garelli, *Gilgameš*, 153–59.

Dayan, Moshe. "The Spirit of the Warriors" (in Hebrew). *Stories of Heroism: Twenty Years of Independence* 11, 50–63. Ministry of Defense, 1968.

Debus, Jörg. *Die Sünde Jerobeams: Studien zur Darstellung Jerobeams und der Geschichte des Nordreichs in der deuteronomistischen Geschichtsschreibung*. Göttingen: Vandenhoeck & Ruprecht, 1967.

Delekat, L. "Tendenz und Theologie der David-Salomo-Erzählung." In Maass, *Das ferne und nahe Wort*, 22–36.

de Liagre Bohl, F. M. Th. "Bijbelse en Babylonische Dichtkunst: een Onderzoek." *Jaarbericht van het Vooraziatische-Egyptisch Genootschap "Ex Oriente Lux"* 15 (1957–58): 133–53.

———. "La Métrique de l'épopée babylonienne." In Garelli, *Gilgameš*, 145–52.

de Man, Paul. *Blindness and Insight: Essays in the Rhetoric of Contemporary Criticism*, 2d ed. Minneapolis: University of Minnesota, 1983.

Denton, Robert C., ed. *The Idea of History in the Ancient Near East*. New Haven: Yale University Press, 1955.

de Vries, Simon J. "David's Victory Over the Philistines as Saga and as Legend." *Journal of Biblical Literature* 92 (1973): 23–36.

Dietrich, Walter. *Prophetie und Geschichte: Eine redaktionsgeschichtliche Untersuchung zum deuteronomistischen Geschichtswerk*. Forschungen zur Religion und Literatur des Alten und Neuen Testaments 108. Göttingen: Vandenhoeck und Ruprecht, 1972.

Dodd, C. H. *The Authority of the Bible*. London: Nisbet, 1928.

Douglas, Mary. *Purity and Danger: An Analysis of Concepts of Pollution and Taboo*. New York: Praeger, 1966.

Eichrodt, W. "Ist die typologische Exegese sachgemässe Exegese?" *Vetus Testamentum* Supplements 4 (1956): 161–81.

Eissfeldt, Otto. *Geschichtsschreibung im Alten Testament: Ein kritischer Bericht über die neueste Literatur dazu*. Berlin: Evangelische Verlagsanstalt, 1948.

———. *The Old Testament: An Introduction*. Trans. P. R. Ackroyd. New York: Harper & Row, 1965.

Eslinger, Lyle M. "Hosea 12:5a and Genesis 32:29: A Study in Inner Biblical Exegesis." *Journal for the Study of the Old Testament* 18 (1980): 91–99.

Falkenstein, Adam. "Der sumerische und der akkadische Mythos von Inannas Gang zur Unterwelt." In Erwin Graf, ed., *Festschrift Werner Caskel*, 97–110. Leiden: Brill, 1968.

Fishbane, Michael. *Biblical Interpretation in Ancient Israel*. New York: Oxford University Press, 1985.

———. "Revelation and Tradition: Aspects of Inner-Biblical Exegesis." *Journal of Biblical Literature* 99 (1980): 343–61.

———. *Text and Texture: Close Readings of Selected Biblical Texts*. New York: Schocken Books, 1979.

Flanagan, James W. "Court History or Succession Document? A Study of 2 Sam. 9–20 and 1 Kings 1–2." *Journal of Biblical Literature* 91 (1972): 172–81.

Fohrer, Georg. "Tradition und Interpretation im Alten Testament." *Zeitschrift für die alttestamentliche Wissenschaft* 73 (1961): 1–30.

Fokkelman, J. P. *Narrative Art in Genesis*. Assen: Van Gorcum, 1975.

Freedman, D. N. "The Babylonian Chronicle." *The Biblical Archaeologist* 19 (1956): 50–60.

Frei, Hans. *The Eclipse of Biblical Narrative*. New Haven: Yale University Press, 1974.

Frye, Northrop. *The Great Code: The Bible and Literature*. New York: Harcourt, Brace, Jovanovich, 1982.

Gardner, Helen. *The Business of Criticism*. Oxford: Clarendon, 1959.

Garelli, Paul, ed. *Gilgameš et sa légende*. Paris: Imprimerie Nationale, 1960.

Garsiel, Moshe. *The First Book of Samuel: A Literary Study of Comparative Structures, Analogies and Parallels*. Ramat-Gan: Revivim, 1985.

———. *The Kingdom of David: Studies in History and Historiography* (in Hebrew). Tel-Aviv: Don, 1975.

Gaster, Theodore H. *Thespis: Ritual, Myth and Drama in the Ancient Near East*. New York: Henry Schuman, 1950.

Girard, René. *The Scapegoat*. Trans. Yvonne Freccero. Baltimore: Johns Hopkins University Press, 1986.

———. *Violence and the Sacred*. Trans. Patrick Gregory. Baltimore: Johns Hopkins University Press, 1977.

Gordon, Cyrus H. *The Ancient Near East*. New York: Norton, 1965.

Gottwald, Norman. *The Hebrew Bible: A Socio-Literary Introduction*. Philadelphia: Fortress, 1985.

———. "Social Matrix and Canonical Shape." *Theology Today* 42 (1985), 307–21.

Gradwohl, Roland. "Das 'Fremde Feuer' von Nadab und Abihu." *Zeitschrift für die alttestamentliche Wissenschaft* 75 (1963): 288–96.

Grapow, Hermann. *Studien zu den Annalen Thutmosis des Dritten und zu ihnen verwandten historischen Berichten des Neuen Reiches.* Abhandlungen der Deutschen Akademie der Wissenschaften zu Berlin, Phil.-hist. Kl., 1947 no. 2. Berlin: Akademie-Verlag, 1949.

Grayson, A. K. "Assyria and Babylonia." *Orientalia* n.s. 49, no. 2 (1980): 140–94.

———. *Assyrian and Babylonian Chronicles.* Texts from Cuneiform Sources 5. Locust Valley, NY: Augustin, 1970.

Gros Louis, Kenneth R. R., ed. *Literary Interpretations of Biblical Narratives.* 2 vols. Nashville: Abingdon, 1974, 1982.

Gunkel, Hermann. *Das Märchen im Alten Testament.* Tübingen: Mohr, 1917.

———. "Fundamental Problems of Hebrew Literary History" (1906). In *What Remains of the Old Testament,* trans. A. K. Dallas, 57–68. New York: Macmillan, 1928.

———. *The Legends of Genesis: The Biblical Saga and History.* Trans. W. H. Carruth. New York: Schocken Books, 1901.

Gunn, David M. *The Story of King David: Genre and Interpretation.* Journal for the Study of the Old Testament Supplements 6. Sheffield, 1978.

———. "On Oral Tradition: A Response to John Van Seters." *Semeia* 5 (1976): 155–63.

Gurney, O. R. "Hittite Kingship." In Hooke, *Myth, Ritual, and Kingship,* 105–12.

Güterbock, H. G. "Die historische Tradition und ihre literarische Gestaltung bei Babyloniern und Hethitern bis 1200." *Zeitschrift für Assyriologie* n.F. 8 (1934): 1–91, and n.F. 10 (1938): 45–149.

Hagan, H. "Deception as Motif and Theme in 2 Sm 9–20; 1 Kgs 1–2." *Biblica* 60 (1979): 301–26.

Halpern, B. Review of Van Seters, *Journal of Biblical Literature* 104 (1985): 506–9.

Haran, Menachem. *Temples and Temple-Service in Ancient Israel.* Oxford: Clarendon, 1978.

Hayes, John, and Carl Holladay. *Biblical Exegesis: A Beginner's Handbook.* Atlanta: John Knox, 1982.

Hecker, Karl. *Untersuchungen zur akkadischen Epik.* Alter Orient und Altes Testament Supplement Series 8. Kevelaer: Butzon & Bercker; Neukirchen-Vluyn: Neukirchner Verlag, 1974.

Heidel, Alexander. *The Gilgamesh Epic and Old Testament Parallels,* 2d ed. Chicago: University of Chicago Press, 1949.

Hempel, Johannes. "Glaube, Mythos und Geschichte im Alten Testament." *Zeitschrift für die alttestamentliche Wissenschaft* 65 (1963): 109–67.

Herrmann, S. "Das Werden Israels." *Theologische Literaturzeitung* 87 (1965): 561–74.

Hertzberg, Hans Wilhelm. "Die Nachgeschichte alttestamentlicher Texte innerhalb des Alten Testaments." In *Beiträge zur Traditionsgeschichte und Theologie des Alten Testaments*, 69–80. Göttingen: Vandenhoeck & Ruprecht, 1962.

Heschel, Abraham. *The Prophets*. New York: Harper & Row, 1969.

Hillers, Delbert R. *Covenant: The History of a Biblical Idea*. Baltimore: Johns Hopkins University Press, 1969.

Hoffmann, Hans-Detlef. *Reform und Reformen: Untersuchungen zu einem Grundthema der deuteronomistischen Geschichtsschreibung*. Abhandlungen zur Theologie des Alten und Neuen Testaments 66. Zurich: Theologischer Verlag, 1980.

Hoffman, Yair. "Between Conventionality and Strategy: On Repetition in Biblical Narrative." *Hasifrut* 8 (1979), 89–99 (in Hebrew; Eng. summary, ii).

Hoffner, Harry A. "Histories and Historians of the Ancient Near East: The Hittites." *Orientalia*, n.s. 49 (1980): 283–332.

Hölscher, Gustav. *Geschichtsschreibung in Israel: Untersuchungen zum Jahwisten und Elohisten*, rev. ed. Lund: Gleerup, 1952.

Hooke, S. H., ed. *Myth, Ritual, and Kingship: Essays on the Theory and Practice of Kingship in the Ancient Near East and in Israel*. Oxford: Clarendon, 1958.

Huffmon, Herbert B. "The Treaty Background of Hebrew Yada'." *Bulletin of the American Schools of Oriental Research* 181 (Feb. 1966): 31–37.

Humphreys, W. Lee. "The Rise and Fall of King Saul: A Study of an Ancient Narrative Stratum in 1 Samuel." *Journal for the Study of the Old Testament* 18 (1980): 74–90.

———. "The Tragedy of King Saul: A Study of the Structure of 1 Samuel 9–31." *Journal for the Study of the Old Testament* 6 (1978): 18–27.

Jacobsen, Thorkild. "Death in Ancient Mesopotamia." In Alster, *Death in Mesopotamia*, 19–24.

Janssen, Enno. *Juda in der Exilszeit: Ein Beitrag zur Frage der Entstehung des Judentums*. Forschungen zur Religion und Literatur des Alten und Neuen Testaments, n.F. 51. Göttingen: Vandenhoeck & Ruprecht, 1956.

Jason, Heddy. "The Story about David and Goliath: Is It a Folk-Epic?" *Hasifrut* 6 (1976), 23–41 (in Hebrew; Eng. summary, iv).

Jensen, Peter. *Das Gilgamesch-Epos in der Weltliteratur.* Strasbourg: Trübner, 1906.

———. *Moses, Jesus, Paulus: Drei Varianten des babylonische Gottmenschen Gilgamesch,* 2d ed. Frankfurt: Neuer Frankfurter Verlag, 1909.

———. *Gilgamesch-Epos, jüdäische Nationalsagen, Ilias und Odyssee.* Ex Oriente Lux 3. Leipzig: Pfeiffer, 1924.

Jordan, Constance. "Montaigne's 'Chasse de Cognoissance': Language and Play in the *Essais.*" *Romanic Review* 71 (1980): 265–80.

Kiel, Yehudah. *The Book of Samuel* (in Hebrew). Jerusalem, 1981.

Kilian, Rudolf. "Die Priesterschrift: Hoffnung auf Heimkehr." In Josef Schreiner, ed., *Wort und Botschaft: Eine theologische und kritische Einführung in die Probleme des Alten Testaments,* 226–43. Würzburg: Echter-Verlag, 1967.

Klopfenstein, M. A. *Die Lüge nach dem Alten Testament: Ihr Begriff, Bedeutung und Beurteilung.* Zurich: Gotthelf-Verlag, 1964.

Knight, Douglas A., and Gene M. Tucker, eds. *The Hebrew Bible and Its Modern Interpreters.* Philadelphia: Fortress, 1985.

Koch, Klaus. *Die Priesterschrift von Exodus 25 bis Leviticus 16: Eine überlieferungsgeschichtliche und literarkritische Untersuchung.* Forschungen zur Religion und Literatur des Alten und Neuen Testaments 53. Göttingen: Vandenhoeck & Ruprecht, 1959.

———. *The Growth of the Biblical Tradition: The Form-Critical Method.* Trans. S. M. Cupitt. New York: Scribner's, 1969.

Kristeva, Julia. *Powers of Horror: An Essay on Abjection.* Trans. Leon Roudiez. New York: Columbia University Press, 1982.

Kroll, Wilhelm. "Die Kreuzung der Gattungen." In *Studien zum Verständnis der römischen Literatur,* 202–24. Stuttgart: Metzler, 1924.

Kugel, James L. *The Idea of Biblical Poetry: Parallelism and Its History.* New Haven: Yale University Press, 1981.

Kugel, James L., and Rowan A. Greer. *Early Biblical Interpretation,* ed. Wayne Meeks. Philadelphia: Westminster, 1986.

Kuhl, Curt. "Die 'Wiederaufnahme': Ein literarkritisches Prinzip?" *Zeitschrift für die alttestamentliche Wissenschaft* 64 (1952): 1–11.

Labat, René. *Les Religions du Proche-Orient asiatique.* Paris: Fayard-Denael, 1970.

Laessøe, Jørgen, "The Atraḥasīs Epic: A Babylonian History of Mankind." *Bibliotheca Orientalis* 13 (1956): 90–102.

Lambert, W. G. "The Theology of Death." In Alster, *Death in Mesopotamia,* 53–66.

Langlamet, F. "David et la maison de Saül." *Revue Biblique* 86 (1979): 194–213, 385–436, 481–513; 87 (1980): 161–210; 88 (1981): 321–32.

———. "Pour ou contre Salomon?" *Revue Biblique* 83 (1976): 321–79, 481–529.

Leibovitz, Nahum. *Studies on the Book of Genesis* (in Hebrew). Jerusalem, 1966.

Lods, Adolphe. *Histoire de la littérature hébraïque et juive.* Paris: Payot, 1950.

Lust, Johan. "The Story of David and Goliath in Hebrew and Greek." *Ephemerides Theologicae Lovaniensis* 59 (1983), 5–25.

Maass, F., ed. *Das ferne und nahe Wort.* Rost Festschrift; Beihefte zur Zeitschrift für die alttestamentliche Wissenschaft 105. Berlin: Töpelmann, 1967.

Machinist, P. "Literature as Politics: The Tukulti-Ninurta Epic and the Bible." *Catholic Biblical Quarterly* 38 (1976): 455–82.

McCarter, P. Kyle. *I Samuel.* Anchor Bible 8. Garden City, New York: Doubleday, 1980.

———. *II Samuel.* Anchor Bible 9. Garden City, New York: Doubleday, 1984.

McEvenue, Sean E., S. J. *The Narrative Style of the Priestly Writer.* Analecta Biblica 50. Rome: Biblical Institute Press, 1971.

McKnight, Edgar. *Meanings in Texts: The Historical Shaping of a Narrative Hermeneutics.* Philadelphia: Fortress, 1978.

Miller, Patrick D., and J. J. M. Roberts. *The Hand of the Lord: A Reassessment of the "Ark Narrative" of 2 Samuel.* Baltimore: Johns Hopkins University Press, 1977.

Miscall, Peter D. *The Workings of Old Testament Narrative.* Philadelphia: Fortress, 1983.

Montaigne, *Essais.* In *Oeuvres Complètes,* ed. Albert Thibaudet and Maurice Rat. Bibliothèque de la Pléiade, 1962.

Moran, W. L., S. J. "The Ancient Near Eastern Background of the Love of God in Deuteronomy." *Catholic Biblical Quarterly* 25 (1963): 77–87.

Mowinckel, Sigmund. "Israelite Historiography." *Annual of the Swedish Theological Institute* 2 (1963): 4–26.

———. *Erwägungen zur Pentateuch Quellenfrage.* Oslo: Universitetsforlaget, 1964.

Muilenberg, James. "Form Criticism and Beyond." *Journal of Biblical Literature* 88 (1969): 1–18.

Naidoff, Bruce D. "A Man to Work the Soil: A New Interpretation of Genesis 2–3." *Journal for the Study of the Old Testament* 5 (1978): 2–14.

Neusner, Jacob. *The Idea of Purity in Ancient Judaism.* Leiden: Brill, 1973.

Nicholson, E. W. *Exodus and Sinai in History and Tradition.* Richmond: John Knox, 1973.

Njal's Saga. Trans. Magnus Magnusson and Hermann Palsson. Baltimore: Penguin, 1960.

Noth, Martin. *A History of Pentateuchal Traditions.* Trans. Bernhard W. Anderson. Englewood Cliffs, NJ: Prentice-Hall, 1972.

Nougayrol, J. "L'Épopée babylonienne." *Atti del Convegno Internazionale sul tema: La Poesia Epica e la sua formazione,* Problemi attuali di scienza e cultura, Quaderno n. 139, 852–58. Rome, 1970.

Oden, R. A. Review of Van Seters. *Interpretation* 38 (1984): 296–99.

Perlitt, Lothar. *Bundestheologie im Alten Testament.* Wissenschaftliche Monographien zum Alten und Neuen Testament 36. Neukirchen-Vluyn: Neukirchener Verlag, 1969.

Petersen, D. L. Review of Van Seters. *Catholic Biblical Quarterly* 47 (1985): 336–40.

Pickthall, Mohammed Marmaduke, trans. and ed. *The Meaning of the Glorious Koran.* New York: New American Library, n.d.

Plant, W. Gunther, et al. *The Torah: A Modern Commentary.* New York: Union of American Hebrew Congregations, 1981.

Polzin, Robert. *Late Biblical Hebrew: Toward an Historical Typology of Biblical Hebrew Prose.* Missoula, MT: Scholars Press, 1976.

_____. *Moses and the Deuteronomist: A Literary Study of the Deuteronomic History,* Part 1. New York: Seabury, 1980.

Porter, J. R. *Moses and Monarchy: A Study in the Biblical Tradition of Moses.* Oxford: Blackwell, 1963.

_____. "Old Testament Historiography." In Anderson, *Tradition and Interpretation,* 125–62.

_____. "Pre-Islamic Arabic Historical Traditions and the Early Historical Narratives of the Old Testament." *Journal of Biblical Literature* 87 (1968): 17–26.

Propp, Vladimir. *The Morphology of the Folktale,* 2d ed. Trans. L. Scott. Austin: University of Texas, 1968.

Rabinowitz, Isaac. " 'Word' and Literature in Ancient Israel." *New Literary History* 4 (1972): 119–39.

Rainey, A. F. "The Order of Sacrifices in Old Testament Ritual Texts." *Biblica* 51 (1970): 485–98.

Redford, D. B. "Studies in Relations Between Palestine and Egypt during the First Millennium B.C." In Wevers and Redford, *Studies,* 141–56.

Reiner, Erica, "City Bread and Bread Baked in Ashes." In *Languages and Areas: Studies Presented to George V. Bobrinskoy,* Committee on Southern Asian Studies, eds. 116–20. Chicago: University of Chicago Press, 1967.

Rendtorff, Rolf. "Genesis 8:21 und die Urgeschichte des Jahwisten." In *Gesammelte Studien zum Alten Testament*, 188–97. Munich: Theologische Bücherei, 1975.

———. *Das überlieferungsgeschichtliche Problem des Pentateuch.* Beihefte zur Zeitschrift für die alttestamentliche Wissenschaft 147. Berlin: de Gruyter, 1977.

———. *Die Gesetze in der Priesterschrift: Eine gattungsgeschichtliche Untersuchung.* Forschungen zur Religion und Literatur des Alten und Neuen Testaments, n.F.44. Göttingen: Vandenhoeck & Ruprecht, 2d ed., 1963.

———. "Literarkritik und Traditionsgeschichte." *Evangelische Theologie* 27 (1967): 138–53.

———. *The Old Testament: An Introduction.* Trans. John Bowden. Philadelphia: Fortress, 1985.

———. "Pentateuchal Studies on the Move." *Journal for the Study of the Old Testament* 3 (1977): 43–46.

———. "The 'Yahwist' as Theologian? The Dilemma of Pentateuchal Criticism." *Journal for the Study of the Old Testament* 3 (1977): 2–10.

Richter, Wolfgang. *Exegese als Literaturwissenschaft: Entwurf einer alttestamentlichen Literaturtheorie und Methodologie.* Göttingen: Vandenhoeck & Ruprecht, 1971.

Ricoeur, Paul. " 'Original Sin': A Study in Meaning." In *The Conflict of Interpretations*, 269–86. Evanston, IL: Northwestern University Press, 1974.

———. *The Symbolism of Evil.* Trans. Emerson Buchanan. Boston: Beacon, 1969.

Riemschneider, Margarete. *Die Welt der Hethiter.* Stuttgart: Kilpper, 1954.

Robertson, David. *The Old Testament and the Literary Critic.* Philadelphia: Fortress, 1977.

Rofé, Alexander. *The Book of Balaam (Numbers 22:2–24:25): A Study in Methods of Criticism and the History of Biblical Literature and Religion* (in Hebrew). Jerusalem: Simor, 1979.

———. "Joshua 20: Historico-Literary Criticism Illustrated." In Tigay, *Empirical Methods*, 131–47.

———. *The Prophetical Stories: The Narratives about the Prophets in the Hebrew Bible—Their Literary Types and History* (in Hebrew). Jerusalem: Magnes, 1982.

Rose, Martin. *Deuteronomist und Jahwist: Untersuchungen zu den Berührungspunkten beider Literaturwerke.* Abhandlungen zur Theologie des Alten und Neuen Testaments 67. Zurich: Theologischer Verlag, 1981.

Rost, Leonhard. *Die Überlieferung von der Thronnachfolge Davids* (1926). Reprinted in *Das kleine Credo und andere Studien zum Alten Testament,* 119–253. Heidelberg: Quelle & Meyer, 1965.

Ryken, Leland. "Literary Criticism of the Bible: Some Fallacies." In Gros Louis, *Literary Interpretations,* vol. 1, 24–40.

Sanders, James A. *Torah and Canon.* Philadelphia: Fortress, 1972.

Schmid, Hans Heinrich. *Der sogenannte Jahwist: Beobachtungen und Fragen zur Pentateuchforschung.* Zurich: Theologischer Verlag, 1976.

———. "In Search of New Approaches in Pentateuchal Research." *Journal for the Study of the Old Testament* 3 (1977): 33–42.

Schmid, Herbert. *Mose: Überlieferung und Geschichte.* Beihefte zur Zeitschrift für die alttestamentliche Wissenschaft 110. Berlin: Töpelmann, 1968.

Schmidt, W. H. *Einführung in das Alte Testament,* 2d ed. Berlin: de Gruyter, 1982.

Schneidau, Herbert N. *Sacred Discontent: The Bible and Western Tradition.* Baton Rouge: Louisiana State University Press, 1976.

Schulte, Hannelis. *Die Entstehung der Geschichtsschreibung im Alten Israel.* Beihefte zur Zeitschrift für die alttestamentliche Wissenschaft 128. Berlin: de Gruyter, 1972.

Scodel, Ruth. "The Achaean Wall and the Myth of Destruction." *Harvard Studies in Classical Philology* 86 (1982): 33–50.

Seeligmann, I. L. "Hebräische Erzählung und biblische Geschichtsschreibung." *Theologische Zeitschrift* 18 (1962): 305–25.

———. "Menschliches Heldentum und göttliche Hilfe: Die doppelte Kausalität im alttestamentlichen Geschichtsdenken." *Theologische Zeitschrift* 19 (1963): 385–411.

Sheppard, Gerald T. "Canonization: Hearing the Voice of the Same God through Historically Dissimilar Traditions." *Interpretation* 36 (1982): 21–33.

Simon, Uriel. "The Poor Man's Ewe Lamb: An Example of a Juridical Parable." *Biblica* 48 (1967): 207–42.

Sjöberg, Åke, *Der Mondgott Nanna-Suen in der sumerischen Überlieferung,* 1.Teil: Texte. Stockholm: Almqvist & Wiksell, 1960.

Smend, Rudolph. "Das Gesetz und die Völker: Ein Beitrag zur deuteronomistischen Redaktionsgeschichte." In Wolff, *Probleme,* 494–509.

————. *Yahweh War and Tribal Confederation.* Trans. M. G. Rogers. Nashville: Abingdon, 2d. ed., 1970.

Smith, Morton. "The Present State of Old Testament Studies." *Journal of Biblical Literature* 88 (1969): 19–35.

Soggin, J. Alberto. *Introduction to the Old Testament.* Trans. John Bowden. Philadelphia: Westminster, 1976.

Speiser, E. A. "Ancient Mesopotamia." In Denton, *Idea of History,* 35–76. Reprinted in his *Oriental and Biblical Studies,* 270–312. Ed. J. J. Finkelstein and Moshe Greenberg. Philadelphia: University of Pennsylvania Press, 1967.

————. "The Biblical Idea of History in Its Common Near Eastern Setting." *Israel Exploration Journal* 7 (1957): 201–16. Reprinted in his *Oriental and Biblical Studies,* 187–210.

————. *Genesis.* Anchor Bible 1. Garden City, NY: Doubleday, 1964.

Starobinski, Jean. "The Struggle with Legion: A Literary Analysis of Mark 5:1–20." *New Literary History* 4 (1973): 331–56.

Stendahl, Krister. "The Bible as a Classic and the Bible as Holy Scripture." *Journal of Biblical Literature* 103 (1984): 3–10.

Sternberg, Meir. *The Poetics of Biblical Narrative: Ideological Literature and the Drama of Reading.* Bloomington: Indiana University Press, 1985.

Sturluson, Snorri. *The Prose Edda.* Trans. Jean Young. Berkeley: University of California Press, 1954.

Tadmor, Hayim. "Observations on Assyrian Historiography." In *Essays on the Ancient Near East in Memory of Jacob Joel Finkelstein.* Memoirs of the Connecticut Academy of Arts and Sciences 19 (1977): 209–13.

Thornton, T. C. G. "Solomonic Apologetic in Samuel and Kings." *Church Quarterly Review* 169 (1968): 159–66.

Tigay, Jeffrey H., ed. *Empirical Models for Biblical Criticism.* Philadelphia: University of Pennsylvania, 1985.

————. *The Evolution of the Gilgamesh Epic.* Philadelphia: University of Pennsylvania Press, 1982.

Tov, Emanuel. "The Composition of 1 Samuel 16–18 in the Light of the Septuagint Version." In Tigay, *Empirical Models,* 97–130.

————. *The Hebrew and Greek Texts of Samuel.* Jerusalem: Academon, 1980.

————. "The Literary History of the Book of Jeremiah in the Light of Its Textual History." In Tigay, *Empirical Models,* 211–37.

————. *The Septuagint Translation of Jeremiah and Baruch: A Discussion of an Early Revision of the LXX of Jeremiah 29–52 and Baruch 1:1–*

3:8. Harvard Semitic Monographs 8. Missoula, MT: Scholars, 1976.

―――. *The Text-Critical Use of the Septuagint in Biblical Research*. Jerusalem Biblical Studies 3. Jerusalem: Simor, 1981.

Tsevat, M. "Common Sense and Hypothesis in Old Testament Study." *Hebrew Union College Annual* 47 (1976): 217–30.

Valentin, Heinrich. *Aaron: Eine Studie zur vor-priesterschriftlichen Aaron-Überlieferung*. Göttingen: Vandenhoeck & Ruprecht, 1978.

Van Seters, John. *Abraham in History and Tradition*. New Haven: Yale University Press, 1975.

―――. *In Search of History: Historiography in the Ancient World and the Origins of Biblical History*. New Haven: Yale University Press, 1983.

―――. "Oral Patterns and Literary Convention in Biblical Narrative." *Semeia* 5 (1976): 139–54.

―――. "Problems of Orality in the Literary Analysis of the Court History of David." *Journal for the Study of the Old Testament* 1 (1976): 22–29.

―――. "The Yahwist as Theologian? A Response." *Journal for the Study of the Old Testament* 3 (1977): 15–19.

Veijola, Timo. *Das Königtum in der Beurteilung der deuteronomistischen Historiographie: Eine redaktionsgeschichtliche Untersuchung*. Helsinki: Suomalainen Tiedeakatemia, 1977.

―――. *Die ewige Dynastie: David und die Entstehung seiner Dynastie nach der deuteronomistischen Darstellung*. Helsinki: Suomalainen Tiedeakatemia, 1975.

Vink, J. G. "The Date and Origin of the Priestly Code in the Old Testament." In Vink et al., *The Priestly Code and Seven Other Studies*, 1–144. Leiden: Brill, 1969.

von Rad, Gerhard. "The Beginnings of Historical Writing in Ancient Israel." In *The Problem of the Hexateuch and other Essays*, trans. E. Dicken, 166–204. New York: McGraw-Hill, 1966.

―――. "The Form-Critical Problem of the Hexateuch" (1938). In *The Problem of the Hexateuch*, 1–78.

―――. "Typological Interpretation of the Old Testament." In Westermann, *Essays on OT Hermeneutics*, 17–39.

von Soden, W. "Der hymnisch-epische Dialekt des Akkadischen." *Zeitschrift für Assyriologie*, n.F.6 (1931): 163–227 and n.F.7 (1933): 90–183.

―――. "Ein Zwiegespräch Hammurabis mit seiner Frau." *Zeitschrift für Assyriologie*, n.F.15 (1950): 153–55.

Wagner, Norman E. "Abraham and David?" In Wevers and Redford, *Studies*, 117–40.

———. *A Literary Analysis of Genesis 12–36*. Ph.D. diss., University of Toronto, 1965.

———. "A Response to Professor Rolf Rendtorff." *Journal for the Study of the Old Testament* 3 (1977), 20–27.

Weimar, Peter, and Erich Zenger. *Exodus: Geschichten und Geschichte der Befreiung Israels*. Stuttgarter Bibelstudien 75. Stuttgart: KBW Verlag, 1975.

Weiser, Artur. "Die Legitimation des Königs David." *Vetus Testamentum* 16 (1966): 325–54.

Wellhausen, Julius. *Prolegomena to the History of Ancient Israel* (1878). Trans. Black and Menzies. New York: Meridian, 1957.

Wenham, G. J. Review of Schmid. *Journal for the Study of the Old Testament* 3 (1977): 57–60.

West, M. L. "Prolegomena" to Hesiod, *Theogony*, 1–107. Oxford: Clarendon, 1966.

Westermann, Claus, ed. *Essays on Old Testament Hermeneutics*. Trans. James Luther Mays. Richmond: John Knox, 2d. ed., 1964.

———. *Genesis 1–11: A Commentary*. Trans. John Scullion. Minneapolis: Augsburg, 1984.

Wevers, J. W., and D. B. Redford, eds. *Studies on the Ancient Palestinian World*. Toronto Semitic Texts and Studies 2. University of Toronto Press, 1971.

Whybray, R. N. "Response to Professor Rendtorff." *Journal for the Study of the Old Testament* 3 (1977): 11–14.

———. *The Succession Narrative: A Study of II Samuel 9–20; I Kings 1 and 2*. Studies in Biblical Theology, 2d ser. no. 9. London: SCM, 1968.

Widengren, G. "Oral and Written Literature among the Hebrews in the Light of Arabic Evidence, with Special Regard to Prose Narratives." *Acta Orientalia* 23 (1959): 201–62.

Willis, J. T. "The Function of Comprehensive Anticipatory Redactional Joints in 1 Samuel 16–18." *Zeitschrift für die alttestamentliche Wissenschaft* 85 (1973): 294–314.

Winnett, F. V. *The Mosaic Tradition*. University of Toronto Press, 1949.

———. "Re-examining the Foundations." *Journal of Biblical Literature* 84 (1965): 1–19.

Wolf, Herbert Martin. *The "Apology of Hattušiliš" Compared With Other Political Self-Justifications of the Ancient Near East*. Ph.D. diss., Brandeis University, 1967.

Wolff, Hans Walter. "The Kerygma of the Yahwist." In Brueggemann and Wolff, *Vitality of OT Traditions,* 41–66.

———. ed. *Probleme biblischer Theologie.* Von Rad Festschrift. Munich: Kaiser, 1971.

Würthwein, E. *Die Erzählung von der Thronfolge Davids—theologische oder politische Geschichtsschreibung?* Theologische Studien 115. Zurich: Theologischer Verlag, 1974.

Zakovitch, Yair. "Assimilation in Biblical Narrative." In Tigay, *Empirical Models,* 175–96.

———. "For Three—and for Four." Jerusalem: Makor, 1979.

Zimmerli, Walther. "Promise and Fulfillment." In Westermann, *Essays on OT Hermeneutics,* 89–122.

Index